MW01040091

Philosophy of Religion

Philosophy of Religion:

Classic and Contemporary Issues

Edited by

Paul Copan and Chad Meister

Blackwell
Publishing

© 2008 by Blackwell Publishing Ltd

BLACKWELL PUBLISHING
350 Main Street, Malden, MA 02148-5020, USA
9600 Garsington Road, Oxford OX4 2DQ, UK
550 Swanston Street, Carlton, Victoria 3053, Australia

The right of Paul Copan and Chad Meister to be identified as the Authors of the Editorial Material in this Work has been asserted in accordance with the UK Copyright, Designs, and Patents Act 1988.

All rights reserved. No part of this publication may be reproduced, stored in a retrieval system, or transmitted, in any form or by any means, electronic, mechanical, photocopying, recording or otherwise, except as permitted by the UK Copyright, Designs, and Patents Act 1988, without the prior permission of the publisher.

Designations used by companies to distinguish their products are often claimed as trademarks. All brand names and product names used in this book are trade names, service marks, trademarks, or registered trademarks of their respective owners. The publisher is not associated with any product or vendor mentioned in this book.

This publication is designed to provide accurate and authoritative information in regard to the subject matter covered. It is sold on the understanding that the publisher is not engaged in rendering professional services. If professional advice or other expert assistance is required, the services of a competent professional should be sought.

First published 2008 by Blackwell Publishing Ltd

1   2008

Library of Congress Cataloging-in-Publication Data

Philosophy of religion : classic and contemporary issues / edited by Paul Copan and Chad Meister.
    p. cm.
    Includes bibliographical references and index.
    ISBN 978-1-4051-3989-2 (hardcover : alk. paper) – ISBN 978-1-4051-3990-8 (pbk. : alk. paper) 1. Religion – Philosophy. I. Copan, Paul. II. Meister, Chad, 1965–
BL51.P334   2007
210—dc22

                                                                    2007014537

A catalogue record for this title is available from the British Library.

Set in 10 on 13 pt Galliard
by SNP Best-set Typesetter Ltd., Hong Kong
Printed and bound in Singapore
by Utopia Press Pte Ltd

The publisher's policy is to use permanent paper from mills that operate a sustainable forestry policy, and which has been manufactured from pulp processed using acid-free and elementary chlorine-free practices. Furthermore, the publisher ensures that the text paper and cover board used have met acceptable environmental accreditation standards.

For further information on
Blackwell Publishing, visit our website:
www.blackwellpublishing.com

Contents

Notes on Contributors

Pamela Sue Anderson is Reader in Philosophy of Religion, University of Oxford, and Fellow of Regent's Park College. She is the author of *Ricoeur and Kant* (Scholars) and *A Feminist Philosophy of Religion* (Blackwell). She is co-editor, with Beverley Clack, of *Feminist Philosophy of Religion: Critical Readings* (Routledge), and she has published articles in various journals including *The International Journal for the Philosophy of Religion, Sophia*, and *Feminist Theory*.

Bruce Ellis Benson is Professor and Chair of the Philosophy Department at Wheaton College. He has written a number of articles and books, including *The Improvisation of Musical Dialogue: A Phenomenology of Music* (Cambridge University Press) and *Graven Ideologies: Nietzsche, Derrida and Marion on Modern Idolatry* (InterVarsity Press). He has edited *Hermeneutics at the Crossroads: Interpretation in Christian Perspective* with Kevin J. Vanhoozer and James K. A. Smith (Indiana University Press) and *The Phenomenology of Prayer* with Norman Wirzba (Fordham University Press). His book *Pious Nietzsche: Decadence and Dionysian Faith* is forthcoming with Indiana University Press.

Robin Collins is Professor of Philosophy at Messiah College where he specializes in philosophy of science and philosophy of religion. He has written articles on religion and science and has contributed to a large number of anthologies, including most recently Bernard Carr's edited work, *Universe or Multiverse?* (Cambridge University Press) and the *Oxford Handbook of Science and Religion* (Oxford University Press). He is currently working on a book on the argument for design from physics and cosmology tentatively entitled *The Well-Tempered Universe: God, Fine-tuning, and the Laws of Nature*.

Paul Copan is Pledger Family Chair of Philosophy and Ethics at Palm Beach Atlantic University. He has edited with Paul K. Moser *The Rationality of Theism* (Routledge), and with Chad Meister *The Routledge Companion to Philosophy of*

Religion (Routledge). He has co-authored with William Lane Craig *Creation Out of Nothing: A Biblical, Philosophical, and Scientific Exploration* (Baker), and has written works related to the philosophy of religion including *Loving Wisdom: Christian Philosophy of Religion* (Chalice Press), *"True for You, But Not for Me"* (Bethany) and *"That's Just Your Interpretation"* (Baker). He has contributed to various edited works and has also written articles and book reviews for journals including *Review of Metaphysics, Faith and Philosophy, Philosophia Christi*, and *Perspectives on Science and the Christian Faith.*

William Lane Craig is Research Professor of Philosophy at Talbot School of Theology. He has written numerous books and articles in philosophy of religion, including *The Cosmological Argument from Plato to Leibniz* (Macmillan), *The Kalam Cosmological Argument* (Macmillan), *Theism, Atheism, and Big Bang Cosmology* (Clarendon Press) with Quentin Smith, and *God, Time, and Eternity* (Kluwer).

Paul Draper is Professor of Philosophy at Purdue University and follows Quentin Smith as editor of *Philo*. He has published in a variety of journals and edited collections, including *American Philosophical Quarterly, Faith and Philosophy, Nous*, and William J. Wainwright (ed.) *The Oxford Handbook of Philosophy of Religion* (Oxford University Press). He is currently co-editing the second edition of Blackwell's *A Companion to Philosophy of Religion* and is working on a book entitled *The Evidential Problem of Evil.*

Gavin Flood is Academic Director of the Oxford Centre for Hindu Studies and Professor of Religion at the University of Stirling where he teaches Indian religions, Sanskrit, and theory and method in the study of religions. He is the author of several books including *An Introduction to Hinduism* (Cambridge University Press) and *The Ascetic Self: Subjectivity, Memory and Tradition* (Cambridge University Press), and he is the editor of *The Blackwell Companion to Hinduism* (Blackwell). He has also published papers in Religious Studies journals such as *Religion and Numen* and in Indological journals such as *The Indo-Iranian Journal.*

Robin Le Poidevin is Professor of Metaphysics at the University of Leeds. His books include *Arguing for Atheism* (Routledge), *Travels in Four Dimensions: The Enigmas of Space and Time* (Oxford University Press), and, as editor, *Questions of Time and Tense* (Clarendon Press) and *The Philosophy of Time* (Oxford University Press). He has also published in numerous journals including *Mind, Philosophical Quarterly, Analysis*, and *Religious Studies.*

William E. Mann is Marsh Professor of Intellectual and Moral Philosophy at the University of Vermont. His published works include *The Blackwell Guide to the Philosophy of Religion* (Blackwell), *Augustine's Confessions: Critical Essays* (Rowman & Littlefield), "Divine Sovereignty and Aseity," in William J. Wainwright (ed.),

The Oxford Handbook of Philosophy of Religion (Oxford University Press), and "Anselm on the Trinity," in Brian Davies and Brian Leftow (eds.), *The Cambridge Companion to Anselm* (Cambridge University Press).

Chad Meister is Head of Philosophy at Bethel College where he specializes in philosophy of religion. His publications include *Building Belief: Constructing Faith from the Ground Up* (Baker), *Introducing Philosophy of Religion* (Routledge), *The Philosophy of Religion Reader* (Routledge), and *The Routledge Companion to Philosophy of Religion*, co-edited with Paul Copan (Routledge). He is also book review editor for *Philosophia Christi*.

Paul K. Moser is Professor and Chairperson of Philosophy at Loyola University of Chicago. His publications include *Philosophy After Objectivity* (Oxford University Press) and *Knowledge and Evidence* (Cambridge University Press). He is co-author of *The Theory of Knowledge* (Oxford University Press). His edited works include *A Priori Knowledge* (Oxford University Press) and *Rationality In Action* (Cambridge University Press). He is also co-editor of *Human Knowledge* (Oxford University Press), *Moral Relativism* (Oxford University Press), and *Divine Hiddenness* (Cambridge University Press).

Harold Netland is Professor of Philosophy of Religion and Intercultural Studies at Trinity Evangelical Divinity School. His publications include *Dissonant Voices: Religious Pluralism and the Question of Truth* (Eerdmans) and *Encountering Religious Pluralism: The Challenge to Christian Faith and Mission* (InterVarsity) as well as a number of articles in journals such as *Faith and Philosophy* and *Religious Studies*. He also co-edited *Christianity and the Religions* (William Carey Library).

Graham Oppy is Associate Dean of Research in the Faculty of Arts at Monash University. He has published in many journals and books including *Mind*, *Nous*, *Philosophy and Phenomenological Research*, *British Journal for Philosophy of Science*, and D. Baker (ed.) *Plantinga's Philosophy of Religion* (Cambridge University Press). He has published *Ontological Arguments and Belief in God* (Cambridge University Press), *Arguing About Gods* (Cambridge University Press), and *Philosophical Perspectives on Infinity* (Cambridge University Press). He has also recently contracted to co-edit a five-volume history of Western philosophy of religion that is due to appear in 2009.

John Polkinghorne is emeritus President of Queen's College, Cambridge, and an Anglican priest. He has a PhD in physics and is a Fellow of the Royal Society. He has written numerous articles and authored/edited many books exploring the relationship between science and religion, including *The Faith of a Physicist* (Fortress), *Belief in God in an Age of Science* (Yale University Press), *Science and the Trinity* (Yale University Press), and *Exploring Reality* (Yale University Press).

Katherin A. Rogers is Associate Professor of Philosophy at the University of Delaware. She has written several books: *Perfect Being Theology* (Edinburgh University Press), *The Neoplatonic Metaphysics and Epistemology of Anselm of Canterbury* (Edwin Mellen), and *The Anselmian Approach to God and Creation* (Edwin Mellen). She has also published in various journals including *International Philosophical Quarterly*, *Religious Studies*, *Philosophy*, *Faith and Philosophy*, and *American Catholic Philosophical Quarterly*.

Joseph Runzo is Professor of Philosophy and Religious Studies at Chapman University. He holds the position of Life Fellow at Clare Hall, Cambridge University, and is Executive Director of Global Ethics and Religion Forum. Among his many publications are *Reason, Relativism and God* (Macmillan), *World Views and Perceiving God* (Macmillan), and *Global Philosophy of Religion: A Short Introduction* (Oneworld Publications). He is also co-editor, with Nancy Martin, of the *Library of Global Ethics and Religion* (Oneworld). He is currently completing *War and the Destruction of the Soul* on human rights and the ethics of war.

Quentin Smith is Professor of Philosophy at Western Michigan University. He has written many books and articles, including *Language and Time* (Oxford University Press) and *Ethical and Religious Thought in Analytic Philosophy of Language* (Yale University Press), and has co-authored, with William Lane Craig, *Theism, Atheism, and Big Bang Cosmology* (Clarendon Press) and with Nathan Oaklander, *Time, Change, and Freedom: An Introduction to Metaphysics* (Routledge). He is philosophy editor for Prometheus Books and former editor-in-chief of *Philo*. He has won numerous awards for his work in time and cosmology.

Charles Taliaferro is Professor of Philosophy at St Olaf College. He has published many books and articles, including *Consciousness and the Mind of God* (Cambridge University Press), *Contemporary Philosophy of Religion* (Blackwell), and *Evidence and Faith: Religion and Philosophy Since the Seventeenth Century* (Cambridge University Press). He is also co-editor of *The Companion to Philosophy of Religion* (Blackwell), and is book review editor for *Faith and Philosophy*.

René van Woudenberg is Professor of Philosophy at the Free University of Amsterdam where he specializes in epistemology and metaphysics. He has written five books in Dutch, and is co-editor, with Terence Cuneo, of *The Cambridge Companion to Thomas Reid* (Cambridge University Press). He is also co-editor, with Sabine Roeser and Ron Rood, of *Basic Belief and Basic Knowledge: Papers in Epistemology* (Ontos Verlag).

Introduction

Paul Copan and Chad Meister

Philosophy of Religion Today

Philosophy of religion is undergoing a renaissance; we are witnessing a resurgence of interest in religious thought by scholars and students, both religious adherents and skeptics alike. This philosophical awakening is reflected in the plethora of books and articles recently published from a wide variety of viewpoints. But given its widespread interest, it is somewhat ironic that many scholars would not agree on what philosophy of religion actually means and includes. Some would incorporate topics typically discussed in religion and theology courses as philosophy of religion material. Others would separate them into distinct disciplines and categories.

For purposes of this volume, philosophy of religion will be understood to be simply the philosophical reflection on religious ideas. These terms – "philosophical reflection" and "religious ideas" – need clarification. "Philosophical reflection" in this context includes the careful analyses of terms, positions, reasons, and evidences for claims and hypotheses. These analyses themselves involve fundamental issues about the nature of what is real (metaphysics) and how we can know about things (epistemology).

Regarding these fundamental issues, philosophy of religion and, indeed, philosophy itself have taken new directions in recent decades. Back in the 1950s and 1960s, the main philosophical issues focused on logical positivist critiques of both traditional philosophy and religious studies (logical positivists held, among other things, that for a claim to be true and meaningful it must be empirically verifiable). Metaphysical reflection on religious topics was widely considered to be absurd, and religious ideas and language were often taken to be meaningless. Due to the influence of such intellectual leaders as John Hick and Alvin Plantinga, however, by the early 1970s the field began taking a significant turn. Nowadays, it is commonplace to see monographs, journals, anthologies, and companions addressing themes in theistic metaphysics and religious epistemology.

"Religious ideas" in this context involve the primary issues that have been discussed and debated within the religious traditions throughout the centuries – issues regarding alleged encounters with the divine, the relation between science and religion, conflicting truth claims among the different religious traditions, the nature and existence of God or the Ultimate Reality, and the meaning of human existence, among other topics. These are not ethereal concepts merely debated among philosophers. To the contrary, they are fundamental issues in the life and thought of living traditions – traditions which have deep, existential meaning and ongoing significance for contemporary humanity.

This volume, then, is a philosophical reflection on religious ideas, and it includes many of these central issues. Most of the chapters are devoted to ideas which have typically been of interest in the West – traditional *theistic* themes. But non-Western religious concerns are also becoming increasingly prominent, as are continental and feminist points of view. So we have included them here. The essays are written by leading scholars from differing backgrounds and perspectives who have been carefully selected given their status, expertise, and ability to write clearly and with authority. While they are fresh and important works in the field, and thus of interest to scholars, they have been written in a way that is accessible to students and others with an interest in philosophy of religion.

The topics covered are divided into four broad categories: (1) religious experience and knowledge, (2) the existence of God, (3) the nature and attributes of God, and (4) emerging themes.

Religious Experience and Knowledge

The history of religion is rife with individuals claiming to have had encounters with the divine or transcendent. These encounters come in a variety of forms and are typically depicted as religious, or numinous, or mystical experiences. But how would one go about determining the veracity of such experiences? Is this kind of question even warranted? Furthermore, what is the relation between religious experiences and religious beliefs? Do ineffable experiences warrant belief in God? In chapter 1, William Mann explores these very important issues.

While religion deals with experience of one type (personal encounters with the divine), science deals with experience of another type (encountering nature via experimentation and examination). But do these two domains ever intersect? Does knowledge about the natural world, for example, offer any insight into the nature of God? And what is the relationship between science and theology? These are some of the significant questions John Polkinghorne addresses in chapter 2.

Whether through religious experiences, scientific investigation, or other means, religious adherents hold beliefs. But do such beliefs require propositional evidence to be justified or intellectually respectable? A number of recent and prominent philosophers have challenged this assumption and argue that religious belief – more specifically, belief in God – is properly basic and thus needs no further justification. In chapter 3, René van Woudenberg examines this view and looks at both what its adherents believe and why they believe this way.

Religious truth claims, as with religious experiences, are not limited to one religion; they can be found in all the great religious traditions. If many of these experiences and claims are veridical (true), does this support religious pluralism (a position in which divergent points of view in religion are held to be equally savingly true)? And what sense can be made of the conflicting truth claims within the different traditions? In chapter 4, Joseph Runzo examines this issue and notes six possible answers.

In chapter 5, Harold Netland also addresses the subject of conflicting truth claims in religion, but he focuses primarily on one possible solution. He examines religious exclusivism – namely, the claim that the means of salvation or liberation is located within one particular faith rather than many – and he contrasts exclusivism with both inclusivism and pluralism.

The Existence of God

Once again, as in previous centuries, natural theology (arguments for the existence and nature of God that are generally accessible apart from special revelation or sacred scriptures) is prominent in the study of religion. Such arguments, whether for or against God's existence, take a variety of forms. One such form, the cosmological argument (from the Greek words *cosmos* = universe, and *logos* = rational account), concentrates on the question, "Why is there something rather than nothing?" In chapter 6, William Lane Craig presents two different versions of the cosmological argument: a Leibnizian version which emphasizes the principle of sufficient reason, and a *kalam* version which argues against the possibility of an infinite temporal regress of events.

Another argument for God's existence is called the teleological, or design, argument (from the Greek words *telos* = goal or end, and *logos*). According to this type of argument, one can infer a designer of the universe given the apparent design in the universe. There are various versions of the teleological argument, and in chapter 7, Robin Collins provides one based on the alleged fine-tuning of the universe. He argues that the laws of nature, the constants of physics, and the initial conditions of the universe are finely tuned on a "razor's edge" for conscious life on planet earth.

Since its inception in 1078 CE by the Benedictine monk Anselm, the ontological argument (from the Greek words *ontos* = being, and *logos*) has fascinated and intrigued philosophers and theologians alike. Graham Oppy offers an exposition of several different versions of this argument in chapter 8. While there have never been many serious defenders of the argument, some very prominent thinkers have defended it in recent times. For a number of reasons, including advances in modal logic, interest in this ancient argument is on the rise.

In chapter 9, Paul Copan presents the moral argument. He defends the argument and explores a range of topics relevant to it, including the existence and nature of moral beliefs, the distinction between *knowing* objective moral values and *being* moral creatures, the relation between naturalism and objective moral values, evolutionary ethics, and the Euthyphro dilemma.

Of course, not everyone believes that the evidence more plausibly supports theism. To the contrary, a number of philosophers argue that the evidence favors naturalism (the view that natural entities have only natural causes). One type of evidence which seems, *prima facie*, to support naturalism is all the evil and suffering in the world. In chapter 10, Paul Draper addresses this topic. He first examines several prominent arguments from evil against God's existence and explains why he finds them deficient. He then presents his own Bayesian version (a type of argument based on probability theory) of the argument.

In chapter 11, Quentin Smith goes further in showing that naturalism is a plausible position. He argues that while the notion of a self-caused simple being (such as God) makes no sense, it is nevertheless reasonable to believe that the universe did cause itself to exist. He utilizes recent work in Big Bang cosmology, most notably the hypothetical "cosmic singularity," in developing his argument.

The Nature and Attributes of God

Debates in natural theology sometimes play a significant role in determining whether one considers theism to be reasonable to believe or not. Just as important, however, is the question of whether the very concept of God makes sense. In chapter 12, Charles Taliaferro tackles this issue. He examines the coherence of theism – that is, whether the attributes of God are intelligible, and whether it is *possible* that a maximally great being could possess these attributes.

Some philosophers have argued not only that it is unlikely that God exists given what the term "God" means, but that it is *impossible* that God exists – that is, that the properties traditionally attributed to God are incompatible with one another or incoherent (either individually or taken as a whole). In chapter 13, Robin Le Poidevin considers this question of whether God is an impossibility. He first explores the meaning of the phrase "God is a perfect being" and then looks at difficulties related to it.

One major conundrum theists have faced for centuries is this: if God is omniscient, then he knows now what you will do tomorrow. But if he infallibly knows now what you will do then, how can you truly have a choice in the matter? So, it seems that you can have either free will or God's omniscience, but not both. Katherin Rogers examines this dilemma in chapter 14.

Another problem for theists is that we generally recognize that we are finite persons; we are born at some point, we live for a time, and then we die. But if the God of theism exists, where is he in all this? Why can't we see God? Why doesn't God make himself readily known and available? In chapter 15, Paul Moser looks at death and divine hiddenness. He contrasts theism with materialism (the view that the physical universe is all there is), and lays out the alternatives from which to choose.

Emerging Themes

The field of philosophy of religion is not static; it is alive and flourishing and continues to evolve in new and exciting directions. For example, until very recently one simply didn't see the phrase "continental philosophy of religion" ("continental philosophy" referring to philosophical work done on the European continent). This is not to say that European philosophers have not been reflecting philosophically on religious ideas – far from it. But the way they have been so reflecting is markedly different from the analytical style of "Anglo-American" philosophers. Even the concerns of the two are often dissimilar. And, unfortunately, continental thought has largely been ignored by those in the analytic tradition.

Bruce Benson in chapter 16 addresses this topic. Rather than focusing on justifying religious belief and experience, he works through the ideas of several key continental thinkers in order to focus on central continental concerns, namely, the relation of faith and reason and the role of the self in relation to God. Though these issues have been addressed by Anglo-American analytic philosophers, European thinkers approach them quite differently, and Benson captures their spirit and method.

Another phrase that is fairly recent in the field is "Eastern philosophy of religion." Of course, thinkers in the East have been philosophizing about religious ideas for millennia; so to consider this an emerging theme is in one sense a gross misnomer. However, *Eastern* ideas regarding religion have been, by and large, ignored by analytic philosophers of religion until quite recently. Philosophy of religion in the East spans 3,000 years and a multitude of countries; so even a cursory presentation of all the important themes would not be possible. Instead, Gavin Flood in chapter 17 centers in on some of the main topics in philosophy of religion that have arisen in South and East Asia.

One emerging theme in the field that *is* fairly recent is feminist philosophy of religion. Indeed, in most branches of philosophy, feminist thinkers have now made important inroads and contributions – transforming concepts, reshaping epistemic and spiritual practices, and correcting a multitude of injustices. In chapter 18, Pamela Sue Anderson raises a number of important feminist concerns, including whether gender is an accidental property, God's relation to gender, gender inequality in religion, and more.

As the different chapter titles and topics indicate, the scope of this volume is broad. But the aim is narrow: to provide a number of central topics in philosophy of religion, both classic and contemporary issues, discussed by leading philosophers of religion in a manner that is clear, concise, and thought-provoking. Questions are provided at the end of each chapter, as are annotated recommended readings, in order to further your engagement with the material.

We hope that through these essays, further readings, and discussions on the themes presented here, you will join in the dialectic that has been ongoing in philosophy of religion across the ages.

Part I

Religious Experience
and Knowledge

Chapter 1

The Epistemology of Religious Experience

William E. Mann

The title of this essay draws attention to religious *experience*, not religious *belief*. There is a difference. One would expect an essay on the epistemology of religious belief to confront such justificatory issues as the relation between reason and faith, the question whether an epistemically responsible agent's degrees of belief in various propositions must track the strength of the evidence the agent has for those propositions, and the role of revelation, testimony, and miracles in the formation of religious belief. If one concentrates on religious experience instead, then these justificatory issues tend to recede into the background. But different justificatory issues then come to the forefront. This essay will explore some of those issues.

Perhaps the most obvious justificatory issue confronting religious experience concerns its status. Put most bluntly, the problem is this: even if we assume that there is a class of experiences properly denominated "religious," are any members of the class likely to be veridical? Charles Dickens's classic, *A Christmas Carol*, provides a somewhat secular analogue of the problem facing religious experience. Jacob Marley's ghost observes to Ebenezer Scrooge,

> "You don't believe in me."
> "I don't," said Scrooge.
> "What evidence would you have of my reality beyond that of your own senses?"
> "I don't know," said Scrooge.
> "Why do you doubt your senses?"
> "Because," said Scrooge, "a little thing affects them. A slight disorder of the stomach makes them cheats. You may be an undigested bit of beef, a blot of mustard, a crumb of cheese, a fragment of an underdone potato. There's more of gravy than of grave about you, whatever you are!" (Dickens [1843] 1984: 47–8)

Scrooge is not denying that his experience is *as if* he is confronting a supernatural spirit. His denial consists rather in the claim that the *cause* or *source* of his experience is nothing supernatural. As readers of Dickens know, Scrooge soon comes to abandon his skeptical hypothesis, taking the vivid representations of Marley's ghost and the Ghosts of Christmas Past, Present, and Future as veridical – indeed, as granting to him a cognitive access to the world that he could not otherwise have had. Scrooge's enhanced perception brings about a change in will, transforming him from a heartless skinflint into a compassionate, joyous human being.

We can discern three elements in this encapsulation of *A Christmas Carol*: the *phenomenology* of Scrooge's experiences, their *psychological impact* on him, and the question of their *veridicality*. We should note in passing that these three elements can vary independently of each other. It may just have been, for all that Dickens's text says, that Marley's "ghost" *was* nothing more than an illusory experience induced by an undigested bit of beef. Yet the illusory experience might be phenomenologically identical to an experience Scrooge would have had if he had encountered the genuine article, Marley's ghost. Moreover, an illusory experience can have a profound impact, even in cases in which the experiencer knows, or comes to know, that the experience is illusory.

We might expect, then, to find the same elements present in an account of putative religious experiences, even though the ways in which the elements play out in religious experiences may differ from the ways they play out in ghostly experiences.

Psychological Impact

It is difficult to imagine someone who says, sincerely, "I've just had one of those annoying religious experiences. I do wish I could be free of them. They're so insipid and boring." The testimony of experiencers is virtually unanimous in depicting such experiences as profound and life-changing. To the observation that perhaps one would become blasé about the experience if only it occurred frequently enough, Christian mystics have a ready answer: the experience is but a fleeting and diluted foretaste of the beatific vision, the eternal bliss that one may come to enjoy in communion with God.

Phenomenology: Non-Sensory Character

Marley's ghost manifests some of the properties stereotypical of what one is supposed to encounter in ghostly experiences, including a transparent body, an ability to pass through solid objects and float on air, a voice capable of bewailing its possessor's awful fate, a capacity to inspire dread among the living. Although stereotypical, the properties may not be essential. Popular culture provides examples of putative ghostly experiences in which some or all of these properties are absent.

When we try to identify the properties, stereotypical or essential, that characterize religious experiences, we find two circumstances that complicate the process.
The first is the phenomenon of religious diversity. Some religions are theistic, and
of those some are polytheistic while others – notably Judaism, Christianity, and
Islam – are monotheistic. Other religions, for example, Buddhism and some varieties of Hinduism, are non-theistic. Reports of religious experiences coming from
different religious traditions are thus quite varied. The variety gives rise to the
suspicion that the reports themselves are not phenomenologically pure; that they
have been processed, consciously or unconsciously, through the religious attitudes
of the experiencer. The suspicion is, to put it more aggressively, that the reports
come to us as tendentious *interpretations*, interpretations that may involve altera-
tion, suppression, or augmentation of the experience. Thus if we survey the myriad
reports that reasonably qualify as reports of religious experiences, we may find no
features common to the content of all of them. I propose to shelve this topic for
now, with a promise to return to it when we discuss veridicality.

The second complicating circumstance is that many reports of religious experience allege that the experience involved no sensory properties. Here is one example,
reported by an anonymous source, that appears in William James's *The Varieties
of Religious Experience*:

> When all at once I experienced a feeling of being raised above myself, I felt the pres-
> ence of God . . . as if his goodness and his power were penetrating me altogether. . . . I
> think it well to add that in this ecstasy of mine God had neither form, color, odor,
> nor taste; moreover, that the feeling of his presence was accompanied with no deter-
> minate localization. . . . But the more I seek words to express this intimate inter-
> course, the more I feel the impossibility of describing the thing by any of our usual
> images. At bottom the expression most apt to render what I felt is this: God was
> present, though invisible; he fell under no one of my senses, yet my consciousness
> perceived him. (James 1902: 68)

James's witness "felt" the presence of God without seeing, hearing, smelling,
tasting, or touching God. Yet the "feeling" was not like some objectless emotion.
The object of the experience was God, who made his presence known, but not
through the mediation of any of the senses. The witness finds it impossible to
describe the experience "by any of our usual images." Perhaps that is because our
stock of descriptive concepts is derived in whole or in large part from our sensory
experience of the world. If that is so, one might reasonably think that reports like
that of James's witness can reveal nothing about the content or object of the
experience. And then one might conclude, not without reason, that the notion of
an experience without a sensory content is baffling if not incoherent.

No one has done more recently to defend the intelligibility of the notion of a
non-sensory religious experience than William Alston (1991; 2005). I shall not
reproduce his considerations here. I believe that receptivity to their possibility can
be heightened by appeal to a case of a non-sensory, *non-religious* experience. By

its nature, such an experience would be extraordinary, but then so are the sorts of religious experiences on which we will focus.

Oliver Sacks reports the case of brain-damaged twins, conventionally catego-rized as "idiot savants," who were inaccurate in the performance of simple tasks of addition and subtraction and incapable of understanding the elementary arith-metical operations of multiplication and division. Yet in one of Sacks's observations of them, he found them verbally exchanging and individually *savoring* seemingly random six-digit numbers. Sacks copied down the numbers and discovered, by consulting a table of prime numbers, that every one of them was prime. The next day Sacks joined in the twins' "conversation" by presenting them with an eight-digit prime. Accepting him into their circle, they escalated the procedure by eventually generating 20-digit . . . what? Primes? Sacks had no way of knowing, since his table of primes stopped at 10 digits. Sacks says of them:

> They are not calculators, and their numeracy is "iconic." . . . They have, I believe, a most singular imagination – and not the least of its singularities is that it can imagine only numbers. They do not seem to "operate" with numbers, non-iconically, like a calculator; they "see" them, directly, as a vast natural scene. (Sacks 1985: 196)

The most natural thing to say about this case is that the twins are discovering primes for themselves. The unusual capacity that they have enables them to gain rapid access to a realm of abstract objects, objects which, in virtue of their abstract-ness, are not discernible by any of the bodily senses. (One can see a numeral, but not a number.) Nonetheless, the numbers are in some sense *there*, waiting to be grasped: the twins' feats are discoveries, not inventions. And the twins' grasping of prime numbers is a palpable experience.

There are of course disanalogies between what the twins can experience and what people subject to religious experience claim to experience. First, the twins seem to have been capable of encountering prime numbers almost at will. Subjects of religious experience claim, for the most part, that religious experiences are unpredictable, some coming unbidden, others failing to occur even after elaborate preparation and personal discipline. Theists in particular insist on this point, claim-ing that religious experiences are granted by a God whose reasons for acting are well beyond their ken. Second, there is a clear, objective, external check for the veridicality of the twins' experiences: look up their numbers in a table of primes or run their numbers through a computer program designed to test for primes. There is no similarly clear and objective check for the veridicality of religious experiences. But the point of the case of the twins was merely to make more plausible the notion of an experience that is non-sensory, and the point appears to withstand the disanalogies.

For the remainder of our discussion of the phenomenology of religious experi-ence let us narrow the topic by excluding the following sorts of cases. *Divine disclosure of factual knowledge*: it would be remarkable if an archangel were to reveal that the number of stars in the Milky Way is 152,333,761,429. Even more remarkable would be the efforts required to establish the identity of our informant as a genuine, truth-telling archangel. *Seeing divinity in nature*: a natural phenomenon such as a sunset can be religiously moving. But such an experience would be at best an indirect way of apprehending divinity. (Compare this to claiming to hear Marley's ghost in the sound of trees groaning in the wind.) The sort of case on which we will focus will be a putative case of the direct apprehension of divinity. *Non-theistic cases*: a Neo-Platonist, through a regimen of spiritual discipline, might claim to know The One, that which is beyond being, while insisting that The One is not to be confused with the deity of Judaism, Christianity, or Islam. We will touch upon claims like this one when we examine the issue of veridicality.

Phenomenology: Direct Awareness and Ineffability

Return to the case reported by James's anonymous source cited earlier. It is an example of what might be called the gold standard of theistic mystical experiences, namely, union with God. We have previously focused on the experience's non-sensory character. There are two other features of it that are intimately connected to this feature. One is that James's witness insists that he was directly aware of God, that God was at least as evidently present to him as these printed words are now present to you. The other feature is the ineffability of the experience. James's witness is literally at a loss for words to describe it, except to say that it was of God. There is a quartet of epistemological assumptions that are attractive in their own right and which, taken together, highlight the predicament of James's witness.

Thought as Propositional: The first assumption is that having a thought is a matter of entertaining a proposition. We may construe "thought" here very broadly, to include beliefs, desires, emotional attitudes, and the like. And we may remain agnostic about what exactly a proposition is: it might be a concrete utterance or inscription or it might be something more abstract, to which the utterance or inscription refers. On this assumption, whenever one thinks about Carthage, one must be eliciting some propositional attitude towards some proposition about Carthage, for example, believing that Carthage is in North Africa, or fearing that Carthage is a center of moral corruption.

Propositional Complexity: On this assumption, propositions themselves are complex, compounded out of simpler ingredients, variously identified as terms, ideas, or concepts. Suppose that Beatrice believes that roses are red. The proposition that is the object of Beatrice's belief is a complex formed from the terms, "rose" and "red" (alternatively, the ideas or concepts of a rose and redness), structured by the predication relation (alternatively, by the inherence relation). Notice that this presupposition entails that one cannot have a thought if one does not have some competency with the ideas or concepts that are integral to the thought.

Thinking as Internal Speaking: The third assumption is that thinking, or the entertaining of propositions, is a kind of internal *speaking*, a sort of unvocalized soliloquy. The language of thought, "mentalese," need not correspond to any natural language. Beatrice, whose natural language competence extends only to English, and Dietrich, who understands only German, may despite their linguistic limitations think the same thought when Beatrice hears "Snow is white" and Dietrich hears "*Schnee ist weiss.*"

Concept Empiricism: The fourth and final assumption is that all our concepts, all the materials of our mental life, are necessarily derived from sense experience. According to this assumption, there are no innate ideas: all the thoughts that we have involve exclusively concepts that we originally acquired from empirical sources.

According to these four assumptions, then, ordinary thought is discursive, conducted in something that either is a language or is very much like a language. Thinking is an activity of putting together or taking apart propositions that are analogous to the sentences of a natural language. Propositions themselves are "molecular" entities whose "atomic" constituents are concepts. Finally, the concepts that are available for discursive thought must have gotten into the repertoire by way of ordinary sense experience.

Now let us reconsider James's witness in light of these assumptions. Because the experience had no sensory content, the witness cannot describe it, given the limits placed on his descriptive powers by *Concept Empiricism*. This inability is not merely a lapse in public communication: if *Concept Empiricism* is true, he cannot even depict the experience to himself – thus the ineffability. However, the other two features of the experience, the of-God feature and the non-sensory feature, seem to be hard to square with our four assumptions. There is no obvious way in which the witness is entitled to claim with certainty that the experience was of God. And the assumption of *Concept Empiricism* seems to raise again the issue of the intelligibility of a non-sensory experience. What in the world *could* be the content of a non-sensory experience?

Eckhart's solution

Think of the witness's predicament as also a predicament for God. If God is an essentially immaterial being, how can he impart knowledge of himself to beings whose concepts can only derive from interaction with material objects? God can impart knowledge by means of ordinary and extraordinary sensory images; sunsets would be an example of the former, a six-winged seraph an example of the latter. But sensory images can only give indirect knowledge of God, and they can lead one mistakenly to project properties inherent only to the imagery onto the imagery's cause. They cannot disclose God himself. The great German mystic, Meister Eckhart (1260–1328), sets up the problem in this way by describing ordinary thinking:

Whatever the soul does, it does through agents. It understands by means of intelligence. If it remembers, it does so by means of memory. If it is to love, the will must be used and thus it acts always through agents and not within its own essence. Its results are achieved through an intermediary. The power of sight can be effectuated only through the eyes, for otherwise the soul has no means of vision. It is the same with the other senses. They are effectuated through intermediaries. . . . When the agents of the soul contact creatures, they take and make ideas and likenesses of them and bear them back again into the self. It is by means of these ideas that the soul knows about external creatures. Creatures cannot approach the soul except in this way and the soul cannot get at creatures, except, on its own initiative, it first conceive ideas of them. Thus the soul gets at things by means of ideas and the idea is an entity created by the soul's agents. Be it a stone, or a rose, or a person, or whatever it is that is to be known, first an idea is taken and then absorbed, and in this way the soul connects with the phenomenal world. (Eckhart 1941: 96–7)

According to Eckhart's account, whenever the soul acts, some encapsulated part of the soul is the agent responsible for the soul's activity. The soul's "agents" are the various faculties it possesses that enable the soul to do what it does. Coming to understand a proposition, for example, is what the faculty of "intelligence" (or intellect, or understanding) can do. Once understood, the proposition may or may not be remembered: that depends on the faculty of memory, which in itself is incapable of understanding, just as the faculty of understanding cannot remember. Eckhart clearly is willing to extend this facultative view to the senses. One sees by means of the faculty of vision, a faculty that, more obviously than in the cases of understanding and memory, cannot operate except by means of sense organs specifically dedicated to the faculty. But there is this difference between the sensory faculties and faculties like intelligence, memory, and will. The sensory faculties work by interaction with the created world. Their function is to produce ideas (or concepts) of the creatures they encounter for the consumption of the faculties of intelligence, memory, and will. The latter faculties operate by analyzing, combining, storing, and judging these ideas, all of which, if *Thought as Propositional* is true, is a matter of trafficking in propositions. The account that Eckhart sketches lays stress on two features of the soul's ordinary operations. First, the agents of the soul are active, yet, second, the agents always operate with and on intermediaries, namely, ideas instead of things, or propositions instead of the states of affairs the propositions represent. Given this second feature, it follows that as long as the soul operates in the ordinary way, it cannot have direct and unmediated knowledge of God.

Eckhart's solution is to describe a way in which God can bypass the soul's ordinary operations:

In Being, however, there is no action and, therefore, there is none in the soul's essence. The soul's agents, by which it acts, are derived from the core of the soul. In that core is the central silence, the pure peace, and abode of the heavenly birth, the place for this event: this utterance of God's word. By nature the core of the soul is sensitive to nothing but the divine Being, unmediated. Here God enters the soul with all he has and not in part. He enters the soul through its core and nothing may touch that core except God himself. No creature enters it, for creatures must stay outside in the soul's agents, from whence the soul receives ideas, behind which it has withdrawn as if to take shelter. . . . When all the agents [of the soul] are withdrawn from action and ideation, then this word is spoken. Thus he said: "Out of the silence, a secret word was spoken to me." [Wisd. of Sol. 18:14–15] The more you can withdraw the agents of your soul and forget things and the ideas you have received hitherto, the nearer you are to [hearing this word] and the more sensitive to it you will be. If you could only become more unconscious of everything all at once and ignore your own life, as St. Paul did when he could say: "Whether in the body, or out of it, I cannot tell: God knoweth!" [2 Cor. 12:3] His spirit had so far withdrawn all its agents that the body was forgotten. Neither memory nor intellect functioned, nor the senses, nor any [of the soul's] agents which are supposed to direct or grace the body. (Eckhart 1941: 97–9)

The soul, for Eckhart, is not merely the collection of all its faculties. Behind the faculties lies the soul's core, or essence. Like the faculties, the core is encapsulated; it is receptive to "nothing but the divine Being, unmediated." Unlike the faculties, it is not active. In order for the soul's core to function properly, the soul must shut down all the clamor for attention that comes to it from its agents. It must, that is, cease perceiving, cease intellection, cease remembering, cease willing. Mystics have prescribed various sorts of regimens, many of them contemplative in nature, designed to achieve cessation of the soul's activities. Only with that cessation is the soul's core most apt to receive God's direct, unmediated contact, to enter into union with God. A word of caution is in order here: in spite of what Eckhart has just said, I suspect that he would not subscribe to either of these propositions:

A   If one succeeds in shutting down all the soul's faculties, then one will experience union with God.
B   If one experiences union with God, then one must have succeeded in shutting down all the soul's faculties.

Not (A), because whether one achieves union with God depends on God's will; nothing is sufficient to induce the union without God's cooperation. Not (B), because God might decide to grant an experience of union even while the faculties are still in operation (as may have happened in the case of James's witness).

Veridicality

There is a difference between a claim's being true and a person's being justified in believing that the claim is true. It may be true that the number of stars in the Milky Way is 152,333,761,429, but I have no justification for believing it.

Conversely, I may be justified in believing that the sun will rise tomorrow even if it is false. Consider now the claim, "James's witness had an experience of union with God." What would make the claim true? It would not be enough that James's witness had an experience *as if* being united with God. At a minimum, the experience would have to be *caused by* God. But how could the witness, or anyone else for that matter, be in a position to know that the experience was caused by God and not brought about in some other way? Only by knowing, at a minimum, that God exists. But now we confront a skeptical dilemma. To characterize the experience robustly as union with God presupposes God's existence, while to characterize it less robustly is to concede that James's witness might have been mistaken. There are two kinds of skeptical attitude that might be taken with respect to the possibility of James's witness being mistaken. The *skeptic about theism* can allow that there is something extraordinary, and not just phenomenologically speaking, about the experience, but that what is extraordinary is not divine. The *debunking skeptic* will insist that while the experience is phenomenologically extraordinary, it is nonetheless hallucinatory, having a thoroughly mundane origin, analogous to Scrooge's undigested bit of beef. In any case, the dilemma concludes by maintaining that the experience cannot be cited as evidence for God's existence.

Let us set the stage for further development of a skeptical challenge by citing some passages from another of Eckhart's sermons:

> The Father ceaselessly begets his Son and, what is more, he begets me as his Son – the self-same Son! Indeed, I assert that he begets me not only as his Son but as himself and himself as myself, begetting me in his own nature, his own being. . . . [W]hatever is changed into something else becomes identical with it. If, therefore, I am changed into God and he makes me one with himself, then, by the living God, there is no distinction between us. . . . Some people imagine that they are going to see God as if he were standing yonder and they here, but it is not to be so. God and I: we are one. (Eckhart 1941: 181–2)

The claims made here are not merely hyperbolic; from the viewpoint of orthodox Christianity, they verge on heresy. Christianity, along with Judaism and Islam, insists on a sharp division between creation and its creator. Creatures are imperfect and ephemeral; their creator is perfect and eternal. The created world is thus not identical with God, nor could it or any part of it ever become identical with God. Theists who believe in this sharp division will claim that Eckhart has confused union with identity. Becoming united with God is one thing, extraordinary in itself. Becoming God is another thing, impossible for Eckhart, impossible for anyone.

Stace's skepticism about theism

Now a skeptic about theism can offer a diagnosis of what is wrong with claims that theistic mystics make about union with God. Eckhart, ironically, was onto something. His claims about identity were right, but he misidentified what it was with which he experienced identity. He came to realize the essential identity of all things, and thus of himself with all things. But, given his Christian background and the weight of Church authority, he interpreted the object of his experience as God. This diagnosis is put forward by W. T. Stace:

> In Christianity the Roman church was so powerful that in general it succeeded in enforcing its will upon the mystics. An Eckhart may tend toward heretical language and get himself into trouble. But the vast majority of the great Catholic mystics were submissive and managed to give an interpretation of "union with God" which could be accommodated to strict orthodoxy. And even Eckhart in his defense defers to the Church and attempts to explain away his pantheism. (Stace 1960b: 128)

> The whole multiplicity of things which comprise the universe are identical with one another and therefore constitute only one thing, a pure unity. The Unity, the One, we shall find, is the central experience and the central concept of all mysticism, of whichever type, although it may be more emphasized or less in different particular cases, and sometimes not even mentioned explicitly. The unity is perceived, or directly apprehended. That is to say, it belongs to the experience and not to the interpretation, in so far as it is possible to make this distinction. (Stace 1960a: 66)

Stace is a skeptic about theism, not a debunking skeptic. Stace's aim is reductionistic. There is, according to Stace, a "universal core" to all mystical experience, in all religious or philosophical traditions in all places at all times. Part of this core consists in the experience of an "undifferentiated unity." In this experience, all distinctions vanish, and one becomes aware that all things are one and identical. Thus Christian mystics, for example, have the same experience as, say, Hindu mystics. The difference is that the Christian mystics' religion forbids them from claiming identity with God. Hence they claim something less than identity, namely, union. It might then seem as though Christian mystics are browbeaten and hypocritical. Not necessarily, says Stace, for there is an important distinction between an experience and its interpretation. You and I might experience the same phenomenon but put different interpretations on what we experience. You might infer that Mary is sad while I might think that she is angry. In an analogous fashion, Stace suggests that the Hindu mystic and the Christian mystic really have the same experience, but the Christian mystic, brought up in the Christian tradition, unreflectively puts an interpretation on his experience that makes it compatible with his theistic beliefs. There is no insincerity or hypocrisy here. The case just shows that how we interpret an experience is quite often a function of the influence of background belief that we bring to the experience. So, according to Stace, both the Hindu mystic and the Christian mystic experience an undifferentiated unity which involves an identity of self with the All, but the Christian mystic feels constrained to put an interpretation on the experience.

You probably have already noticed that Stace's Christian mystic does not simply put an interpretation on the experience; according to Stace, the interpretation is not true to the experience. The experience, according to Stace, just *is* an awareness of identity. Hence the Christian mystic's insistence on union, not identity, turns out to be a misunderstanding of his own experience, an embellishment of the phenomenological facts.

It is certainly true that one can misunderstand one's experiences. John sincerely reports that he succeeded in impressing Mary favorably. Mary emphatically disagrees. Either John is mistaken or Mary is. How can we tell? We might initially favor Mary's testimony, except for the fact that romantic comedies thrive on the misidentification of one's emotions – "You're in love and you don't even realize it!" In cases like John and Mary's, we can look for subsequent behavior to determine who is mistaken. If Mary consistently shuns John, we are entitled to infer that John is mistaken. If, on the other hand, Mary begins to seek out John's company for no ulterior reason that we can discern, then perhaps John is not mistaken. But, to put it charitably, prospects are dim for using subsequent behavioral criteria to determine whether the theistic mystic or the non-theistic mystic is right. What would we look for? A certain jauntiness in the step of one mystic that is not present in the other? It would seem that any behavioral difference that one might point out would be absurdly arbitrary as evidence. As Stace rightly acknowledges, the only evidence we have available to us is testimony – in particular, the reports of the mystics themselves. This acknowledgment underscores the weight Stace must place on his distinction between theistic interpretation and pure, uninterpreted phenomena. The distinction will not bear the weight. Here is why.

Imagine the philosopher, T. W. Pime, who agrees with Stace's claim that theistic and non-theistic mystics undergo the same mystical experience. But the experience, according to Pime, is an experience of union with God, not identity with the All, or with God, or with anything else. What about the testimony of the non-theistic mystic to the effect that the experience is an experience of identity of the self with the All? By Pime's lights the testimony incorporates an interpretation placed on the experience by the non-theistic mystic. Pime has some ancillary hypotheses ready to explain this mystic's behavior. Perhaps the mystic has not yet heard about God. Or perhaps he is pressured into saying what he says by his peer group. No matter; Pime's point is that the non-theistic mystic misinterprets his experience, since the experience is, by fiat, an experience of union with God.

I suggest that Pime's theory is at least as plausible as Stace's. A defender of Stace may protest that Pime's theory is more metaphysically extravagant than Stace's, inasmuch as Pime's theory presupposes the existence of a supernatural being while Stace's does not. But Stace's view has its own metaphysical costs. When Stace says that "the whole multiplicity of things which comprise the universe are identical with one another and therefore constitute only one thing," Stace means this: "If the things are symbolized as *A*, *B*, *C*, etc., then all are one because *A* is identical with *B* – although it at the same time remains different from it, and so with the rest" (Stace 1960a: 66). If we take Stace seriously, it follows that you and I and Alpha Centauri are identical, that is, numerically one and the same thing. This is not simply to say that you, I, and Alpha Centauri are all *parts* of a greater whole. It is to say that you are the whole, I am the whole, and Alpha Centauri is the whole. Stace's view receives high marks for simplicity, for according to it there is only one thing, insusceptible to fragmentation into many. But the view receives low marks for credibility. Perhaps as a sop to our ordinary ways of perceiving and thinking about the world, Stace assures us in the next breath that you, I, and Alpha Centauri are all different from each other. Far from reassuring, this addition to Stace's initial claim makes his view incoherent. There may be maneuvers one can make on Stace's behalf that would render his view coherent, but one may be excused for suspecting that by the time the maneuvers are in place, Stace's view will be at least as extravagant as Pime's.

The debunking skeptic

We have little space and time to deal with Stace and Pime. I would like to conclude with two observations. First, even if we have fought the skeptic about theism to a standoff, the debunking skeptic has not been engaged. Recall the skeptical dilemma posed earlier. One of its horns was the claim that if we accept what amounts to Pime's theory about religious experiences, then we presuppose the existence of God, and thus the experiences cannot be used as evidence of God's existence. Now the principle the skeptic invokes here is less than compelling. The skeptic surely cannot mean to appeal to this principle:

1   If an experience is an experience of entity E, then the experience cannot be used as evidence for the existence of E.

(1) is false because it disallows a person's sighting of an ivory-billed woodpecker to count as evidence for the bird's existence. The skeptic must have in mind a more limited principle, perhaps something like this:

2   If an experience is alleged to be an experience of an entity E, and the content of the experience cannot in principle be confirmed by other observers, then the experience cannot be used as evidence for the existence of E.

Unlike (1), (2) will allow the sighting of an ivory-billed woodpecker to count as evidence for its existence. Unfortunately for the skeptic it does not bar the mystic from taking his experience as evidentiary. For the mystic can claim that other observers, either by training or by God's grace, can have the same experience. Nor should it trouble the mystic if few people, statistically speaking, ever do have religious experiences, for there are many cases of ordinary perceptual experience that require training and opportunity for their success; for example, the observation of a subatomic particle in a cloud chamber or the discrimination between cancerous and non-cancerous cells in a biopsy. It is within the mystic's intellectual rights to appeal to what Richard Swinburne has called the Principle of Credulity: "In the absence of special considerations, if it seems to a subject that *x* is present, then probably *x* is present" (Swinburne 1979: 254). Perhaps there is some plausible version of the debunking skeptic's principle that will defeat the Principle of Credulity and fuel the skeptic's dilemma, but it is not our problem: let us leave the task of discovery to the debunking skeptic.

Second, notice that Stace and Pime share in the same reductionistic assumption, namely that all mystics, no matter where or when they happen to be located, experience the same thing: all difference is in interpretation. Why accept the assumption? (Of course Pime is a creature of fiction, created to challenge the obviousness of Stace's view. But the question stands even when the only protagonist is Stace.) Why assume that Christian and Hindu are undergoing the same experience? In order to deal adequately with this question, we should be prepared to give an account of the identity conditions for experiences, the conditions, in other words, under which experiences are the same or different.

In conclusion, let me offer an example of how debate about such an account might proceed. A natural initial proposal would be to suggest that Christian mystical experience and Hindu mystical experience are the same if they have exactly the same phenomenological and affective content, that is, stripped of all interpretation, the two experiences "look" and "feel" exactly the same. Such a proposal would at best specify a necessary condition. Think of this analogy: by sheer accident, Jones, a careless house painter, spills paint on a drop cloth that results in something qualitatively identical to Jackson Pollock's *Shimmering Substance*. When you look at Jones's production you see something that is perceptually indiscriminable from Pollock's painting; your perceptual experience is phenomenologically identical to the experience you would have if you were confronting *Shimmering Substance*. Yet in seeing Jones's drop cloth, you have not thereby seen *Shimmering Substance*. The reason is that your experience was not caused by Pollock's painting. I suspect that theistic mystics would insist on the analogous condition that an experience of union with God must be brought about by God. Even if a phenomenologically identical experience could be induced by drugs, the experience would be counterfeit.

Are identity of content and causal origin necessary and sufficient conditions for identity of experience? I do not know. Here, as in the case of skepticism, there is more work to be done.

Questions for Reflection

1   What are the differences between an experience's phenomenology, its psychological impact, and its veridicality? (Illustrate the differences in an experience that is not a religious experience.)
2   Do you think there can be any experiences that have no sensory content? Why, or why not?

3   People who have had mystical experiences claim that the experiences defy description. Yet they frequently write at length about the experiences. Is their activity of writing consistent with their claim that what they are writing about is ineffable?
4   With respect to religious experience, what is the difference between the skeptic about theism and the debunking skeptic?
5   Is it a telling criticism of mystical experiences that very few people have them?

References

Alston, W. P. (1991) *Perceiving God: The Epistemology of Religious Experience*. Ithaca, NY: Cornell University Press.
—— (2005) "Mysticism and Perceptual Awareness of God." In W. E. Mann (ed.), *The Blackwell Guide to the Philosophy of Religion*. Malden, MA: Blackwell Publishing.
Dickens, C. ([1843] 1984) "A Christmas Carol." In C. Dickens, *A Christmas Carol and Other Christmas Stories*. New York: Signet Classics.
Eckhart, M. (1941) *Meister Eckhart: A Modern Translation*, trans. R. B. Blakney. New York: Harper & Row.
James, W. (1902) *The Varieties of Religious Experience*. New York: Longmans, Green, and Co.
Sacks, O. (1985) *The Man Who Mistook His Wife for a Hat and Other Clinical Tales*. New York: Summit Books.
Stace, W. T. (1960a) *Mysticism and Philosophy*. London: Macmillan Press.
—— (1960b) *The Teachings of the Mystics*. New York: Mentor Books.
Swinburne, R. (1979) *The Existence of God*. Oxford: Oxford University Press.

Further Reading

Katz, S. T. (ed.) (1978) *Mysticism and Philosophical Analysis*. New York: Oxford University Press. (A collection of essays by scholars in philosophy and in religious studies, mostly on epistemological issues arising from mystical experience.)
Pike, N. (1992) *Mystic Union: An Essay on the Phenomenology of Mysticism*. Ithaca, NY: Cornell University Press. (A detailed discussion of different kinds of mystic union, along with a critical assessment of Stace's views.)
Smart, N. (1967) "Mystical Experience." In W. H. Capitan and D. D. Merrill (eds.), *Art, Mind, and Religion*. Pittsburgh: University of Pittsburgh Press. (Disagrees with Zaehner's experiential pluralism and offers an analysis of how he thinks Zaehner went wrong.)
Zaehner, R. C. (1957) *Mysticism Sacred and Profane*. Oxford: Oxford University Press. (Argues that not all religious experiences are identical; one of the targets of Stace.)

Chapter 2

Religion and Science

John Polkinghorne

In a form recognizably continuous with its practice today, science originated in Western Europe in the seventeenth century. Galileo's combination of mathematical argument with empirical observation established a paradigm style that was to prove of immense fruitfulness. Francis Bacon had given philosophical encouragement to the exploration (and exploitation) of nature, but it has been argued that the Christian doctrine of creation, with its expectation of a deep order in the world reflecting the Mind of its Creator, together with its insistence that this order had been freely chosen by God so that it was necessary to look to see what its character actually was, also played a significant role in enabling the rise of modern science (Jaki 1986). It is certainly the case that most of the scientific pioneers of that period were persons of religious faith, even if some had their difficulties with the Church authorities (Galileo) or with Christian orthodoxy (Newton). A favorite metaphor in seventeenth-century discourse was to speak of the Two Books that God had written, nature and scripture. Both were worthy to be read; neither would mislead if read correctly, nor could they be in conflict since they had the same Author.

However, the post-Newtonian development of mechanical philosophy, particularly in France, broke the harmony between science and religion. Charles Darwin's publication of the *Origin of Species* in 1859 is often portrayed as the final parting of the ways. This judgment depends upon accepting an inaccurate caricature, as if all the scientists immediately embraced evolutionary thought and all the theologians resolutely opposed it. In fact, the issues were, and have remained, much more subtle than that (Brooke 1991). The natural dialogue partner for science is theology (intellectual reflection on religion), and there is a vigorous contemporary conversation going on between the two, whose present phase dates from the stimulus given by publications such as those by Eric Mascall (1956) and Ian Barbour (1966).

Philosophical Issues

The "Two Books" metaphor suggests a degree of cousinly relationship between science and theology, and this has been an important theme in recent writing. Both science and theology are seen to be engaged in the rational exploration of experience, though clearly their investigations deal with different kinds of experience. Science's concern is with the world encountered in an impersonal mode that lays it open to experimental manipulation and interrogation. Theology is concerned with the transpersonal meeting with the infinite reality of God, One who is not to be put to the test since encounter with the divine involves finite beings in an irreducible experience of awe and mystery. Scientific questions relate to inquiry into the processes by which things happen; theological questions relate to issues of meaning and purpose – whether there is something going on in what is happening. Despite these differences, science and theology share a common commitment to the quest for truthful understanding, attained through motivated belief.

Much writing on science and religion comes from scientist-theologians, people whose formation was in one of the sciences before they ventured into interdisciplinary work. Scientist-theologians often adopt the stance of a commitment to critical realism (Barbour 1974; Peacocke 1984; Polkinghorne 1991). Both science and theology involve a subtle and sensitive interplay between experience and its interpretation. The acknowledged role of interpretation frustrates the heroic (but ultimately failed) attempt of modernism to follow René Descartes in appealing to sure and certain ideas unproblematically accessible to all, in the hope that they could serve as the foundation of knowledge. The acknowledged role of experience in controlling the shape of thought delivers the search for understanding from any exaggerated postmodernist assertion of mere cultural construction. Neither in science nor in theology is it given to human beings to attain absolute truth, but verisimilitude, an account reliable for some but not every purpose, is within our grasp. The philosopher who has been found particularly helpful in articulating critical realism has been Michael Polanyi (1958). He tells us that he wrote *Personal Knowledge* to explain how he might commit himself to what he believed scientifically to be true, while knowing that it might be false. Theologians can accept a similar description of the task of "faith seeking understanding" (to use a celebrated phrase due to Anselm). More specifically, John Polkinghorne (1994) has set out an approach to Christian theology based on what he calls "bottom-up thinking," in which revelation is understood to be the record of particularly transparent experiences of the divine presence, carefully evaluated as providing motivations for doctrinal understanding.

Some writers on science and theology, most notably Barbour (1966; 1998), have appealed specifically to the process philosophy of A. N. Whitehead (1978) as a philosophical basis for theological discourse. Others, however, find that the apparent episodic character of Whitehead's event-based metaphysic fits poorly with quantum physics, whose subtle kind of continuity is only to a limited degree punctuated by occasions of discontinuity (macroscopic measurements). Moreover, the God of process theology acts solely by persuasive influence, seeking to exercise a "lure" on the outcome of individual events ("actual occasions"), while the final initiative for what actually happens is held to lie with the event itself. (There is a panpsychic tinge to process thought – namely, in its aspiration to combine protons and persons in a single continuum of being – which does not seem wholly repudiated by using "panexperientialism" as an indicator that no claim is being made that atoms possess actual consciousness.) The God of process thought appears to be a Pleader on the margins of occurrence, and much theological thinking calls for a stronger account of divine providential action than that.

A concept of philosophical theology that has found wider, but by no means universal, acceptance in the science and theology community, has been panentheism, carefully to be distinguished from pantheism. The latter identifies God and the universe, in the spirit of Benedict Spinoza's phrase *deus sive natura*. Panentheism, by contrast, asserts the world to be "in" God in some sense, but also acknowledges that God exceeds the world. The comparative popularity of this idea has partly been the result of a reaction against the ideas of classical theology (such as in the tradition associated with Thomas Aquinas), which tended to emphasize to an exaggerated degree the transcendent otherness of deity, so that Aquinas could say that though God acted on creatures, creatures in no way acted on God. Yet the blurring of a distinction between Creator and creatures poses problems for theology, both in relation to the problem of evil and suffering and in relation to the eschatological hope of a creaturely destiny beyond death. Consequently, others in the science and theology community have concluded that all that is needed by way of correction to classical theology is an enhanced understanding of divine immanence, expressing God's close presence to creation but preserving a vital distinction between God and the world.

Creation

Two errors have bedeviled discussion of creation in the interaction between science and religion. One originated on the religious side, the other among the scientists.

It was only in the later Middle Ages, and then reinforced in Reformation times, that interpreters of the Bible increasingly confined themselves to a narrowly literal reading of the text. Earlier generations had adopted a more flexible approach. For example, Augustine understood the "days" of creation to be long periods of time, and he believed that God had originally created "seeds" that would in due course germinate to produce the rich variety of nature. In approaching scripture it is important to pay attention to the genre of what is being read. The Bible is a library of many different kinds of writing, rather than a single homogeneous book. The irony of contemporary "creationism" is that its erroneous attempt to treat chapters 1 and 2 of Genesis as if they were divinely dictated scientific texts actually does violence to the nature of scripture. The character of these two chapters is theological rather than scientific, as the contrast between the two accounts of creation there given should make clear. The purpose of Genesis 1 is to assert that nothing exists save by the will of God ("And God said, Let there be . . .") and that humans are made in the divine image, while the older story of Genesis 2 gives a more intimate account of the relationship between human beings and God.

The error so often made by scientists is failing to recognize that the doctrine of creation is concerned with ontological origin rather than temporal beginning. Its concern is to answer G. W. Leibniz's great question, "Why is there something rather than nothing?", and not with who it was who started off the Big Bang. Hence the discovery by cosmology that our universe has a finite age (14 billion years), while scientifically interesting, is not particularly theologically significant. The originators of the now discredited steady-state theory of the universe were mistaken in thinking they were making a blow against theism, as was also Stephen Hawking when he suggested that his speculative quantum cosmology, which asserts that the universe has a finite age but no precisely dateable beginning, impugned belief in a Creator. Theology understands God to be as much the Creator today as God was 14 billion years ago.

Modern theology sets alongside the traditional concept of creation *ex nihilo*, a complementary concept of continuous creation, a historically unfolding process of increasing fertility. It was only in the nineteenth century that science began to recognize that the past had been very different from the way things are now, so that time is not just the index of occurrence, but the womb from which the present has emerged. Darwin's great evolutionary insights into the history of life were supplemented in the twentieth century by cosmology's (initially reluctant) recognition that the universe itself has had an evolving history. It started extremely simple, an almost uniform expanding ball of energy emerging from the singularity of the Big Bang, and it has taken 14 billion years of cosmic history to evolve into its present rich complexity.

Shortly after the publication of the *Origin of Species*, two Anglican clergymen, Charles Kingsley and Frederick Temple, coined a phrase that encapsulates the theological way to think about an evolutionary universe. They said that, instead of creating a ready-made world, God had done something cleverer than that in creating a world in which creatures could "make themselves." This pregnant insight has been particularly developed and explored by Arthur Peacocke (1978; 1993).

Christian theology has to find a middle way between two unacceptably extreme pictures of God's relationship to creation. God can neither be the spectatorial God of deism, simply watching things happen in indifferent detachment, nor the Cosmic Tyrant whose creation is a cosmic puppet theatre in which the divine Puppeteer pulls every string. If the divine character is love, then creatures must have been given some due degree of independence to be themselves and to make themselves. A particularly significant theme in much twentieth-century theology has been the recognition that the act of creation is a kenotic act on the part of the Creator, a divine self-limitation through which God allows creatures to exercise the gift of creaturely freedom (Polkinghorne 2001).

This kenosis (emptying) of divine power, allowing the created other to be, implies that not all that God allows to happen in creation will be in accordance with the divine positive will. The problems of theodicy (justifying God in the face of evil and suffering) have been of particular significance in the century of two world wars and the Holocaust. In relation to moral evil (the chosen cruelties and neglects of humankind), appeal has been made to the "free-will defense," the claim that a world of freely choosing beings is a better world than one populated by perfect automata, however terrible some of those choices may prove to be. Theology gains some insight here, though the assertion is not one that can be made without a quiver in the voice (see chapter 10, The Argument from Evil).

What then about physical evil (disease and disaster)? Here the responsibility of the Creator may seem to be more direct. Scientific understanding offers theology some help. A world in which creatures make themselves may be a great good, but it has a necessary cost. The shuffling explorations of potentiality through unfolding evolutionary process cannot avoid having ragged edges and blind alleys. There is a necessary shadow side that even God cannot eliminate. The processes of genetic mutation, which in germ cells have driven the evolution of complexity, will in some somatic cells induce malignancy. Tectonic plates, whose existence facilitates the circulation of mineral resources vital to life, will also sometimes, in accordance with their nature, slip and produce earthquakes. Polkinghorne (1989) has called this collection of insights the "free-process defense" in relation to natural evil.

The central question of theodicy is "If God is good and almighty, whence comes evil?" The response of a coherent doctrine of creation requires a reassessment of the meaning of "almighty." The word does not signify arbitrary divine power, but it asserts God's unlimited ability to act *in accordance with the divine nature*. The rational God cannot decree that $2 + 2 = 5$, nor can the loving God act as a despot. No external influence can act to limit God, but internally the Creator is self-limited to permit creatures to be themselves and to make themselves. Some twentieth-century theologians have extended kenotic thinking to qualify not only divine power, but also a divine engagement with temporality. Classical theology envisaged God as wholly outside time, able to survey from an eternal viewpoint the whole of creation's history laid out before the divine atemporal gaze "all at once." While theologians will wish to assert divine eternity, signifying that God is not in thrall to time as all creatures are, yet much contemporary theology, including process theology but not limited to it, has supposed that there is also a temporal pole in the divine nature, expressing the Creator's gracious choice to engage with the unfolding history of creation. If this is so, some have gone on to see this as implying a kenosis of divine omniscience. In a world of true becoming, it is claimed, even God does not yet know the unformed future, for it is not yet there to be known. On this view, God possesses a current omniscience, knowing all that is now knowable, but not an absolute omniscience, knowing all that will ever be knowable (Swinburne 1977). Needless to say, the claim is contentious.

Science's exploration of the universe has brought to light its deeply relational character. General relativity ties together space, time, and matter in a single unified account. Quantum entanglement (Polkinghorne 2002a) shows that once entities have interacted with each other, they effectively constitute a single system, however far they may separate spatially. The extreme sensitivity of chaotic systems to the fine detail of circumstance shows that they can never properly be treated in isolation from their environment. These discoveries about creation are certainly consistent with the insight of Trinitarian theology that the Creator's nature itself is intrinsically relational (Polkinghorne 2004), even if they clearly do not entail that conclusion.

Natural Theology

Natural theology is the attempt to learn something of God by considering general experience rather than specific acts of revelatory disclosure. Typically it appeals to the exercise of reason and the inspection of the world. The later Middle Ages and the beginning of the nineteenth century were two great periods of the flourishing of natural theology. The former included Anselm's ontological argument, defining God as "that than which no greater can be conceived" and asserting that it is greater to exist than not to do so (see chapter 8, The Ontological Argument). However, Immanuel Kant was surely right to argue that existence cannot act as a defining predicate. In reality, Anselm could establish no more than that, if there actually is a maximal being, that being possesses aseity, being in itself, independently of anything else. The other great medieval natural theologian was Aquinas. His "Five Ways" in which to prove the existence of God look to very general features of the world, such as the existence of change, said to call for an unchanging God as the ground of the world's persistence. Only the fifth way is more specific, appealing to an idea of design manifested in the apt functioning of living beings.

The argument from design was wholeheartedly endorsed in the second period of flourishing, forming the basis of the writings of William Paley and the authors of the Bridgewater Treatises (Brooke 1991). However, Darwin undermined this approach when he showed how the patient sifting and accumulation of small differences could, over long periods of time, lead to the appearance of design without a need for the direct intervention of a Designer.

The contemporary scene in science and religion has witnessed a revival of natural theology, both at the hands of scientist-theologians and also by some scientists who stand outside any faith tradition (Davies 1992). Its form, however, is significantly revised from that which preceded it. Talk of "proofs" of God's

existence has given way to the more modest claim that theism offers more com-
prehensively explanatory insight than is possible for atheism. Natural theology is
seen to be persuasive rather than logically coercive. At the same time, its insights
are offered as complementary to science rather than in direct competition with it.
Scientific questions – such as the development of the eye, whose delicately effective
optical system had been seen by Paley as a manifestation of divine design – are
now expected to receive scientific answers. The so-called "God of the gaps,"
invoked as the source of what the science of the time could not yet explain in
terms of natural process, has been found to be no more than a pseudo-deity, ever
disappearing with the advance of knowledge. In any case, he was a theological
mistake, for the true God is not an invisible artificer, but the Ordainer and Sustainer of the whole natural order. Instead, the new natural theology looks beyond
science to those aspects of the world which science, by its own self-limited nature,
has bracketed out of its discourse so that it is unable to explain them. Two meta-
questions, arising from scientific experience but lying outside its narrow power to
address, have been the focus of the new natural theology. They relate to the
observed character of the laws of nature, which is seen to be such that it is intellectually unsatisfying to follow David Hume's advice and to treat these laws simply
as given brute fact.

The first metaquestion concerns the deep intelligibility of the universe, which
makes it so profoundly transparent to scientific inquiry. The evolutionary necessity
to survive in a given environment furnishes an adequate explanation of how the
human mind is able to achieve a rough and ready understanding of everyday
experience. Yet it seems highly implausible to suppose that our ability to understand regimes such as that of quantum physics, remote from direct impact on
everyday life and requiring counterintuitive ways of thinking for their comprehension, is simply a happy spin-off from mundane survival needs. Many scientists
are deeply impressed by the mystery of cosmic intelligibility. Albert Einstein
once said that the only incomprehensible thing about the universe is its
comprehensibility.

And not only is the world transparent to our inquiry, but it also proves to be
rationally beautiful, frequently rewarding scientists with the experience of wonder
as a recompense for the hours of weary labor spent in research. In fundamental
physics it has been found time and again that only equations endowed with the
unmistakable quality of mathematical beauty correspond to theories able to persuade us of their verisimilitudinous character through their long-term fruitfulness
of explanation. Paul Dirac, one of the founding figures of quantum theory, once
said that it was more important to have mathematical beauty in your equations
than to have them fit experiment! This was certainly not because empirical
adequacy was irrelevant. Yet, if at first sight it seemed to be absent, it was at
least conceivable that there had been some mistake in the calculations or in the
experiments, but if beauty were lacking, nothing could be expected to remedy
that defect. Another Nobel prizewinner, Eugene Wigner, once asked, "Why is
mathematics so unreasonably effective?" How can it be that this abstract discipline

provides the key to unlock the secrets of the physical universe? Natural theology renders intelligible the rational transparency and rational beauty of the cosmos, seeing them as signs of the Mind of the Creator that lies behind the wonderful order of the world.

The second metaquestion asks why the universe is so special. Although life took some 10 billion years to appear, there is a real sense in which the universe was pregnant with its possibility from about the Big Bang onwards. Only because the laws of nature operating in our world took a very precise, "finely tuned," quantitative form was it possible for carbon-based life to develop anywhere within the universe (see chapter 7, The Teleological Argument). Such a remarkable fact surely calls for some kind of explanation. Two metascientific suggestions have been made. The idea of a multiverse, a vast portfolio of many separate universes, all with different laws of nature, suggests that it is simply by chance that our world is the one in that immense array where circumstances were right for carbon-based life. The proposal has great ontological prodigality, invoked to do a single piece of explanatory work. By contrast, the second explanation, offered by natural theology, that this universe is a creation that has been endowed by its Creator with just the laws that have enabled it to have a fruitful history, is ontologically parsimonious and forms part of a cumulative case for theism, offering many other explanatory insights (such as why the world is profoundly intelligible).

Divine Action

The limited resources appealed to by natural theology imply that the insights it can offer will be similarly circumscribed. Its picture of God cannot amount to much more than the great Cosmic Mathematician, a concept as consistent with the God of deism as it is with the providentially active God of theism. Yet it is the latter to whom most of the adherents of the world faiths address their prayers. But can one really believe today in a God who acts in history, given all that science can tell us about the regularity of the physical world?

Throughout the 1990s, the attention of the science and theology community was focused on the issue of how divine action might take place in the world described by modern science (Russell, Murphy, and Peacocke 1995; Russell et al. 2001). The mechanical paradigm that had seemed to be the implication of Newtonian theory had been rendered obsolete by the discovery in the twentieth century of intrinsic unpredictabilities present in nature. They first came to light in microscopic processes subject to quantum uncertainty (Polkinghorne 2002a) and then, in a different form, in the macroscopic processes described by chaos theory (Gleick 1988). It is important to recognize that in both these regimes the unpredictabilities are *intrinsic*, incapable of being removed by more precise calculation or more exact observation. The physical world has turned out to be something more subtle than a clockwork universe. The critical question is whether it is also more supple in its causal structure, open to effects that go beyond science's traditional account of the exchange of energy between constituents.

Unpredictability is an epistemological property, expressing a limit on what can be known about future behavior. It is a question for metaphysical decision what this might be held to imply for the ontological character of causal structure. Physics constrains metaphysics, but it does not determine it. The point is clearly illustrated by arguments about the interpretation of quantum theory. The mainstream approach, commonly called the Copenhagen interpretation because of its association with Niels Bohr, treats quantum physics as intrinsically indeterministic. Yet there is another interpretation of equal empirical adequacy, due to David Bohm, which is deterministic and in which unpredictability arises simply from unavoidable ignorance of certain factors ("hidden variables"). Both approaches incorporate Heisenberg's uncertainty principle, but for Bohr it is an expression of ontological indeterminacy, while for Bohm it is an epistemological principle of ignorance. The choice between the two can only be made on metascientific grounds, such as perceived economy and lack of contrivance.

There is a similar option to treat the unpredictabilities of chaos theory as signs of an ontological suppleness. Polkinghorne (1998: ch. 3) has taken this view, but others have not adopted it, perhaps influenced by the deterministic character of the Newtonian equations whose study led to the recognition of mathematical chaos. Yet Newtonian physics is only an approximation, and so it cannot be used to settle the issue. If chaotic unpredictability is treated in the same way that the majority treat quantum unpredictability, it leads to the expectation of new macroscopic causal principles whose character is holistic rather than reductionistic (since chaotic systems are effectively not isolatable from their environment). These principles are related to the internal patterns in which energy flows, rather than to external inputs of energy (since that is the form that differences between the unpredictable future behaviors of a chaotic system actually take).

At first sight, one might have hoped to advance the discussion by combining quantum and chaotic unpredictabilities, since the future behavior of chaotic systems soon comes to depend upon fine details at the level of Heisenberg's uncertainty principle. However, quantum chaology has not progressed because the two theories do not readily fit together (Berry 2001). Quantum theory has a scale, set by Planck's constant, but the fractal character of chaotic dynamics means that it is scale-free. This mismatch illustrates a more general point, that the investigations of physics into the causal structure of the world are often patchy, with connections between different regimes frequently problematic and ill-understood. Another example is provided by the measurement problem in quantum theory: How does it come about that a cloudy microscopic quantum system, on each occasion of measurement using macroscopic apparatus, yields a definite answer, though not the same answer on each such occasion? Eighty years after the discovery of modern quantum theory, this reasonable question still lacks a full and agreed answer. We are far from a complete understanding of the relationship between classical physics and quantum theory.

The discussions of the 1990s did not provide a well-articulated theory of either human or providential agency, but they did "defeat the defeaters." Science has not established causal closure in terms of its traditional reductionistic picture of the exchange of energy between constituents, and there is metaphysical room for belief in additional causal principles of a holistic, top-down kind, consistent with both human and divine action in the world. Information (the specification of patterned holistic behavior) is coming to be recognized as a fundamental concept in science, and one may associate agency with a form of "active information."

The picture of agency exercised within the cloudy unpredictabilities of nature has implications for theology. There is a degree of veiling involved that means that it is not possible to analyze and itemize what is happening in an exhaustive fashion, as if one could say that nature did this, human action did that, and God did the third thing. Providence may be discernible by faith, but it will not be demonstrable by experiment. While there are many clouds in the world, there are also many reliable clocks. These have permitted science to pursue its investigations, and theology can see them as signs of the Creator's faithfulness. God will not capriciously set these regularities aside, and this implies that there are some things that it is not sensible to pray for. Long ago in Alexandria, Origen said that one should not pray for the cool of spring in the heat of summer.

Eschatology

Cosmologists not only look back to the universe's origin in the Big Bang, but they also peer into the cosmic future. When they do so, they see it all ending in futility. Many tens of billions of years hence, a time will come when all carbon-based life will have perished from the universe, most probably through increasing cold and dilution brought about by ceaseless cosmic expansion. This scientific prognostication puts a serious question to theology about what it might suppose to be the Creator's true intentions for creation.

Recent work in science and religion has paid an increasing attention to the issues of eschatology, asking whether there is indeed a coherent hope of a destiny beyond death, either for human individuals or for the universe itself (Polkinghorne and Welker 2000; Polkinghorne 2002b; Peters, Russell, and Welker 2002). Christian thinking acknowledges that there is no natural hope of such a destiny, of a kind that science could incorporate into the story it has to tell. Only if there is a further story, telling the tale of the faithfulness of God (and in Christian belief exemplified in the resurrection of Jesus Christ), can there be hope of life beyond death, brought about by the divine eschatological act of resurrection into God's new creation. The concern of the discussions in the science and theology community has been to explore whether such a hope indeed seems to be a coherent possibility.

Consideration of the case of individual human destiny soon shows that the idea requires a combination of both continuity and discontinuity. If Abraham will indeed live again in the kingdom of God, then there must be sufficient continuity to ensure that it is truly the patriarch himself, and not just some new being given the old name. But there must also be sufficient discontinuity to ensure that Abraham is not made alive again simply in order to die again.

The carrier of continuity between this world and the next has usually been supposed to be the human soul. In much traditional thinking, the soul was conceived in Platonic terms as a detachable spiritual substance, released from the fleshly body at the moment of death. However, such a dualist picture of human nature has become increasingly problematic with the recognition of such matters as the influence of drugs and brain damage on personality, and human evolutionary kinship with the animals. Today a psychosomatic picture of human nature is much more persuasive. This is accepted by many contemporary theologians, and it would have caused no shock to most of the writers of the Bible, since Hebrew thought saw human beings as animated bodies, rather than incarnated souls. In that case, some reconceptualization of the soul is called for.

The question of what constitutes the continuity of the person is a complex one, even in this life. It is certainly not material continuity, since the atoms in our bodies are in a state of constant flux through physiological processes. The "real person" must be constituted by something like the almost infinitely complex information-bearing pattern carried at any one moment by those ever-changing atoms. Such a concept is difficult to articulate with any degree of precision, but the idea is consistent with the growing scientific recognition of the significance of information, and it represents a revival in modern dress of the Aristotelian-Thomistic notion of the soul as the "form" of the body. As far as natural understanding is concerned, the soul-pattern will not possess an intrinsic immortality, for it will dissolve with the decay of the body that carried it. However, it is a coherent theological hope that this individual pattern will not be allowed to be lost, but it will be preserved in the memory of the faithful God. This of itself would not be the continuation of the life of the individual since, if human beings are psychosomatic unities, full humanity requires embodiment of some kind. However, if new life is not to lead simply to new death, this embodiment must be in some new form of "matter."

This is the point at which discontinuity comes into play. Mortality in this present world essentially arises from the operation of the second law of thermodynamics, driving a relentless drift from order to disorder. Increasing entropy results from the statistical fact that there are very many more disorderly forms of matter than there are orderly, so that disorder always wins in the end. Yet it seems a perfectly coherent possibility that the Creator could bring into being a new kind of "matter," endowed with such powerful self-organizing principles that it would no longer be subject to the thermodynamic drift to disorder. If that is the case, two critical questions still remain to be answered.

The first is where this "matter" might come from. The theological expectation is that it arises from an eschatological transformation of the matter of the present universe. In other words, ultimate human and cosmic destinies lie together in a world of new creation, an insight foreshadowed for the Christian by the fact that Christ's risen and glorified body is the transformation of his dead body.

The second question asks why, if the new creation is to be free from death and transience, did the Creator bother with the mortal world of the old creation. The theological response is that God's creative purpose is necessarily two-step. This evolving world, in which death is the inevitable cost of new life, is one in which creatures make themselves, living at some distance from the veiled presence of their Creator. The life of the world to come will have a different character because in it creatures will have entered into a new and more intimate relationship with their Creator, not imposed upon them but freely accepted.

Eschatological exploration has a necessarily speculative component, but for Christian theology it rests on the foundation of the faithfulness of God revealed in the resurrection of Jesus Christ.

World Faiths

The discussion here has been presented principally in Christian terms, though on matters such as creation and natural theology there would be substantial agreement between the three Abrahamic faiths. Discussion of science and religion must be concerned with more than generalized notions, and it needs to engage with the specificities of particular religious belief. Of the world faiths, Christianity is probably the one that attaches the greatest importance to an academic approach to questions of belief, and so a great deal of the discussion of science and theology has, so far, taken place within the Christian fold. It is to be hoped that in the future the insights of the other traditions will make an increasing contribution. At the same time, discussion of science and religion issues offers the faiths a serious meeting place for what will surely be their increasing mutual dialogue in the course of the twenty-first century, without immediately moving to possible confrontation arising from the puzzling cognitive clashes that there appear to be between their core accounts of the nature of sacred reality.

Questions for Reflection

1   How similar, and how different, are science and theology? How should they relate to each other?
2   What reasons might there be to speak of the universe as a creation?
3   How should religion understand evolution?
4   Could a scientist pray and expect God to respond by acting in the world?
5   Can one make sense of the hope of a destiny beyond death?

References

Barbour, I. G. (1966) *Issues in Science and Religion*. London: SCM Press.
—— (1974) *Myths, Models and Paradigms*. London: SCM Press.
—— (1998) *Religion and Science*. London: SCM Press.
Berry, M. V. (2001) "Chaos and the Semiclassical Limit in Quantum Theory." In R. J. Russell, P. Clayton, K. Wegter-McNelly, and J. C. Polkinghorne (eds.), *Quantum Mechanics*. Vatican City: Vatican Observatory.
Brooke, J. H. (1991) *Science and Religion*. Cambridge: Cambridge University Press.
Davies, P. W. (1992) *The Mind of God*. New York: Simon and Schuster.
Gleick, J. (1988) *Chaos*. London: Heinmann.
Jaki, S. (1986) *Science and Creation*. Edinburgh: Scottish Academic Press.
Mascall, E. L. (1956) *Christian Theology and Natural Science*. London: Longmans.
Peacocke, A. R. (1978) *Creation and the World of Science*. Oxford: Oxford University Press.
—— (1984) *Intimations of Reality*. Notre Dame: University of Notre Dame Press.
—— (1993) *Theology for a Scientific Age*. London: SCM Press.
Peters, T., R. J. Russell, and M. Welker (eds.) (2002) *Resurrection*. Grand Rapids: Eerdmans.
Polanyi, M. (1958) *Personal Knowledge*. London: Routledge and Kegan Paul.
Polkinghorne, J. C. (1989) *Science and Providence*. London: SPCK.
—— (1991) *Reason and Reality*. London: SPCK.
—— (1994) *Science and Christian Belief*. London: SPCK. Also published as (1996) *The Faith of a Physicist*. Minneapolis: Fortress.
—— (1998) *Belief in God in an Age of Science*. New Haven, CT: Yale University Press.
—— (ed.) (2001) *The Work of Love*. Grand Rapids: Eerdmans.
—— (2002a) *Quantum Theory: A Very Short Introduction*. Oxford: Oxford University Press.
—— (2002b) *The God of Hope and the End of the World*. New Haven, CT: Yale University Press.
—— (2004) *Science and the Trinity*. New Haven, CT: Yale University Press.
Polkinghorne, J. C., and M. Welker (eds.) (2000) *The End of the World and the Ends of God*. Harrisburg, PA: Trinity Press International.
Russell, R. J., N. Murphy, and A. R. Peacocke (eds.) (1995) *Chaos and Complexity*. Vatican City: Vatican Observatory.
Russell, R. J., P. Clayton, K. Wegter-McNelly, and J. C. Polkinghorne (eds.) (2001) *Quantum Mechanics*. Vatican City: Vatican Observatory.
Swinburne, R. (1977) *The Coherence of Theism*. Oxford: Oxford University Press.
Whitehead, A. N. (1978) *Process and Reality* (corr. edn.). New York: Free Press.

Further Reading

Barbour, I. G. (1997) *Religion and Science*. New York: HarperCollins. (A comprehensive account of the thinking of a modern pioneer.)
Peacocke, A. R. (1994) *Theology for a Scientific Age*. Minneapolis: Augsburg Fortress Press. (A biologist's approach, particularly helpful in relation to evolutionary insight.)

Polkinghorne, J. C. (1994) *Science and Christian Belief / The Faith of a Physicist.* Princeton: Princeton University Press. (A physicist's approach to Christian belief, based on a "bottom-up" argument from evidence to interpretation.)

—— (2002) *The God of Hope and the End of the World.* New Haven, CT: Yale University Press. (Discussion of the nature of the soul and the credibility of the hope of a destiny beyond death.)

Rolston, H. (1999) *Genes, Genesis and God.* Cambridge: Cambridge University. Press. (A philosopher of evolutionary biology discusses values and their origins in nature and in human history.)

Chapter 3

Reformed Epistemology

René van Woudenberg

Religious believers hold beliefs. Many of them, for example, believe there is a God, a being whose understanding has no measure, whose power has no limits, and whose goodness is holy and without bounds. Call this theistic belief, or bare theism. Virtually all religious believers hold beliefs beyond bare theism. Christians, for example, believe that God created the heavens and the earth – as do adherents of Judaism and Islam. Christians furthermore believe, as it is expressed in the Apostles' Creed, that Jesus Christ is the Son of God, and that through his redemptive suffering and glorious resurrection from the dead there is forgiveness of sins and everlasting life. But next to these "doctrinal" beliefs, the ordinary believer may, upon doing what he knows is wrong, form the belief that God disapproves of what he has done.

One question that has haunted religious belief in the Western world is whether holding such beliefs is, or can be, justified, or rational, or intellectually respectable. Many who have addressed this question have made an important assumption. They have held that if religious belief is to have any of the merits mentioned, it needs to be based on propositional evidence. One particularly striking formulation of the assumption is due to W. K. Clifford who urged that "It is wrong, always, and everywhere, to believe anything upon insufficient evidence" (Clifford 1901: 186). On the basis of this it has been claimed that religious beliefs are, or at least can be, respectable. After all, there are many arguments for God's existence, for example ontological arguments, cosmological arguments, arguments from design, from desire, and many more (see Part II, The Existence of God). On the basis of the same assumption, however, it is claimed that religious beliefs are unjustified, irrational, and intellectually despicable, especially the existence of evil seems to be powerful evidence against theistic belief (see chapter 10, The Argument from Evil).

The aim of this chapter is to present a way of thinking about the intellectual respectability of religious belief that involves a rather striking departure from the assumption mentioned in the previous paragraph – namely, Reformed epistemology.

Its intellectual fathers (there seem to be no such mothers) include Alvin Plantinga, Nicholas Wolterstorff, and, at some remove, William Alston and George Mavrodes. The order of business is as follows. First, the assumption referred to, which I shall call "the evidentialist assumption," is explained and then criticized. Next, a particular way of thinking about the respectability of religious belief is presented that takes its cue from such Reformed theologians as John Calvin and Herman Bavinck, one that certainly isn't foreign to the Catholic tradition. Finally, a number of concluding and critical remarks will be made.

The Evidentialist Assumption Stated

The assumption that religious belief is rational or justified only insofar as it is based on propositional evidence is part and parcel of what has come to be known as "classical foundationalism" – a certain way of thinking about justification, belief, and knowledge that can be traced back to at least René Descartes and John Locke (Wolterstorff 1997; Plantinga 2000: ch. 3). According to the classical foundationalist, there is a great divide between two types of belief, between two ways of believing a proposition. There are, first, beliefs that we have because we have followed or devised an argument for them. I believe, for example, that $37 \times 21 = 777$ because I have followed an argument: I have just calculated the product. There are many things we believe on the basis of arguments, especially when we are doing science. Upon performing a number of experiments, Robert Boyle came to believe that for any fixed and closed volume of gas, there is a direct relation between its temperature and its pressure: the higher the temperature, the greater the pressure. Let us call beliefs that we have because of some line of reasoning we performed *inferential* or *non-basic beliefs*.

The classical foundationalist holds that if we are to have non-basic beliefs, we will have to have *basic* beliefs as well, i.e., beliefs that we have but not because we have arguments for them. To be sure, there are many such beliefs. Upon noticing the blooming of the magnolia in my garden, I may find myself with the belief that the magnolia in my garden is blooming; but in the typical case this belief is not the result of having made a perhaps quick and silent argument to myself. I don't think "That seems to be my garden, and that seems to be a blooming magnolia in it; usually when I seem to see my garden and a blooming magnolia in it, then it is really my garden (as opposed to yours, for example) and a blooming magnolia (as opposed to, perhaps, a sycamore) in (as opposed to adjacent to) it; currently there is nothing unusual; therefore there is a blooming magnolia in my garden." That is typically not the sort of process that precedes and leads to my perceptual beliefs. Something similar holds for memory beliefs. Being in a certain frame of mind, I may remember that one of my earliest teachers was named Verrips and accordingly believe that she was thus named. But there is no arguing or reasoning involved. This belief is "basic" in the intended sense, as are many beliefs about "other minds" – such as your belief "Mary is in pain" – and many *a priori* beliefs – such your belief that 2 + 2 = 4 and that every number that is greater than seven is also greater than three (Plantinga 1993: 65–77). So, there are numerous clear and uncontroversial examples of basic beliefs (see van Woudenberg, Roeser, and Rood 2005).

Now beliefs may be basic in the sense intended but at the same time improper to embrace. I may believe without evidence or argument that the Queen of Holland is right now hosting an old friend of hers. This belief would be basic but improper as well: it is a belief I had better not have. Which beliefs, then, are basic – and properly so? According to the classical foundationalist only those beliefs whose object (or content) is either a proposition that is self-evident, "evident to the senses," or incorrigibly reporting from one's own experience. Examples of propositions that will be self-evident to the vast majority of adult human beings are:

1   2 + 2 = 4.
2   Nothing can be red all over and green all over at the same time.
3   The property of being prime is different from the property of being composite.

The defining characteristic of a self-evident proposition is that the moment one grasps or understands it, one sees it to be true. And, of course, the moment one sees a proposition to be true, one will be believing it is true. Whether or not a proposition is self-evident is person relative. If you don't grasp, for example, what *being prime* comes to, you won't see that (3) is true, but if you do, you will.

Examples of propositions that are "evident to the senses" include:

4   That window is broken.
5   There is an apple pie in the oven.

The hallmark of these propositions is that their truth value can be determined by using our senses, i.e., by looking, hearing, touching, tasting, or smelling. One can determine the truth value of (4) by looking at the window, and the truth value of (5) by smelling a hard-to-describe but characteristic smell. It should be noted that not all empirical propositions are evident to the senses. That the earth revolves around the sun is an empirical proposition, but not evident to the senses.

Finally, examples of propositions that are incorrigible reports from experience include:

6   It seems to me that the window is broken.
7   I seem to hear an A 440 Hz (i.e., middle A, or the A above middle C).

These propositions seem to be such that if one believes them, one cannot be mistaken about them. Due to fatigue, drugs, or hallucinations I may mistakenly believe that the window is broken. But I cannot be mistaken in my belief that it *seems* to me that it is. There may be no window, and hence I may not see a window, but it could still be incontrovertible that I seem to see that the window is broken. Proposition (6) enjoys some kind of immunity from error that (4) lacks – it is, as they say, incorrigible. The defining characteristic of an incorrigible proposition is that, firstly, it is not possible that one believes it while it is false, and, secondly, it is not possible that one disbelieves it while it is true.

The classical foundationalist, then, holds that only those basic beliefs are *proper* that have as their object (or content) propositions of any one of these three types. Like basic beliefs, non-basic beliefs too can be either proper or improper. Which ones are properly non-basic? The classical foundationalist's answer is that it is only those beliefs that are appropriately based upon a foundation of properly basic beliefs. And, roughly speaking, belief B is appropriately based provided it follows deductively, inductively, or probabilistically from what is properly basic.

We can now see the relation between classical foundationalism and the evidentialist assumption: the assumption presupposes and is in fact part of classical foundationalism. Hence, on this assumption, the intellectual respectability of religious beliefs depends on whether or not there are good arguments for theistic conclusions that start from propositions that are self-evident, evident to the senses, or incorrigible reports from experience.

The Evidentialist Assumption Rejected

As I noted earlier on, both theists and atheists have embraced the evidentialist assumption and have, on its basis, argued both for and against the intellectual respectability of belief in God. But is there any reason to think the assumption is correct? Two reasons have been advanced for thinking it is not (Plantinga 1983: 59–63; Plantinga 2000: 93–9; Wolterstorff 1997: ix–xv).

First, the evidentialist assumption is part of classical foundationalism (CF), which may be stated as follows:

CF: Belief B is intellectually respectable for subject S if and only if either (a) B's content (the proposition believed) is properly basic for S, or (b) B's content follows from, or is probable with respect to, what is properly basic for S.

Now CF implies that many of our ordinary, non-religious, beliefs are not intellectually respectable. For example, I believe I had a grapefruit for breakfast this morning. I believe this because I clearly remember it. But the proposition *I had a grapefruit for breakfast this morning* is not properly basic for me. For, first, it is not self-evident; it is not that upon grasping the proposition, I see that it must be true. Neither, second, is it an incorrigible report from my experience; it is not such that I cannot be mistaken about it. Nor, third, is it evident to my senses; it is not that I now have a sense experience that induces belief in it. So, my belief is not properly basic on CF. But then perhaps it follows from, or is probable with respect to, what is properly basic for me? Perhaps it is intellectually respectable in that way? But it is hard to see how that could be. Suppose I believe that *I seem to remember that I had a grapefruit for breakfast this morning*. Surely this belief is properly basic for me. However, this proposition, as can be learned from the history of philosophy between Descartes and Thomas Reid, does not imply *I had a grapefruit for breakfast this morning*. Nor is the latter proposition probable with respect to the former. For, as Descartes argued, it is illegitimate to conclude from the way things seem to how they are. After all, an evil demon may "feed" me the belief that it seems to me that I had a grapefruit for breakfast this morning; in that case it would be wrong to conclude from this that I actually had a grapefruit for breakfast this morning. And the point is that neither I, nor anybody else, can ever exclude the evil demon scenario. On CF, then, my belief is not intellectually respectable. Now, either my belief is not respectable, or CF is wrong. But surely, the Reformed epistemologist argues, my belief is respectable. Hence CF is wrong. This argument, then, has the character of a *reductio ad absurdum* of CF.

An even more telling criticism of CF is that it is, as Plantinga says, "self-referentially incoherent." To see the problem we have to ask ourselves whether CF itself is intellectually respectable. That will be the case if and only if CF meets condition (a) or (b). Now CF itself doesn't seem to be self-evident or evident to the senses, nor is it an incorrigible report from experience. It furthermore doesn't seem to follow from, or to be probable with respect to, what *is* self-evident, or evident to the senses, or incorrigible reports from experience. So, CF gives us a reason to think that CF itself is not intellectually respectable. Anybody who embraces CF has a reason to reject it.

So, there is no reason to accept CF, and, by implication, no reason to accept the evidentialist assumption that that religious belief is intellectually respectable if and only if one has propositional evidence for it. But where does one go from here? If one rejects the evidentialist's assumption, how shall one think about the intellectual respectability of religious beliefs? Doesn't rejection of the evidentialist assumption imply that any belief whatsoever, even of the craziest kind, can be intellectually respectable? The next section spells out the key elements of the Reformed epistemologist's reply.

The Possibility of Properly Basic Religious Belief

First, the problem with CF is not, as some have argued, that it makes a distinction between basic and non-basic beliefs, but rather that it gives too few (kinds of) beliefs the basic status. This is a point that the eighteenth-century Scottish philosopher Thomas Reid, one source of inspiration for Reformed epistemologists, had already made against CF adherents such as Descartes, Locke, and Hume. He argued that next to the beliefs that CF assigns proper basicality, many more have that status. Consider, for instance, memory beliefs (such as my belief that I had a grapefruit for breakfast this morning) and many beliefs about other minds (such as your belief that your friend Lizzy is a person and not a conscious automaton). These basic beliefs are not the result of, say, having worked out an analogical argument for other minds. But they are no less intellectually respectable for that. Many moral beliefs too are properly basic (see chapter 9, The Moral Argument). We believe it is wrong to hurt somebody else just for the fun of it, and for most of us this belief is basic; it is not based on propositional evidence that speaks for it. We believe it in much the same way we believe that $2 + 2 = 4$: we *see* it to be true upon apprehending it.

But if so many kinds of beliefs can be, and in fact are, properly basic, then why could not religious beliefs be properly basic as well? Nineteenth-century Dutch Reformed theologian Herman Bavinck suggested exactly this:

> We receive the impression that belief in the existence of God is based entirely on these proofs. . . . The contrary, however, is the truth. There is not a single object the existence of which we hesitate to accept until definite proofs are furnished. Of the existence of self, of the world round about us, of logical and moral laws, etc., we are so deeply convinced because of the indelible impressions which all these things make upon our consciousness that we need no arguments or demonstration. Spontaneously, altogether involuntarily: without any constraint or coercion, we accept that existence. Now the same is true in regard to the existence of God. The so-called proofs are by no means the final grounds of our most certain conviction that God exists. This certainty is established only by faith; that is, by the spontaneous testimony which forces itself upon us from every side. (Bavinck 1951: 78–9)

And John Calvin wrote:

> God himself has implanted in all men a certain understanding of his divine majesty. Ever renewing its memory, he repeatedly sheds fresh drops. . . . Therefore, men one and all perceive that there is a God and that he is their Maker. . . . Since from the beginning of the world there has been no region, no city, in short, no household, that could do without religion, there lies in this a tacit confession of a sense of deity inscribed in the hearts of all.
>
> . . . [T]his conviction . . . that there is some God, is naturally inborn in all, and is fixed deep within, as it were in the very marrow. . . . [F]rom this we conclude that it is not a doctrine that must first be learned in school, but one of which each of us is master from his mother's womb and which nature itself permits no one to forget. (Calvin 1960: 43–4)

According to these theologians, belief in God's existence in typical cases does not result from proof or demonstration. It is spontaneous and involuntary, says Bavinck, even if uncoerced. Calvin says it is a naturally inborn conviction, not a doctrine that must be taught at school. This suggests they hold that in the typical case belief in God is *basic*. But can it ever be *properly* basic? Both Bavinck and Calvin suggest that it can. Bavinck refers to the fact that belief in our own existence, as well as in the existence of the world, is both basic and proper, and he clearly thinks that theistic belief is in the same boat. Calvin says much the same thing when he says that God implanted in us a tendency or disposition to believe in him, a *sensus divinitatis*, as he calls it. And, of course, if God has done so, the beliefs engendered by that disposition cannot be improper. Reformed epistemologists agree and have worked out this idea with great care.

In order to see how, it is useful to review Plantinga's response to what he calls "the Great Pumpkin objection" which may be stated as follows: "If belief in God can be claimed to be properly basic, then why can't the same be claimed for just any old belief, for example the crazy belief that the Great Pumpkin returns every Halloween?" The response is that a basic belief is proper *only in certain circumstances*. Belief B may be properly basic in circumstance C, but not in circumstance C*. That you are reading a book right now is properly basic for you in your current situation, but not in a situation where you are playing the piano, or hiking the Pennine Way. What the Reformed epistemologist claims is that there are situations in which belief in God is properly basic, and furthermore that those situations occur rather frequently. But this need not commit him to the claim that the Great Pumpkin belief can be properly basic in any circumstance, nor to the claim that for any belief whatsoever there are circumstances in which it is properly basic. Again, all he claims is that belief in God can be properly basic.

It would be very nice if we had a *criterion* by means of which we would be able to tell whether or not a certain belief B is properly basic in circumstances C, C*, C**, etc. – a criterion that helps us to separate the sheep from the goats. But how do we arrive at such a criterion? Since we cannot simply *see* what criterion does the job, there appears to be no alternative to a broadly *inductive* approach. That is, there is no alternative to gathering examples of pairs of beliefs and circumstances, such that the former are properly basic in the latter, as well as examples of pairs such that the former are *not* properly basic in the latter, as well as examples of pairs where it is unclear whether or not the former are properly basic in the latter. Given these different kinds of examples, we may then try to see what all of the examples of the first sort have in common and in which respects they differ from the examples of the second sort, etc., and in this inductive way formulate a criterion of proper basicality. It must be noted that this procedure doesn't ensure that everyone will agree on the examples. The Reformed epistemologist holds that belief in God is properly basic in a wide variety of circumstances. But surely atheists like Bertrand Russell and Richard Dawkins and Daniel Dennett disagree. And isn't this a drawback for this inductive approach? Surely not! The procedure is entirely sound, as reasonable atheists will agree: this is a proper way to find a criterion for proper basicality. It does indicate, however, that the inductive way of finding the criterion for proper basicality is not *polemically* useful. One cannot, criterion in hand, persuade others who don't already agree that theistic belief is properly basic in a wide variety of circumstances.

The claim that belief in God can be properly basic does not mean that such belief is capricious, haphazard, or irrational (in one of the many senses of that word), nor that it is insensitive to arguments. Such belief is not capricious or haphazard, for even if it is basic, it is occasioned by someone's being in certain circumstances, or somewhat more precisely, by someone's faculties being activated by certain circumstances. A parallel might be helpful. I now believe I had a grapefruit for breakfast this morning, and this belief of mine is basic: I haven't formed it on the basis of propositional evidence. Still, it isn't capricious, for it is occasioned by, first, my actually having had a grapefruit for breakfast this morning and, second, by my having a clear memory of this event. Likewise, belief in God, says the Reformed epistemologist, is not capricious or haphazard even if basic. For there are many conditions and circumstances that occasion, trigger, or call forth belief in God, such as guilt, gratitude, danger, a sense of God's presence, a sense that he speaks, perception of various parts of the universe. As Plantinga says,

> Upon reading the Bible, one may be impressed with a deep sense that God is speaking to him. Upon having done what I know is cheap, or wrong, or wicked, I may feel guilty in God's sight and form the belief *God disapproves of what I have done.* Upon confession and repentance I may feel forgiven, forming the belief *God forgives me for what I have done.* . . . When life is sweet and satisfying, a spontaneous sense of gratitude may well up within the soul; someone in this condition may thank and praise the Lord for his goodness, and will of course have the accompanying belief that indeed the Lord is to be thanked and praised. (Plantinga 1983: 80; see Alston 1991 for a similar argument)

And arguments *are* relevant to basic belief in God. It might be that one's basic belief is cast into doubt by contrary evidence or counterargument. Again a parallel may clear the way. Suppose I believe, in the basic way, that I had a grapefruit for breakfast this morning, but later on I am confronted with the fact that yesterday the last grapefruit was eaten, or that there haven't been grapefruits in the house for quite a few days. Then I have a defeater for my initial belief that will now stop being intellectually respectable for me unless I have a defeater for my defeater. Likewise, one's basic belief in God will stop being intellectually respectable if one has an undefeated defeater for it. Since many such putative defeaters are arguments, many defeater defeaters will likewise be argumentative in nature. Hence, arguments can be, and in fact are, relevant to belief in God, even if it is basic. Reformed epistemologists have accordingly put a lot of energy in considering and criticizing putative defeaters of theistic belief, such as the argument from evil (Plantinga 2000: 154–99).

Warranted Belief

From the late 1980s onwards, Plantinga has expounded an epistemological theory, the core notion of which is "warrant" (Plantinga 1993). This theory has a very wide scope, but it is also relevant for the issue of the intellectual respectability of religious beliefs. I will first present a *Reader's Digest* version of the theory, and then explain its relevance for religious beliefs. Warrant, in Plantinga's theory, is the name for that quality or quantity that distinguishes knowledge from mere true belief. So, if one has knowledge, then, on this theory, one has warranted true belief. And a belief is warranted, provided the following conditions are met. First, the belief is produced by a faculty or cognitive mechanism that functions properly (i.e., as it is supposed to function, in accord with its design plan). Second, the mechanism involved works in an appropriate cognitive environment. Third, the design plan of the faculty involved is successfully aimed at truth. The underlying idea of the first condition is that we are endowed with faculties or other mechanisms that produce beliefs in us. There is, for instance, *memory* that engenders in us numerous beliefs about the past, or beliefs about what one had for breakfast this morning. And there is *perception*, which, upon having hard-to-describe sensations, produces in us beliefs that, say, the magnolias are blooming or that the coach is nearing. Furthermore, *reason* provides us with numerous a priori beliefs such as that $6 + 1 = 7$. Additionally, *inductive reasoning* is a procedure that gives us such beliefs as that all crows are black, that the sun will rise tomorrow, etc. The list goes on.

The first condition for warranted belief tells us that for each of these faculties or mechanisms, there is a way they are supposed to work; for each there is a design plan that specifies how it should work. This is important, for each can malfunction in many ways. When extremely tired or under the influence of some drug, my memory won't function as it should. When suffering a severe headache, I won't as ably engage in inductive reasoning as when I am without pain. So, a belief has warrant only if it is produced by a mechanism that works the way it should work. But more is needed. For the faculties need to work in an appropriate environment. Visual perception won't do what it should, and hence doesn't function properly, in the dark. This is what the second condition says. But still more is required for warranted belief – namely, that the faculty is aimed at truth. It may be the case that we are endowed with mechanisms that produce beliefs, all right, but which don't serve the goal of truth but some other goal, such as affording psychological comfort or enhancing survival. What is needed for warranted belief is that the mechanism involved aims at truth – and generally succeeds (i.e., that a high percentage of the beliefs it produces are true). This is what the third condition tells us.

Now for the application. Belief in God, the Reformed epistemologist maintains, is occasioned by what Calvin has called the *sensus divinitatis*, a belief-forming faculty that is indigenous to all of us. Moreover, that faculty, he maintained, is successfully aimed at truth and produces basic belief in a wide array of circumstances we happen to find ourselves in.

Still, there are many people who claim to be without discernible theistic belief. How can this be if all of us are endowed with this *sensus*? Due to a wide variety of causes, all of our faculties can function improperly, or their proper function can be impeded. Certain types of brain damage, for example, might forestall that

I remember certain past events I was involved in. Likewise, the Reformed epistemologist holds, the *sensus divinitatis* can be impeded. The most important cause for this impediment is that we human being have fallen into sin, a calamitous condition that alienates us from God and makes us unfit for communion with him (Plantinga 2000: 199–240). One of the cognitive consequences of sin is that the *sensus divinitatis* has been damaged and deformed, so that we no longer know God in the same natural and unproblematic way in which we know each other and the world around us. Sin furthermore induces in us a resistance to the deliverances of the *sensus*, so that often we don't pay attention to its still small voice, even if it speaks clearly and insistently.

An Epistemological Model for Specifically Christian Beliefs

So far we have only been dealing with theism, the belief that there is a God. But although by far most religious believers are theists, they believe many things in addition to the existence of God. Christians, for example, believe that we human beings are somehow mired in rebellion and sin and that, as a consequence, we need redemption and salvation, and that God has arranged for that through the sacrificial suffering, death, and resurrection of Jesus Christ, the unique Son of God. Are these beliefs intellectually respectable? And if so, how shall we think about the epistemology of these specifically Christian beliefs? How does one get such beliefs? Can they enjoy warrant?

In response to questions like these, Alvin Plantinga has devised a model which he calls the Aquinas/Calvin (A/C) model – thus paying tribute to two who inspired it – a model that he believes to be true, or at least close to the truth, although he doesn't claim to have shown that it is. What he does claim to have shown is that the model is possible and that there aren't any cogent objections to it.

So, how does a person acquire these specifically Christian beliefs? According to the A/C model, these beliefs don't come to one just by way of perception, reason, the *sensus divinitatis*, or any other cognitive faculty with which we are originally endowed. They come instead by way of the work of the Holy Spirit who causes men and women to believe the great truths of the gospel. These beliefs aren't occasioned by the normal operation of our natural faculties but come as a supernatural gift. More specifically, these beliefs result from a cognitive process that involves three ingredients. First, there is scripture, in which God proposes many things for our belief, the most important of which is the gospel, the stunning good news about the way God has provided for salvation from the mire of sin. Second, there is the work of the Holy Spirit in the heart of the believer, the work of repairing the ravages of sin and making her accept the great truths of the gospel. Finally, there is, as a result of the prompting of the Spirit, faith described by Calvin as "a firm and certain knowledge of God's benevolence toward us."

The specifically Christian beliefs acquired in this way are typically basic beliefs, they aren't arrived at on the basis of argument or reasoning. And if the process that occasions Christian belief functions as it ought to – in an appropriate environment and furthermore aimed at truth – those beliefs will have warrant. As is the case with theistic belief, reasoning may be relevant for specifically Christian beliefs as well. For if there are defeaters for those beliefs, then they will lose their warrant (partly or entirely) if there are no defeater defeaters. So the Reformed epistemologist claims that both theistic and specifically Christian beliefs are innocent until proven guilty, and the task is not to prove these beliefs to be true, but to show that objections against them are unconvincing.

"Intellectual Respectability"

Along these lines Reformed epistemology accounts for the intellectual acceptability of religious beliefs. But how shall we understand "intellectual acceptability"? What does it mean for a belief to be "intellectually respectable"? One explanation is that a belief has this quality provided it is "justified," and a belief is justified provided one is epistemically responsible in forming and holding the belief, and one is responsible in having a belief provided one hasn't flouted one's intellectual duties. Now can religious beliefs, understood as basic beliefs, be justified in this sense? That surely looks to be the case. After all, there is no duty to the effect that one forms one's belief in accordance with the CF requirements. And if we suppose that a believer knows of the many criticisms that have been leveled against religious belief but is utterly unmoved by them, and at the same time has an awareness of God, occasionally seems to catch a glimpse of the work of the Holy Spirit, etc., then surely she isn't going contrary to any intellectual duty of hers. Accordingly, she is justified in her belief.

Another way to construe "intellectual acceptability" is in terms of rationality, and a belief is rational (in at least one of its senses) provided it results from faculties that are truth-directed and functioning properly. Can religious beliefs be rational in this sense? Marx, Freud, and many others have claimed they cannot. According to them, religious beliefs result either from faculties or mechanisms that are not truth-directed (wishful thinking, projection, as Freud has it) or from malfunctioning faculties or mechanisms (which, according to Marx, is due to a perversion of society). Hence religious belief is irrational. Reformed epistemologists, by contrast, deny this and have made a case for the claim that religious belief is, or at the very least can be, rational in the sense that it doesn't result from malfunction, nor from mechanisms directed at something other than truth (Plantinga 2000: part III; Wolterstorff 1995: 261–80; Alston 1991).

Concluding Remarks

As was to be expected, Reformed epistemology has evoked much discussion and numerous criticisms – that belief in God can never be properly basic; that CF is not self-referentially incoherent; that religious belief does require propositional evidence in order to be intellectually respectable; that not all believers have beliefs that are so robust that they will consider them to be properly basic (which has implications for the inductive strategy of formulating a criterion for proper basicality); that Reformed epistemology neglects the social dimension of religious belief; that it neglects the role of the intellectual virtues in the acquisition of belief (cf. Zagzebski 1993: 281–90; McLeod 1993).

Likewise, Plantinga's theory of warrant and proper function has been criticized on many points – that warrant is not necessary for knowledge; that this theory leads to skepticism; that it shares in the problems that attach to externalist theories generally. These criticisms have been expanded upon, and Plantinga has offered substantial replies to them. (See Kvanvig 1996; Beilby 2002; book symposia 1993 and 1995. On responses to Alston's epistemology of religious belief, see Battaly and Lynch 2005). Also of interest is Plantinga's evolutionary argument against naturalism (Plantinga 1993: ch. 12; Beilby 2002).

Reformed epistemology has been the subject of numerous discussions. And there is ample warrant that it will continue to be so in the future.

Questions for Reflection

1   As a matter of sociological fact, do you think that the set of believers with basic belief in God is bigger than the set of believers with non-basic belief in God?

2   Mr T says: "My belief in God is intellectually respectable, it is properly basic for me, I have it, even though, like so many other of my intellectually respectable beliefs, I haven't derived it from beliefs that I have." Mrs A, who was addressed by this little speech, replies: "Well, that might be all very fine for you, but for me things don't go that way. I don't believe in God, and hence I don't believe in God in that way. Furthermore, there is nothing in your speech that might motivate me to start believing in God, nothing that urges me to consider belief in God as a live option." What has the Reformed epistemologist to say in response to Mrs A?

3   It is widely held that knowledge excludes luck. According to Plantinga's theory, someone's belief in God counts as knowledge, provided it is generated by faculties that *de facto* happen to be truth-directed and reliably so. Now suppose someone's theistic belief is generated by such faculties: is this really knowledge? For hasn't the anti-luck condition been violated? After all, isn't it sheer luck that the faculties that generate theistic belief are *de facto* truth-directed, and even reliably so?

4   Suppose you think that belief in God can be properly basic. Does this commit you to holding that the traditional arguments for the existence of God are without value, or never come to any good, or never establish their conclusions, or never make their conclusion probable?

References

Alston, W. P. (1991) *Perceiving God: The Epistemology of Religious Experience*. Ithaca, NY: Cornell University Press.

Battaly, H. D., and M. Lynch (eds.) (2005) *Perspectives on the Philosophy of William P. Alston*. Lanham, MD: Rowman & Littlefield.

Bavinck, H. (1951) *The Doctrine of God*. Grand Rapids: Eerdmans.

Beilby, J. (ed.) (2002) *Naturalism Defeated? Essays on Plantinga's Evolutionary Argument Against Naturalism*. Ithaca, NY: Cornell University Press.

Book symposium (1993) on A. Plantinga, *Warrant and Proper Function* and *Warrant: The Current Debate*. In *Noûs* 27/1.

Book symposium (1995) on A. Plantinga, *Warrant and Proper Function* and *Warrant: The Current Debate*. In *Philosophy and Phenomenological Research* 55/2.

Calvin, J. (1960) *Institutes of the Christian Religion*. Philadelphia: Westminster Press.

Clifford, W. K. (1901) "The Ethics of Belief." In W. K. Clifford, *Lectures and Essays*, vol. 2. London: Macmillan.

Kvanvig, J. L. (ed.) (1996) *Warrant in Contemporary Epistemology: Essays in Honor of Plantinga's Theory of Knowledge*. Lanham, MD: Rowman & Littlefield.

McLeod, M. (1993) *Rationality and Theistic Belief: An Essay on Reformed Epistemology*. Ithaca, NY: Cornell University Press.

Plantinga, A. (1977) *God and Other Minds*. Ithaca, NY: Cornell University Press.

—— (1983) "Reason and Belief in God." In A. Plantinga and N. Wolterstorff (eds.), *Faith and Rationality: Reason and Belief in God*. Notre Dame: University of Notre Dame Press.

—— (1993) *Warrant and Proper Function*. New York: Oxford University Press.

—— (2000) *Warranted Christian Belief*. New York: Oxford University Press.

Plantinga, A., and N. Wolterstorff (1983) *Faith and Rationality: Reason and Belief in God*. Notre Dame: University of Notre Dame Press.

Pritchard, D. (2005) "Reforming Reformed Epistemology." In R. van Woudenberg, S. Roeser, and R. Rood (eds.), *Basic Belief and Basic Knowledge: Papers in Epistemology*. Frankfurt: Ontos Verlag.

Van Woudenberg, R., S. Roeser, and R. Rood (eds.) (2005) *Basic Belief and Basic Knowledge: Papers in Epistemology*. Frankfurt: Ontos Verlag.

Wolterstorff, N. (1995) *Divine Discourse: Philosophical Reflections on the Claim that God Speaks*. Cambridge: Cambridge University Press.

—— (1997) *John Locke and the Ethics of Belief*. Cambridge: Cambridge University Press.

—— (2003) *Thomas Reid and the Story of Epistemology*. Cambridge: Cambridge University Press.

Zagzebski, L. (ed.) (1993) *Rational Faith: Catholic Responses to Reformed Epistemology*. Notre Dame: University of Notre Dame Press.

Further Reading

Kvanvig, J. L. (1996) *Warrant in Contemporary Epistemology*. Lanham, MD: Rowman & Littlefield. (A number of the finest epistemologists take issue with Plantinga's theory of warrant, and Plantinga responds to them.)

Mavrodes, G. (1988) *Revelation in Religious Belief.* Philadelphia: Temple University Press. (Discusses the central Reformed epistemologist's ideas in connection with various views of revelation, arguing that Reformed epistemology involves a "causation model" of revelation.)

McLeod, M. (1993) *Rationality and Theistic Belief.* Ithaca, NY: Cornell University Press. (A book-length study of Reformed epistemology.)

Zagzebski, L. (ed.) (1993) *Rational Faith.* Notre Dame: University of Notre Dame Press. (A number of responses from Catholic philosophers on Plantinga's and Wolterstorff's claim that belief in God can be properly basic.)

Chapter 4

Religious Pluralism

Joseph Runzo

Introduction

"Religious pluralism" is a complex notion which raises challenging issues both for religion and for the philosophy of religion in the global twenty-first century. There are at least four things to consider when dealing with the issue of religious pluralism. First, there is the fact of the pluralistic phenomena of the religious life of humankind. Second, for those who are especially interested in religious matters, the fact of religious pluralism raises the "problem of religious pluralism," that is, the problem of conflicting religious truth claims. Third, in response to the problem of religious pluralism, there are a number of comparative theories about religion, one of which is called "religious pluralism." And fourth, there is the overarching question of why it matters, and especially why it matters morally, how one responds to the conflicting truth claims of the religions of the world.

The religious life of humankind is both remarkably pervasive and remarkably diverse. The overwhelming majority of humans – approximately five out of every six people – are religious, and the remaining sixth of the world's population also responds to religious ideas, either with puzzlement or rejection. Yet while humans can plausibly be identified as the "religious animals," there is great diversity within this underlying unity. At the start of the twenty-first century, there are nearly 2 billion nominal Christians, divided between approximately 1 billion Roman Catholics, and nearly half a billion each of Orthodox Christians and Protestants. There are 1.2 to 1.3 billion Muslims, about 80 percent of whom are Sunni and 20 percent Shiite. There are about a billion Hindus, some 350 million Buddhists divided between forms of Theravada and Mahayana, roughly 14 million Jews, 25 million Sikhs, perhaps 20 million Jains, 6 million Baha'i, and approximately 500,000 Zoroastrians (Parsis). In addition, there are indigenous traditions, like the Yoruba tradition of western Africa which has its own diaspora and nearly as many adherents as Buddhism. Finally, the Chinese traditions of Confucianism and Daoism are widely influential in the areas of the world directly affected by

Chinese culture (e.g., China, Tibet, Mongolia, Korea, Japan, Vietnam, Cambodia, and Malaysia).

None of these traditions has an even distribution around the globe. While Christianity is predominant in Armenia, Ethiopia, Europe, and the former European colonies – such as those in the Americas, South Africa, Lesotho, Rwanda, Burundi, Kenya, Australia, New Zealand, Papua New Guinea, and the central Philippines – it has never made significant inroads into the large populations of Japan, China, and India, or into the central global band across northern Africa and central Asia since Islam spread to those areas. Likewise Islam, having once spread rapidly from the Middle East across northern Africa and Asia to its current stronghold in Indonesia, has not been particularly successful in the Americas or Russia or China, or in Japan or the southern Pacific. Hinduism, which has followed the large Indian-Hindu population around the world, is still concentrated on the Indian subcontinent. Similar geographic restrictions apply, *mutatis mutandis*, to other religious traditions.

It is evident that the religious tradition which one follows is largely determined by such factors as where one lives, one's family background, one's ethnic background, and one's historical period. These facts of religious pluralism can raise the "problem of religious pluralism" if one is concerned about the *truth* of religious claims and/or the *relevance* of religious life to the meaning of one's own life. For then, the mutually conflicting systems of truth claims of the world's religions confront us with a tripartite question: is only one system of religious truth claims correct, or is more than one system correct, or are all religious systems mistaken?

Defining Pluralism

When we speak of religious pluralism, we do not mean pluralism as a doctrine in religious metaphysics which contrasts with monism (e.g., with a view like Spinoza's; also see chapter 17, Eastern Philosophy of Religion) or perhaps with dualism (views like Manichaeism and Gnosticism). Rather, current interest in religious pluralism is part of a new, wider philosophical interest in pluralism in the sense of the willingness to take divergent points of view or perspectives into account as bearers of the truth. Nicholas Rescher defines pluralism as

> the doctrine that any substantial question admits of a variety of plausible but mutually conflicting responses. . . . [E]pistemic pluralism in particular . . . raises the question of whether the truth is something that admits not only of different *visions* but of different *versions*, whether there are different and incompatible truths or simply different and incompatible opinions regarding the monolithic truth. (Rescher 1993: 79)

Epistemic pluralists hold that we have no direct access to "The Truth" and that our conceptions of truth are dependent on the conceptual scheme or worldview which we bring to experience.

Thus while in the abstract the distinction between vision and version of the truth may be all-important, nevertheless in the concrete, for us here and now, it is a distinction without a difference. The truth, like the Bible, may be one, but it is, again like the Bible, a one that admits of many constructions and interpretations. For all practical purposes . . . a plurality of beliefs about the truth (a plurality of visions) is a plurality of formulations of the true (a plurality of versions). (Rescher 1993: 79)

The modern pluralist philosophical perspective can be traced back to Immanuel Kant's distinction between *phenomena* and *noumena* and his emphasis on the mind's ineluctable conceptual contribution to experience. This Kantian epistemology opened the way to a pluralist revolution in Western thought. One of the tributaries which joined the stream, as it were, of the Kantian revolution can be found in American pragmatism and such works as William James's *The Varieties of Religious Experience* (1902) and *A Pluralistic Universe* (1909). As James succinctly enunciates a pluralist epistemology, "Why in the name of common sense need we assume that only one . . . system of ideas can be true? The obvious outcome of our total experience is that the world can be handled according to many systems of ideas" (James 1902: 120). Ludwig Wittgenstein's later emphasis on the variety of coherent language-games heavily influenced both British and American philosophical thinking throughout the latter half of the twentieth century, while the work of American philosophers like W. V. O. Quine on the relativity of truth to conceptual schemes and then others like Richard Rorty (1981) continued the pragmatist influence. These philosophical currents were joined by anthropological and sociological currents as well. Consequently, as Calvin Schrag observes, contemporary pluralism has moved into a "post metaphysical age" and is "more attuned to the diversity of social practices and the multiple roles of language, discourse, and narrative in the panoply of human affairs" (Schrag 1995).

This more recent emphasis on the pluralism of viable human perspectives has brought Western thought closer to the long-standing Asian traditions of pluralism. Hinduism, the oldest extant world religion, is traditionally a philosophically inclusive tradition. When traveling in India, a Hindu might well inquire about one's *istadevata* – i.e., "the god of one's choice." Whatever one's answer, including an avowal of atheism, Hindus will typically consider that chosen "god" to be encompassed by Hinduism, another among countless manifestations of the one Reality which is Brahman. Even Buddhism, which explicitly rejected the ideas of *atman* (soul) and Brahman, is regarded as part of Hinduism: the earthly Buddha, Sakyamuni Buddha, is treated as one of the 10 *avatars* (incarnations) of Vishnu, who is in turn one of the primary manifestations of Brahman. And Buddhism itself, the self-described Middle Way, values flexibility, prescribing *upaya* (skillful means) to explain Buddhist principles to non-Buddhists using terms Buddhists would not ordinarily accept. Jainism, the other major "axial age" offshoot of Hinduism, has its own metaphysics but also centrally espouses the doctrine of *anekantavada* (non-onesidedness) which holds that all views are subject to revision (Ram-Prasad 2001).

Finally, if we turn to the Chinese traditions, Daoism has always been inclusively flexible, unlike its more rigid Confucian philosophical partner, though we find a more pluralistic openness in Neo-Confucian religiosity, represented in the well-known words of Chang Tsai: "that which fills the universe I regard as my body and that which directs the universe I consider as my nature. All people are my brothers and sisters, and all things are my companions" (Wei-Ming 1985: 157).

Religion and Truth Claims

The *world religions* – those traditions which are concerned with the relation of all humans to a Transcendent, which have persisted over time and spread worldwide, and which accept converts – all have some historical blending and borrowing *vis-à-vis* other traditions. Still, each world religion has its own distinct vital core beliefs. The doctrines of the Incarnation and the Trinity distinguish Christianity from the other Abrahamic faiths; the doctrine of impermanence and the rejection of a substance ontology distinguishes Buddhism from Hinduism; the hierarchical role ethics of Confucianism distinguishes it from Taoism, and so on. Moreover, the vital core beliefs of one world religion are often *prima facie* incompatible with the vital core beliefs of other world religions.

There are six possible responses, religious and non-religious, to the conflicting truth claims of vital core beliefs among the world religions:

1 Religious antipathy: all world religions are mistaken.
2 Religious subjectivism: every individual perspective within each world religion is correct, and every individual perspective is correct and incontrovertible insofar as it is good for the individual who adheres to it.
3 Religious exclusivism: only one world religion is correct, and all others are mistaken.
4 Religious pluralism: ultimately all world religions are correct, each offering a different path and partial perspective *vis-à-vis* the one Ultimate Reality.
5 Religious inclusivism: only one world religion is fully correct, but other world religions participate in or partially reveal some of the truth of the one correct religion.
6 Religious henofideism: one has a faith commitment that one's own world religion is correct, while acknowledging that other world religions may be correct.

If we imagine different views of the best dual-carriageway/freeway route into a major city like London or Los Angeles as an analogy, the relation between these six responses becomes apparent (Runzo 2001: 41–2). Travelers with antipathy discount the view that there is a London or Los Angeles ("the Transcendent"). Exclusivist travelers believe that there is only one real route to the city. The subjectivist traveler believes that all routes, large and small, lead to the city and are just a matter of personal preference. The pluralist traveler says that if you imagine London or Los Angeles from a "God's eye view," you will see that all the major dual-carriageways or freeways do, indeed, lead to the city. Inclusivist travelers favor one route to the city, but believe that other major routes are branch routes which inevitably feed into their favored route. Henofideist travelers are firmly committed to their favored route into the city, and though they do not accept the possibility of having a "God's eye view," they take into account the reports of other travelers, and allow for the possibility that there are alternative successful routes to the city.

Now, those committed to the religious life need to take religious antipathy seriously as a challenge to religious truth claims. (It is better to refer here to religious "antipathy" rather than "atheism," since atheism is both restricted to theistic views and a misleading term, referring either to a conscious disbelief in God or to a lack of belief in God. The latter includes Buddhists who are, however, not religiously antipathetic.) The apparently incommensurate, conflicting truth claims of the diverse world religions – and the constant doctrinal bickering among strands, sects, and denominations within each tradition – certainly lend *prima facie* credence to a "plague on all your houses" response. That said, here we may set religious antipathy aside in order to compare the five remaining theories which do regard many religious truth claims as veridical. Of the remaining five, we can discount religious subjectivism. As Wittgenstein's "private language" argument shows, concepts are social constructs (Wittgenstein 1958). Since truth claims depend on concepts and concepts are social constructs, a radical subjectivism about truth – the idea that religious truth could be strictly personal or "private" and not subject to external judgment – is incoherent.

For the religious person, the choice of which of the remaining four positions to take requires steering between a stifling provincialism and narrow-mindedness, on the one side, and a ruinous vagueness and weakened commitment, on the other side. The goal is to be faithful to one's own religious worldview without making unjustifiable claims which are either too dismissive, in the first instance, or too facilely condoning of other religious worldviews, in the second instance.

Religious Pluralism and Religious Exclusivism

Of the four remaining theories, religious pluralism would seem to be the most accepting of religious diversity. Religious pluralism has been most famously developed by John Hick who, citing Jalalu'l-Din Rumi's statement that "the lamps are different, but the light is the same," says that "the great post-axial faiths constitute different ways of experience, conceiving and living in relation to an ultimate divine Reality which transcends all our varied visions of it" (Hick 1989: 235–6). In Rescher's terms, Hick attempts to avoid the apparent conflict among the truth claims of the world religions by accepting different *visions* of Ultimate Reality while de-emphasizing them as different *versions*. As Peter Byrne notes, the religious pluralist outlook has three minimal elements: belief in the existence of a Transcendent, belief in "a basic cognitive equality" among traditions as a "vehicle of salvation," and agnosticism about "the specifics of any confessional stance toward religion" (Byrne 1995: 11).

Hick reduces the cognitive significance of religious truth claims by arguing that "To the extent that [the religious notions of] a *persona* or *impersona* is in soteriological alignment with the Real, an appropriate response to that deity or absolute is an appropriate response to the Real" (Hick 1989: 248). Thus, religious pluralism suggests that the transformative power of religion – its "soteriological alignment" – is more important than the truth of its metaphysical claims, but also that "The theological task of interpreting and understanding one's own religion must be done in conversations with others" (Knitter 1995: 24).

A number of objections have been mounted to religious pluralism. One opponent is the religious exclusivist, who is generally opposed to pluralist approaches but in particular tends to see the question of the truth of religious claims as paramount and religious doctrine as delineating truths which are *essential* for salvation (Griffiths 1990). This preeminent emphasis of exclusivism and of the narrower sort of "closed inclusivism" discussed below on the cognitive component of religion is more amenable to the Western emphasis on orthodoxy rather than the typically Asian orientation toward orthopraxy. However, it is important to note that inclusivism and henofideism both retain a strong place for the cognitive.

Exclusivists typically argue that pluralist orientations undermine religious commitment by undermining the cognitive content of religion (see chapter 5, Religious Exclusivism). While firmness of belief is a clear strength of exclusivism, it does not follow from the pluralist acceptance of the possible rationality of others' beliefs, given the other's epistemic circumstances, that the pluralist's own beliefs are thereby less rational or should be abandoned. As Rescher notes, "it does not follow that the pluralist needs to be disloyal to his own standards . . . any more than it follows that my acknowledging your spouse to be appropriate *for you* constitutes on my part an act of disloyalty to my own" (Rescher 1993: 123). After all, even if only one is correct, two people can be rationally justified in holding different beliefs when there are different grounds available to each for justification. Additionally, the three pluralist perspectives of (a) religious pluralism, (b) religious inclusivism (in the form of "open inclusivism"), and (c) religious henofideism all hold that, to some extent, being right does not mean that others must be wrong or that others being right about certain doctrines you disagree with must mean that *you* are wrong. This follows from the view that different religious worldviews may be not only different visions but even different coherent versions of the truth.

Certain salient historical factors call the plausibility of religious exclusivism into question, lending support to a religious pluralist perspective. Not only is the religious tradition a person follows usually a product of where and when they were

born – making the religious exclusivist's claimed possession of the only truth ser-
endipitous – but religious traditions themselves are the result of the merging of
two or more traditions and/or draw heavily on the tradition out of which they
arose. Thus, Hinduism arose out of Indo-Aryan religious traditions interacting
with the indigenous traditions of India around 1500 BCE; contemporary Confucianism has Daoist and Buddhist influences; Christianity arose in the first century
CE from Hebrew religious traditions in the context of both Greek philosophy (see
elements of the gospel of John) and Zoroastrian ideas (hell and a last judgment);
and Islam draws on both Hebrew and Christian scriptures.

Another kind of merging and/or connectedness of religious traditions which
militates against exclusivist claims is the result of religious transitions in a person's
own life. Even if a person does not convert to another tradition within her lifetime,
many people change sectarian commitments within a tradition, and many develop
their religious outlooks through the accretion of concepts, rituals, myths, and even
scriptural sources from other traditions they encounter. Thus, Jesuits may come
to employ Buddhist meditative methods, or Hindus may accept Jesus as a divine
incarnation, all the while retaining the vital core beliefs of their "home" tradition.
Against the validity of these personal transitions, the insistence on religious exclusivism will seem unrealistic and parochial to the pluralist. As Paul Tillich suggests
regarding Christianity, "Theologians have become careless in safeguarding their
idea of a personal God from slipping into 'henotheistic' mythology (the belief in
one god who, however, remains particular and bound to a particular group)"
(Tillich 1963: 91). The Japanese Christian novelist Shusaku Endo illustrates this
problem in *Deep River*, when the protagonist Otsu goes to France to study theology and finds that an exclusively European understanding of Christianity is forced
on him:

> My Japanese sensibilities have made me feel out of harmony with European Chris-
> tianity. . . . these people reject anything they cannot slice into categories. . . . As a
> Japanese, I can't bear those who ignore the great life force that exists in Nature. . . .
> ultimately what I have sought is nothing more than the love of [God], not any of
> the other innumerable doctrines mouthed by the various churches. (Endo 1994:
> 118–19)

Religious Inclusivism and Religious Henofideism

Religious inclusivism and religious henofideism attempt to avoid the parochialism
of exclusivism without undermining commitment to one's own tradition.
Gavin D'Costa has developed a rigorous notion of Christian inclusivism which
includes

> an openness that seeks to explore the many and various ways in which God has spoken
> to all his children in the non-Christian religions and an openness that will lead to the

positive fruits of this exploration transforming, enriching and fulfilling Christianity.
(D'Costa 1986: 136)

D'Costa illustrates his idea of how the Christian religious inclusivist should
encounter other religious traditions with the following lines from T. S. Eliot:

> We shall not cease from exploration
> And the end of all our exploring
> Will be to arrive where we started
> And know the place for the first time.
> (T. S. Eliot, quoted in D'Costa
> 1986: 137)

We might call this kind of inclusivism "closed inclusivism," for there is a closed
circle which prohibits extensive transformation of one's own tradition through
contact with other world religions. The "openness" D'Costa speaks about is not
between spiritual equals. Interaction with other traditions is seen as a way to
enhance one's already held views by observing how they are present in the lives
of others.

Another sort of inclusivism we might designate "open inclusivism." This is held,
for example, by Karl Rahner in his proposal that adherents of religious traditions
other than Roman Catholicism can be "anonymous Christians." In Rahner's view,
this is an appropriate interpretation of Catholic doctrines like that in the Vatican
II Dogmatic Constitution *Nostra Aetate*:

> The Catholic Church rejects nothing which is true and holy in [the other world reli-
> gions]. She looks with sincere respect upon those ways of conduct and of life, those
> rules and teachings which, though differing in many particulars from what she holds
> and sets forth, nevertheless often reflect a ray of that Truth which enlightens all men.
> (Abbott 1966: 662)

For Rahner and other Christian open inclusivists, a Buddhist might be progressing
toward the salvation Roman Catholicism articulates (just as for a Buddhist open
inclusivist, a Christian could be an "anonymous Buddhist" who is progressing
toward liberation.)

For the open religious inclusivist, his own tradition is the ultimate fulfillment
of the partial progress other traditions provide toward salvation or liberation.
However, it is important to keep in mind that neither open inclusivism nor henofideism (nor, for that matter, pluralism) is proposing a syncretic religion, an
amalgam of the world traditions. As the Fourteenth Dalai Lama has said of
Christianity and Buddhism, "If [the] view of integration envisions all of society
following some sort of composite religion which is neither pure Buddhism nor
pure Christianity, then I would have to consider this form of integration impossible" (Gyatso 2001). Open inclusivism, henofideism and pluralism all preserve a

distinctiveness between world religious traditions, reflecting William James's suggestion that "the world can be handled according to many systems of ideas."

Turning now to henofideism, Keith Ward expresses what might be characterized as a henofideistic Christian appraisal of other world religions after rejecting Hick's religious pluralist assessment that all world religions are "equally authentic manifestations of ultimate truth":

> The rational course is to commit oneself to a tradition of revelation, which delivers one from the pretense that one can work out the truth entirely for oneself. Such commitment should, however, involve an acceptance that the Supreme Reality has not been silent in the other religions of the world, which delivers one from a myopia which confines God to one small sector of human history. (Ward 1994: 324)

Here the henotheism Tillich warns against is avoided, yet a strong faith commitment to a specific "tradition of revelation" is retained. (In contrast, D'Costa rejects the notion of "alternative revelations" [D'Costa 2000].) Ward then explains his idea of a possible "convergent spirituality" – "a convergence in common core beliefs, as complementary images come to be more widely recognized" – using an *anekantavada*-like perspective, that is, "an acceptance of the partiality and inadequacy of all human concepts to capture the object of [the quest for unity with supreme perfection] definitively" (Ward 1994: 339). Since the henofideist takes other world religions to be possible versions of the truth, the henofideist can engage in a completely open interaction with other traditions, willing to synergistically shape her present religious understanding with understandings in other traditions. To see the importance of this, we now turn to ethics and contemporary human rights challenges.

Religious Pluralism and Human Rights

Whether one should choose to adopt a pluralist theory regarding the truth claims of other traditions is not merely an epistemological question. For instance, the Jain notion that all things are imbued with *jiva* (soul) entails the radical non-violence (*ahimsa*) of Jainism. Similarly, central to the more theistic Hindu *bhakti* tradition is the notion of *nishkama karma* – moral action out of a sense of duty motivated by love of God:

> Implicit in the whole teaching scheme of the [*Bhagavad*] *Gita* is the belief that there is no other way to establish non-attachment than through a new attachment, which is greater in quality and power. . . . One overcomes that narrow clinging to results, the passionate involvement with the consequences of one's own action, only when that passion is replaced by one directed to the Divine. (Deutsch 1968: 163)

As these examples illustrate, one's conception of the self, the Transcendent, the end goal of life, and so on, frame and delimit one's ethics. Since metaphysics importantly drives ethics, what view one holds of the truth of the metaphysical claims of other religious traditions importantly determines how one sees both the religious ethics of one's own tradition as well as that of other traditions. To the extent that other traditions can accept the Jain notion of *jiva* or the *bhakti* Hindu notion of duty motivated by love of God, other religious traditions will be able to accept the ethical reasoning of Jainism and *bhakti* Hinduism.

Pluralist perspectives are more conducive than anti-pluralist perspectives for open human rights dialogue. Indeed, as shared problems of violence, tyranny, natural disasters and pandemics have been more frequently addressed across religious and cultural divides, human rights dialogue has, in turn, become a focal point for encouraging a pluralistic approach to ethical issues (Grelle 2005: 133). The promotion of human rights is a definitive form of good works in our global world, and as St Theresa of Avila puts it, "good works and good works alone . . . are the sign of every genuine favour [from God] and of everything else that comes from God" (St Theresa of Avila 1961: 228). The consequences of taking one of the three pluralist positions (a)–(c) versus an exclusivist position regarding the conflicting truth claims of the world religions become apparent when we consider that an effective global ethic for human rights which will be widely acceptable depends on religious traditions working with each other (and with the secular).

Exclusivist (and closed inclusivist) religious views may hinder interreligious moral dialogue, but Rescher points out that even within a pluralistic orientation, there may be a moral duty to "stick by our own opinions:"

> If someone lies ill and unconscious in the street and you propose forming a circle to say incantations, then I, persuaded that summoning a doctor is the thing to do, would be acting in a morally reprehensible way if I acceded to your view of the matter in the interests of consensus. (Rescher 1993: 123)

Rescher is surely right about our moral duty to not act against our deepest moral convictions. But if religious communities are not open to human rights conversation with other religious communities unless there is consensus with their own traditional interpretations of morality, a global human rights ethic will founder on the rock of exclusivism. For example, Islamic exclusivists like the "puritans" (e.g., Wahhabists) and the "apologists" (e.g., Sayyid Qutb) demand consensus about morality, but find it only within the close confines of *shari'a* and so reject dialogue with Western human rights advocates (Abou El Fadl 2003). However, as Rescher also points out, truth consensus is not a reasonable goal for the pluralist. So what would be a proper goal for the diverse world religions to pursue in order to support a global human rights ethic within a pluralistic perspective?

The point of moral action for the sake of another is *to help the other to the best of one's ability*. Hence, in moral matters, sometimes the best consensus one can reach is to agree to disagree about ethics in order to act together morally to aid the poor, the vulnerable, the oppressed. We might call this "axiological consensus." Arguing about whether God or *dharma* or self-cultivation is the reason to prevent genocide or to aid the destitute, instead of working to prevent genocide or to aid the destitute, is itself immoral. Similarly, religious groups which tightly tie desperately needed medical aid or education to proselytizing in developing countries devalue human rights concerns in a desire for ideological truth consensus.

Nostra Aetate opens with this statement of its purpose:

> the Church is giving deeper study to her relationship with non-Christian religions. In her task of fostering unity and love among men, and even among nations, she gives primary consideration in this document to what human beings have in common and to what promotes fellowship among them. (Abbott 1966: 660)

The need to openly explore human commonality is perhaps even clearer at the start of the twenty-first century than it was in the 1960s. With respect to human rights in particular, there is a moral duty both to adhere to our commitments and to work to lessen differences and find commonality with others for unity of action. This moral duty is concisely expressed by the Christian philosopher Brian Hebblethwaite in an open inclusivist statement:

> The Christian has no monopoly of the ways of God with humankind. There may well be forms of the religious life that encapsulate and manifest values understressed in the Christian tradition; and Christianity's historically dynamic and eschatologically oriented moral faith needs to be complemented by oriental cosmic wisdom. (Hebblethwaite 1997: 61–2)

Now, anyone who is strongly committed to a particular way of religious life – say, Buddhism – *will*, as they should, hold the moral principles of their tradition to be right. For to abandon the moral implications of a religion is to abandon the religion. How then could there be a global ethic across religious traditions in view of both the strength of religious commitment in people's lives and the diversity of ethical perspectives across traditions? The first thing to observe is that the world religions largely agree about morality, about what is right and wrong, morally good and morally bad. From disapprobation for stealing and murder to the general moral principle of the "golden rule," there is much axiological consensus across the world religions. Religious pluralism *vis-à-vis* moral matters is primarily found in the sphere of ethics – that is, the disagreement among the world religions is primarily a matter of the *reasons* given for moral judgments and moral principles. This pluralism of religious ethics arises, in turn, from underlying differences in religious metaphysics upon which the ethical reasoning is based. Despite this, humans can act together in moral matters insofar as they are willing to take the moral point of view and to set aside ideological differences for greater ends despite a lack of complete truth consensus.

Moral Responsibility and Religious Pluralism

With the rise of the modern secular nation-state, the development of non-governmental organizations, and the formation of international legal bodies such as the United Nations, the International Criminal Court, etc., religion has been unseated from the head of the moral leadership table. What then do the world religions bring to the table to add to human rights discussion as we begin the twenty-first century? If the world religions do no more than serve as a multitude of alternative expressions of morality to secular humanism, then their role is restricted. Against this I have argued that the world religions can make at least six significant contributions to human rights (Runzo 2006):

1   The world religions serve as one important avenue to articulate certain rights.
2   The world religions encourage the moral virtue of benevolence which lies at the heart of taking the moral point of view.
3   The world religions emphasize responsibility to others as the deeper foundation of rights.
4   The world religions add the call to love or compassion as integral to relationship with the Transcendent and a motivation for benevolence.
5   The world religions offer institutional structures, myths, symbols, rituals and texts to support human rights.
6   The world religions offer moral-religious saints as models for the commitment to human rights.

The more open any religious tradition is to other traditions, the more effective will be its contribution in each of these areas. It is widely recognized that pluralistic individuals like the Fourteenth Dalai Lama, Martin Luther King, Jr., Mahatma Gandhi, Mother Teresa, and Archbishop Desmond Tutu are moral-religious saints who serve as exemplars of the kind of contribution which the deeply religious can bring to human rights. It is not incidental to any of these individuals' moral commitments that they are religious. Yet it is also not always equally evident that the diverse world religions themselves have a clear role in human rights.

For example, for Buddhists, talk about "rights" seems self-centered, and they "may question whether talk of 'inalienable rights' implies some unchanging, essential Self that 'has' these, which is out of accord with Buddhism's teaching on the nature of selfhood" (Harvey 2000: 119). It might appear, then, that Buddhist metaphysics prevents pluralist human rights dialogue. Buddhism, like the other world religions, emphasizes moral responsibility and "as rights imply duties, Buddhists are happier talking directly about the duties themselves: about 'universal duties,' or, to use a phrase much used by the Dalai Lama, 'universal responsibilities'" (Harvey 2000: 119). In contrast to the contemporary Western language of "rights," in the South and East Asian societies shaped by Hinduism, Buddhism, Jainism, Confucianism and Daoism, the central moral notion traditionally is not *rights*, but rather one's *role* in society and one's moral responsibilities to others. However, this need not divide Western and Asian *religious* approaches to human rights. For this Asian moral orientation corresponds to the *traditional* Western religious emphasis on moral obligations, and this can provide an underlying commonality across the pluralism of the traditions to support human rights as a moral responsibility.

Another point of moral agreement among the world religions is the emphasis on benevolence, or taking others into account in one's actions, not just out of self-interest but because one respects them as persons (Runzo 2003). Thus, in the *Analects*, Confucius says, "Do not impose on others what you yourself do not desire"; the Hindu epic the *Mahabharata* says: "One should never do that to another which one regards as injurious to one's own self. This, in brief, is the rule of the *dharma*" (Chapple 1993: 16); and in the gospel of Mark, Jesus proclaims the second commandment, "You shall love your neighbor as yourself." This benevolent relationality – what Buddhists call "compassion" – which is enjoined by all the world religions can sustain human rights commitments.

While being genuinely religious entails being moral, the world religions go far beyond simply supporting morality and human rights. In spite of religious pluralism, the world religions all agree that the source of meaning in life is relationship to a Transcendent – God, Allah, Brahman, the Dharmakaya, etc. – and in this they move beyond secular humanism in the commitment to human rights. This axiological consensus among the world religions, despite their metaphysical differences, is elegantly summarized by Khaled Abou El Fadl for the Islamic tradition:

> Why should a Muslim commit himself/herself to the rights and well-being of a fellow human being? The answer is because God has already made such a commitment when God invested so much of the God-self in each and every person. This is why the Qur'an asserts that whoever kills a fellow human being unjustly it is as if he/she has murdered all of humanity – it is as if the killer has murdered the divine sanctity and defiled the very meaning of divinity. (Abou El Fadl 2003: 338)

This is why each person, despite the diversity of humankind, matters and why, from a pluralistic perspective, it matters to take seriously the religious pluralism of humankind.

Questions for Reflection

1   Why might the antireligious secular humanist still want to promote a religious pluralist perspective among those who are religious?

2   How might a religious exclusivist or a closed inclusivist deal with the historical
    and sociological fact that the religious tradition one follows is usually the same
    as one's parents' tradition, or is a prevailing tradition in the region in which
    one lives?
3   To what extent is the pluralist correct that all the world religions are progress-
    ing toward the same end goal?
4   Which of the theories about religion – exclusivism, pluralism, inclusivism, or
    henofideism – might best promote interreligious human rights dialogue?
    Why?
5   What difference does it make to your understanding of the meaning of your
    life what other people who have very different religious views, or who have
    antireligious views, think gives human life meaning?

References

Abbott, W. (1966) *The Documents of Vatican II*. New York: America Press.

Abou El Fadl, K. (2003) "The Human Rights Commitment in Modern Islam." In
    J. Runzo, N. Martin and A. Sharma (eds.), *Human Rights and Responsibilities in the
    World Religions*. Oxford: Oneworld Publications.

Byrne, P. (1995) *Prolegomena to Religious Pluralism: Reference and Realism in Religion*.
    New York: St Martin's Press.

Chapple, C. (1993) *Nonviolence to Animals, Earth and Self in Asian Traditions*. Albany,
    NY: State University of New York Press.

Confucius (1979) *The Analects*, trans. D. C. Lau. London: Penguin.

D'Costa, G. (1986) *Theology and Religious Pluralism: The Challenge of Other Religions*.
    Oxford: Blackwell.

—— (2000) *The Meeting of Religions and the Trinity*. Maryknoll, NY: Orbis Books.

Deutsch, E. (trans. and ed.) (1968) *The Bhagavad Gita*. New York: University Press of
    America.

Endo, S. (1994) *Deep River*. New York: New Direction Books.

Grelle, B. (2005) "Culture and Moral Pluralism." In W. Schweiker (ed.), *The Blackwell
    Companion to Religious Ethics*. Oxford: Blackwell.

Griffiths, P. (1990) "The Uniqueness of Christian Doctrine Defended." In G. D'Costa
    (ed.), *Christian Uniqueness Reconsidered: The Myth of a Pluralistic Theology of
    Religions*. Maryknoll, NY: Orbis Books.

Gyatso, T. (His Holiness the Fourteenth Dalai Lama) (2001) "Buddhism and Other
    Religions." In M. Peterson, W. Hasker, B. Reichenbach and D. Basinger (eds.),
    Philosophy of Religion. New York: Oxford University Press.

Harvey, P. (2000) *An Introduction to Buddhist Ethics*. Cambridge: Cambridge University
    Press.

Hebblethwaite, B. (1997) *Ethics and Religion in a Pluralistic Age*. Edinburgh: T. &
    T. Clark.

Hick, J. (1989) *An Interpretation of Religion: Human Responses to the Transcendent*.
    London: Macmillan.

James, W. (1902) *The Varieties of Religious Experience: A Study of Human Nature*. London: Longmans.

—— (1909) *A Pluralistic Universe*. New York: Longmans.

Knitter, P. (1995) *One Earth, Many Religions: Multifaith Dialogue and Global Responsibility*. Maryknoll, NY: Orbis Books.

Ram-Prasad, C. (2001) "Multiplism: A Jaina Ethics of Toleration for a Complex World." In J. Runzo and N. Martin (eds.), *Ethics in the World Religions*. Oxford: Oneworld Publications.

Rescher, N. (1993) *Pluralism: Against the Demand for Consensus*. Oxford: Oxford University Press.

Rorty, R. (1981) *Philosophy and the Mirror of Nature*. Princeton: Princeton University Press.

Runzo, J. (2001) *Global Philosophy of Religion: A Short Introduction*. Oxford: Oneworld Publications.

—— (2003) "Secular Rights and Religious Responsibilities." In J. Runzo, N. Martin and A. Sharma (eds.), *Human Rights and Responsibilities in the World Religions*. Oxford: Oneworld Publications.

—— (2006) "Human Rights and the World Religions." In *SHAP Journal of World Religions in Education*.

Schrag, C. (1995) "Pluralism." In R. Audi (ed.), *The Cambridge Dictionary of Philosophy*. Cambridge: Cambridge University Press.

St Theresa of Avila (1961) *Interior Castle*, trans. E. A. Peers. Garden City, NY: Image.

Tillich, P. (1963) *Christianity and the Encounter of the World Religions*. New York: Columbia University Press.

Ward, K. (1994) *Religion and Revelation*. New York: Oxford University Press.

Wei-Ming, T. (1985) *Confucian Thought*. Albany, NY: State University of New York Press.

Wittgenstein, L. (1958) *Philosophical Investigations*, trans. G. E. M. Anscombe. Oxford: Blackwell.

Further Reading

Byrne, P. (1995) *Prolegomena to Religious Pluralism: Reference and Realism in Religion*. New York: St. Martin's Press. (An analysis of philosophical consequences of religious pluralism.)

Hick, J. (2004) *An Interpretation of Religion: Human Responses to the Transcendent*. 2nd edn. New Haven, CT: Yale University Press. (The most comprehensive statement of Hick's paradigmatic religious pluralism.)

Rescher, N. (1993) *Pluralism: Against the Demand for Consensus*. Oxford: Oxford University Press. (A concise defense of philosophical pluralism and a rejection of the drive for rationalistic consensus.)

Runzo, J. (2001) *Global Philosophy of Religion: A Short Introduction*. Oxford: Oneworld Publications. (A comparative analysis of central philosophical ideas and religious values in the world religions.)

Runzo, J. and N. Martin (eds.) (2000) *The Meaning of Life in the World Religions*. Oxford: Oneworld Publications. (Essays by prominent scholars on the meaning and value of life as understood in each of the world religions.)

Ward, K. (1994) *Religion and Revelation*. New York: Oxford University Press. (Vol. 2 in Ward's important tetralogy setting out a pluralistic, systematic philosophical theology.)

Chapter 5

Religious Exclusivism

Harold Netland

One of the more striking things about contemporary religion is the sheer diversity of religious expression. Religious diversity is evident in dietary restrictions, dress, social relationships, artistic expression, rituals, and architecture. But such visible differences grow out of more fundamental differences in worldview, or ways in which each religion understands reality. The major religions teach that humankind, and in some cases the cosmos at large, is suffering under some kind of undesirable predicament and that, if proper steps are followed, an ultimately good and desirable state can be achieved. Religions typically offer comprehensive visions of what is religiously ultimate, the nature of the problem afflicting humankind, and the remedy for this predicament. "A religion proposes a diagnosis of a deep, crippling spiritual disease universal to non-divine sentience and offers a cure. A particular religion is true if its diagnosis is correct and its cure is efficacious" (Yandell 2004: 191). Furthermore, Christian, Islamic, Hindu, and other traditions emphasize that accepting the right beliefs about the diagnosis and cure is important; having a correct understanding of the way things are is an essential part of attaining the soteriological goal.

But the religions notoriously disagree, offering conflicting diagnoses and cures. Religions traditionally have been more or less exclusive in maintaining that their particular perspective on reality is true and efficacious in ways that others are not. Since the mid-twentieth century, with increased awareness of religious others, a cluster of theological and philosophical questions pertaining to religious diversity have attracted attention. Much of the debate has been conducted in the West and addresses the relation of Christian faith to other religions. This chapter will focus upon one approach to these issues, religious exclusivism, as it has been developed in discussions on Christianity and other religions.

The Traditional Taxonomy

Serious discussion by Christians of other religions goes back at least to the sixteenth century. Nevertheless, it has become customary in recent literature to distinguish three broad paradigms for understanding the relation of Christian faith to other religions – exclusivism, inclusivism, and pluralism. The terms seem first to have been used by Alan Race in *Christians and Religious Pluralism* (1982), and have been widely adopted since then.

Although there is no uniformly accepted definition of the terms, *exclusivism* is typically understood as the position which maintains that religious truth and salvation are restricted primarily, if not exclusively, to Christianity. Thus, Christian exclusivism embraces the following claims: (1) The Bible comprises God's distinctive written revelation, and where the claims of scripture are incompatible with those of other faiths the latter are to be rejected; (2) Jesus Christ is the unique incarnation of God, fully God and fully man, and only through the person and work of Jesus Christ is there possibility of salvation; (3) God's saving grace is not mediated through the teachings, practices, or institutions of other religions. With some modifications, exclusivism can be said to reflect the dominant position of the Church, Protestant and Roman Catholic, until the twentieth century. It is today primarily identified with evangelical Protestants.

The term "exclusivism" is often understood in negative terms, with exclusivists frequently characterized as dogmatic, narrow-minded, intolerant, ignorant, and arrogant. Thus, more recently, advocates of this position have adopted the term "particularism" rather than "exclusivism" as less offensive, although the change in terminology has not been widely adopted. The relation between exclusivism and tolerance will be considered below.

In the nineteenth and twentieth centuries more open perspectives on other religions became widespread, first among theologically more liberal Protestants and then, with Vatican II (1962–5), in Roman Catholicism. *Inclusivism* refers to a broad spectrum of views which embrace the following principles: (1) There is a sense in which Jesus Christ is unique, normative, or superior to other religious figures, and in some sense it is through Christ that salvation is made available; (2) God's grace and salvation, which are somehow based upon Jesus Christ, are also available and efficacious through other religions; (3) thus other religions should be regarded positively as part of God's purposes for humankind. There is enormous diversity among inclusivists over how these principles are to be understood and applied to other religions. Some develop an inclusivist theology of religions within traditional Trinitarian understandings of God and the incarnation; others modify or abandon traditional doctrines, especially in Christology. But the core of inclusivism is the desire to maintain in some sense the uniqueness and normativity of Jesus Christ while simultaneously acknowledging that God's saving grace is present and effective in and through other religions. Versions of inclusivism are dominant within mainline Protestant traditions and Roman Catholicism, and can also be found among some evangelicals.

By the 1970s and 1980s, however, a growing number of Western theologians were calling for explicit rejection of an assumption common to both exclusivism and inclusivism – that there is something significantly superior, or normative, about Jesus Christ and Christianity. *Religious pluralism*, which breaks with both exclusivism and inclusivism, maintains that the major religions should be regarded as more or less equally effective and legitimate alternative ways of responding to the one divine reality (see chapter 4, Religious Pluralism). "Religious pluralism" is sometimes used simply as a descriptive term, referring to the obvious religious diversity in our world. But as used here, it goes beyond mere recognition of diversity to include the claim that there is rough parity among the religions with respect to truth and soteriological effectiveness. Salvation, liberation, or enlightenment are said to be present and effective in all religions. No single religion can legitimately claim to be superior to others, for all religions are in their own ways complex historically and culturally conditioned human responses to the one divine reality. Variations of this view have become widespread on a popular level in the West and find sophisticated philosophical defense in the writings of John Hick (Hick 2004).

The taxonomy of exclusivism, inclusivism, and pluralism was developed by Western thinkers in the debate over Christianity and other religions. While discussions about religious others have not been as prominent in religions such as Islam, Hinduism, or Buddhism as in Christianity, analogues to the three approaches can be found there as well. Many traditions in Islam, Hinduism, and Buddhism, for example, are exclusivist in restricting truth and soteriological effectiveness to their own traditions. But there are also more inclusivist or even pluralist perspectives on other religions found among Muslims, Hindus, and Buddhists.

Although use of the three categories is widespread and can be helpful in sorting out the many views held by Christian thinkers on other religions, the taxonomy is somewhat misleading and simplistic. The broad range of questions concerning religious others and the many, often highly nuanced, perspectives on these issues cannot be forced into three neat categories.

It is significant that adoption of the three categories is fairly recent, only since the 1980s. Earlier nineteenth- and twentieth-century Christians' discussions of other religions were not constrained by the categories, and thus the issues were often formulated in other ways. Moreover, there is little consistency in use of the terms in the literature. Many – including most evangelicals – define the categories simply in terms of salvation. But even here there is not consistency, as "exclusivism" is often used for the view that only those who hear the gospel of Jesus Christ in this life and respond explicitly in faith to Christ can be saved. But many evangelicals reject this definition of exclusivism and recent discussions of soteriology have become sufficiently nuanced that trying to classify them in terms of just a few categories is misleading.

Furthermore, defining the categories in terms of salvation makes it difficult to address other questions demanding attention. Paul Griffiths (2001) helpfully distinguishes questions of truth from those of salvation, suggesting that the exclusivist/inclusivist distinction be construed in terms of each. With respect to truth, for example, exclusivism holds that true religious claims are found only among the teachings of one's own religion, whereas inclusivism maintains that it is possible that both one's own and other religions teach truth. What Griffiths calls open inclusivism affirms the possibility that some other religions might teach truths not already contained within one's own religion; closed inclusivism denies this (Griffiths 2001: xiv–xv).

In enlarging the categories to include questions of truth as well as salvation, however, it becomes even more difficult to classify particular thinkers without qualification. One might, for example, be exclusivist in maintaining that only those with an explicit relationship to Jesus Christ can be saved while also being an open inclusivist in acknowledging that other religions contain truths not explicitly found within Christianity. Moreover, since religions involve more than just matters of truth and salvation, questions about, for example, the moral value or social utility of other religions should also be addressed. But it is difficult to see how the three categories can be defined so that they reflect accurately the very diverse responses we can expect from such widely ranging questions. Thus, while the standard taxonomy can be helpful, the three positions should not be understood as clearly defined, mutually exclusive categories so much as distinct points on a continuum of perspectives, with particular thinkers falling into one or another category depending upon the particular issue under consideration.

Aspects of Religious Exclusivism

It is helpful to distinguish three aspects of exclusivism. The first, corresponding to the definition of Christian exclusivism above, is *theological exclusivism*, which maintains that religious truth and attainment of the soteriological goal are primarily restricted to a particular religion. Many traditions within Islam, Hinduism, Buddhism, and Christianity are theologically exclusive in this sense.

Formal exclusivism refers to the fact that any claim about the way things are which is intended to be true in a non-relative sense excludes something; to affirm that p is to deny that not-p. To claim that desire results in rebirth excludes the contradictory claim that desire does not result in rebirth. Any meaningful affirmation about reality, however trivial or ambiguous, excludes *something*. In this formal sense, all religious and non-religious worldviews, to the extent that they make claims about reality which are intended to be true, are exclusive.

In light of this, some have argued that inclusivist or pluralist perspectives on other religions are really simply variations of exclusivism (D'Costa 1996; 2000). Contrary to what Hick asserts, there cannot be a genuinely pluralistic perspective since pluralism "is always some or other form of explicit or implicit exclusivist tradition-specific narrative" (D'Costa 2000: 90). Insofar as they maintain that their own perspective is correct and incompatible alternatives should be rejected, pluralism and inclusivism ultimately collapse into exclusivism. Now there is a legitimate, although trivial, point here. Pluralists and inclusivists, like exclusivists, reject perspectives incompatible with their own. But to conclude from this that inclusivism and pluralism both reduce to exclusivism is to ignore the very real substantive differences between the three positions in their respective understandings of the relation between Christianity and other religions (Hick 1997). Thus, although Hick's pluralism is exclusive in the formal sense, the picture it presents of the relation among the religions and the epistemological and ontological commitments it embraces, are significantly different from exclusivism or inclusivism.

Finally, *social exclusivism* refers to assumptions or practices associated with a particular religious tradition which are exclusive with respect to social or interpersonal relations. Theological commitments in a particular tradition, for example, might result in restricting membership in the relevant group to believers, or prohibiting marriage with those outside the group, or in regulating association with certain classes of people. Some such practices might be relatively benign – the restriction of the office of Baptist pastor to Baptist Christians or of Islamic mullah to Muslims. Others might be morally repugnant but nevertheless protected by law – such as the exclusion of Jews or African Americans from membership in white supremacist organizations on racial grounds. Social exclusivism sometimes involves elitist and arrogant attitudes toward those who are different, but it need not do so. One can, for example, maintain that only believing Baptist Christians should be Baptist pastors and still be humble, gracious, and irenic in relations with religious others.

With these distinctions in mind, two further points should be noted. First, given the various senses in which a religious tradition or believer can be exclusive we should be careful about labeling a particular position as simply exclusive without qualification. One might be exclusive in some senses but not in others. For example, one might be theologically exclusive but not socially exclusive in the sense of restricting association with those outside the group. Or one might be theologically exclusive with respect to truth but not salvation (a soteriological universalist might also be a theological exclusivist). Conversely, one might acknowledge that there is much truth, goodness, and value in non-Christian religions and also insist that salvation is restricted to those with explicit faith in Christ.

Furthermore, although exclusivism is often identified with intolerance, the two concepts must be distinguished. Theological exclusivists are frequently dismissed today as intolerant for their (supposed) judgmental attitudes in rejecting beliefs of other religions. But tolerance and intolerance are not properties of beliefs as such but rather of behavior. It is not accepting or rejecting a particular belief that marks one as tolerant or intolerant. For if this were the case, then any time one disagreed with someone's beliefs one would be intolerant; the only way to be tolerant would be to accept all beliefs or withhold judgment about competing beliefs. If religious exclusivism is necessarily intolerant for the Christian exclusivist, then it follows that anyone – Buddhist, Wiccan, atheist, or religious pluralist – who maintains that her beliefs about religious matters are true and other incompatible beliefs false is also similarly morally blameworthy. But surely this is intellectual suicide, not tolerance.

John Horton reminds us that tolerance involves "the deliberate decision to refrain from prohibiting, hindering, or otherwise coercively interfering with conduct of which one disapproves, although one has the power to do so" (Horton

1998: 429–30). One can be theologically exclusive, believing that religious truth and salvation are largely restricted to one's own tradition, and still be appropriately tolerant of others, honoring freedom of conscience and religious expression. Whether in practice theological exclusivists are tolerant in their treatment of other religious groups is of course another matter. Tolerance of religious diversity – the freedom to believe and practice according to one's conscience, or even to reject religion entirely – is a modern phenomenon (Zagorin 2003). There is no question that institutional Christianity from the fifth through the seventeenth centuries was often highly intolerant in its treatment of Jews, Muslims, and dissenters. Whether such intolerance was greater than that found in Islam, Hinduism, or Buddhism throughout their histories, or than the intolerance of atheistic totalitarian regimes of the twentieth century, is an empirical question for social historians. The point here is simply that there is no necessary connection between theological exclusivism and intolerance.

The Problem of Conflicting Truth Claims

Religious exclusivism grows out of exposure to religious diversity and disagreement. Some religious disagreements are relatively insignificant. Judaism and Islam, for example, disagree over the identity of the son of Abraham who was to be sacrificed: the Hebrew scriptures identify him as Isaac whereas Islamic tradition insists it was Ishmael.

Other disagreements, however, are far more consequential. Both Islam and Christianity maintain that Jesus is to be esteemed, but they disagree sharply over his identity and nature. Christians accept Jesus as the unique incarnation of the eternal, creator God – Jesus as fully God and fully man. Muslims reject this as blasphemous; although Jesus was a great prophet, he was still only a man. Furthermore, Muslims and Christians disagree over the factual question whether Jesus was actually crucified, for many Muslims understand Surah 4:155–9 of the Qur'an to be ruling out Jesus' death on the cross. This cannot be dismissed as a minor disagreement, for the atoning work of Jesus Christ on the cross is at the heart of the Christian gospel. Even more basic disagreements emerge when we compare theistic religions with non-theistic ones. Judaism, Christianity, and Islam all believe in an all-powerful creator God, but this is explicitly denied in many Buddhist, Jain, Hindu, and Shinto traditions. Christianity teaches that the root problem confronting humankind is sin against a holy and righteous God. Hindu, Buddhist, and Jain traditions typically hold that the problem is a deeply embedded ignorance about the true nature of reality, although they disagree among themselves over the nature of this reality and whether, for example, there are enduring souls or persons.

Given such competing claims, it has generally been accepted that not all of the central assertions made by the religions can be true; at least some are false. Thus, religious exclusivism – whether Christian, Islamic, or Hindu – maintains that its own perspective is true and that other religious claims incompatible with it are to be rejected as false or incomplete. This conclusion, however, has the unhappy consequence that large numbers of sincere, morally good, respectable, and intelligent people are simply mistaken in some of their fundamental beliefs about reality. In an era of increasing globalization, in which we are far more aware of religious diversity than before, this implication strikes many as problematic.

Can We Avoid the Problem of Conflicting Truth Claims?

The problem of conflicting truth claims, it is sometimes said, presupposes a particular view of religious language and religious truth which ought to be rejected. Abandoning these problematic assumptions removes the problem of conflicting truth claims. Wilfred Cantwell Smith, for example, has argued that we should understand religious truth as personal truth rather than as a property of beliefs or statements (Smith 1962). Religious truth is not to be identified with beliefs or doctrines but rather with the inner faith of the believer. Religious truth is thus a quality in the believer which signifies integrity, sincerity, faithfulness, authenticity, and existentially appropriating one's commitments in life and conduct. "No statement might be accepted as true that has not been inwardly appropriated by its author" (Smith 1974: 35). Personal truth is thus relative to person and context; a statement might be "true for me" but "false for you," depending upon the extent to which each of us existentially appropriates it. The Christian who claims that God exists and the Buddhist who denies this are thus not disagreeing over whether God actually does exist; they are expressing different ways in which each responds existentially to the idea of God's reality.

Two points should be noted in response to Smith's proposal. First, the notion of personal truth does not reflect accurately what religious believers understand themselves to be doing when they make religious statements (Christian 1972). When the Christian speaks about God creating the universe, or the Buddhist says that release from rebirth comes through following the Four Noble Truths, or the Hindu speaks of the effects of *karma* upon subsequent lives, they normally intend to be making genuine assertions about reality. And these assertions are accepted by believers in the respective traditions as reflecting accurately the way reality is. Of course religious believers are expected to appropriate existentially the religious beliefs they accept. But it hardly follows that religious statements are not making claims about reality which are either true or false. Moreover, Smith's notion of personal truth itself presupposes the logically more basic sense of truth as a property of statements or beliefs. For the statement "Allah is a righteous judge" to "become true" in a personal sense for a Muslim, the Muslim would need to appropriate the belief in such a way that his life is congruous with belief in Allah as a righteous judge. But this will happen only if the Muslim accepts that "Allah is a righteous judge" depicts the way reality is – Allah actually exists and is a righteous judge (Wainwright 1984). Smith confuses the question of the truth of a statement with that of a believer's response to the statement.

Similarly, John Hick acknowledges that the major religions offer conflicting truth claims, but he attempts to blunt the force of this by minimizing the significance of such conflicts and offering a new way of understanding religious truth. Hick's thesis is that the major religions are different historically – and culturally – conditioned human responses to the religious ultimate (the Real) and that within each of them the same transformation from self-centeredness to reality-centeredness is taking place (Hick 2004). To the extent that they offer contexts within which such moral transformation occurs, each can be regarded as an appropriate or "true" religion.

Hick recognizes that the religions disagree on at least three levels: disagreements over matters of historical fact (did Jesus really die on the cross?); disputes over matters of "trans-historical fact" (is reincarnation true?); and different conceptions of the religious ultimate (is it a personal God or non-personal Emptiness?) (Hick 2004: chap. 20). If we understand religious language as involving assertions about reality which are literally true or false, then the traditional problem of conflicting truth claims is inescapable. However, Hick suggests two ways of avoiding this conclusion. First, we should acknowledge that resolving such disputes is not essential to salvation, understood as the transformation from self-centeredness to reality-centeredness, and thus such disagreements should not be emphasized. Second, he argues that we should understand religious truth in terms of mythological truth rather than literal truth. A statement is literally true if the state of affairs to which it refers is as the statement asserts it to be. But "a statement about X is mythologically true if it is not literally true but nevertheless tends to evoke an appropriate dispositional attitude to X" (Hick 2004: 348). Thus, "true religious myths are accordingly those that evoke in us attitudes and modes of behaviour which are appropriate to our situation in relation to the Real" (Hick 2004: 248). On this view, the problem of conflicting truth claims is no longer a matter of disputes over objectively existing states of affairs. Rather, the "truth" or "falsity" of religious utterances is a function of their capacity to prompt in us appropriate dispositional responses to the Real.

But there are at least three difficulties with this proposal. First, we note again that most believers do intend to make claims about reality that are true in the sense that they accurately (but not exhaustively) reflect the way things are. Moreover, most believers will insist that, while salvation or enlightenment involves more than this, having a proper understanding of some religious truths is essential to attaining the soteriological goal. And finally, the notion of mythological truth is itself parasitic upon the idea of literal truth; we cannot know what it means to have an appropriate dispositional response to the Real unless we first accept certain statements about the Real as true in a literal, not mythological, sense.

There is a final point that should be observed about Hick's effort to avoid the implications of the problem of conflicting truth claims. Even if Hick's model of religious pluralism is accepted, this does not eliminate the disturbing implication that large numbers of sincere, good, and intelligent religious believers are mistaken in their basic commitments. For a consequence of religious pluralism is that many of the central beliefs of traditional Christianity, Islam, Judaism, Hinduism, Buddhism, and Jainism, for example, are in fact false. Hick himself is quite clear that such central Christian beliefs as Jesus Christ being the unique incarnation of the one Triune God, taken as historically understood within orthodox Christianity, are false. The same holds for core Islamic beliefs such as the Qur'an being dictated to Muhammad by the angel Gabriel; or the Advaita Vedantin claim about our ultimate identity with Nirguna Brahman; or the Zen belief that the experience of *satori* provides direct, unmediated access to Emptiness. Accepting these beliefs might have pragmatic value in shaping behavior, and thus can be regarded as mythologically true, but strictly speaking they are false. Thus, even with pluralism we cannot escape the conclusion that large numbers of sincere, intelligent, and good people are mistaken in their basic religious commitments.

Can Religious Exclusivism be Justified?

Given our awareness of religious diversity today, can it be reasonable for one to insist that religious truth and salvation are to be found primarily within one's own religious tradition? While the same issues pertain to Muslim, Hindu, Buddhist, and other forms of theological exclusivism, we will frame the discussion in terms of Christian exclusivism.

People respond to awareness of religious diversity in different ways. Some are not particularly bothered by it and continue to remain confident in their commitments. Many others, however, find that exposure to other religions raises troubling questions and reduces epistemic confidence in their own tradition. Should it do so?

Does commitment to Christian theological exclusivism, given awareness of widespread religious disagreement, require justification? While many respond affirmatively, others claim that there is no special epistemic obligation to justify such commitments. Alvin Plantinga and other Reformed epistemologists, for example, maintain that there is no need for the Christian believer to demonstrate the truth of Christian theism, or even to provide "sufficient reasons" for Christian faith (see chapter 3, Reformed Epistemology). It can be "entirely right, rational, reasonable, and proper to believe in God without any evidence or argument at all (Plantinga 1983: 17). For the Christian in appropriate circumstances, belief in God can be "properly basic" and thus be epistemically appropriate apart from any appeal to supporting evidence. More recently, Plantinga has developed a theory of warrant, understood as the quality which distinguishes mere true belief from knowledge, and has applied this to Christian belief (Plantinga 2000). In brief, a belief is warranted only if it is produced by our epistemic faculties when they are operating properly, in accordance with their design plan, in appropriate contexts. In such cases the Christian can be warranted in her beliefs even if she has no argument or evidence for those beliefs.

Does exposure to widespread religious diversity alter the relevant circumstances, so that the believer who is confronted by religious disagreement is under an epistemic obligation to justify his religious beliefs which do not obtain in the absence of awareness of such diversity? Plantinga insists that even when one is aware of radical religious diversity, the Christian exclusivist need not defend his beliefs by appealing to reasons for accepting Christian claims (Plantinga 1995; 2000: 422–57). Awareness of diversity, while perhaps having the psychological effect of reducing confidence in one's initial beliefs, does not produce a special epistemic obligation to justify such belief.

Let us assume that Plantinga is correct in saying that, in general, it can be entirely reasonable for belief in God to be properly basic for someone in appropriate circumstances. A consequence of this, however, seems to be that in principle adherents of any religion can similarly claim that *their* religious beliefs are properly basic for them and thus can be held without any justifying reasons. It is difficult to see why belief in God can be properly basic for Christians but core beliefs of other religions cannot also be properly basic for their adherents. But if this is acceptable, we are left with a very weak sense of rationality according to which adherents of various religions can all be regarded as (equally?) reasonable in holding their respective beliefs, even if at least some of these beliefs are mutually incompatible. David Tien, for example, shows that on Plantinga's model of warrant the Neo-Confucianist Wang Yangming's religious beliefs, which conflict with Christian theism, can also be regarded as warranted (Tien 2004).

This leads to a second issue. Treating a belief as "properly basic," and thus not in need of further epistemic justification, is not controversial when there is a clear consensus on the appropriateness of the belief, but it becomes problematic when the belief in question is the subject of widespread disagreement. Thus although there is little controversy over accepting "In general, memory is reliable" as properly basic, this is not the case with "God the creator exists." While it is not necessary to justify a particular belief when there is a consensus about its truth or appropriateness, when one becomes aware of widespread disagreement over the belief, and is confronted with claims which undermine the belief, then some justification for maintaining that belief is in order (Basinger 2002: chs. 2–3; Griffiths 2001: ch. 3). Spelling out just when this is required and what constitutes adequate justification is notoriously difficult, but it does seem that awareness of religious diversity and contrary claims should prompt some reconsideration of one's beliefs. In some cases this might result in renewed confidence in the appropriateness of one's initial beliefs; in others it might demand modification of one's views.

There is an important challenge to religious exclusivism that argues for religious skepticism from the fact of religious disagreement. Widespread religious disagreement is sometimes said to undermine the claims of religious exclusivism by providing positive reasons for rejecting the assertions of any particular religion. Given the problem of conflicting truth claims, and the absence of any clear procedure for adjudicating such conflicts satisfactorily, the wisest course surely is to dismiss all claims as false or at least to withhold judgment about their truth.

This response to religious diversity is usually based upon the epistemic parity thesis, which maintains that evidential and rational considerations relevant to religious belief are such that no particular religious tradition can be said to be rationally superior to others; the data are sufficiently ambiguous that the major religions enjoy more or less epistemic parity. Since we cannot settle religious disputes in a non-arbitrary manner, we should simply withhold judgment and not accept any claim as more likely to be true than others. The parity thesis can be used to support either a general agnosticism about all religions or religious pluralism (Byrne 2004).

But should the epistemic parity thesis be accepted simply because of religious disagreement? Religious ambiguity means that it can be just as rational to interpret the universe as a Christian theist or a Vedantin Hindu or a Theravadin Buddhist, and so on, depending upon one's particular circumstances and experiences. But why accept this? Is it really the case that the proposition "God exists" has no greater evidential or rational support than its denial? Is it really just as reasonable to accept as veridical purported experiences of Nirguna Brahman among Hindus or of Emptiness among Buddhists as it is to accept purported experiences of the personal God of Christian theism? Deeply rooted disagreement by itself does not entail that there is no single perspective more likely to be true than others, or that all religious perspectives have roughly the same epistemic support. If, as many philosophers maintain, central beliefs of the religions can be assessed in terms of rationality and truth and some perspectives have much stronger epistemic support than others, then the epistemic parity thesis should be rejected. Keith Yandell (Yandell 1993; 1999), for example, argues that certain introspective enlightenment experiences at the heart of Advaita Vedanta Hinduism and Buddhism *cannot* be veridical and self-authenticating as claimed, and that the notion of *anatman* (no self) in classical Buddhism is incoherent. He argues further that there are positive reasons for accepting some versions of theism, including evidence from reports of numinous experiences of God across cultures. If he is correct, then the world is not as religiously ambiguous as the parity thesis suggests.

Whether a particular expression of Christian exclusivism is justified depends upon two distinct sets of issues. First, there is the question whether particular doctrinal beliefs (e.g. Jesus Christ is the only savior for all humankind; God revealed himself to the biblical prophets in ways unparalleled in other religions) are justified. Included here are the internal disputes over whether exclusivist or inclusivist views on other religions ought to be accepted. Such issues are settled largely by appeal to authoritative sources and criteria internal to Christian faith itself – the scriptures and theological heritage of the Church.

But there is also a second, more basic, issue: Should one accept Christian theism in the first place? Christian theological exclusivism will only be justifiable if the broader framework within which it is embedded – Christian theism – is justifiable. Discussion of this set of issues is, of course, beyond the scope of this chapter. It seems clear, however, that given our awareness of religious diversity, questions of the justification of Christian faith cannot be considered apart from the challenges posed by widespread religious disagreement. The plausibility of Christian theism is in part a function of its capacity to withstand challenges from religious diversity. What is needed in such contexts is what Ninian Smart called "worldview analysis," the cross-cultural and interreligious analysis of competing worldviews in terms of truth and rationality, and "soft natural theology," or the attempt to show in appropriate ways that there are good reasons for accepting Christian theism rather than other alternatives (Smart 1992; 1995; Netland 2004).

Questions for Reflection

1   What are some advantages and disadvantages to keeping the standard categories of "exclusivism," "inclusivism," and "pluralism" to describe various positions on other religions?
2   Many assume that theological exclusivism and social exclusivism inevitably lead to intolerance of religious others. Is this the case? Why or why not?
3   The author claims that given the problem of conflicting truth claims among the religions, any position we adopt regarding the relationship among the religions (including religious pluralism) entails that at least some claims of some religions are false. Why is this? Do you agree?
4   Given widespread religious diversity and disagreement, is it reasonable to think that one particular religion might be distinctively true or rational? What would be involved in defending the claim that one religion is more likely to be true than the others?
5   Can one be a theological exclusivist, as defined in this chapter, and still be genuinely accepting of religious diversity in the social and cultural dimensions? Why or why not?

References

Basinger, D. (2002) *Religious Diversity: A Philosophical Assessment*. Burlington, VT: Ashgate.
Byrne, P. (2004) "It Is Not Reasonable to Believe that Only One Religion is True." In M. L. Peterson and R. J. VanArragon (eds.), *Contemporary Debates in Philosophy of Religion*. Oxford: Blackwell.
Christian, W. A. (1972) *Oppositions of Religious Doctrines: A Study in the Logic of Dialogue Among Religions*. London: Macmillan.
D'Costa, G. (1996) "The Impossibility of a Pluralist View of Religions." *Religious Studies* 32, 223–32.
—— (2000) *The Meeting of Religions and the Trinity*. Maryknoll, NY: Orbis Books.
Griffiths, P. (2001) *Problems of Religious Diversity*. Oxford: Blackwell.
Hick, J. (1997) "The Possibility of Religious Pluralism: A Reply to Gavin D'Costa." *Religious Studies* 33, 161–66.
—— (2004) *An Interpretation of Religion: Human Responses to the Transcendent*. 2nd edn. New Haven, CT: Yale University Press.

Hick, J., and P. F. Knitter (eds.) (1987) *The Myth of Christian Uniqueness: Toward a Pluralistic Theology of Religions.* Maryknoll, NY: Orbis Books.

Horton, J. (1998) "Toleration." In E. Craig (ed.), *Routledge Encyclopedia of Philosophy.* Vol. 9. London: Routledge.

Knitter, P. (1985) *No Other Name? A Critical Survey of Christian Attitudes Toward the World Religions.* Maryknoll, NY: Orbis Books.

Netland, H. (2001) *Encountering Religious Pluralism.* Downers Grove, IL: InterVarsity Press.

—— (2004) "Natural Theology and Religious Diversity." *Faith and Philosophy* 21:4, 503–18.

Okholm, D. L., and T. R. Philips (eds.) (1996) *Four Views on Salvation in a Pluralistic World.* Grand Rapids, MI: Zondervan.

Plantinga, A. (1983) "Reason and Belief in God." In A. Plantinga and N. Wolterstorff (eds.), *Faith and Rationality: Reason and Belief in God.* Notre Dame: University of Notre Dame Press.

—— (1995) "Pluralism: A Defense of Religious Exclusivism." In T. Senor (ed.), *The Rationality of Belief and the Plurality of Faith.* Ithaca, NY: Cornell University Press.

—— (2000) *Warranted Christian Belief.* New York: Oxford University Press.

Race, A. (1982) *Christians and Religious Pluralism: Patterns in the Christian Theology of Religions.* Maryknoll, NY: Orbis Books.

Smart, N. (1992) "Soft Natural Theology." In E. Thomas (ed.), *Prospects for Natural Theology: Studies in Philosophy and the History of Philosophy.* Washington, DC: The Catholic University of America Press.

—— (1995) "The Philosophy of Worldviews, or the Philosophy of Religion Transformed." In T. Dean (ed.), *Religious Pluralism and Truth: Essays in Cross-Cultural Philosophy of Religion.* Albany, NY: State University of New York Press.

Smith, W. C. (1962) *The Meaning and End of Religion.* San Francisco: Harper & Row.

—— (1974) "A Human View of Truth." In J. Hick (ed.), *Truth and Dialogue in World Religions: Conflicting Truth Claims.* Philadelphia: Westminster Press.

Tien, D. W. (2004) "Warranted Neo-Confucian Belief: Religious Pluralism and the Affections in the Epistemologies of Wang Yangming (1472–1529) and Alvin Plantinga." *International Journal for Philosophy of Religion* 55, 31–55.

Wainwright, W. J. (1984) "Wilfred Cantwell Smith on Faith and Belief." *Religious Studies* 20:3, 353–66.

Yandell, K. (1993) *The Epistemology of Religious Experience.* New York: Cambridge University Press.

—— (1999) *Philosophy of Religion: A Contemporary Introduction.* London: Routledge.

—— (2004) "How to Sink in Cognitive Quicksand: Nuancing Religious Pluralism." In M. L. Peterson and R. J. VanArragon (eds.), *Contemporary Debates in Philosophy of Religion.* Oxford: Blackwell.

Zagorin, P. (2003) *How the Idea of Religious Toleration Came to the West.* Princeton: Princeton University Press.

Further Reading

Griffiths, P. (1991) *An Apology for Apologetics: A Study in the Logic of Interreligious Dialogue.* Maryknoll, NY: Orbis Books. (Griffiths provides an incisive analysis of religious discourse and truth and argues that religious communities have epistemic and moral obligations to defend the truth of their religious claims against competitors.)

Hick, J., and B. Hebblethwaite (eds.) (2001) *Christianity and Other Religions: Selected Readings*. Rev. edn. Oxford: Oneworld Publications. (This is a helpful collection of writings on theology of religions by some leading Christian theologians.)

Neill, S. (1961) *Christian Faith and Other Faiths*. New York: Oxford University Press. (Written a half century ago, Neill's classic work is a clear and irenic statement of a Christian "exclusivist" position on other religions.)

Quinn, P. L., and K. Meeker (eds.) (2000) *The Philosophical Challenge of Religious Diversity*. New York: Oxford University Press. (Collected here are discussions of epistemological and ontological issues relating to religious diversity and religious pluralism by some of the leading analytic philosophers of religion.)

Part II
The Existence of God

Chapter 6

The Cosmological Argument

William Lane Craig

Introduction

In his biography of Ludwig Wittgenstein, Norman Malcolm reports:

> He said that he sometimes had a certain experience which could best be described
> by saying that "when I have it, *I wonder at the existence of the world.* I am then inclined
> to use such phrases as 'How extraordinary that anything should exist!' or 'How
> extraordinary that the world should exist!'" (Malcolm 1958: 70)

The mystery of the existence of the universe, which according to Aristotle
lay at the very root of philosophy, is one which even thoughtful naturalists
cannot avoid. Derek Parfit agrees that "No question is more sublime than
why there is a Universe: why there is anything rather than nothing" (Parfit
1998: 24).

This question led G. W. Leibniz (1951: 415; 237–9) to posit the existence
of a necessary being, which carries within itself the sufficient reason for its
existence and which constitutes the sufficient reason for the existence of everything else in the world. Leibniz identified this being as God. Leibniz's critics,
on the other hand, have typically claimed that the space-time universe is itself at
least factually necessary (Hick 1960: 733–4) – that is to say, eternal, uncaused,
incorruptible, and indestructible – while dismissing the demand for a logically
necessary being. Thus, David Hume (1947: ch. 9, par. 190) queried, "Why
may not the material universe be the necessarily existent Being . . .?" Indeed,
"How can anything, that exists from eternity, have a cause, since that relation
implies a priority in time and a beginning of existence?" There is no warrant for
going beyond the universe to posit a supernatural ground of its existence. As
Bertrand Russell put it so succinctly in his BBC radio debate with Frederick
Copleston, "The universe is just there, and that's all" (Russell and Copleston
1964: 175).

A Leibnizian Argument

But is that really all? On the Hume-Russell view the universe is a brute contingent, eternally existing without reason or cause. We are simply left with no explanation of the existence of the universe. Leibniz would have rejected such a view on the basis of his Principle of Sufficient Reason, which states that "no fact can be real or existent, no statement true, unless there be a sufficient reason why it is so and not otherwise." Although Leibniz's principle has some intuitive warrant, critics have rejected Leibniz's principle as stated in *The Monadology* on the grounds that not every fact can have an explanation, for there cannot be an explanation of what we might call the Big Contingent Conjunctive Fact (BCCF) which is itself the conjunction of all the contingent facts there are. For if such an explanation states a contingent fact, then it, too, must have a further explanation, which is impossible, since the BCCF includes all the contingent facts there are. But if the explanation states a necessary fact, then the fact explained by it must also be necessary, which is impossible, since the BCCF is contingent. Therefore, not every fact can have an explanation.

Some theists have responded to this objection by agreeing that one must ultimately come to some explanatory stopping point which is simply a brute fact, a being whose existence is unexplained. For example, Richard Swinburne (1991: ch. 7) claims that in answering the question "Why is there something rather than nothing?" we must finally come to the brute existence of some contingent being. This being will not serve to explain its own existence (and, hence, the question goes unanswered), but it will explain the existence of everything else. Swinburne argues that God is the best explanation of why everything other than the brute Ultimate exists because as a unique and infinite being God is simpler than the variegated and finite universe. Hume and Russell got it right in thinking that there must be a brute Ultimate, but they erred in identifying such an inexplicable given with the physical universe.

Other theists have sought to defend the Leibnizian argument without retreating to the dubious position that God is a contingent being. They have either challenged the assumption that there is a BCCF or sought to provide an acceptable explanation of it. For example, Alexander Pruss (2006) has argued that it may well be that the existence of a BCCF is inherently paradoxical (cf. the set of all truths), so that its existence cannot just be assumed. But if there is such a fact, he argues, then its explanation may be found in the necessary truth that God has weighed the reasons for creating each world and has freely chosen which world to create. Moreover, the claim that the BCCF cannot be explained by some contingent truth assumes that no contingent truth can be self-explained. William Vallicella (1997) suggests that the reason the BCCF is true may be simply because each of its conjuncts is true; nothing more is needed to explain why the BCCF is true than the truth of its atomic constituents, each of which has an explanation for its truth. Hence, Leibniz's formulation of the Principle of Sufficient Reason is quite defensible.

This debate is, in the end, somewhat academic, since the cosmological argument does not depend for its success on anything so strong as Leibniz's own version of the Principle of Sufficient Reason. For example, the proponent of a Leibnizian cosmological argument could generate his argument by holding that, for any contingently existing thing, there is an explanation why that thing exists. Or again, he could assert that everything that exists has an explanation of its existence, either in the necessity of its own nature or in an external cause. Or, more broadly, he might maintain that in the case of any contingent state of affairs, there is either an explanation for why that state of affairs obtains or else an explanation of why no explanation is needed. All of these are more modest, non-paradoxical, and seemingly plausible versions of the Principle of Sufficient Reason.

So we might formulate a simple version of a Leibnizian cosmological argument as follows:

1   Any thing that exists has an explanation of its existence, either in the necessity of its own nature or in an external cause.
2   If the universe has an explanation of its existence, that explanation is God.
3   The universe exists.
4   Therefore the explanation of the existence of the universe is God.

Premise (1) is a modest version of the Principle of Sufficient Reason which circumvents the typical objections to strong versions of that principle. For (1) merely requires any existing *thing* to have an explanation of its existence. This premise is compatible with there being brute *facts* about the world. What it precludes is that there could exist things which just exist inexplicably. According to (1) there are two kinds of being: necessary beings, which exist of their own nature and so have no external cause of their existence, and contingent beings, whose existence is accounted for by causal factors outside themselves. Numbers might be prime candidates for the first sort of being, while familiar physical objects fall under the second kind of being.

This principle seems quite plausible, at least more so than its contradictory. One thinks of Richard Taylor's illustration of finding a translucent ball while walking in the woods (Taylor 1991: 100–1). One would find the claim quite bizarre that the ball just exists inexplicably; and increasing the size of the ball, even until it becomes co-extensive with the cosmos, would do nothing to obviate the need for an explanation of its existence.

Crispin Wright and Bob Hale (1992: 128), while recognizing that explicability is the default position and that exceptions to the requirement of an explanation therefore require justification, nonetheless maintain that an exemption is justified in the case of the contingent universe because the demand for an explanation of the contingent universe is pre-empted by the restrictive principle that *the explanation of the obtaining of a (physical) state of affairs must advert to a causally prior state of affairs in which it does not obtain*. This principle would require that any explanation of the existence of the universe must advert to a causally prior state of affairs in which the universe does not exist. But since a physically empty world would not cause anything, the demand for an explanation of the universe becomes absurd and thus the demand for an explanation is preempted. This line of reasoning plainly begs the question in favor of atheism. For apart from that assumption, there is just no reason to think that a causally prior state of affairs must be a physical state of affairs. The theist will regard Wright and Hale's principle as not at all restrictive, since the explanation of why the physical universe exists can and should be provided in terms of a causally prior non-physical state of affairs involving God's existence and will.

Premise (2) is, in effect, the contrapositive of the typical atheist retort given by Hume and Russell that on the atheistic worldview the universe simply exists as a brute contingent thing. Atheists typically assert that, there being no God, the universe just exists inexplicably. In affirming that if atheism is true, then the universe has no explanation of its existence, atheists are also affirming the logically equivalent claim that if the universe has an explanation of its existence, then atheism is not true, that is to say, God exists. Hence, most atheists are implicitly committed to (2).

Moreover, (2) seems quite plausible in its own right. For if the universe, by definition, includes all of physical reality, then the cause of the universe must (at least causally prior to the universe's existence) transcend space and time and therefore cannot be temporal or material. But there are only two kinds of things that could fall under such a description: either an abstract object or else a mind. But abstract objects do not stand in causal relations. Whether we are talking about mathematical objects, universals, propositions, or any other of a host of abstract objects which many philosophers deem to exist, it belongs conceptually to such objects that they are causally effete and so cannot effect anything. By contrast, minds are the causes with which we are the most intimately acquainted of all causes, as we experience the causal efficacy of our own willings. It therefore follows that the explanation of the existence of the universe is an external, transcendent, personal cause – which is one meaning of "God."

Finally, (3) states the obvious, that there is a universe. It follows that God exists.

It is open to the atheist to reply to this Leibnizian argument that while the universe has an explanation of its existence, that explanation lies not in an external ground but in the necessity of its own nature; in other words, (2) is false. This is, however, an extremely bold suggestion which atheists have not been eager to embrace. We have, one can safely say, a strong intuition of the universe's contingency. A possible world in which no concrete objects exist certainly seems conceivable. We generally trust our modal intuitions on other matters with which we are familiar; if we are to do otherwise with respect to the universe's contingency, then the non-theist needs to provide some reason for such skepticism other than his desire to avoid theism.

Moreover, we have good grounds for thinking that the universe does not exist by a necessity of its own nature. It is easy to conceive of the non-existence of any and all of the macroscopic objects we observe in the world; indeed, prior to a certain point in the past none of them did exist. As for fundamental particles or the building blocks of matter, be they quarks or strings, it is easy to conceive of a world in which all of the present microscopic constituents of macroscopic objects were replaced by other quarks or strings. A universe consisting of a totally different collection of quarks, say, seems quite possible. If that is the case, then the universe does not exist by a necessity of its own nature, since a universe composed of a wholly different collection of quarks is not the same universe as ours. This is the case whether we think of the universe as an object in its own right, just as a block of marble is not identical to a block of the same shape constituted of different marble, or as an aggregate or group, just as a flock of birds is not identical to a similar flock composed of different birds, or even as nothing at all over and above the quarks themselves. Since quarks are the fundamental building blocks of material objects, one cannot say, as one might of macroscopic objects, that while they are contingent, the stuff of which they are made is necessary, for there is no further stuff beyond them. No atheist will, I think, have the temerity to suggest that some quarks, though qualitatively similar to ordinary quarks, have the special occult property of being metaphysically necessary. It is all or nothing here. But no one thinks that every quark exists by a necessity of its own nature. It follows that neither does the universe composed of such quarks exist by a necessity of its own nature.

Perhaps it will be said, as Bede Rundle has in fact said (Rundle 2004), that while nothing exists by a necessity of its own nature, nevertheless it is necessary that something or other exist. Rundle agrees with the theist (albeit for different reasons) that it is broadly logically impossible that nothing exist; but the proper conclusion to be drawn from this fact is not that a necessary being exists, but that, necessarily, some contingent being or other exists. In short, premise (1) is, on Rundle's view, false after all.

Alexander Pruss (2005: 210) has pointed out that Rundle's view has an extremely untoward consequence. It is plausible that no conjunction of claims about the non-existence of various things entails, say, that a unicorn exists. After all, how could the fact that certain things do not exist entail that some other thing does exist? But on Rundle's view the conjunction "There are no mountains, there are no people, there are no planets, there are no rocks, . . . [including everything that is not a unicorn]" entails that there is a unicorn! For if it is necessary that contingent beings exist, and none of the other contingent beings listed exist, then the only thing left is a unicorn. Hence, a conjunction about the non-existence of certain things entails that a unicorn exists, a most implausible consequence.

Moreover, on Rundle's view there is nothing which would account for *why* there exist contingent beings in every possible world. Since there is no metaphysically necessary being, there is nothing that could cause contingent beings to exist in every possible world and no explanation why every world includes contingent beings. There is no strict logical inconsistency in the concept of a world devoid of contingent beings. What accounts for the fact that in every possible world contingent beings exist? Given the infinity of broadly logically possible worlds, the odds that in all of them contingent beings just happen inexplicably to exist is infinitesimal. Hence, the probability of Rundle's hypothesis is effectively zero. Rundle cannot avoid this difficulty by asserting that the reason why contingent beings exist is that matter necessarily exists, for none of the fundamental building blocks of matter does seem to exist by a necessity of its own nature, so that matter itself is contingent. The probability that matter inexplicably happens to exist in every world is vanishingly small.

The premises of this Leibnizian argument thus all seem more plausible than their negations. It therefore follows logically that the explanation for why the universe exists is to be found in God.

An Argument from *Kalam*

In fact, the Hume-Russell view is even more implausible than the above remarks suggest. For in asserting that the universe exists without explanation or cause, Hume and Russell were presupposing that the universe has existed, in Hume's words, "from eternity," that is to say, the universe never began to exist. Given the beginningless and endless existence of the universe, we can give the naturalist a run for his money when he asserts that it is a brute contingent. But if the universe had a beginning, then it seems incredible to think that it came into being uncaused out of nothing. Neither can its existence be construed as metaphysically necessary; otherwise it would have always existed. Hence, if the universe had a beginning, one is compelled to find the explanation of its existence in an ultramundane cause that brought it into being.

This type of cosmological argument was a centerpiece of the intellectual movement in medieval Islamic theology called *kalam* (which means "word" and by extension designates the statement of some theological position). Interest in this form of the cosmological argument has been re-awakened in our day by astronomical discoveries which provide empirical evidence unknown to the medievals in support of the argument's key premise. A simple version of the *kalam* cosmological argument might run as follows:

1 Whatever begins to exist has a cause.
2 The universe began to exist.
3 Therefore, the universe has a cause.

Conceptual analysis of what it means to be a cause of the universe then helps to establish some of the theologically significant properties of this being.

Premise (1) seems obviously true – at the least, more so than its negation. It is rooted in the metaphysical intuition that something cannot come into being from nothing. To suggest that things could just pop into being uncaused out of nothing is to quit doing serious metaphysics and to resort to magic. Furthermore, if things could really come into being uncaused out of nothing, then it becomes inexplicable why just anything and everything does not come into existence uncaused from nothing. Finally, the first premise is constantly confirmed in our experience. Atheists who are scientific naturalists thus have the strongest of motivations to accept it.

Often it is said that quantum physics furnishes an exception to premise (1), since on the subatomic level events are said to be uncaused. This objection, however, is based on misunderstandings. In the first place, not all scientists agree that subatomic events are uncaused. A great many physicists today are quite dissatisfied with this view (the so-called Copenhagen Interpretation) of quantum physics and are exploring deterministic theories (like that of David Bohm). Thus, quantum physics is not a proven exception to premise (1). Second, even on the traditional, indeterministic interpretation, particles do not come into being out of nothing. They arise as spontaneous fluctuations of the energy contained in the quantum vacuum, which constitutes an indeterministic cause of their origination. Thus, there is no basis for the claim that quantum physics proves that things can begin to exist without a cause, much less that the universe could have sprung into being uncaused from literally nothing.

Premise (2), the more controversial premise, may be supported by both deductive, philosophical arguments and inductive, scientific arguments.

First deductive argument

The first argument we shall consider for premise (2) is argument (2.1), based on *the impossibility of the existence of an actual infinite*. We may formulate the argument as follows:

2.11 An actual infinite cannot exist.
2.12 An infinite temporal regress of events is an actual infinite.
2.13 Therefore an infinite temporal regress of events cannot exist.

Since the universe is not distinct from the temporal series of past events, it follows that the universe must have begun to exist.

Consider premise (2.11). By an actual infinite, one means any collection having at a time t a number of definite and discrete members which is greater than any natural number 0, 1, 2, 3, ... It is usually alleged that (2.11) has been falsified by Georg Cantor's work on the actual infinite and by subsequent developments in set theory. But the ontological finitist can legitimately respond that this allegation not only begs the question against intuitionistic denials of the mathematical existence of the actual infinite, but, more seriously, it begs the question against non-Platonist views of the ontology of mathematical objects. These are distinct questions, and most non-Platonists would not go to the intuitionistic extreme of denying mathematical legitimacy to the actual infinite; they would simply insist that acceptance of the mathematical existence of certain entities does not imply an ontological commitment to the metaphysical reality of such objects. Cantor's system and set theory may be taken to be simply a universe of discourse, a mathematical system based on certain adopted axioms and conventions. On anti-realist views of mathematical objects such as Balaguer's Fictionalism (Balaguer 1998; 2001; 2004) or Chihara's Constructivism (Chihara 1990; 2004) there are no mathematical objects at all, let alone an infinite number of them. One may consistently hold that while the actual infinite is a fruitful and consistent concept within the postulated universe of discourse, it cannot be transposed into the spatio-temporal world, for this would involve counterintuitive absurdities.

Perhaps the best way to support this premise is by way of thought experiments, like the famous Hilbert's Hotel – a brainchild of the great German mathematician David Hilbert – which illustrate the various absurdities that would result if an actual infinite were to be instantiated in the real world (Gamow 1946: 17). The absurdity in this case is not merely practical and physical; it seems ontologically absurd that a hotel exist which is completely full and yet can accommodate untold infinities of new guests just by moving people around. Worse, if such a hotel could exist in reality, then it would lead to situations which would not be warranted by transfinite arithmetic and finally to logical contradictions. For while in transfinite arithmetic the inverse operations of subtraction and division of infinite quantities from or by infinite quantities are not permitted, these could occur with a real hotel occupied by real people. In such cases one winds up with logically impossible situations, such as subtracting identical quantities from identical quantities and finding non-identical differences.

Howard Sobel (2004: 186–7) observes that such situations bring into conflict two "seemingly innocuous" principles, namely:

(i)   There are not more things in a multitude M than there are in a multitude M′ if there is a 1–1 correspondence of their members.

and

(ii) There are more things in M than there are in M′ if M′ is a proper submultitude of M.

We cannot have both of these principles along with:

(iii) An actually infinite multitude exists.

For Sobel the choice to be taken is clear: "The choice we have taken from Cantor is to hold on to (i) while restricting the proper submultiplicity condition to finite multiplicities. In this way we can 'have' comparable infinite multitudes."

But the choice taken from Cantor of which Sobel speaks is a choice on the part of the mathematical community to reject intuitionism in favor of infinite set theory. Intuitionism (which allows only the potential infinite) would too radically truncate mathematics to be acceptable to most mathematicians. But, as already indicated, that choice does not validate metaphysical conclusions. The metaphysician wants to know why, in order to resolve the inconsistency among (i)–(iii), it is (ii) that should be jettisoned (or restricted). Why not instead reject (i), which is a mere set-theoretical convention, or restrict it to finite multiplicities? More to the point, why not reject (iii) instead of the apparently innocuous (i) or (ii)? It certainly lacks the innocuousness of those principles, and giving it up would enable us to affirm both (i) and (ii). We can "have" comparable infinite multiplicities in mathematics without admitting them into our ontology. In view of the absurdities which ontologically real actual infinite multitudes would engender, we are better off without them.

Sobel thus needs some *argument* for the falsity of (ii). It is insufficient merely to point out that if (i) and (iii) are true, then (ii) is false, for that is merely to re-iterate the incompatibility of the three propositions. The opponent of (iii) may argue that if (iii) were true, then (i) would be true with respect to such a multitude, as Sobel believes; and that if (i) and (iii) were true, then the various counterintuitive situations would result; therefore if (iii) were true, the various counterintuitive situations would result. But because these situations are really impossible, it follows that (iii) is not possibly true. In order to refute this reasoning, one must do more than point out that if (i) and (iii) are true, then (ii) is false, for that is merely to reiterate that if an actual infinite were to exist and the principle of correspondence were valid with respect to it, then the relevant situations would result, which is not in dispute.

The truth of (2.12) seems obvious. It therefore follows that the series of past events must be finite and have a beginning.

Second deductive argument

The second philosophical argument we shall consider on behalf of premise (2) is argument (2.2), based on *the impossibility of the formation of an actual infinite by successive addition*. We may formulate the argument as follows:

2.21   The series of events in time is a collection formed by successive addition.
2.22   A collection formed by successive addition cannot be actually infinite.
2.23   Therefore, the series of events in time cannot be actually infinite.

Since the series of events in time is not distinct from the universe, it follows that the universe began to exist.

It may seem that (2.21) is rather obvious, but it does presuppose the truth of a tensed theory of time. Since advocates of a tenseless theory of time deny the reality of temporal becoming, they deny that the past series of events was formed by successive addition. There are, however, powerful reasons to think that the tenseless theory of time is mistaken and that temporal becoming is real (Craig 2000a; 2000b; 2001).

The key premise, then, is (2.22). Sometimes this is called the impossibility of traversing the infinite. In order for us to have "arrived" at today, temporal existence has, so to speak, traversed an infinite number of prior events. But before the present event could arrive, the event immediately prior to it would have to arrive; and before that event could arrive, the event immediately prior to it would have to arrive; and so on *ad infinitum*. No event could ever arrive, since before it could elapse there will always be one more event that had to have happened first. Thus, if the series of past events were beginningless, the present event could not have arrived, which is absurd.

It is frequently objected that this sort of argument illicitly presupposes an infinitely distant starting point in the past and then pronounces it impossible to travel from that point to today, whereas in fact from any given point in the past, there is only a finite distance to the present, which is easily traversed (Mackie 1982: 93; Sobel 2004: 182). But proponents of the argument have not in fact assumed that there was an infinitely distant starting point in the past. To traverse a distance is to cross every proper part of it. As such, traversal does not entail that the distance traversed has a beginning or ending point or a first or last part. The fact that there is *no beginning* at all, not even an infinitely distant one, seems only to make the problem worse, not better. To say that the infinite past could have been formed by successive addition is like saying that someone has just succeeded in writing down all the negative numbers, ending at − 1. And, proponents of the argument may ask, how is the claim that from any given moment in the past there is only a finite distance to the present even relevant to the issue? For the question is how the *whole* series can be formed, not a finite portion of it. To think that because every *finite* segment of the series can be formed by successive addition the whole *infinite* series can as well is to commit the fallacy of composition.

Given the truth of the premises, it follows that the temporal series of past, physical events is not infinite and that the universe began to exist.

First inductive argument

A third argument for (2) is an inductive argument based on evidence for the expansion of the universe. The Big Bang model does not describe the expansion of the material content of the universe into a pre-existing, empty space, but rather the expansion of space itself. As one extrapolates back in time, space-time curvature becomes progressively greater until one arrives at a singularity, at which space-time curvature becomes infinite. It therefore constitutes an edge or boundary to space-time itself.

Twentieth-century cosmology has witnessed a long series of failed attempts to craft plausible models of the expanding universe which avert the absolute beginning predicted by the standard model. While such theories are possible, it has been the overwhelming verdict of the scientific community than none of them is more probable than the Big Bang theory (Craig forthcoming). There is no mathematically consistent model which has been so successful in its predictions or as corroborated by the evidence as the traditional Big Bang theory. For example, some theories, like the Oscillating Universe or the Chaotic Inflationary Universe, do have a potentially infinite future but turn out to have only a finite past. Vacuum Fluctuation Universe theories cannot explain why, if the vacuum was eternal, we do not observe an infinitely old universe. The same difficulty attends the so-called Pre-Big Bang scenario. The No-Boundary Universe proposal of James Hartle and Stephen Hawking still involves an absolute origin of the universe in the finite past even if the universe does not begin in a singularity, as it does in the standard Big Bang theory. Recently proposed Ekpyrotic Cyclic Universe scenarios based on string theory or M-theory have also been shown, not only to be riddled with problems, but to imply the very origin of the universe which its proponents sought to avoid. There is no doubt that one who asserts the truth of (2) rests comfortably within the scientific mainstream.

Second inductive argument

A fourth argument for (2) is also an inductive argument, appealing to thermodynamic properties of the universe. According to the second law of thermodynamics, processes taking place in a closed system tend toward states of higher entropy, as their energy is used up. Already in the nineteenth century scientists realized that the application of the law to the universe as a whole implied a grim eschatological conclusion: given sufficient time, the universe would eventually come to a state of equilibrium and suffer heat death. But this projection raised an even deeper question: if, given sufficient time, the universe will suffer heat death, then why, if it has existed forever, is it not now in a state of heat death?

The advent of relativity theory altered the shape of the eschatological scenario but did not materially affect this fundamental question. Astrophysical evidence indicates overwhelmingly that the universe will expand forever. As it does, it will become increasingly cold, dark, dilute, and dead. Eventually the entire mass of the universe will be nothing but a cold, thin gas of elementary particles and radiation, growing ever more dilute as it expands into the endless darkness, a universe in ruins.

Very recent discoveries provide strong evidence that there is effectively a positive cosmological constant which causes the cosmic expansion to accelerate rather than decelerate. Paradoxically, since the volume of space increases exponentially, allowing greater room for further entropy production, the universe actually grows farther and farther from an equilibrium state as time proceeds. But the acceleration only hastens the cosmos's disintegration into increasingly isolated patches no longer causally connected with similarly marooned remnants of the expanding universe.

These recent discoveries have made the traditional problem even more acute. Restricting their attention to our causally connected patch of the universe and taking as their point of departure Henri Poincaré's argument that in a closed box of randomly moving particles every configuration of particles, no matter how improbable, will eventually recur, given enough time, Dyson, Kleban, and Susskind (2002) argue for the inevitability of cosmological Poincaré recurrences, allowing the process of cosmogony to begin anew within our causal patch. "The question then is whether the universe can be a naturally occurring fluctuation, or must it be due to an external agent which starts the system out in a specific low entropy state?" (p. 4). They recognize that the central weakness of the fluctuation hypothesis is that there are "far more probable ways of creating liveable ('anthropically acceptable') environments" than those that begin in a low entropy condition. Therefore, the fluctuation hypothesis is unacceptably improbable. They acknowledge, "Another possibility is that an unknown agent intervened in the evolution and for reasons of its own restarted the universe in the state of low entropy characterizing inflation. However, even this does not rid the theory of the pesky recurrences. Only the first occurrence would evolve in a way that would be consistent with usual expectations" (pp. 20–1). But so saying, they have misconstrued the hypothesis. The hypothesis was not of an external agent which "restarted" the universe but of "an external agent which *starts the system out* in a specific low entropy state" (p. 4). On such a hypothesis "Some unknown agent initially started the inflation high up on its potential, and the rest is history" (p. 2). On this hypothesis the recurrence problems do even not arise. By contrast, Dyson, Kleban, and Susskind are finally driven to suggest that "Perhaps the only reasonable conclusion is that we do not live in a world with a true cosmological constant" (p. 21), a desperate hypothesis which flies in the face of the evidence.

Thus, the same pointed question raised by classical physics persists: if in a finite amount of time the universe *will* achieve a cold, dark, dilute, and lifeless state, then why, if it has existed for *infinite time*, is it not *now* in such a state? If one is to avoid the conclusion that the universe has not in fact existed forever, then one must find some scientifically plausible way to overturn the findings of physical cosmology so as to permit the universe to return to its youthful condition. But no realistic and plausible scenario is forthcoming (Craig forthcoming). Most cosmologists agree with physicist Paul Davies that whether we like it or not, we seem forced to conclude that the universe's low entropy condition was simply "put in" as an initial condition at the moment of creation (Davies 1974: 104; cf. Penrose 1981: 249; 1982: 4–5).

We thus have good philosophical and scientific grounds for affirming the second premise of the *kalam* cosmological argument.

It follows logically that the universe has a cause. Conceptual analysis of what properties must be possessed by such an ultramundane cause enables us to recover a striking number of the traditional divine attributes, revealing that if the universe has a cause, then an uncaused, personal Creator of the universe exists, who *sans* the universe is beginningless, changeless, immaterial, timeless, spaceless, and enormously powerful (Craig 2006).

Conclusion

The Leibnizian and *kalam* cosmological arguments are powerful, complementary arguments which make it plausible to believe that the answer to the mystery of the existence of the universe is to be found in an uncaused, metaphysically necessary, personal Creator of the universe, who *sans* the universe is beginningless, changeless, immaterial, timeless, spaceless, and enormously powerful, and who brought the universe into being a finite time ago.

Questions for Reflection

1 Is the "mystery of existence," which lies at the root of the Leibnizian version of the cosmological argument, a question that troubles you? Your acquaintances? If not, why not? If so, what answer do you or they give to it?
2 Provide some thought experiments of your own to illustrate what it would be like in the concrete realm for an actual infinite to exist or to be formed by successive addition.
3 Summarize the astrophysical evidence in support of a beginning of the universe.
4 What arguments might be given in support of the contention that the cause of the universe is "an uncaused, personal Creator . . . , who *sans* the universe is beginningless, changeless, immaterial, timeless, spaceless, and enormously powerful"?

References

Balaguer, M. (1998) *Platonism and Anti-Platonism in Mathematics*. New York: Oxford University Press.

—— (2001) "A Theory of Mathematical Correctness and Mathematical Truth." *Pacific Philosophical Quarterly* 82, 87–114.

—— (2004) "Platonism in Metaphysics." In E. N. Zalta (ed.), *Stanford Encyclopedia of Philosophy*. Also available at the following URL: http://plato.stanford.edu/archives/sum2004/entries/platonism/.

Chihara, C. (1990) *Constructibility and Mathematical Existence*. Oxford: Clarendon Press.

—— (2004) *A Structural Account of Mathematics*. Oxford: Clarendon Press.

Craig, W. L. (2000a) *The Tensed Theory of Time*. Dordrecht: Kluwer Academic Publishers.

—— (2000b) *The Tenseless Theory of Time*. Dordrecht: Kluwer Academic Publishers.

—— (2001) *Time and Eternity*. Wheaton, IL: Crossway.

—— (2006) "Naturalism and Cosmology." In A. Corradini, S. Galvan, and E. J. Lowe (eds.), *Analytic Philosophy without Naturalism*. New York: Routledge.

—— (forthcoming) "Cosmology and Naturalism." In B. Gordon and W. Dembski (eds.), *The Nature of Nature*.

Davies, P. (1974) *The Physics of Time Asymmetry*. London: Surrey University Press.

Dyson, L., M. Kleban, and L. Susskind (2002) "Disturbing Implications of a Cosmological Constant." Available at the following URL: http://arXiv.org/abs/hep-th/0208013v3.

Gamow, G. (1946) *One, Two, Three, Infinity*. London: Macmillan.

Hick, J. (1960) "God as Necessary Being." *Journal of Philosophy* 57, 725–33.

Hume, D. (1947) *Dialogues Concerning Natural Religion*. Indianapolis: Bobbs-Merrill.

Leibniz, G. (1951) *The Monadology and Other Philosophical Writings*, trans. R. Latta. London: Oxford University Press.

Mackie, J. L. (1982) *The Miracle of Theism*. Oxford: Clarendon Press.

Malcolm, N. (1958) *Ludwig Wittgenstein: A Memoir*. London: Oxford University Press.

Parfit, D. (1998) "Why Anything? Why This?" *London Review of Books* 20:2, 24.

Penrose, R. (1981) "Time-asymmetry and Quantum Gravity." In C. J. Isham, R. Penrose, and D. W. Sciama (eds.), *Quantum Gravity 2*. Oxford: Clarendon Press.

—— (1982) "Some Remarks on Gravity and Quantum Mechanics." In M. J. Duff and C. J. Isham (eds.), *Quantum Structure of Space and Time*. Cambridge: Cambridge University Press.

Pruss, A. (2005) "Critical Notice of Bede Rundle, *Why Is There Something Rather than Nothing?*" *Philosophia Christi* 7:1, 209–13.

—— (2006) *The Principle of Sufficient Reason*. Cambridge: Cambridge University Press.

Rundle, B. (2004) *Why Is There Something Rather than Nothing?* Oxford: Oxford University Press.

Russell, B., and F. Copleston (1964) "The Existence of God." In John Hick (ed.), *The Existence of God*. New York: Macmillan.

Sobel, J. H. (2004) *Logic and Theism*. Cambridge: Cambridge University Press.

Swinburne, R. (1991) *The Existence of God*. Rev. edn. Oxford: Clarendon Press.

Taylor, R. (1991) *Metaphysics*. 4th edn. Englewood Cliffs, NJ: Prentice-Hall.

Vallicella, W. (1997) "On an Insufficient Argument Against Sufficient Reason." *Ratio* 10, 76–81.

Wright, C., and B. Hale (1992) "Nominalism and the Contingency of Abstract Objects." *Journal of Philosophy* 89, 111–35.

Further Reading

Burrill, D. (1967) *The Cosmological Argument*. New York: Doubleday. (An anthology of historical and contemporary readings.)

Craig, W. L. (1979) *The Kalam Cosmological Argument*. London: Macmillan. Republished edn. (2000) Eugene, OR: Wipf & Stock. (Resuscitates the argument for a first cause based on the finitude of the past.)

—— (1980) *The Cosmological Argument from Plato to Leibniz*. London: Macmillan. Republished edn. (2001) Eugene, OR: Wipf & Stock. (Historical survey and typology of various cosmological arguments.)

Craig, W. L., and Q. Smith. (1993) *Theism, Atheism, and Big Bang Cosmology*. Oxford: Clarendon Press. (Pits an advocate of the *kalam* argument against an equally determined atheist in a series of exchanges.)

Pruss, A. (2006) *The Principle of Sufficient Reason*. Cambridge: Cambridge University Press. (Most thorough examination of the question of why something exists rather than nothing.)

Sobel, J. H. (2004) *Logic and Theism*. Cambridge: Cambridge University Press. (Best critique of theistic arguments on offer today.)

Chapter 7

The Teleological Argument

Robin Collins

Introduction

Historically, the teleological argument has been considered one of the strongest arguments for the existence of an intelligence behind or within the universe. In the West it dates back to Heraclitus (500 BCE), whereas in the East it dates back to various schools of Hindu philosophy in the early centuries CE. The design argument reached its highpoint of popularity in the West with the publication by William Paley (1743–1805) of his *Natural Theology* ([1802] 1970). Much, but not all, of Paley's case for design, however, was based on the intricate structure of plants and animals, and thus was severely undercut by Darwin's theory of evolution. Except for some recent claims by advocates of the so-called intelligent design movement, and a few others, most scientists and philosophers accept that life on earth can be adequately explained by evolution by chance plus natural selection. Whether this is actually the case, however, is beyond the scope of this chapter to address.

In the second half of Paley's treatise, he offered another design argument based on the overall structure of the universe. This version of the argument has gained new strength in the last 50 years. Particularly, physicists have discovered at least three features of the universe that many think point to a transcendent intelligence:

1   The so-called fine-tuning of the laws, constants, and initial conditions of the universe for conscious, embodied life (CEL), such as human beings.
2   The extraordinary beauty and elegance of the laws and mathematical structure of the universe.
3   The intelligibility and discoverability of the basic structure of nature.

We will briefly look at each of these in turn, and then at why one could claim they count as significant evidence for theistic design. After doing this, we will look at

several major objections raised to this sort of design argument. We will start with
the fine-tuning for CEL.

Fine-Tuning for CEL

The fine-tuning for CEL refers to the fact that the laws of nature, the constants
of physics, and the initial conditions of the universe are balanced on a "razor's
edge" for the existence of CEL. A key assumption underlying this claim is that
the existence of CEL requires the existence of forms of matter with a high degree
of stable, reproducible complexity. We will first look at the fine-tuning of the laws
for CEL.

Fine-Tuning of laws for CEL

To say that the laws are fine-tuned for CEL means that if we did not have just
the right combination of laws, CEL would probably be impossible. For example,
according to current physics, there are four forces in nature – gravity, the weak
force, electromagnetism, and the strong nuclear force that binds protons and
neutrons together in an atom. The existence of each of at least three of these forces
is necessary for CEL, and probably the fourth. If gravity did not exist, masses
would not clump together to form stars or planets; if the electromagnetic force
didn't exist, there would be no chemistry; if the strong nuclear force didn't exist,
protons and neutrons could not bind together and hence no atoms with an atomic
number greater than hydrogen would exist. Other principles of physics also appear
necessary for CEL. For example, as Princeton University physicist Freeman Dyson
has pointed out (Dyson 1979: 251), if the Pauli-exclusion principle didn't exist –
which is what keeps two electrons from occupying the same energy state in an
atom – all electrons would occupy the lowest atomic energy state, and thus no
complex atoms could exist. Thus, if any of these fundamental laws or principles
were missing, complex chemistry, and therefore the existence of CEL, would
probably be rendered impossible.

Fine-tuning of constants

Next, consider the fine-tuning for CEL of the constants of physics. The constants
of physics are fundamental numbers that when plugged into the laws of physics
determine the basic structure of the universe. An example of a fundamental constant is Newton's gravitational constant G, which determines the strength of
gravity via Newton's law $F = Gm_1m_2/r^2$. Many of the fundamental constants must
fall into a *relatively* narrow range in order for CEL to exist.

To illustrate this fine-tuning, consider gravity. Using a standard measure of
force strengths – which turns out to be roughly the relative strength of the various
forces between two protons in a nucleus – gravity is the weakest of the forces, and

the strong nuclear force is the strongest, being a factor of 10^{40} – or 10 thousand billion, billion, billion, billion – times stronger than gravity. If we increased the strength of gravity a billion-fold, for instance, the force of gravity on a planet with the mass and size of the earth would be so great that organisms anywhere near the size of human beings, whether land-based or aquatic, would be crushed. (The strength of materials depends on the electromagnetic force via the fine-structure constant, which would not be affected by a change in gravity.) Even a much smaller planet of only 40 feet in diameter – which is not large enough to sustain organisms of our size – would have a gravitational pull of 1,000 times that of earth, still too strong for organisms of our brain size, and hence level of intelligence, to exist. As astrophysicist Martin Rees notes, "In an imaginary strong gravity world, even insects would need thick legs to support them, and no animals could get much larger" (Rees 2000: 30). Of course, a billion-fold increase in the strength of gravity is a lot, but compared to the total range of the strengths of the forces in nature (which span a range of 10^{40} as we saw above), it is very small, being one part in 10 thousand, billion, billion, billion. Indeed, other calculations show that stars with lifetimes of more than a billion years, as compared to our sun's lifetime of 10 billion years, could not exist if gravity were increased by more than a factor of 3,000. This would have significant intelligent-life-inhibiting consequences (Collins 2003).

The most impressive case of fine-tuning for CEL is that of the cosmological constant. The cosmological constant is a term in Einstein's equation of general relativity that, when positive, acts as a repulsive force, causing space to expand and, when negative, acts as an attractive force, causing space to contract. If it were too large, space would expand so rapidly that galaxies and stars could not form, and if too small, the universe would collapse before CEL could evolve. In today's physics, it is taken to correspond to the energy density of empty space. The fine-tuning for CEL of the cosmological constant is estimated to be *at least* one part in 10^{53}, that is, one part in a hundred million, billion, billion, billion, billion, billion. To get an idea of how precise this is, it would be like throwing a dart at the surface of the earth from outer space, and hitting a bull's-eye one trillionth of a trillionth of an inch in diameter, less than the size of an atom. Nobel prize-winning physicist Steven Weinberg, a critic of fine-tuning, himself admits that the fine-tuning of the cosmological constant is highly impressive (Weinberg 2001: 67; Collins 2003). Further examples of the fine-tuning for CEL of the fundamental constants of physics can also be given, such as that of mass difference between the neutron and the proton. If, for example, the mass of the neutron were slightly increased by about one part in 700, stable hydrogen burning stars would cease to exist (Leslie 1989: 39–40; Collins 2003).

Other types of fine-tuning for CEL

Two other types of fine-tuning should be mentioned. One is that of the initial conditions of the universe, which refers to the fact that the initial distribution of mass-energy – as measured by entropy – must fall within an exceedingly narrow range for CEL to occur. Although no one has calculated the CEL-permitting range for entropy, Roger Penrose, one of Britain's leading theoretical physicists, claims that "in order to produce a universe resembling the one in which we live, the Creator would have to aim for an absurdly tiny volume of the phase space of possible universes" (Penrose 1989: 343). How tiny is this volume? According to Penrose, if we let $x = 10^{123}$, the volume of phase space would be about $1/10^x$ of the entire volume (p. 343). (Phase space is the space that physicists use to measure the various possible configurations of mass-energy of a system.) This precision is much, much greater than the precision that would be required to hit an individual proton given that the entire visible universe were a dartboard.

Finally, in his book *Nature's Destiny*, biochemist Michael Denton extensively discusses various higher-level features of the natural world, such as the many unique properties of carbon, oxygen, water, and the electromagnetic spectrum, that appear optimally adjusted for the existence of complex biochemical systems (Denton 1988: 300).

Summary of the evidence for the fine-tuning for CEL

It should be pointed out that some scientists, such as Steven Weinberg, have been skeptical of some of the prominent cases of fine-tuning in the literature (Weinberg 2001). In several prominent cases of purported fine-tuning, this skepticism is warranted, but in other cases the arguments based in physics for the fine-tuning are solid (Collins 2003). Nonetheless, even if none of the cases of purported fine-tuning was well-established, one could argue that the argument would still have significant force. As philosopher John Leslie has pointed out, "clues heaped upon clues can constitute weighty evidence despite doubts about each element in the pile" (Leslie 1988: 300).

Beauty, Elegance, and Discoverability of the Laws

The beauty and elegance of the laws of nature also have been claimed to suggest design, though no one has yet developed this argument in detail (see Davies 1984 and Polkinghorne 1998 on the elegance of the laws of nature as suggestive of design; for detailed development this argument, see Collins 2002). The apparent beauty of the laws of nature has been acknowledged by both theists and atheists. Nobel Prize-winning physicist Steven Weinberg, a convinced atheist, devotes a whole chapter of his book, *Dreams of a Final Theory*, to explaining how the criteria of beauty and elegance are commonly used with great success to guide physicists in formulating laws. As Weinberg points out, "mathematical structures that confessedly are developed by mathematicians because they seek a sort of beauty are often found later to be extraordinarily valuable by the physicist" (Weinberg 1994: 153). Today, this use of beauty and elegance as a guide is particularly evident in the popularity of superstring theory as providing the most fundamental account of physical reality, which is almost entirely motivated by considerations of elegance, having no experimental support in its favor (Greene 1999: 214). Indeed, one of the most prominent theoretical physicists of this century, Paul Dirac, has gone so far as to claim, as Einstein did, that "it is more important to have beauty in one's equations than to have them fit experiment" (Dirac 1963: 47). The beauty, elegance, and ingenuity of mathematical equations make sense if the universe was purposefully designed like an artwork, but arguably appear surprising and inexplicable under the non-design hypothesis. As Weinberg states, "sometimes nature seems more beautiful than strictly necessary" (Weinberg 1994: 250).

Some have claimed that the beauty we see in nature is merely subjective, like seeing the Big Bear or Big Dipper in the random pattern of stars in the night sky. To say that the beauty of the mathematical structure of nature is merely subjective, however, fails to account for the seemingly amazing success of the criterion of beauty in producing predictively accurate theories, such as Einstein's general theory of relativity. We would not expect merely subjective impressions to lead to highly successful theories.

Finally, the laws of nature themselves seem to be carefully arranged so that they are intelligible, and in addition discoverable, by beings with our level of intelligence – like solving a clever puzzle. This has been stressed by many prominent physicists. Albert Einstein, for example, famously remarked that "the eternal mystery of the world is that it is comprehensible. . . . The fact that it is comprehensible is a miracle" (in Calaprice 1996: 197). Similarly, in his famous essay, "The Unreasonable Effectiveness of Mathematics in the Physical Sciences," Eugene Wigner, one of the principal founders of quantum mechanics, famously claimed that "The miracle of the appropriateness of the language of mathematics for the formulation of the laws of physics is a wonderful gift which we neither understand nor deserve" (Wigner 1960: 14). Work on articulating detailed examples of this intelligibility and discoverability has just begun in the last 10 years. For example, philosopher Mark Steiner's recent book, *The Applicability of Mathematics as a Philosophical Problem*, is devoted to this issue, where he concludes that the world is much more "user-friendly" for the discovery of its fundamental mathematical structure than seems explicable under naturalism (Steiner 1998: 176).

Summary of Argument for Design: Method of Inference

All these features of the laws of nature, let alone the fact that our best theories seem to require that the universe has a beginning, give the impression in many people's minds that the universe was created by some transcendent intelligence. One way of casting the form of inference here is in terms of what philosophers call a *cumulative case argument* in which many factors, such as the fine-tuning, beauty, intelligibility, and discoverability of the laws of nature, all point in the same direction, and seem difficult to explain on any other hypothesis. In this sense, the teleological argument based on the above features of the universe is similar to the sort of arguments offered for scientific theories, such as the theory of evolution by descent with modification. As evolutionary biologist and geneticist Edward Dodson summarizes the case for evolution, understood as the thesis of common ancestry:

> All [pieces of evidence] concur in *suggesting* evolution [the thesis of common ancestry] with varying degrees of cogency, but most can be explained on other bases, albeit with some damage to the law of parsimony. The strongest evidence for evolution is the concurrence of so many independent probabilities. That such different disciplines as biochemistry and comparative anatomy, genetics and biogeography should all point toward the same conclusion is very difficult to attribute to coincidence. (Dodson 1984: 68)

At this point, one might want to inquire further as to why each feature mentioned above counts as evidence in favor of design. What rule of inference is being used? One rule of inference is that if a body of data E is inexplicable under one hypothesis H_1, but is explicable under another hypothesis H_2, then it counts as evidence in favor of H_1 over H_2. The fine-tuning of the universe for CEL, and the beauty, elegance, intelligibility, and discoverability of the laws of nature each seem inexplicable under naturalism (or in the case of the fine-tuning for CEL, what I call the naturalistic-single-universe hypothesis – see the next section). Theists, however, have traditionally held that God is the greatest possible being and hence is perfectly good and has a perfect aesthetic sense. Since both the existence of CEL and beauty are positive goods, it makes sense that a God with these characteristics would create a universe that is set just right for the existence of CEL and that has an elegant underlying mathematical structure. Further, given that God is the ultimate cause of both the universe and the human mind, it makes sense that the universe would be intelligible to us. Consequently, one could argue, since these features of our universe make sense under theism, but are inexplicable under naturalism, they provide evidence for theism over naturalism.

This way of articulating the argument, however, does not capture the full force of the argument, since it is not merely that the above features of the universe are inexplicable under atheism that suggests design, but also that they appear to be very improbable or surprising. This in turn leads to an additional way of articulating why these features of the universe supposedly count as evidence for theism over naturalism in terms of a standard principle of confirmation theory called the *likelihood principle*. According to this principle, a body of data E supports one hypothesis, H_1, over another, H_2, if the probability of the data E on the first hypothesis (H_1) is greater than the probability of E on the second hypothesis (H_2), with the degree of support being proportional to the degree to which the data are

more probable under the one hypothesis than the other. Below, we will articulate
this version of the design argument for the case of the fine-tuning of the constants
of physics since it has been the most discussed in the literature (see chapter 2,
Religion and Science).

Elaboration of Fine-Tuning for CEL Argument

First, in developing the likelihood version of the fine-tuning design argument,
it is critical to point out that the sort of probability being used is not statistical
probability. Rather, the probability being used is what philosophers call *epistemic*
probability, which can be thought of as a measure of rational degrees of expectation. For example, when scientists say that the theory of evolution is *probably* true,
they are clearly not talking about statistical probability: they are *not* referring to
some repeatable trial in which the theory turns out true with some relative frequency. Rather, they are saying something to the effect that given the total body
of available evidence, a rational person should have more confidence than not that
the theory of evolution is true.

   Given this notion of epistemic probability, the likelihood version of the fine-
tuning argument can then be stated as follows:

1   The existence of CEL-permitting universe with fine-tuned constants is not
    epistemically improbable under theism.
2   The existence of a CEL-permitting universe with fine-tuned constants is very
    epistemically improbable under the naturalistic-single-universe hypothesis
    (NSU). (The NSU is the hypothesis that there is only one universe and it exists
    as a brute fact without any transcendent explanation.)
3   From premises (1) and (2) and the likelihood principle, it follows that the
    fine-tuning data provide significant evidence in favor of the design hypothesis
    over the NSU.

Several further features of this argument need to be articulated. First, since we
are dealing with epistemic probability, to say that the existence of a CEL-permitting universe is more probable under theism than under the NSU is to say something to the effect that of itself, the theistic hypothesis should rationally lead us
to expect the existence of such a universe more than the NSU. The reason is that,
as mentioned above, given that the existence of CEL has some positive ethical
value, the perfectly good God hypothesized by traditional theism would have
some reason to create a universe containing such beings. This is enough to make
the existence of such a universe unsurprising under theism. On the other hand,
under NSU we have no reason to think that a universe would exist whose values
fall into the CEL-permitting range instead of any other part of the theoretically
possible range of values for these constants. Thus, given that the CEL-permitting
range is very small in comparison, it seems highly surprising – that is, epistemically

very improbable – for the universe that happens to exist to have CEL-permitting values for its constants.

Of course, much more work needs to be done to make this argument from comparative epistemic probabilities rigorous, but that is beyond the scope of this paper (for more on this, see Collins forthcoming). Even if it cannot be made rigorous, however, it still would be as powerful as many arguments in science, since these sorts of non-rigorous arguments based on perceived improbabilities are pervasive in science. For example, as the above quotation by Edward Dodson illustrates, the support for the thesis of common ancestry (evolution) is based on the claim that a variety of features of the world – such as the structure of the tree of life – would not be improbable if evolution is true, but would be very improbable under the other viable non-evolutionary hypotheses, such as special creation. This improbability is not statistical improbability, nor can it be justified by an appeal to statistical improbability, since we have no statistics regarding the relative frequency of life on a planet having these features under either the evolutionary hypothesis or some non-evolutionary hypothesis. Neither do we have any model from which to derive those statistics. Rather, it should be understood as a form of epistemic probability – e.g., as claiming that various features of the world would be very *unexpected* under the various contender non-evolutionary hypotheses, but not under the evolutionary hypothesis. Clearly, these judgments of epistemic probability are not and cannot be rigorously justified, even though scientists must rely on them in deciding what theory to adopt.

Third, the argument does not say that the fine-tuning evidence proves that the universe was designed, or even that it is likely that the universe was designed. Indeed, of itself it does not even show that we are epistemically warranted in believing in theism over the NSU. In order to justify these sorts of claims, one would have to look at the full range of evidence both for and against the design hypothesis, something we are not doing in this essay. Rather, the argument merely concludes that the fine-tuning significantly *supports* theism *over* the NSU. In this way, the evidence of fine-tuning is much like fingerprints found on the gun: although they can provide strong evidence that the defendant committed the murder, one could not conclude merely from them alone that the defendant is guilty; one would also have to look at all the other evidence offered. Perhaps, for instance, 10 reliable witnesses claimed to see the defendant at a party at the time of the shooting. In this case, the fingerprints would still count as significant evidence of guilt, but this evidence would be counterbalanced by the testimony of the witnesses.

Objections to the Fine-Tuning for CEL Argument

We will now consider a few common objections to the fine-tuning for CEL argument.

Other forms of life objection

One common objection to the fine-tuning for CEL argument is that there could be other forms of life of which we have not conceived. One response is that, as pointed out above, the fine-tuning argument is really about the existence of CEL. The fine-tuning argument only assumes that CEL requires a large amount of stable, reproducible complexity in order to have evolved. For example, if the cosmological constant is too large, matter would disperse so rapidly in the universe that no stars would form, and thus there would not be any energy sources to support the evolution of CEL.

Grand unified theory objection

Another common objection is that, as far as we know, the values of the fundamental parameters will eventually be explained by some grand unified theory. Hence, it is argued, we do not need to invoke a designer to explain why these parameters have CEL-permitting values. As astrophysicists Bernard Carr and Martin Rees note, however, "even if all apparently anthropic coincidences could be explained [in terms of such a unified theory], it would still be remarkable that the relationships dictated by physical theory happened also to be those propitious for life" (Carr and Rees 1979: 612). Accordingly, a theist could respond by claiming that the development of a grand unified theory would not undercut the case for design, but would only serve to deepen our appreciation of the ingenuity of the creator. Instead of separately fine-tuning each individual constant, in this view, the designer simply carefully chose those laws that would yield CEL-permitting values for each parameter.

Many universes objection

Probably the most widely advocated objection to considering fine-tuning for CEL as evidence for design is the proposal that there are a very large number of universes, each with different values for the fundamental parameters of physics. If such multiple universes exist, it would be no surprise that the parameters in one of them would have just the right values for the existence of CEL. An analogy is lottery tickets: if enough were generated, it would be no surprise that one of them would turn out to be the winning number. Further, it is no surprise that we observe that *our* universe has these values, since they are necessary for our existence.

How did these universes come into existence? By far the most common response is to postulate some kind of physical process, what I will call a "universe generator," that brought the universes into existence (e.g., Rees 2000). Against the naturalistic version of the universe-generator hypothesis, one could argue that the universe generator itself must be "well designed" to produce even one CEL-sustaining universe. After all, even a mundane item such as a bread-making machine, which only produces loaves of bread instead of universes, must be well designed as an appliance *and* have just the right ingredients (flour, yeast, gluten, and so on) in just the right amounts to produce decent loaves of bread. Indeed, as has been argued in more detail elsewhere (Collins 2002), if one carefully examines the most popular version of this scenario, that arising out of inflationary cosmology combined with superstring theory (e.g., Susskind 2005), one finds that it contains just the right ultimate laws governing superstrings to generate CEL-permitting universes. Change these ultimate laws, and no CEL-sustaining universes would be produced.

The other answer to where the universes came from is what I call the metaphysical many-universes hypothesis, according to which all these universes exist as a brute fact. Typically, advocates of this view – such as the late Princeton University philosopher David Lewis (Lewis 1986) and University of Pennsylvania astrophysicist Max Tegmark (Tegmark 1998; 2003) – claim that every possible world exists (Lewis) or that "everything that exists mathematically exists physically" (Tegmark 1998: 1). Tegmark calls his hypothesis the "ultimate ensemble hypothesis," and claims it explains why there exists a universe such as ours in which the laws of nature and the parameters of physics are life-permitting.

Besides claiming that this hypothesis requires more faith than belief in God, a theist could argue that neither it, nor the universe-generator hypothesis, can explain the other design-indicating features of our universe mentioned above, such as why *our* universe appears to have an elegant, intelligible, and discoverable underlying mathematical structure. The universe-generator scenario simply assumes this as a brute fact. Under the metaphysical many-universes hypothesis, on the other hand, there will be many, many universes that contain observers in which the laws are not elegant, and thus it does not explain the seemingly surprising fact that we exist in a universe with an elegant and discoverable underlying mathematical structure.

Further, besides seeming largely constructed simply to get around the evidence for fine-tuning, the metaphysical many-universes hypothesis has a difficult time explaining the order in the universe, such as the low entropy of its initial state. Even though a low entropy state is probably necessary for life, as many physicists have pointed out in response to a similar hypothesis raised by Ludwig Boltzman in the early 1900s, it is vastly more likely for such a low entropy bubble to exist around the planet on which life evolves than for the whole universe to start off in such a state (e.g., Davies 1974: 103.). Thus, under this hypothesis, we would not expect the whole universe to be in such a low entropy state since the vast majority of universes with observers in them would only have local islands of low entropy around those observers. (For the argument against this hypothesis based on the universe's order, see Schlesinger 1984; for a response, see Lewis 1986: 115–23).

Despite these objections to the non-theistic interpretations of the above two versions of the many-universes hypothesis, theists should not reject the idea of many-universes in and of itself. For the theist, the existence of many universes could be claimed to support the view that creation reflects the *infinite creativity* of the creator, who not only creates a reality with an enormous number of planets and galaxies, but also one with many universes.

Who designed God objection

Another objection commonly raised against the design argument is what I call the "Who designed God" objection. Advocates of this objection claim that the designer of an artifact must be at least as complex, intricate, "well ordered," or "well designed" as the artifact itself, and hence God must be more intricate, well designed, complex, etc., than the universe. Thus, it is argued, if the universe is in need of explanation, then God is even more in need of an explanation. One is better off, therefore, simply stopping the explanatory regress at the universe and accepting it as a brute fact. To add God to the mix simply increases the amount of unexplained complexity.

One response a theist could give is that we often take evidence as confirming a hypothesis, even if the hypothesis being confirmed involves postulating a large amount of unexplained complexity. For example, we would take the existence of complex physical structures resembling houses and machines on Mars as evidence of extraterrestrial life, even if such life forms were far more complex than the structures being explained. Another, and I believe better, response to this argument is that, at least in the case of God, it is unclear that the designer of an artifact must be as complex as the artifact itself. For example, medieval philosophers such as Thomas Aquinas held that God was absolutely simple, without any internal complexity, using arguments independent of the design argument. Further, one could argue, following Richard Swinburne (e.g., Swinburne 1979: 93–8; 1996: 38–69), that although God is not absolutely simple, the God hypothesis is much simpler than the hypothesis that the universe is simply a brute fact, and thus does decrease the amount of unexplained complexity one must hypothesize. These sorts of arguments are addressed in more detail in Collins (2005; see also, www. fine-tuning.org).

Conclusion

In this paper, I have presented the modern teleological argument based on the fine-tuning of the cosmos for conscious, embodied life, and the beauty, elegance, and discoverability of the underlying mathematical order of nature. It should be stressed that one cannot conclude from the version of the design argument that I have articulated to the existence of the omnipotent, omniscient, and perfectly good God of traditional theism, or even to the position that belief in such a deity is epistemically justified. To do this, one would not only have to look at all the evidence both for and against the existence of God, but also would have to argue that such a God provides a better (or more likely) explanation of these features of the universe than other explanations, such as a morally indifferent, non-omnipotent deity. Although Richard Swinburne has attempted to do this (e.g., Swinburne 1979: 93–8 and 1996: 38–69), we cannot evaluate his arguments here (see Part II, The Existence of God; see also chapter 13, The Impossibility of God?). All one can conclude regarding the version of the teleological argument that I have presented is that these features of the universe offer significant evidence for theism over naturalism. Furthermore, whether this argument can be made sufficiently philosophically rigorous, and adequately answer all the objections raised against it, will depend on the outcome of the current exciting philosophical work being done on the argument.

Questions for Reflection

1   Of the evidence presented by Collins for some sort of divine design of the universe, what strikes you as the strongest and the weakest? Why?
2   If you were an atheist, how would you respond to the version of the teleological argument that Collins presents? Do you think the response is adequate? Why or why not?
3   In your opinion, how does the strength of the teleological argument compare with what you think is the strongest argument against the existence of God? Explain your answer.
4   What objection to the fine-tuning for CEL argument do you find most powerful? Do you find the responses Collins presents to this objection adequate? Explain your answer.
5   Does the teleological argument purport to establish the existence of an all powerful, all good God? If not, do you think that it nonetheless establishes something significant? Explain your answers.

References

Calaprice, A. (ed.) (1996) *The Quotable Einstein*. Princeton: Princeton University Press.
Carr, B. J., and M. J. Rees (1979) "The Anthropic Cosmological Principle and the Structure of the Physical World." *Nature* 278 (April 12), 605–12.
Collins, R. (2002) "The Argument from Design and the Many-Worlds Hypothesis." In W. L. Craig (ed.), *Philosophy of Religion: A Reader and Guide*. New Brunswick, NJ: Rutgers University Press. Also available at the following URL: http://www.fine-tuning.org.
—— (2003) "The Evidence for Fine-Tuning." In N. Manson (ed.), *God and Design: The Teleological Argument and Modern Science*. New York: Routledge.
—— (2005) "Hume, Fine-Tuning and the Who Designed God? Objection" In J. Sennett and D. Groothius (eds.), *In Defense of Natural Theology: A Post-Humean Reassessment*. Downers Grove, IL: InterVarsity Press.
—— (forthcoming) *The Well-Tempered Universe: God, Fine-tuning, and the Laws of Nature*.

Davies, P. (1974) *The Physics of Time Asymmetry*. Berkeley, CA: University of California Press.

—— (1984) *Superforce: The Search for a Grand Unified Theory of Nature*. New York: Simon and Schuster.

Denton, M. (1998) *Nature's Destiny: How the Laws of Biology Reveal Purpose in the Universe*. New York: Free Press.

Dirac, P. A. M. (1963) "The Evolution of the Physicist's Picture of Nature." *Scientific American* 208:5 (May), 45–53.

Dodson, E. (1984) *The Phenomena of Man Revisited: A Biological Viewpoint on Teilhard de Chardin*. New York: Columbia University Press.

Dyson, F. (1979) *Disturbing the Universe*. New York: Harper and Row.

Greene, B. (1999) *The Elegant Universe: Superstrings, Hidden Dimensions, and the Quest for the Ultimate Theory*. New York: W. W. Norton and Company.

Leslie, J. (1988) "How to Draw Conclusions from a Fine-Tuned Cosmos." In R. Russell, W. R. Stoeger, and G. V. Coyne (eds.), *Physics, Philosophy and Theology: A Common Quest for Understanding*. Vatican City: Vatican Observatory Press.

—— (1989) *Universes*. New York: Routledge.

Lewis, D. (1986) *On the Plurality of Worlds*. New York: Blackwell.

Paley, W. ([1802] 1970) *Natural Theology: Or, Evidences of the Existence and Attributes of the Deity, Collected from the Appearances of Nature*. Farnborough, England: Gregg International.

Penrose, R. (1989) *The Emperor's New Mind: Concerning Computers, Minds, and the Laws of Physics*. New York: Oxford University Press.

Polkinghorne, J. (1998) *Belief in God in an Age of Science*. New Haven, CT: Yale University Press.

Rees, M. (2000) *Just Six Numbers: The Deep Forces that Shape the Universe*. New York: Basic Books.

Schlesinger, G. (1984) "Possible Worlds and the Mystery of Existence." *Ratio* 26, 1–18.

Steiner, M. (1998) *The Applicability of Mathematics as a Philosophical Problem*. Cambridge, MA: Harvard University Press.

Susskind, L. (2005) *The Cosmic Landscape: String Theory and the Illusion of Intelligent Design*. New York: Little, Brown and Company.

Swinburne, R. (1979) *The Existence of God*. Oxford: Clarendon Press.

—— (1996) *Is There a God?* Oxford: Oxford University Press.

Tegmark, M. (1998) "Is 'the Theory of Everything' Merely the Ultimate Ensemble Theory?" *Annals of Physics* 270, 1–51. Also available at the following URL: http://arxiv.org/abs/gr-qc/9704009.

—— (2003) "Parallel Universes." *Scientific American* 288:5 (May) 40–51.

Weinberg, S. (1994) *Dreams of a Final Theory*. Reprint edn. New York: Vintage Books.

—— (2001) "A Designer Universe?" *The Skeptical Inquirer* (September–October 2001), 64–8. Originally published in the *New York Review of Books* (October 21, 1999).

Wigner, E. (1960) "The Unreasonable Effectiveness of Mathematics in the Natural Sciences." *Communications on Pure and Applied Mathematics* 13, 1–14. Also available at the following URL: http://www.dartmouth.edu/~matc/MathDrama/reading/Wigner.html.

Further Reading

Barrow, J., and F. Tipler (1986) *The Anthropic Cosmological Principle*. Oxford: Oxford University Press. (A classic and lengthy discussion by two well-known physicists of the idea that the universe is adjusted just right for the existence of intelligent observers and the possible consequences of this.)

Davies, P. C. W. (1982) *The Accidental Universe*. Cambridge: Cambridge University Press. (A short book by a well-known theoretical physicist elaborating on some of the main evidences for cosmic fine-tuning.)

—— (1993) "The Intelligibility of Nature." In R. J. Russell, N. Murphy, and C. J. Isham (eds.), *Quantum Cosmology and the Laws of Nature: Scientific Perspectives on Divine Action*. 2nd edn. Berkeley, CA: The Center for Theology and the Natural Sciences Publications. (A discussion of the intelligibility of nature and why it poses a problem for naturalism.)

Holder, R. (2004) *God, the Multiverse, and Everything: Modern Cosmology and the Argument from Design*. Hampshire, England: Ashgate. (This book argues that theism is the best explanation for the fine-tuning of the cosmos, with particular attention given to the many-universes hypothesis.)

Manson, N. (ed.) (2003) *God and Design: The Teleological Argument and Modern Science*. New York: Routledge. (Twenty-one authors vigorously debate the merits of divine teleology from the realm of biology to cosmology.)

Chapter 8

The Ontological Argument

Graham Oppy

According to common philosophical understanding, a successful ontological argument would be an argument that established the existence of God using nothing more than the resources of logical reasoning. That is, according to common philosophical understanding, a successful ontological argument would be an argument that had nothing but truths of logic – i.e., truths that can be known *a priori* by any reasonable cognitive agent – for its premises, and reached the conclusion that God exists using nothing but logically impeccable inferences from those premises. Hence, according to common philosophical understanding, a successful ontological argument would show that there is a sense in which it is a logical theorem – a truth provable *a priori* by any reasonable cognitive agent – that God exists.

Given this common philosophical understanding, we can say that the aim of those who put forward what they call "ontological arguments" is to show that, merely in virtue of being reasonable in the formation of beliefs that it holds on the basis of reason alone, any reasonable cognitive agent holds beliefs that jointly entail that God exists. Moreover, we can observe that a successful ontological argument will be such that none of its premises can be reasonably rejected by a reasonable cognitive agent; and it will be such that no reasonable being can reasonably deny that the conclusion of the argument is entailed by the premises of the argument; and it will have the conclusion that God exists.

The last claim in the previous paragraph is not *exactly* right. Many so-called "ontological arguments" do not end with the words "Therefore God exists." Often enough, so-called "ontological arguments" end with the words "Therefore so-and-so exists," where "so-and-so" is something that at least some theists will suppose is identifiable with God. This qualification is important for some interpretations of some so-called "ontological arguments," where there is room for reasonable disagreement about whether "so-and-so" is properly identified with God.

No one who understands the ambitious aim of ontological arguments should be surprised to hear that the majority verdict of philosophers throughout the ages has been that no so-called "ontological argument" is successful. John Locke speaks for the majority of *theistic* philosophers when, concerning Descartes's "ontological argument" he writes: "It is an ill way of establishing [God's existence] and silencing atheists." But, of course, even if this verdict is correct – something that can only be decided on the basis of case-by-case examination of so-called "ontological arguments" that have been proposed down the centuries – it is a further question whether there is a successful ontological argument that awaits discovery. Many opponents of so-called "ontological arguments" have tried to show, on the basis of *a priori* considerations, that there could not be a successful ontological argument; these *a priori* counterarguments are hardly in better standing than the so-called "ontological arguments" themselves. Moreover, even though there is fairly widespread agreement that no so-called "ontological argument" that has been proposed thus far is successful, there is considerable disagreement about the shortcomings of these arguments: even if philosophers are in broad agreement that particular so-called "ontological arguments" are unsuccessful, they are certainly not in agreement about why it is that those arguments are unsuccessful.

One further reason for being cautious in embracing majority verdicts concerning so-called "ontological arguments" is the caliber of some of the philosophers who have defended these arguments. Anselm, Descartes, Leibniz, Gödel, and Plantinga are not intellectual lightweights; when they claim that there are successful ontological arguments, we have good reason to look carefully at the particular arguments that they offer. However, when we turn to a careful examination of these paradigmatic defenses of so-called "ontological arguments," we immediately encounter serious difficulties.

In the case of Anselm and Descartes, the principle difficulty is that it is not at all easy to be confident that one is making proper application of modern analytical techniques to the "ontological arguments" that are defended by these authors. In the current literature, there are many wildly discrepant readings of Anselm's *Proslogion* 2 argument and Descartes's *Meditation* 5 argument. One point worth noting here is that there is a tendency for non-theists to find, in these texts, arguments that commit relatively elementary errors of reasoning; there is a much wider variation in the responses to these arguments on the part of logically adept theistic commentators.

In the case of Gödel, the principal difficulty is that the argument is technically complicated; one needs to have a reasonably extensive understanding of twentieth-century developments in logic in order to begin to understand the argument. There has been extensive recent discussion of this argument, including discussion of the attitude that Gödel himself took towards it. It is not at all clear that Gödel himself supposed that the argument constitutes a "successful proof" in the sense discussed above. (I shall not discuss Gödel's proof further in the present article.)

And, in the case of Plantinga, while the argument that he presents is clear and straightforward, it is much less clear what he is getting at when he claims that the

Graham Oppy

"ontological argument" that he presents is "successful." Indeed, since Plantinga himself concedes that his argument certainly does *not* meet the standards for "successful proof" set out earlier, one might take the view that there is no room at all for thinking that his "ontological argument" remains live.

There are, of course, many other "ontological arguments" that have been presented and defended in recent times; there is no way of doing full justice to the extant literature in a brief review article like this one. Interested readers might choose to consult Oppy (1995; 2006) for a much more comprehensive set of analyses.

Anselm

In *Proslogion* 2, Anselm writes:

> Even the fool is convinced that something than which nothing greater can be conceived is in the understanding, since when he hears this, he understands it; and whatever is understood is in the understanding. And certainly that than which a greater cannot be conceived cannot be in the understanding alone. For if it is even in the understanding alone, it can be conceived to exist in reality also, which is greater. Thus if that than which a greater cannot be conceived is in the understanding alone, then that than which a greater cannot be conceived is itself that than which a greater can be conceived. But surely this cannot be. Thus without doubt something than which a greater cannot be conceived exists, both in the understanding and in reality.

This argument has been variously represented. Here are five quite recent representations:

Chambers (2000):

1 There is a thing x, and a magnitude m, such that x exists in the understanding, m is the magnitude of x, and it is not possible that there is a thing y and a magnitude n such that n is the magnitude of y and n > m.
2 For any thing x and magnitude m, if x exists in the understanding, m is the magnitude of x, and it is not possible that there is a thing y and magnitude n such that n is the magnitude of y and n > m, then it is possible that x exists in reality.
3 For any thing x and magnitude m, if m is the magnitude of x, and it is not possible that there is a thing y and a magnitude n such that n is the magnitude of y and n > m, and x does not exist in reality, then it is not possible that if x exists in reality then there is a magnitude n such that n is greater than m and n is the magnitude of x.
4 (Hence) there is a thing x and a magnitude m such that x exists in the understanding, and x exists in reality, and m is the magnitude of x, and it is not possible that there is a thing y and a magnitude n such that n is the magnitude of y and n > m. (From (1), (2), and (3).)

Millican (2004):

1 The phrase "a-nature-than-which-no-greater-nature-can-be-thought" is clearly understood by the Fool, and apparently makes sense.
2 If a phrase "A" is clearly understood and apparently makes sense, then we can take it to successfully denote some specific nature.
3 A nature which is instantiated in reality is greater than one which is not instantiated in reality.
4 It is obviously impossible to think of a nature that is greater than a-nature-than-which-no-greater-nature-can-be-thought.
5 (Hence), a-nature-than-which-no-greater-nature-can-be-thought must indeed be instantiated in reality. (From (1), (2), (3), and (4).)

Sobel (2004):

1 At least one thing than which nothing greater can be thought exists in the mind.
2 Existing both in the mind and in reality is greater than existing in the mind alone.
3 (Therefore) at least one thing than which nothing greater can be thought exists both in the mind and in reality. (From (1) and (2).)

Everitt (2003):

1 When the fool hears the words "A being-than-which-nothing-greater-can-be-thought," he understands these words.
2 Whatever is understood is in the mind.
3 If a being-than-which-nothing-greater-can-be-thought existed only in the fool's mind, it could also be thought of as existing in reality as well, and this is greater.
4 (Hence) a being-than-which-nothing-greater-can-be-thought exists both in the mind and in reality. (From (1), (2), and (3).)

Leftow (2005):

1 Someone thinks of a possible object which is something than which no greater can be thought.
2 If a possible something than which no greater can be thought is thought of but not actual, it could have been greater than it actually is.
3 (So) there actually exists something than which no greater can be thought. (From (1) and (2).)

There are various reasons why authors arrive at such different representations of Anselm's *Proslogion* 2 argument. The text itself is rather elusive. Moreover, given that the text is elusive, it is highly tempting for interpreters to read their own assumptions into the text to arrive at an interpretation that they find satisfying.

Despite the difficulties involved in the interpretation of *Proslogion* 2, I think that it is possible to show that the argument that is actually presented in the text is unsuccessful. Consider Anselm's claim that even the Fool is convinced that something than which nothing greater can be conceived exists in the understanding. What is the best way to represent the content of the belief that is here attributed to the Fool? I take it that it is something like this:

[In the understanding] [There exists an x] [It is not the case that] [It is conceivable that] [There exists a y] [y > x]. Here, "[In the understanding]" is a sentential operator whose scope governs all of the remaining materials – quantifiers, operators, etc. – that occur in the sentence. Moreover, "[In the understanding]" operates in the same way as "[According to the fiction]," by providing protection against the incurring of ontological commitment via occurrences of quantifiers that lie within its scope. (Compare: [In the understanding] [There is an x] [x lives at the North Pole, wears a red suit, and delivers presents to children at Christmas]. It certainly does not follow from this claim that [There is an x] [In the understanding] [x lives at the North Pole, wears a red suit, and delivers presents to children at Christmas]. One who asserts the former claim is by no means committed to the latter.)

However, if this is how Anselm's initial claim is meant to be understood, then it seems to me that it is quite clear that his argument is unsuccessful. What Anselm's *reductio* argument requires is the assumption that [There is an x] [In the understanding] [It is not the case that] [It is conceivable that] [There exists a y] [y > x]. But, first, Anselm's preliminary considerations provide us with no reason to suppose that this claim is true, even if we concede that the Fool must allow that [In the understanding] [There exists an x] [It is not the case that] [It is conceivable that] [There exists a y] [y > x]. And, second, there is good reason for the Fool to deny the claim that Anselm imputes to him: the Fool does not and should not accept that *there is* something *of* which he understands that nothing greater than *it* can be conceived; his mere *understanding* of the expression "something than which nothing greater can be conceived" does not require his commitment to the *existence* of any beings of any kind.

Perhaps it might be objected: surely we can allow to Anselm his (tacit) assumption that *there are* things that exist only in the understanding. But, if we do make this concession to Anselm, then we are faced with a series of questions. Suppose we allow that [There is an x] [In the understanding] [x lives at the North Pole, wears a red suit, and delivers presents to children at Christmas]. How is this concession consistent with the evident truth that Santa Claus does not exist? What properties should we suppose that an x of the kind in question possesses, i.e., what properties does it *really* have (given that, of course, *there is no one* who lives at the North Pole and who delivers presents to children at Christmas)?

It might be suggested that some version of Meinong's theory of objects can be used to provide answers to these questions: there are non-existent objects; hence, in particular, there is a non-existent x which has the properties that it lives at the North Pole, wears a red suit, and delivers presents to children at Christmas.

However, while there are *consistent* theories of this kind, the price of consistency is the adoption of constraints that rule out the possibility of successful ontological arguments that adopt these theories. That we need some constraints is evident. Given the description "the really existent Santa Claus," we cannot allow that the Meinongian Santa Claus referred to by this description really exists, on pain of violating evident common sense. So consistent Meinongian theories adopt one of a range of protective mechanisms. For example, some Meinongians invoke a distinction between *characterizing* and *non-characterizing* properties. Characterizing properties are those properties whose presence in a description is guaranteed by the theory to be true of the Meinongian object picked out by that description; non-characterizing properties are properties whose presence in a description is not guaranteed by the theory to be true of the Meinongian object picked out by that description. In particular, of course, all "real existence" entailing properties are non-characterizing properties; this is what allows our Meinongian to say that, if there is a Meinongian object picked out the description "the really existent Santa Claus," then the Meinongian object picked out by that description does not have the property of really existing. But then, of course, the Fool has a ready response to Anselm's ontological argument: if the property "being that than which no greater can be conceived" is existence entailing, then it is also non-characterizing – and so there can be no guarantee from the principles of the Meinongian theory of objects that the Meinongian object picked out by the description "that than which no greater can be conceived" really exists. (Other Meinongian theorists choose different protective mechanisms; but, in every case, the upshot is the same: the measure invoked to avoid the difficulties posed by "the really existent Santa Claus" derails the relevant versions of Anselm's ontological argument.)

Of course, even if it is plausible to suppose that Anselm's text actually contains an unsuccessful argument, it certainly does not follow that the various arguments that other philosophers have read into the text are unsuccessful. On the contrary, a proper discussion of "ontological arguments" requires that each of the available formulations needs to be carefully considered on its own terms. While I cannot discuss all of the above examples of arguments derived from Anselm's text – though I can refer the reader to analyses of these, and many other formulations (Oppy 1995; 2006) – I would like to close this section with a comment on Leftow's formulation.

Leftow claims that his argument "survives objections" (Leftow 2005: 111). However, on his own admission, he makes no attempt to show that his first premise – essentially, the claim that it is possible that there is something than which nothing greater can be conceived – is something that reasonable people are required to accept simply in virtue of being rational cognitive agents. To the objection that insistence on this first premise simply begs the question against those who do not accept that there is a being than which no greater can be conceived – and who *consequently* do not accept that it is *possible* that there is a being than which no greater can be conceived – Leftow says:

Every argument asserts rather than justifies its own premises. If we need reason to believe [that it is possible that there is something than which nothing greater can be conceived] . . . this shows not that [our] argument begs the question, but merely that another argument is needed, on behalf of one of its premises. (Leftow 2005: 91)

But this really amounts to nothing more than the claim that there *might* be a successful ontological argument out there awaiting discovery; even Leftow tacitly concedes that there is *no* reason for the Fool to be persuaded by the argument that he has given *so far*.

Descartes

In *Meditation* 5, Descartes writes:

> If from the fact alone that I can draw from my thought the idea of a thing, it follows that all that I recognise clearly and distinctly as belonging to that thing does indeed belong to it, cannot I derive from this an argument and a proof demonstrating the existence of God? It is certain that I no less find the idea of God in me, that is to say, the idea of a supremely perfect being, than that of any figure or number whatsoever. And I know no less clearly and distinctly that an actual and eternal existence belongs to his nature, than that all I can demonstrate of any figure or number truly belongs to the nature of that figure or number. . . . There is no less contradiction in conceiving a God, that is to say, a supremely perfect being, who lacks existence, that is to say, who lacks some particular perfection, than in conceiving a mountain without a valley. (Descartes [1637] 1968; 143)

As in the case of Anselm's *Proslogion* 2 argument, Descartes's *Meditation* 5 argument has been quite variously represented in the recent literature. Again, the text is rather elusive. And, again, because the text is elusive, it is highly tempting for interpreters to read their own assumptions into the text to arrive at an interpretation that they find satisfying. Here are some recent representations of the argument:

Dore (1997):

1 The concept of a supremely perfect being is, in part, the concept of a person who has all those properties which are such that it is better than not that a person jointly possesses them.
2 The concept of existence is the concept of such a property.
3 (Hence) a supremely perfect being exists. (From (1) and (2).)

Everitt (2003):

1 God is by definition a being with all perfections.
2 Existence is a perfection.
3 (So) God has the perfection of existence, i.e. God exists. (From (1) and (2).)

Sobel (2004):

1   A supremely perfect being has every perfection.
2   Existence is a perfection.
3   (Hence) a supremely perfect being exists. (From (1) and (2).)

Leftow (2005):

1   If God does not exist, a being with all perfections lacks a perfection.
2   "A being with all perfections lacks a perfection" entails a contradiction.
3   (Hence) God exists. (From (1) and (2).)

1   For all x, if being F is part of the concept of x, then Fx.
2   It is part of the concept of God that if God's nature is what it is, God exists. (From (1).)
3   God's nature is what it is.
4   (So) God exists. (From (2) and (3).)

1   If the "true and immutable nature" of x includes being F, then Fx.
2   The "true and immutable nature" of God includes existence.
3   (So) God exists. (From (1) and (2).)

If anything, it seems to me that these arguments do less justice to Descartes's text than the recent representations of Anselm's *Proslogion* 2 argument do to Anselm's text. But, despite the interpretative difficulties, I think that it is possible to show that the actual argument that Descartes gives is unpersuasive.

Suppose that a non-theist grants to Descartes that we can frame the idea of God. Suppose that our non-theist also grants to Descartes that it is "part of the idea of God" that God is a supremely perfect being. And, finally, suppose that our non-theist grants to Descartes that anything that is a supremely perfect being is actually, eternally – and even necessarily – existent. Does it follow that our non-theist is rationally required to grant to Descartes that there is a supremely perfect being? Not at all. What our non-theist grants initially is that [According to the relevant idea] [God is a supremely perfect being]. Given the other claims that are granted to Descartes, what follows, at most, is that, [According to the relevant idea] [God is an actually, eternally – and even necessarily – existent supremely perfect being]. But, of course, it simply doesn't follow from [According to the relevant idea] [God is an actually, eternally – and even necessarily – existent supremely perfect being] that God exists. For, plainly enough, it no more follows from the claim that, [According to the relevant idea][Santa Claus is an existent inhabitant of the North Pole who wears a red suit and delivers presents to children at Christmas] that Santa Claus exists. (And it is undeniable that it is "part of the Santa Claus idea" that Santa Claus exists. The story is *not* that some metaphysically bizarre, non-existent man lives at the North Pole, etc.! Moreover, re-telling the story so that Santa Claus is eternally and/or necessarily existent would make no difference: no amount of heavy-duty metaphysical padding in the *content* of the idea will legitimate the exportation of the claim that Santa

Claus exists from within the scope of the "[According to the relevant idea]" operator.)

Even those people who are disposed to see some merit in Anselm's *Proslogion* 2 argument are typically not disposed to see any merit in Descartes's *Meditation* 5 argument. Leftow (2005) is a good recent example of someone who thinks that Descartes's argument is a failure, but who thinks that Anselm's argument has not yet been shown to fail. Sobel (2004) sees far more merit in Anselm's argument than he sees in Descartes's argument, even though he holds that both arguments fail. Dore (1997) is one of very few people who think that Descartes's *Meditation* 5 argument is compelling.

Plantinga

Plantinga's "successful" modal ontological argument may be stated quite briefly. Say that an entity is *maximally excellent* if it is omnipotent, omniscient, and morally perfect. Say, further, than an entity is *maximally great* if and only if it is maximally excellent in every possible world, i.e., if and only if it is necessarily existent and necessarily maximally excellent. Then Plantinga's argument runs as follows:

1   It is possible that there is a maximally great entity.
2   (Hence) there is a maximally excellent entity. (From (1).)

Under suitable assumptions about the underlying modal logic, this is a valid argument. Moreover, it is clear that, if there can be theists who reasonably believe that there is a maximally great entity, then there certainly can be theists who reasonably believe that it is possible that there is a maximally great entity. Nonetheless, it seems clear that this argument falls well short of being a successful argument for its conclusion. For, as Plantinga himself observes, this argument should be assessed only in conjunction with the following valid argument:

1   It is possible that there is no maximally great entity.
2   (Hence) there is no maximally excellent entity. (From (1).)

Plainly enough, if there can be reasonable non-theists who reasonably believe that there is no maximally great entity, then certainly there can be reasonable non-theists who reasonably believe that it is possible that there is no maximally great entity. So neither of these arguments can reasonably be considered to be persuasive. Moreover, contrary to Plantinga's own claim, neither of these arguments shows anything at all about the reasonableness of accepting the conclusions of these arguments.

It is perhaps worth noting that Plantinga's "successful" modal ontological argument is similar to an argument developed by Charles Hartshorne, and which has been linked by some to an argument devised by Anselm in *Proslogion* 3. There is an enormous literature on the overall structure of Anselm's *Proslogion*, and, in particular, on the relationships that hold between the arguments in *Proslogion* 2 and *Proslogion* 3. And there are other places in which Anselm elaborates upon and defends the arguments of *Proslogion* 2 and *Proslogion* 3. To do full justice to Anselm's "ontological arguments" is an enormous task that has not yet been seriously attempted.

A Priori Objections

As I noted earlier, there are many philosophers who have undertaken to show, on the basis of purely *a priori* considerations, that there *could not* be a successful ontological argument. Most famously, Kant produced often cited *a priori* objections to the possibility of successful ontological arguments. In particular, many philosophers have taken from Kant the idea that there is something wrong with the thought that existence is a property, or a defining property, or a property that can be incorporated into ideas or individual concepts. Kant writes:

> "Being" is obviously not a real predicate; that is, it is not a concept of something which could be added to the concept of a thing. . . . By whatever and however many predicates we may think a thing – even if we completely determine it – we do not make the least addition to the thing when we further declare that this thing is. Otherwise, it would not be exactly the same thing that exists, but something more than we thought in the concept; and we could not, therefore, say that the exact object of my concept exists. (Cited in Oppy 1995: 32–3)

Despite the obvious interpretative difficulties, I think that we can be pretty confident that there is no successful *a priori* objection to the possibility of a successful ontological argument buried in this Kantian text. Focus for a moment on sentences of the form "a is F," where "a" is a singular denoting term, and "F" is a predicate. If we suppose that singular denoting terms and predicates express "concepts," it is clear that we shall need to allow that, in many ordinary cases in which we accept judgments of the form "a is F," it is not the case that the concept associated with "a" *includes* the concept expressed by "F." (Put another way, in many ordinary cases in which we accept a judgment of the form "a is F," it is not the case that our acceptance of this judgment is based on *a priori* considerations.) But, in ordinary cases, involving uncontroversial "predicates," this failure of *inclusion* does nothing at all towards showing that these predicates fail to express real properties, or that "the exact objects of our concepts" do not exist. Bertrand Russell is the exact object of my concept "Bertrand Russell," even though there are many claims of the form "Bertrand Russell is F" that I accept only on *a posteriori* grounds. So there is no reason here to suppose that "exists" cannot be treated as a real predicate.

Perhaps it might be objected that, in the case of other predicates that do form part of our concepts, we can draw secure *a priori* inferences: if "F" is included in my concept of Bertrand Russell, then I know *a priori* that Bertrand Russell is F. And it might be added that there is an evident difficulty in allowing that existence can be incorporated into concepts: given the concept "existent denizen of the North Pole who wears a red suit and distributes presents to children at Christmas," I cannot securely draw the conclusion that Santa Claus exists. However, as we have already noted, there seems to be only two available options at this point. On the one hand, we might insist that it is no more true that Santa Claus lives at the North Pole: for *there are no* permanent denizens of the North Pole. Granted, according to the Santa Claus story, Santa lives at the North Pole; but it does not follow from this uncontroversial claim that there is someone who lives at the North Pole. On the other hand, if we wish to follow Meinong in allowing that it is true that Santa Claus lives at the North Pole even though Santa Claus is a non-existent object, then we need to adopt one of the available protective strategies to ensure that we are not committed to the claim that we know *a priori* that a is F whenever the concept "F" is contained in the concept "a." (No-one wants to allow that we know *a priori* that the really existent Santa Claus really exists; the truth is that there is no really existent Santa Claus.) But, of course, these strategies do not forbid us from incorporating "existence" into our concepts: from the standpoint of these Meinongian theories, there is, after all, nothing in the least problematic about, say, a "really existing George W. Bush" concept that includes real existence. Rather, what these strategies do is to limit the *a priori* inferences that can be drawn from concepts so that Meinongian theories square with evident claims about what *really* does not exist. (While we do not know *a priori* that the really existent George W. Bush really exists, we do know – on *a posteriori* grounds – that the really existent George W. Bush really exists!)

There are other *a priori* objections that have been made to the possibility of a successful ontological argument. In my view, these objections are no more successful than the Kantian objection that we have just been discussing. There are many subtle questions that can be raised about the nature of existence, intentional objects, mind/world relations, the fallacy of begging the question, and the like; but it is not the case that the investigation of any of these questions has thus far led to a successful demonstration that it is knowable *a priori* that there cannot be a successful ontological argument. (Of course, in saying that, I don't mean to deny that it can be shown *a priori* that some particular ontological arguments are unsuccessful. I have argued elsewhere, for example, that this is true of the argument in Maydole (2003). The objections that I have sketched above to the arguments of Anselm and Descartes also fall into this category.)

Parody

Apart from the Kantian objections, the most often discussed objections to ontological arguments are modelled on one of the responses that the monk Gaunilo made to Anselm's ontological argument. Although Gaunilo doesn't quite make his objection in the following terms, we can imagine him presenting the following argument to Anselm:

> Even the fool is convinced that an island than which no greater island can be conceived is in the understanding, since when he hears this, he understands it; and whatever is understood is in the understanding. And certainly that island than which a greater island cannot be conceived cannot be in the understanding alone. For if it is even in the understanding alone, it can be conceived to exist in reality also, which is greater. Thus if that island than which a greater island cannot be conceived is in the understanding alone, then that island than which a greater island cannot be conceived is itself an island than which a greater island can be conceived. But surely this cannot be. Thus without doubt an island than which a greater island cannot be conceived exists, both in the understanding and in reality.

If Anselm's argument succeeded in showing that there is a being than which no greater can be conceived, then surely a very similar argument would succeed in showing that there is an island than which no greater island can be conceived. But it is absurd to suppose that this very similar argument succeeds in showing that there is an island than which no greater island can be conceived. Whence it follows that Anselm's argument cannot succeed in showing that there is a being than which no greater can be conceived.

Responses to Gaunilo's objection have typically taken one of two forms. Some philosophers have claimed that, while the Fool really does understand the expression "being than which no greater can be conceived," he doesn't really understand the expression "island than which no greater island can be conceived." So, for example, we have Plantinga's claim (cited in Oppy 1995: 163–4) that the idea of a greatest possible island is incoherent: "No matter how great an island is, no matter how many Nubian maidens and dancing girls adorn it, there could always be a greater – one with twice as many, for example." Plantinga's particular line of attack is suspect: the greatest possible island will be an island, hence girt by sea, hence of finite size. An island *overcrowded* with whatever it is that makes for greatness of islands will not be the greatest conceivable island. Moreover, the general strategy that underlies Plantinga's response is also dangerous: if, for example, we suppose that a being is greater in proportion to the number of universes that it creates, then the same line of argument would show that the Fool doesn't really understand the expression "being than which no greater can be conceived."

Other philosophers have claimed that, while it is true that real existence is great-making for beings in general, it is not the case that real existence is great-making for islands. Even if the Fool were to concede this claim, the most that would be achieved would be to shift attention to other cases – e.g., beings than which no greater can be conceived except that they know nothing about inaccessible cardinal numbers. Since the Fool would surely be right to insist that real existence is great-making in this case, it seems clear that, on its own, this strategy cannot generate a successful response to Gaunilo's objection.

Of course, the above remarks barely begin to scratch the surface of recent discussions of Gaunilo-style objections to ontological arguments. Philosophers disagree about the effectiveness of this style of objection: for example, Leftow (2005:
92–7) gives an interesting – though, in my view, ultimately unsuccessful – defense
of Anselm against Gaunilo's objection. Philosophers disagree about the range of
its applicability: even if Gaunilo's objection does defeat Anselm's argument, are
there other ontological arguments that cannot be defeated by objections in this
style? And philosophers disagree about the value of these kinds of objections: even
if Gaunilo-style objections do show that there is something wrong with ontological
arguments, surely they don't satisfy our desire to know why it is that ontological
arguments fail.

Concluding Remarks

In the heyday of logical positivism and ordinary language philosophy, there were
many philosophers who were quite happy to bury all discussion of ontological
arguments. Consider, for example, Walter T. Stace's assessment from 1959: "I
simply cannot bear to discuss the dreary logomachy of the ontological argument.
Probably [C. D.] Broad has completely demolished the argument. But I cannot
bring myself to think that it needs demolishing" (cited in Oppy 1995: 202).

Today, the situation is a bit different. While ontological arguments still have
few serious defenders, there is a much wider recognition that there are interesting,
live questions to be taken up in connection with them. And while most recent
discussions of ontological arguments occur in compendiums, companions, ency-
clopedias, and the like (e.g., Dore 1997; Everitt 2003; Sobel 2004; Leftow 2005;
Matthews 2005; Oppy 2006) there has been some interesting activity in the
journals (e.g., Chambers 2000; Maydole 2003; Millican 2004). I think that
we can confidently expect to hear much more about ontological arguments in the
coming decade.

Questions for Reflection

1   What would it be for an argument to "survive objections?" What are the char-
    acteristics that are possessed by successful arguments? What are the standards
    that successful arguments are required to achieve?
2   What, exactly, is wrong with "question-begging" arguments? Is it plausible to
    claim that typical ontological arguments – e.g. the argument of *Proslogion* 2 –
    are "question-begging?" Should Anselm be dismayed by the suggestion that
    his argument is "question-begging?"
3   Is Gaunilo's parody argument for the existence of an island than which no
    greater island can be conceived really on all fours with Anselm's *Proslogion* 2
    argument for the existence of a being than which no greater being can be

conceived? If not, then what is the key difference between the two arguments? Alternatively, if so, then what conclusion should we draw about the success or otherwise of Anselm's *Proslogion* 2 argument?

4   What is it, exactly, for something to be a "real" property? Can the claim that existence is not a "real" property somehow form the basis for a successful (*a priori*) objection to ontological arguments (or, at any rate, to some well-known ontological arguments)?

5   Is there some kind of contradiction involved in "conceiving a supremely perfect being who lacks existence?" If so, does it then follow that there is a supremely perfect being? What options are available to the opponent of ontological arguments who allows that there is a contradiction involved in "conceiving a supremely perfect being who lacks existence?"

References

Chambers, T. (2000) "On Behalf of the Devil: A Parody of St Anselm Revisited." *Proceedings of the Aristotelian Society* 100, 93–113.

Descartes, R. ([1637] 1968) *Discourse on the Method and The Meditations*, trans. F. Sutcliffe. Harmondsworth: Penguin.

Dore, C. (1997) "Ontological Arguments." In P. Quinn and C. Taliaferro (eds.), *A Companion to Philosophy of Religion*. Oxford: Blackwell.

Everitt, N. (2003) "Ontological Arguments." In *The Non-Existence of God*. London: Routledge.

Leftow, B. (2005) "The Ontological Argument." In W. Wainwright (ed.), *The Oxford Handbook of Philosophy of Religion*. Oxford: Oxford University Press.

Matthews, G. (2005) "The Ontological Argument." In W. Mann (ed.), *The Blackwell Guide to Philosophy of Religion*. Oxford: Blackwell.

Maydole, R. (2003) "The Modal Perfection Argument for the Existence of a Supreme Being." *Philo* 6, 299–313.

Millican, P. (2004) "The One Fatal Flaw in Anselm's Argument." *Mind* 113, 437–76.

Oppy, G. (1995) *Ontological Arguments and Belief in God*. Cambridge: Cambridge University Press.

—— (2006) *Arguing about Gods*. Cambridge: Cambridge University Press (chapter 2).

Sobel, J. (2004) *Logic and Theism*. Cambridge: Cambridge University Press (chapters 2–4).

Further Reading

Barnes, J. (1972) *The Ontological Argument*. London: Macmillan. (Very careful analyses of a range of ontological arguments and objections to those arguments. Focuses in particular on Anselm, Descartes, and Kant.)

Charlesworth, M. (1965) *St. Anselm's Proslogion*. Oxford: Oxford University Press. (Scholarly parallel translation and annotation of Anselm's *Proslogion*. There are many translations of *Proslogion* 2–4; this one is indispensable for those who want to see the wider context in which the ontological arguments are set.)

Hartshorne, C. (1965) *Anselm's Discovery: A Re-examination of the Ontological Proof for God's Existence.* La Salle, IL: Open Court. (Written by an enthusiastic defender of Anselm's arguments. Notable for its detailed information about the history of arguments related to those that Anselm gave.)

Plantinga, A. (ed.) (1965) *The Ontological Argument.* New York: Doubleday. (Edited collection of classic works on ontological arguments. Includes extracts from Anselm, Gaunilo, Descartes, Leibniz, Kant, and many others.)

Chapter 9

The Moral Argument

Paul Copan

Introduction

The French Catholic philosopher Jacques Maritain helped draft the United Nations (UN) Universal Declaration of Human Rights (1948), which recognizes "the inherent dignity" and "the equal and inalienable rights of all members of the human family." Further, it declares: "All human beings are born free and equal in dignity and rights. They are endowed with reason and conscience and should act towards one another in a spirit of brotherhood." What is the foundation or basis, though, for such a sweeping affirmation of human dignity and rights? The UN document doesn't say. In light of the philosophical discussion behind the drafting of the Declaration, Maritain wrote: "we agree on these rights, providing we are not asked why. With the 'why,' the dispute begins" (Maritain 1951: 77). Why *do* humans have value? Why think that they, as persons, ought to be treated as ends in themselves rather than objects to be used?

There is a host of related questions that inevitably emerge: Do objective/ universal moral values exist? Were the moral ideals expressed, say, during the Nuremberg trials after the second world war nothing more than the victors' own moral preferences imposed upon the conquered, or would the Nazis have been morally wrong even if they had dominated the world and were successful at convincing all humanity of their ideology? Do human beings have authentic moral obligations to actual duties and the cultivation of virtue, or does our sense of morality spring from survival instincts and complex social structures? Is there any connection between God and objective moral values? Or perhaps, like Platonic forms, could moral values simply be brute facts – just part of the existing metaphysical furniture?

This chapter suggests that a strong case can be made that deeply connects a good God with objective moral values and obligations as well as human rights, dignity, and moral responsibility. A moral universe is far less likely – indeed very difficult to come by – if God does not exist. In contrast to the UN Declaration's mere assertion that human rights and moral obligations exist, there must be some metaphysical grounding for such sweeping declarations. Theists believe that there is an intimate connection between (1) a good God and Creator (the metaphysical foundation) and (2) basic human rights and general moral obligations (which all humans can recognize, even if they do not believe in God). God is the necessarily good Source of all finite goods (by "good" is meant what is desired for its own sake). The Jewish-Christian tradition affirms that human beings, because they are made in the "likeness" or "image of God" (Gen. 1:26–7; James 3:9) are part of God's "very good" creation (Gen. 1:31). Even though, as this tradition argues, human sin has introduced evil and corruption into the world, the goodness of human nature, though damaged and distorted by evil (Graham 2001), still remains.

This chapter will explore a range of topics as they have a bearing on the moral argument for God's existence: the existence and nature of properly basic moral beliefs; the important distinction between *knowing* or recognizing objective moral values and *being* moral, rights-bearing beings; the ill fit of naturalism and objective moral values; the question of evolutionary ethics; and the Euthyphro dilemma.

This version of the moral argument attempts to connect (1) the existence of a morally excellent Being who is worthy of worship and (2) objective moral values and human dignity/rights. If such values exist, then it is extremely likely that some intrinsically valuable Being exists. In other words, if objective moral values exist, then (it is highly probable) that God exists. Such values do exist. Therefore God (most likely) exists.

The Proper Basicality of Moral Values

The Jewish-Christian scriptures assume that human beings are morally responsible agents who can generally know what is good and that they ought to do what is good and avoid what is evil. In the Hebrew scriptures, the prophet Amos (in chapters 1–2) delivers severe warnings from God to surrounding Gentile nations because of their atrocities and crimes against humanity – ripping open pregnant women, breaking treaties, acting treacherously, stifling compassion. The underlying assumption is that these nations – even without God's special revelation – should have known better. In the writings of the apostle Paul, the same assumption is expressed more explicitly:

> For when Gentiles who do not have the Law [of Moses] do instinctively the things of the Law, these, not having the Law, are a law to themselves, in that they show the work of the Law written in their hearts, their conscience bearing witness and their thoughts alternately accusing or else defending them. (Rom. 2:14–15)

There are detractors from the view that objective moral values exist. David Hume claims that reason is "the slave of the passions, and can never pretend to any other office than to serve and obey them" (Hume 1888: 2.3.3, 415). Not only is human reason enslaved to human passion, morality itself is "more properly felt than judg'd of" (3.1.2, 470). Morality for Hume is found within: one can never locate vice "till you turn your reflexion into your own breast, and find a sentiment of disapprobation, which arises in you, towards this action" (3.1.2, 468–9). Like a number of contemporary naturalistic Darwinists, for Hume there is no transcendent morality that cuts across cultural and individual preferences. Morality is subjective, located within "your own breast," and it has no meaning beyond this.

Hume's empiricistic starting point, however, is itself problematic (see Copan 2005). How can one empirically show that all knowledge must be rooted in the empirical (scientific) realm? Such an assertion is a philosophical assumption, not a scientific conclusion. Beyond this, the Scottish philosopher Thomas Reid, who responds at length to Hume, considers basic moral principles (e.g., "treat another as you desire to be treated") to be commonsensical; they are obvious to those who haven't ignored their conscience. For such persons, he claimed he didn't know by what reasoning, demonstrative or probable, he could convince the moral skeptic of her moral duty. Reid claimed that morality was properly basic:

> The sceptic asks me, Why do you believe the existence of the external object which you perceive? This belief, sir, is none of my manufacture; it came from the mint of Nature; it bears her image and superscription; and, if it is not right, the fault is not mine. I ever took it upon trust, and without suspicion. (Reid 1975: 84–5)

As with science, morality begins with certain axioms or first principles. First principles are self-evident to the person who has not hardened his conscience. Reid says that the law of God is written on our hearts (conscience), and to reject its fundamental inclinations is to act unnaturally (Reid 1969: 364–7). The reason the atheist can recognize the same moral truths as the theist is that "the faculty [is] given him by God." Both are made in the same divine image. If God had not bestowed this faculty upon man, "he would not be a moral and accountable being" (Reid 1822: 381). Although basic moral principles (to be kind, selfless, and compassionate; to avoid torturing for fun, raping, or taking innocent human life) are accessible and knowable to morally sensitive human beings, some individuals may be self-deceived or hard-hearted sophists.

Furthermore, it seems that we should reasonably believe what is apparent or obvious to us unless there are overriding reasons to dismiss it (this has been called *the credulity principle*). The use of this notion is appropriate with regard to our *sense* perceptions, our *reasoning* faculty, and our *moral* intuitions/perception. As a general rule of thumb – one we constantly take for granted – these faculties/ capacities are *innocent until proven guilty*. I am wise to accept their reliability/testimony *unless* I have strong reasons to doubt them (see chapter 3, Reformed Epistemology).

Furthermore, if a trustworthy God has created our noetic structure, then we have all the more reason for generally trusting these faculties or capacities rather than constantly doubting their reliability – even though, here and there, we may get things wrong. Indeed, we have been designed to trust our faculties, and constantly failing to trust them is a sign of cognitive malfunction (Plantinga 2000: 185). This can be extended to the moral realm as well. Even if human beings make faulty moral judgments and can be misguided, we would be wrong to abandon the quest for goodness or become moral skeptics: "we cannot always or even usually be totally mistaken about goodness" (Adams 1999: 20). Indeed, atheist philosopher Kai Nielsen comments on the vileness of child abuse and wife-beating:

> It is more reasonable to believe such elemental things to be evil than to believe any skeptical theory that tells us we cannot know or reasonably believe any of these things to be evil. . . . I firmly believe that this is bedrock and right and that anyone who does not believe it cannot have probed deeply enough into the grounds of his moral beliefs. (Nielsen 1990: 10–11)

The existence of "grey areas" does not mean that we can't readily recognize general moral principles. Objective moral values do exist, and morally sensitive persons can recognize them and get a lot right. In making moral judgments, however, we must begin with the clear and move to the unclear, not vice versa. Simply because moral uncertainty or ambiguity exists, this doesn't eclipse the morally obvious. As Dr Samuel Johnson put it, the fact that there is such a thing as twilight does not mean that we cannot distinguish between day and night (Plantinga 2000: 202).

Knowing versus Being

Certain atheists may question how God's non-existence would adversely affect the goodness of compassion, mercy, justice, and other virtues. One can readily affirm the wrongness of rape and deny the existence of God with perfect consistency. One could affirm the objective immorality of, say, rape and deny the existence of God without inconsistency. The claim made here is that even if God didn't exist, we could still know that objective morality exists, and Christians will give the same reasons as atheists about the immorality of rape. Rape is a horrible violation of the victim and of her rights. The atheist appears vindicated since such reasoning does not appeal to God's existence (Martin 2002).

This is too quick. Here it is important to distinguish between *knowing* (epistemology) and *being* (ontology) – and to get clear on which is more fundamental. At one level (*knowing*), the atheist's argument appears to make sense. Because humans have been made in God's image as intrinsically valuable (endowed with rights, dignity, conscience, moral responsibility, and the basic capacity to recognize right and wrong), we should not be surprised that non-theists of all stripes know the same sorts of moral truths about human rights, dignity, and moral obligation. They do not have to believe in God to *know* right from wrong. Such moral recognition comes readily when we are functioning properly and are not suppressing our conscience. Atheists don't need a Bible to recognize basic objective moral values.

However, the atheist's (or non-theist's) defense of objective morality only works at one level – knowledge. The more fundamental level of *being* – that is, the *actual ground* or *basis* (which makes moral knowledge possible) – is inadequate (Copan 2003; 2005). The reason the atheist, theist, Buddhist, or Hindu can recognize basic moral values as objectively right is because each has been made in the divine image. So anyone can *know* that humans have rights and dignity and that we have a moral obligation to live accordingly. The more fundamental question is: how did they come to *be* that way? Why think human beings have rights, value, or dignity if we are the result of valueless, physical processes in a cause-and-effect series from the Big Bang until now? A more plausible scenario that offers a metaphysical grounding for human rights and dignity is that we have been *created* with a *moral constitution* (involving rights, dignity, and moral responsibility) by a supremely valuable being. In other words, if we believe humans have intrinsic (rather than instrumental) value and rights and moral responsibility, the context that appears to offer a more natural fit or a smoother transition is a personal God, the source of value or goodness who creates us as morally responsible agents – rather than a series of impersonal, valueless causes and effects from the Big Bang onwards.

According to the Jewish-Christian tradition, our moral awareness is part of God's *general* self-revelation; a personal God is responsible for this being a morally ordered universe. Even if they don't believe in or acknowledge God's existence, *all* humans are hard-wired the same way: *they are made to function properly when living morally.*

Now, various naturalists have claimed that moral properties or objective moral values somehow supervene upon an organism when it is sufficiently neurologically complex (e.g., Brink 1989; Martin 2002) or once sufficiently complex social configurations arise (e.g., "homeostatic property clusters" in Boyd 1988). Despite this, problems of accounting for the emergence of rights, value, or dignity remain. If intrinsic value does not exist from the outset, its emergence from non-valuable processes is difficult to explain. It doesn't matter how many non-personal and non-valuable components we happen to stack up: from valuelessness, valuelessness comes.

Brink suggests a parallel to support his naturalistic moral realism – namely, the supervenience of the *mental* upon a complex *physical* brain and nervous system: "Assuming materialism is true, mental states supervene on physical states, yet few think that mental states are metaphysically queer" (Brink 1989: 120, 156–67). Such optimism about a natural transition from non-conscious matter to emergent mental properties such as consciousness or intentionality is unwarranted. As naturalistic philosopher of mind Ned Block admits, we have "no conception" – "zilch" – that enables us to explain subjective experience or to *begin* to account for conscious life: "Researchers are *stumped*" (Block 1994: 211, his emphasis). Likewise, Jaegwon Kim, another naturalist, wonders how "a series of physical events, little particles jostling against one another, electric current rushing to and fro" could blossom into "conscious experience": "Why should *any* experience emerge when these neurons fire?" (Kim 1996: 8). It seems that the emergence of consciousness from non-conscious matter in a naturalistic setting is very difficult to account for. The theist has no such challenges if a supremely self-aware Being exists – from consciousness, consciousness comes. Brink's suggested parallel actually reinforces a theistic outlook.

As opposed to the naturalistic supervenience model of moral value, the theist could argue that a *personal* Creator, who creates human *persons* in his image, serves as the ontological basis for the existence of objective moral values, moral obligation, human dignity and rights. Without the existence of a personal God, there would be no persons at all. (Indeed, God is the sufficient reason for why anything exists at all. For if the universe came into existence a finite time ago, the only options appear to be that it was simply uncaused – a metaphysical impossibility – or that something outside the universe caused its existence. See chapter 6, The Cosmological Argument.) And if no persons would exist, then no moral properties would be instantiated or realized in our world:

1 If *persons* (who possess intrinsic value) exist, moral properties are instantiated.
2 A divine creative *personal* (supremely valuable) Being exists (without whose unique act of creation, human persons would never exist).
3 Therefore, moral properties are instantiated.

A personal God, who created human persons in his image, is necessary to ground the instantiation of moral properties: His own existence as a personal Being instantiates these properties, and by virtue of our creation in God's image, we human persons are further instantiations of these properties. Moral categories (right/wrong, good/bad, praiseworthy/blameworthy) get to the essence of who we fundamentally are. They apply to us *as persons*, who have been made to resemble God in certain important (though limited) ways. Moral values – the instantiation of moral properties – and personhood are intertwined: moral properties are instantiated through personhood, which is ontologically rooted in God's personhood.

Various non-theistic moral realists – not to mention some theists (e.g., Layman 1991: 44–52; Swinburne 1977: 204) – maintain that statements such as "*Murder is wrong*" would hold true even if God does not exist. They are simply brute facts or givens. But if, as argued above, there is a deep connection between personhood and objective moral values and if our personhood is rooted in God's specially creating humans, we can offer the following response.

First, we have a much simpler alternative than the "brute-fact" thesis (which assumes an additional, independent moral realm), an explanatory fifth wheel. The moral connection between a good God and humans needs no such superfluous Platonic realm independent of God.

Second, even if we grant that moral facts are just brute givens and necessarily true (just as logical laws are), the huge cosmic coincidence of/ correspondence between these *moral facts* and the eventual evolutionary and highly contingent development of *self-reflective, morally responsible beings* who can recognize them and are obligated to them begs explanation. This moral realm, it appears, was *anticipating* our emergence – a remarkable cosmic coincidence! A less *ad hoc* explanation is that a good God made valuable human beings in his image.

Third, the necessity of moral truths does not diminish their need for grounding in the character of a personal God. God, who necessarily exists in all possible worlds, is the source of all necessary moral truths that stand in asymmetrical relation to God's necessity (Craig, in Wallace 2003: 168–73). So God would still be explanatorily prior to these moral values. It just is not obvious that an independent Platonic realm (or its naturalistic equivalent) containing forms of "Justice" and "Goodness" exists. Fourth, even if this Platonic realm of moral forms exists, there is no good reason to think that valuable, morally responsible human beings should emerge from valueless processes. Theism offers a far more plausible explanation for human value, as it does a better job than non-theistic accounts of explaining human dignity.

Naturalistic philosophers have often appealed to, say, Aristotle's eudaimonistic ethic as an example of an adequate objective ethical system that can safely ignore any God-morality connection. Yet while Aristotle certainly offers important emphases in ethical discussion, critical gaps and shortcomings remain: (1) the questionable notion of intellectual activity (as opposed to relationships) as central to fulfilling our natural human task (*ergon*) or goal (*telos*); (2) the radical evil embedded in human nature that inclines us to self-centeredness and evil – what comes "naturally" may often undermine human flourishing. As it turns out, certain facets of Aristotle's teleological account are deeply enhanced in the context of a Creator's ends or design plan for his creation (Layman 1991: 138–44).

Along with naturalism, it seems difficult to ground human value and dignity and objective moral values in the context of non-theistic Eastern religions. These may advocate a monistic impersonal consciousness (*brahman*) and a denial of any distinctions, or the ultimacy of emptiness (*sunyata*). Ninian Smart, scholar of Asian philosophy and religion, observes that the "concept of the importance of the historical process is largely foreign to these faiths," adding that "the notion of a personal God is altogether less prominent" (Smart 1986: 161). It seems that a personal Creator offers a more adequate grounding for human value and personal virtues such as compassion, love, and kindness than an impersonal ontological foundation.

Naturalism and Moral Realism – an Ill Fit?

Non-theistic moral realists believe that (1) objective moral values and moral obligations *do* exist independent of human minds while (2) God does (or perhaps
may) *not* exist. Real right and wrong, they claim, can be explained without appealing to a personal God. This, however, seems problematic not only for the reasons
articulated above. In addition, the metaphysical inconsistency between naturalism
(or non-theism) and moral realism has been recognized by many naturalists themselves, which further bolsters the theistic hypothesis. Indeed, human beings are
simply advanced animals. Why think then that they have moral obligations while
chimpanzees and gorillas do not? (Someone may posit that certain animals are
"moral patients" while humans are "moral agents," but this still does not
adequately account for the emergence of rights, moral value, responsibility,
and freedom given a naturalistic backdrop of valueless, impersonal processes
at work.)

Bertrand Russell believed that "the whole subject of ethics arises from the pressure of the community on the individual" (Russell 1954: 124). Biologist E. O.
Wilson claims that religious doctrines and faith are "entirely material products of
the mind;" moral feeling, rooted in "the hypothalamus and the limbic system" is
simply a "device of survival in social organisms" (Wilson 1998: 268, 269). Philosopher James Rachels affirms this "scientific" view of ethics: "Man is a moral
(altruistic) being, not because he intuits the rightness of loving his neighbor, or
because he responds to some noble ideal, but because his behavior is comprised
of tendencies which natural selection has favoured" (Rachels 1990: 77). Derk
Pereboom makes clear the implications: "our best scientific theories indeed have
the consequence that we are not morally responsible for our actions. . . . [We are]
more like machines than we ordinarily suppose" (Pereboom 2001: xiii–xiv). Such
views on morality flow quite understandably from metaphysical naturalism.

On the other hand, some non-theistic philosophers have suggested that if objective moral values do exist, this would constitute significant evidence for the existence of God. For example, the Oxonian J. L. Mackie remarked, "Moral properties
constitute so odd a cluster of properties and relations that they are most unlikely
to have arisen in the ordinary course of events without an all-powerful god to
create them" (Mackie 1982: 115). Mackie, an atheist, rejected objective moral
values in favor of "inventing right and wrong" (Mackie 1991). One does not have
to look hard to find atheists who acknowledge the God-morality connection (even
if they reject objective moral values). This lends support to the argument that
objective moral values cannot be separated from God's existence.

Evolutionary Ethics

Naturalists generally claim that moral values are just the result of human evolutionary development. For some (naturalistic moral realists), moral values are *objective*

because moral properties "supervene" or emerge once the human brain and nervous system reach a certain level of complexity. (We have just addressed the unlikelihood of values emerging from valuelessness.) Other naturalists claim that moral values are simply *subjective*. Philosopher of science Michael Ruse asserts that we have developed an "awareness of morality – a sense of right and wrong and a feeling of obligation to be thus governed – because such an awareness is of biological worth" (Ruse 1989: 262). Morality is simply "an aid to survival and reproduction, and has no being beyond this" (p. 268).

Such a subjectivistic view ultimately reduces to ethical relativism; ethics is simply illusory. After all, Westerners may find abhorrent practices such as female circumcision or suttee/sati (a widow's self-immolation on the funeral pyre of her husband, which was outlawed in India under the British Raj), but on what basis should one oppose them? If ethical beliefs are simply hard-wired into us for our fitness and survival, these beliefs are not *true*; they simply *are*.

For the naturalist who, contrary to Ruse and his ilk, claims that objective moral values exist, the pertinent question to ask here is this: *Can we even trust our minds if we are nothing more than the products of naturalistic evolution trying to fight, feed, flee, and reproduce?* Charles Darwin himself was deeply troubled by this:

> With me the horrid doubt always arises whether the convictions of man's mind, which has been developed from the mind of the lower animals, are of any value or at all trustworthy. Would any one trust in the convictions of a monkey's mind, if there are any convictions in such a mind? (Darwin 1887: 315–16)

The evolutionary process is interested in fitness and survival, not in true belief. The problem with naturalistic evolution is that not only is *objective morality* undermined; so is *rational thought*. Our beliefs – moral or epistemic – may help us *survive*, but there is no reason to think they are *true* (Mavrodes 1986: 219).

So we may *believe* that human beings are intrinsically valuable, and this may help the *homo sapiens* species survive, but it may be wholly *false*. We may *believe* with full conviction that we have moral obligations, and this belief may help us survive, but it may be completely *wrong*. We may have the belief that our wills are free and that our choices do make a difference, but, again, we may be in serious *error*. If we are blindly hard-wired by nature to accept certain beliefs because of their survival-enhancing value, then we would not have access to the *truth-status* of these beliefs. They may help us to survive, but how could we know whether they are true or false?

Every waking hour, we depend upon our *rational* faculties to make basic inferences and to guide us towards truth. We take our *sense* perceptions as basically reliable. We tend to assume our general *moral* intuitions to be generally trustworthy. But if we're hard-wired to reproduce and survive, then the reliability of our reason, sense perceptions, and moral intuitions must be called into question. The scandal of such skepticism is this: I am relying on the very cognitive faculties whose unreliability is the conclusion of my skeptical argument (Plantinga 2000: 219n.). I am assuming a trustworthy reasoning process to arrive at the conclusion that I can't trust my reasoning.

Moreover, we believe lots of things that don't help us survive but are still true (e.g., the current temperature at the North Pole). In virtue of the fact that we seek to know the *truth* about many things apart from their survival value suggests that we are living according to a theistic worldview rather than a naturalistic (or, more broadly, a non-theistic) one. We have been made in the image of a truthful, rational Being. So it would make sense that we would be functioning properly when our cognitive faculties are directed at the truth. In our very nature, we are interested in more than just survival. There seems to be a parallel between truth and morality. Commenting on the idea that humans have an "increated" orientation toward truth, Richard Rorty claims this is as "un-Darwinian" as the notion of humans having "a built-in moral compass" or conscience (Rorty 1995).

It appears that a naturalistic evolutionary process that attempts to explain (away) moral values (or our pursuit of truth) is inadequate. Our basic moral intuitions – along with our faculties of reason and sense perception – are generally reliable (unless we're malfunctioning); there is no good reason to deny them. And if we claim that such basic beliefs should be questioned in the name of our impulse to survive and reproduce, then this skeptical conclusion is itself the result of those same impulses.

Naturalism does not inspire confidence in our belief-forming mechanisms. Indeed, naturalism has the potential to undermine our conviction that rationality and objective moral values exist. If our *beliefs* – moral or epistemic – are survival-enhancing by-products of Darwinistic evolution, why think that we actually *have* dignity, rights, and obligations – or that we are thinking rationally? A theistic worldview, on the other hand, does inspire confidence that we can *know* moral (and rational) truths – even if they do not contribute one whit to our survival.

The Euthyphro Problem

In Plato's *Euthyphro* dialogue (10a), Socrates asks: "Is what is holy holy because the gods approve it, or do they approve it because it is holy?" Various philosophers of religion have followed up on this question. They present the dilemma in (roughly) this way: Either (1) God's commands are *arbitrary* (something is good *because* God commands it – and he could have commanded "You *shall* murder/commit adultery"), or (2) there must be some *autonomous moral standard* (which God consults in order to command). Robin Le Poidevin maintains that "we can, apparently, only make sense of these doctrines [that God is good and wills us to do what is good] if we think of goodness as being defined independently of God" (Le Poidevin 1996: 86). Is this so? Are our alternatives reduced to these two – a moral standard that exists completely independent of God (which God must apparently consult when issuing commands) *or* divine arbitrariness or capriciousness?

Although God's commands may serve as a partial guide to living rightly (e.g., God's civil laws to theocratic Israel), God's character is the more ultimate and underlying reality. As Robert M. Adams points out, "It matters what God's attributes are. . . . It makes a difference if you think of commands as coming from someone who completely understands both us and our situation. It matters not only that God is loving but also that he is just" (Adams 1988: 272). Again:

> It is crucial (and plausible on the assumption that God is the supreme Good) that God's commands spring from a design and purpose that is good, and that the behavior that God commands is not bad, but good, either intrinsically or by serving a pattern of life that is very good. It matters to the plausibility of a divine command theory, for example, that we do not believe that God demands cruelty. (Adams 1999: 255)

Indeed, the ultimate resolution to this dilemma is that *God's good character* or *nature* sufficiently grounds objective morality. So we don't need to look elsewhere for such a standard. We have been made in the divine image, without which we would neither (1) be moral beings nor (2) have the capacity to recognize objective moral values. The ultimate solution to the Euthyphro dilemma shifts the grounding of morality from the *commands of God* to something more basic – that is, the *nature* or *character* of God (see chapter 12, The Coherence of Theism). Thus, we human beings (who have been made to resemble God in certain ways) have the capacity to recognize them, and thus his commands – far from being arbitrary – are in accordance with that nature. We would not *know* goodness without God's granting us a moral *constitution*. We have rights, dignity, freedom, and responsibility because God has designed us this way.

As an aside, God's designs for us are for our good and well-being, not our harm. Contrary to the skeptic's caricatures of God as a divine policeman or cosmic killjoy, God issues commands that are rooted in his good nature and are in line with the maximal function and flourishing of human beings (see chapter 15, Divine Hiddenness, Death, and Meaning). Indeed, these commands spring from the love and self-giving nature of God, who is *pro nobis* (for us).

Furthermore, in light of (1) our ability to recognize basic moral values and ideals as well as (2) our moral failures to live up to these ideals, this "moral gap" suggests the need for (3) divine grace to enable us to live as we ought. So rather than Kant's "ought implies can," we failing humans may still cast ourselves upon God's mercy and grace; that is, "ought implies can – *with* divine assistance" (Hare 1996).

There are other points to ponder. What if the naturalistic (or non-theistic) moral realist pushes the Euthyphro dilemma further? Is the very *character* of God good because it is God's character or is it God's character because it is good? (1) If the naturalistic (or non-theistic) moral realist is correct about there needing to be some standard external to God, then she herself cannot escape a similar dilemma: Are these moral values good simply because they are good, or is there an independent standard of goodness to which *they* conform? Her argument offers her no actual advantage over theism. If two entities are sufficient to establish a relation (here, God's good character and objective moral values), inserting yet a third entity – some moral standard independent of God to assess the connection between them – becomes superfluous. The skeptic's demand is unwarranted. (2) The naturalist's query is pointless in this regard also: we must eventually arrive at some self-sufficient and self-explanatory stopping point beyond which the discussion can go no further. Why is this "independent moral standard" any less arbitrary a stopping-point than God's nature? (3) God, who is essentially perfect, does not have obligations to some external moral standard; God simply acts, and it is good. He naturally does what is good. God doesn't fulfill moral obligations but simply expresses the goodness of his nature. (4) The idea that God could be evil or command evil is utterly contrary to the very definition of God (who is intrinsically morally excellent, maximally great, and worthy of worship); if we are talking about "God," then he cannot be some evil creator of the universe. (5) The acceptance of objective values assumes a kind of ultimate goal or design plan for human beings. This would make little sense given naturalism (since we are the products of mindless, unguided processes), but it makes much sense given theism, which presumes a design plan or ideal standard for human beings. (6) Even if there were some moral standard independent of God, it still would fail to account for how humans, given their valueless, unguided, materialistic origins came to be morally valuable, rights-bearing, morally-responsible beings. There seems to be no reason to think that the Euthyphro dilemma poses a serious threat to a theistically rooted ethic (Alston 1990; Copan, 2003; Morris 1987a; Morris 1987b; Wainwright 2005).

Conclusion

Unlike the UN Universal Declaration of Human Rights, which takes human rights and moral obligations for granted, another historic document – the Declaration of Independence – presents the essential grounding for human rights and dignity as being rooted in "our Creator," a personal Being who has uniquely made human beings. A good case can be made that without God, there would be no objective moral values, obligations, human rights and dignity. John Rist has observed that there is "widely admitted to be a crisis in contemporary Western debate about ethical foundations" (Rist 2001: 1). It seems that taking seriously a personal God and Creator, who is the infinite Good and source of all finite goods – including human dignity – would go a long way in providing the needed metaphysical foundation for human rights and objective moral values.

Apart from such a move, it seems that the crisis may become only more pronounced.

Maritain argues that God and objective morality cannot plausibly be separated since God, the Creator of valuable, morally responsible human beings, is the very source of value. Ethical systems – and official documents regarding human rights – that ignore this foundation will necessarily be incomplete:

> The truths which I have just recalled were not discovered and formulated by moral philosophy. They spring from a higher source. They correspond, nevertheless, to an aspiration (a trans-natural aspiration) so deeply rooted in man that many philosophers have undergone its attraction, and have tried to transpose it into purely rational terms, an attempt which, lacking the indispensable data, could only be disappointing. (Maritain 1964: 439)

If objective moral values exist, we have good reason for believing in God. Of course, a successful moral argument does not reveal that the God of Abraham, Isaac, Jacob, and Jesus exists – a full-blown and robust theism. The moral argument, however, can be supplemented with other successful theistic arguments – all the more with particular or special revelation (e.g., in the scriptures and in Jesus of Nazareth). That said, the moral argument does point us to a supreme personal moral Being (1) who is worthy of worship, (2) who has made us with dignity and worth, (3) to whom we are personally accountable, and (4) who may reasonably be called "God."

Questions for Reflection

1   Does the background of a good personal God help to make better explanatory sense of human rights and dignity than naturalistic or non-theistic alternatives? Why or why not?
2   Does the instinct to survive and reproduce offer sufficient grounding for our deepest moral beliefs, or is it perhaps too reductionistic?
3   Why was the distinction made between *being* moral and *knowing* moral truths? Is this an important distinction?
4   Does the Euthyphro dilemma raise serious questions about the God-morality connection, or can this be overcome?
5   If a good personal God does not exist, what are the practical implications regarding moral obligations, human rights and dignity, and the pursuit of justice in society?

References

Adams, R. M. (1988) "Divine Commands and Obligation." *Faith and Philosophy* 4, 262–75.

—— (1999) *Finite and Infinite Goods: A Framework for Ethics.* New York: Oxford University Press.

Alston, W. P. (1990) "Some Suggestions for Divine Command Theorists." In M. D. Beaty (ed.), *Christian Theism and the Problems of Philosophy.* Notre Dame: University of Notre Dame Press.

Block, N. (1994) "Consciousness." In S. Guttenplan (ed.), *A Companion to the Philosophy of Mind.* Oxford: Blackwell.

Boyd, R. N. (1988) "How to Be a Moral Realist." In G. Sayre-McCord (ed.), *Essays on Moral Realism.* Ithaca, NY: Cornell University Press.

Brink, D. O. (1989) *Moral Realism and the Foundation of Ethics.* Cambridge: Cambridge University Press.

Copan, P. (2003) "The Moral Argument." In P. Copan and P. K. Moser (eds.), *The Rationality of Theism.* London: Routledge.

—— (2005) "David Hume and the Moral Argument." In D. R. Groothuis and J. R. Sennett (eds.), *In Defense of Natural Theology: A Post-Humean Assessment.* Downers Grove, IL: InterVarsity Press.

Darwin, C. (1887) "Letter to William Graham Down" (3 July 1881). In F. Darwin (ed.), *The Life and Letters of Charles Darwin Including an Autobiographical Chapter.* Vol. 1. London: John Murray, Abermarle Street.

Graham, G. (2001) *Evil and Christian Ethics.* Cambridge: Cambridge University Press.

Hare, J. (1996) *The Moral Gap.* Oxford: Clarendon Press.

Hume, D. (1888) *A Treatise of Human Nature*, ed. L. A. Selby-Bigge. Reprint. Oxford: Clarendon.

Kim, J. (1996) *Philosophy of Mind.* Boulder, CO: Westview Press.

Layman, S. C. (1991) *The Shape of the Good: Christian Reflections and the Foundation of Ethics.* Notre Dame: University of Notre Dame Press.

Le Poidevin, R. (1996) *Arguing for Atheism.* London: Routledge.

Mackie, J. L. (1982) *The Miracle of Theism.* Oxford: Clarendon Press.

—— (1991) *Ethics: Inventing Right and Wrong.* Reprint. New York: Penguin.

Maritain, J. (1951) *Man and the State.* Chicago: University of Chicago Press.

—— (1964) *Moral Philosophy.* New York: Charles Scribner's Sons.

Martin, M. (2002) *Atheism, Morality, and Meaning.* Amherst, NY: Prometheus.

Mavrodes, G. I. (1986) "Religion and the Queerness of Morality." In R. Audi and W. J. Wainwright (eds.), *Rationality, Religious Belief, and Moral Commitment.* Ithaca, NY: Cornell University Press.

Morris, T. V. (1987a) "Duty and Divine Goodness." In *Anselmian Explorations*, Notre Dame: University of Notre Dame Press.

—— (1987b) "The Necessity of God's Goodness." In *Anselmian Explorations*, Notre Dame: University of Notre Dame Press.

Nielsen, K. (1990) *Ethics Without God.* Rev. edn. Buffalo, NY: Prometheus.

Pereboom, D. (2001) *Living Without Free Will.* Cambridge: Cambridge University Press.

Plantinga, A. (2000) *Warranted Christian Belief.* New York: Oxford University Press.

Pojman, L. P. (2001) *Philosophy of Religion.* Mountain View, CA: Mayfield.

Rachels, J. (1990) *Created From Animals: The Moral Implications of Darwinism.* Oxford: Oxford University Press.

Reid, T. (1822) "Whether Morality Be Demonstrable." In "Essays on the Intellectual Powers of Man" in D. Stewart (ed.), *The Works of Thomas Reid*, Vol. 2, New York: Bangs and Mason.

—— (1969) "Of the First Principles of Morals." In *Essays on the Active Powers of the Human Mind*. Cambridge, MA: MIT Press.

—— (1975) *Thomas Reid's Inquiry and Essays*. K. Lehrer and R. E. Beanblossom (eds.) Indianapolis: Bobbs-Merrill.

Rist, J. (2001) *Real Ethics: Rethinking the Foundations of Morality*. Cambridge: Cambridge University Press.

Rorty, R. (1995) "Untruth and Consequences." *The New Republic* (31 July), 32–6.

Ruse, M. (1989) *The Darwinian Paradigm*. London: Routledge.

Russell, B. (1954) *Human Society in Ethics and Politics*. London: Allen & Unwin.

Smart, N. (1986) "Religion as a Discipline." In D. Wiebe (ed.), *Concept and Empathy*. New York: New York University Press.

Swinburne, R. (1977) *The Coherence of Theism*. Oxford: Oxford University Press.

Wainwright, W. J. (2005) *Religion and Morality*. Burlington, VT: Ashgate.

Wallace, S. W. (ed.) (2003) *Does God Exist? The Craig-Flew Debate*. Burlington, VT: Ashgate.

Wilson, E. O. (1998) *Consilience*. New York: Random House.

Further Reading

Adams, R. M. (1999) *Finite and Infinite Goods: A Framework for Ethics*. New York: Oxford University Press. (Offers a divine/transcendent basis for understanding goodness and moral obligation.)

Copan, P. (2003) "The Moral Argument." In P. Copan and P. K. Moser (eds.), *The Rationality of Theism*. London: Routledge. (A concise defense of the moral argument for God's existence.)

Graham, G. (2001) *Evil and Christian Ethics*. Cambridge: Cambridge University Press. (A study of evil in light of the Christian faith and a discussion of evil's inexplicability using naturalistic categories.)

Mavrodes, G. I. (1986) "Religion and the Queerness of Morality." In R. Audi and W. J. Wainwright (eds.), *Rationality, Religious Belief, and Moral Commitment*. Ithaca, NY: Cornell University Press. (A classic essay on the unlikelihood of objective moral values in a "Russellian" world.)

Rist, J. (2001) *Real Ethics: Rethinking the Foundations of Morality*. Cambridge: Cambridge University Press. (A masterful, wide-ranging survey of ethical theories and their justification, concluding that our ethical alternatives are either Nieztschean or theistic and transcendent.)

Chapter 10

The Argument from Evil

Paul Draper

Consider the condition of sentient beings on earth. Many and perhaps most of these beings either never flourish at all or flourish only very briefly; and many psychologically complex animals, including many human beings, suffer horrifically at least once in their lifetimes. Famine, disease, genetic defects, predators, accidents, and natural disasters, not to mention the wickedness of some human beings, all conspire to make this so. In some cases, horrific suffering is prolonged, as when a little girl is paralyzed in a car accident that takes the lives of both her parents. At a gut level, it seems almost inconceivable that a powerful and wise creator who loves her creatures more perfectly than any parent loves a child would produce a world like this. Yet this is exactly what orthodox monotheists believe. More precisely, this is exactly what must be true, if orthodox monotheism is true. For orthodox monotheism (or "theism" for short) is the view that the natural world depends for its existence on the existence of a "God" – a loving supernatural person who is perfect in power ("omnipotent"), perfect in knowledge ("omniscient"), and perfect in moral goodness ("morally perfect").

It *appears* then that theism can't even begin to make sense of the "facts of evil," and that this is a very powerful if not conclusive reason to reject it. But is this more than just appearance? Can we trust our gut feeling here? Is theism really "testable" in this way, and does it really fail that test? Philosophers who defend affirmative answers to these questions do so in part by constructing what are called "arguments from evil" against theism. Philosophers who defend negative answers to these questions do so either by constructing "theodicies" – attempts to explain why a God might create a world like ours in spite of the evils it contains – or by challenging one of the underlying assumptions upon which arguments from evil rest. In this chapter, I will attempt to formulate a rigorous and challenging argument from evil against theism. I will not, however, take a direct route to accomplishing this task. Instead, in order to motivate my argument, I will first explain why I am not persuaded by other arguments from evil. Then, after formulating my argument, I will sketch some reasons for believing that its premises are true and that its conclusion follows from its premises. I will not, however, attempt to prove that the argument is sound.

MT Arguments

At first glance, it may appear easy to construct a convincing argument from evil against theism. One obvious strategy is to formulate an argument of the following very simple sort:

    1   If God exists, then E does not obtain.
    2   E obtains.
So, 3   God does not exist.

Notice that any argument from evil of this sort will be deductively valid because it will have a valid argument form, namely, modus tollens. For this reason, I will call arguments from evil of this sort "MT arguments." Notice also that, so long as the variable "E" is replaced with some fact about evil that is *known* to obtain, an argument from evil of this sort will be sound if its first premise is true and it will be convincing if we have good reason to believe that its first premise is true. Since an "evil" should be understood in discussions of arguments from evil to mean anything that is bad, including things that are bad solely because they imply the absence of something good, there are countless candidates to replace E. For example, E could be replaced by the fact that evil exists, or that suffering exists, or that undeserved suffering exists, or that horrific suffering exists, or that horrific undeserved suffering exists, or that immorality exists, or that heinous immorality exists, or that some innocent children have been tortured, or that not every sentient being flourishes, or that some sentient beings flourish while most do not. Which replacement for E is chosen may affect the prospects for showing that the first premise of the resulting argument is true. The crucial question is whether this premise can be shown to be true for at least one suitable replacement of E.

It is far from obvious that the correct answer to this question is "yes." The first premise is a conditional statement and so is true only if it is not the case that both its antecedent is true and its consequent false. In other words, it is true only if it is false that both God exists and E obtains. But how can the falsity of the proposition "God exists and E obtains" be established? One approach is to argue that the falsity of this proposition is entailed by the definition of the title "God." In other words, one might try to argue that the existence of a being qualified to bear the title "God" – i.e., the existence of a loving supernatural person who is omnipotent, omniscient, and morally perfect – is logically incompatible with E's obtaining. To argue in this way would be to offer what philosophers have called a "logical argument from evil" against theism. All other arguments from evil are called "evidential arguments from evil."

Logical Arguments from Evil

Although logical arguments from evil seemed promising to a number of philosophers in the 1950s and 1960s (e.g., Mackie 1955), they are rejected by the vast majority of contemporary philosophers of religion, for two reasons. The first is that some serious attempts have been made to demonstrate that the existence of evil and several other more specific facts about evil are logically compatible with God's existence. For example, Alvin Plantinga's famous "Free Will Defense" (Plantinga 1974) persuaded many that it is logically possible that God exist, that God create people with morally significant free will, and that some of those people make morally bad choices. If Plantinga is right that this is logically possible, then God's existence is logically compatible with the existence of evil and (more specifically) with the existence of immorality. Plantinga also tried to extend the Free Will Defense to several other facts about evil. For example, he tried to show that theism is compatible with the amount of moral evil in the world, and he even appealed to the possibility of non-human persons who have free will (e.g., demons) in an attempt to show that theism is compatible with the existence of "natural" evil (i.e., evil that does not result from *human* immorality). The appeal to demons may seem fanciful or even desperate, but one must keep in mind that Plantinga is responding to the *logical* argument from evil. If one's goal is only to prove logical compatibility, then it is legitimate to appeal to any possible state of affairs, no matter how unlikely.

The unpopularity of logical arguments from evil cannot, however, be explained solely by the success of the Free Will Defense or other defenses. For there are many replacements for *E* that no defense has shown to be compatible with theism. Thus, a more fundamental and hence more important reason for the unpopularity of logical arguments from evil is that, even when some fact about evil cannot be shown to be compatible with theism, establishing an incompatibility is no less beyond our abilities (Pike 1963). Granted a God, being omnipotent and morally perfect, could eliminate any evils that he wanted to eliminate and would eliminate any evils that he had no good moral reason to permit; but all that follows from these claims is that a God would eliminate any evil that he had no good moral reason to permit. In order for a logical argument from evil to succeed, it is necessary to show that, for some known fact about evil, it is logically impossible for God to have a good moral reason to permit that fact to obtain. This, however, is precisely what most philosophers nowadays believe cannot be shown.

But why do they believe this? After all, when one examines the sorts of "excuses" that human beings have for not eliminating evil, they all seem to involve imperfect power or imperfect knowledge. For example, human beings avoid blame for destructive tornadoes because they lack the power to prevent them. They avoid blame for not rescuing people lost at sea because they don't know their whereabouts. And, depending on the circumstances, they may avoid blame for evils they know about and have the power to eliminate, such as visits to the dentist, so long as those evils lead to (or result from) greater goods like healthy teeth. These sorts of excuses could not work for an omnipotent and omniscient being. This is obvious in the case of the first two types because they explicitly involve a lack of power or knowledge. But it is no less true about the third case, because "leads to" and "results from" are causal notions and an omnipotent being would not be limited by causal laws. For example, an omnipotent being would never need to use unpleasant dental procedures as a causal means of keeping someone's teeth healthy. Her merely willing that a person's teeth be healthy would suffice to make it so.

Still, it would be a mistake to jump to the conclusion that all good reasons for not eliminating evil involve some lack of power or knowledge. To understand why this would be a mistake, it is crucial to understand that the inability to produce things that are logically impossible to produce, or to know statements that are logically impossible to know, does not count as a *lack* of power or a *lack* of knowledge. In other words, not even an omnipotent and omniscient being would have more power or more knowledge than it is logically possible for a being to have. Next, suppose that some good that is worth my suffering (perhaps it is even a good that benefits me) *logically implies* that I suffer (or at least that the objective chance of my suffering is not zero). For all we know or can prove, there could be such a good, even if it is not known to us. After all, even some goods we know about logically imply evils. For example, my showing fortitude in the face of pain logically implies that I feel pain and thus not even an omnipotent being could produce the good of my showing such fortitude without permitting the evil of my feeling pain. Of course, the good of my showing fortitude in the face of pain is probably not *worth* my feeling pain, but for all we know other goods not only logically imply my suffering but are also worth my suffering. Such goods would be known to an omniscient being even if they are beyond our ken. Further, if there are such goods, then not even an omnipotent and omniscient being could produce them without allowing me to suffer and hence even an omnipotent and omniscient being might have a good moral reason to permit my suffering.

One might object here that no good, no matter how great, could justify allowing horrific evils like the torturing of innocent children. (The character Ivan in Fyodor Dostoevksy's *The Brothers Karamazov* is often interpreted to be making this claim.) Indeed, some philosophers (e.g., Phillips 2004) seem to object to the whole notion of an "outweighing" good. To be sure, this notion should be rejected if it implies that all value can be measured on a single numerical scale or if it presupposes a crude consequentialist understanding of morality. It need not be interpreted in this way, however. In fact, it is even compatible with the position that no good, no matter how great, "outweighs" the harm done to an individual unless it benefits that individual. This last point is important because, for all we know, (1) there may exist goods far more valuable than any we can imagine, (2) these goods may logically imply the existence or risk of horrific evils, and (3) these goods may (if there is life after death) include among their beneficiaries the victims

of horrific evils. If this possibility is taken seriously (and admittedly not all philosophers think it should be taken seriously or even that it is a *possibility*), then it is
hard to be confident that the notion of an *outweighing* good breaks down in the
face of horrific evil, especially given how imprecise and fallible our moral intuitions
are. Therefore, since I believe this possibility should be taken seriously, I do not
see how it is possible to construct a convincing logical argument from evil against
theism, and for that reason the rest of the arguments from evil I discuss in this
chapter will be evidential ones.

Evidential MT Arguments

Notice that an MT argument need not be a logical argument from evil. Some
philosophers have tried to defend the conditional premise of an MT argument
without trying to show that the antecedent of that conditional is a logically sufficient condition of its consequent. Consider, for example, the following
argument:

    1 If God exists, then not all of the members of S exist.
    2 All of the members of S exist.
So, 3 God does not exist.

In this argument, "S" stands for a set containing all of the evils we know about
for which no adequate theodicy has yet been offered. One might try to establish
that the first premise of this argument is true by arguing that, since no *known*
goods justify God's permitting *even one* of the members of S, and since S has very
many members, it follows inductively that no goods at all (whether known or not)
justify God's permitting *all* of the members of S. Therefore, since God's existence
entails that either some goods justify permitting all of the members of S or not
all of the members of S exist, it follows deductively that if God exists, then
not all of the members of S exist (cf. Rowe 1979; 1986).

The second inference (the deductive one) is solid, but the first inference (the
inductive one) is questionable. It involves reasoning from a sample of "known
goods" to a conclusion about all goods whether known or not. Obviously there
is nothing wrong in principle with reasoning from samples to populations, but
such inferences are correct only when one has good reason to believe that one's
sample is representative of the population. One problem here is that we know so
little about the population of all goods that it is hard to be confident that our
sample of known goods is representative of that population (Alston 1991). A
second problem is that any evidence we have that supports theism will *ipso facto*
be evidence that our sample is biased and so may undermine the inference in
question.

An apparently more direct approach to defending the conditional premise in
an MT argument would be to give reasons why a God would be unlikely to permit

some fact about evil to obtain. For example, if the fact in question is that horrific suffering exists, then one might point out that horrific suffering is appallingly bad and that the worse it is, the less likely it is that God would permit it. One might also point out that certain goods that a God would *prima facie* want to exist are incompatible with horrific suffering. For example, one cannot flourish or pursue certain moral goals or have loving interactions with others if one is suffering horrifically (cf. Schellenberg 2000).

Are these good reasons to believe that if God exists, then horrific suffering does not exist? Not as good, perhaps, as they appear. For starters, there is the possibility of strong evidence for God's existence. Any such evidence would, given the existence of horrific suffering, be strong evidence for the falsity of the statement that if God exists, then horrific suffering does not exist. But even if no such evidence exists, giving reasons like the ones described above for believing that a God would be opposed to horrific suffering does not prove that the statement "if God exists, then horrific suffering does not exist" is probably true. Instead, such reasons only show at most that the consequent of that conditional statement is antecedently very probable, given the truth of its antecedent. In short, instead of establishing the probability of a conditional, they establish only a conditional antecedent probability. And the former does not follow from the latter: from the fact that Q is antecedently probable given P, it does not follow that "if P then Q" is probable. Since this mistake in reasoning is frequently made by those who defend the conditional premise of modus tollens arguments, it deserves a name. I will call it the "bogus tollens fallacy."

This is a very easy mistake to make. Suppose, for example, that Detective Garcia is trying to locate a car and is certain that it is owned by either Smith or Jones. In her efforts to figure out which of the two is the owner, she discovers that the car was recently painted green. She then reasons as follows:

1   If Smith owns the car, then it was not recently painted green.
2   It was recently painted green.
So,   3   Smith does not own the car.

In support of the first premise of this modus tollens argument, Garcia notes that it is well-known that Smith really likes red cars. Thus, assuming he is the owner, the car would most likely have been painted red – not green. This may sound convincing, but Garcia has actually committed the bogus tollens fallacy. She has shown that it is antecedently probable that the car would not have been painted green given that Smith owns it, but that doesn't entitle her to conclude that the conditional statement "if Smith owns the car, then it was not painted green" is probably true. To see why, suppose that Garcia also knows, not only that Jones really likes yellow cars but also that he was once struck by a green car and has had a strong aversion to green cars ever since. Then, even though it is antecedently likely that the car was not painted green given that Smith owns it, it is even more likely that it was not painted green given that Smith does not own it. This means that the fact that the car has recently been painted green is actually evidence that Smith is the owner! So what appeared to be evidence for the truth of the conditional premise of Garcia's modus tollens argument in reality provides no good reason at all to believe that this premise is true.

Similarly, from the fact that the non-existence of horrific suffering is antecedently likely given theism, it does not follow even inductively that, if God exists, then horrific suffering does not occur. To draw that conclusion, one would need to show, among other things, that the non-existence of horrific suffering is less likely on the assumption that God does not exist than it is on the assumption that God exists. And showing that is very difficult since, as I will explain in more detail later, it is far from clear what exactly one is assuming to be true when one assumes that the statement "God exists" is false.

Bayesian Arguments from Evil

Problems like these make me doubt the viability of MT arguments. I'm much more optimistic about what I call "Bayesian" arguments from evil. (I call them this because the structure of the reasoning in these arguments can be analyzed, made precise, and defended by appealing to a theorem of mathematical probability called "Bayes' theorem.") I'm more optimistic about these arguments for at least two reasons. First, they conclude only that *other evidence held equal*, theism is very probably false and thus they do not presuppose without justification that there is no offsetting or even outweighing evidence in support of theism. Second, they avoid anything resembling the bogus tollens fallacy by explicitly comparing the probability of certain facts about evil given theism to the probability of those facts given some relevant alternative hypothesis. Bayesian arguments from evil (e.g., Draper 1989) have the following structure:

1   We know that E obtains.
2   E is antecedently many times more probable given some alternative hypothesis H to theism than it is given theism.
So, 3 E reports strong evidence favoring H over theism (i.e., our knowledge that E obtains increases the ratio of the probability of H to the probability of theism many-fold).
4   H is at least as plausible as theism (i.e., H is at least as probable as theism independent of all evidence for and against theism and H).
So, 5   Other evidence held equal, theism is very probably false.

Like MT arguments, Bayesian arguments from evil vary depending on which facts about evil are used to replace the variable E. Unlike MT arguments, however, Bayesian arguments also vary because different hypotheses are chosen to replace the variable H. One natural choice is, of course, atheism. William Rowe (1996), for instance, makes this choice in his most recent argument from evil, which explicitly appeals to Bayes' theorem. Consider, then, the following Bayesian argument from evil:

1   We know that horrific suffering exists.
2   The existence of horrific suffering is antecedently many times more probable on the assumption that God does not exist (atheism) than it is on the assumption that God exists (theism).
So, 3   The existence of horrific suffering is strong evidence favoring atheism over theism.
4   Atheism is at least as plausible as theism.
So, 5   Other evidence held equal, theism is very probably false.

This argument has many virtues. The reasoning is tight and two of its three premises seem unquestionably true. It does, however, have one major flaw. Its second premise is not obviously true and it is hard to see how one could successfully argue for its truth. Good reasons can, I believe, be given for believing that horrific suffering is unlikely given theism, but it is difficult to show that horrific suffering is any less unlikely given atheism. This is difficult to show because the probability of horrific suffering given atheism depends on what is likely to be true on the assumption that theism is false. For example, if theism is false, then perhaps polytheism is true. Or maybe panentheism is true. Or perhaps pantheism. Or naturalism. Indeed, if theism is false, then perhaps what is true is some non-theistic form of supernaturalism that can't even be understood by human beings because of their cognitive limitations. The point is that, even if we could agree on a list of serious possibilities and restrict our attention to those (estimating the probability of horrific suffering given atheism by taking a probability weighted average of the probability of horrific suffering on each of those possibilities) the calculation of the probability of horrific suffering given atheism would be prohibitively complicated. Rowe (1996) cleverly tries to avoid this problem by using an evidence statement ("no good we know of justifies God in permitting [horrific evils]") that is entailed by atheism (and hence has a probability of one given atheism), but Otte (2003) argues convincingly that this strategy violates the requirement of total evidence. (If atheism is not known to be true and yet entails Rowe's evidence statement, then, although we know that Rowe's evidence statement is true, there must be a more specific evidence statement than Rowe's that we also know to be true and which, given the requirement of total evidence, should be used instead of Rowe's evidence statement.)

I submit, then, that the best way to formulate a Bayesian argument from evil is to use a specific alternative hypothesis to theism instead of the general hypothesis that theism is false. This will make the second premise more manageable, although the third premise – step (4) – will as a result be more difficult to defend. The last argument from evil I will formulate in this chapter, the argument I earlier referred to as "my argument," will use (metaphysical) naturalism as the alternative hypothesis to which theism is compared. Naturalism is the hypothesis that natural entities have only natural causes. It does not deny the existence of non-natural entities, but it does deny the existence of "supernatural" entities (e.g., God) – that is, it denies the existence of non-natural entities that affect natural entities. By "natural" entities, I mean physical entities and entities that are either ontologically reducible to physical entities or are caused by physical entities. By "physical entities," I mean entities of the sorts studied in the physical sciences (e.g., atoms) along with any as yet undiscovered entities whose behavior is governed by the fundamental laws of physics. The evidence statement I will use in my argument from evil is the following statement (I'll call it "F"), which reports some known facts about the flourishing, languishing, and suffering of terrestrial organisms:

> F: For a variety of biological and ecological reasons, organisms compete for survival, with some having an advantage in the struggle for survival over others; as a result, many organisms, including many sentient beings, never flourish because they die before maturity, many others barely survive, but languish for most or all of their lives, and those that reach maturity and flourish for much of their lives usually languish in old age; in the case of human beings and probably some non-human animals as well, languishing often involves intense or prolonged suffering.

This yields the following Bayesian argument from evil:

     1 We know that F is true.
     2 F's truth is antecedently many times more probable given naturalism than
        it is given theism.
So, 3 F reports strong evidence favoring naturalism over theism.
     4 Naturalism is at least as plausible as theism.
So, 5 Other evidence held equal, theism is very probably false. (Draper
        2007)

The first premise of this argument is clearly true, but the other two premises – steps (2) and (4) – need to be supported by additional arguments.

The Plausibility of Naturalism and Theism

Let me begin with the premise that naturalism is at least as plausible as theism. Philosophers do not agree on how such a premise should be interpreted in the context of a Bayesian argument. Some philosophers believe that plausibility judgments are purely subjective. We just find ourselves taking some hypotheses seriously while dismissing others out of hand. The former we judge worthy of being tested by evidence, while the latter we ignore. If this is correct, then my argument from evil may still be sound relative to the epistemic situations of those who take naturalism seriously (which includes most contemporary philosophers, including many philosophers who are theists), while it won't be sound relative to the epistemic situations of others for whom naturalism is not a live option.

Other philosophers believe that plausibility judgments are objective. For example, my own view is that the plausibility of a hypothesis should be equated with its intrinsic (epistemic) probability – the probability it has simply by virtue of what it asserts and what we know about the world by means of rational intuition. The intrinsic probability of a hypothesis depends primarily on its scope and simplicity (cf. Swinburne 2001: ch. 4). Scope is a measure of how much a hypothesis purports to tell us about the world that we do not already know by rational intuition. Relative to certain practical goals, the larger the scope of a hypothesis, the better; but relative to the goal of truth, large scope is a vice rather than a virtue. For the more that a hypothesis says that (for all we know by rational intuition) *might be* false, the more likely it is to say something that *is* false, and hence the less likely it is to be true. A hypothesis can be simple in more than one way, and simplicity can make a hypothesis better just by making it easier to use and understand. In this context, however, the simplicity of a hypothesis should be understood to be a measure of the degree of *objective* uniformity that the hypothesis attributes to the world. Understood in this way, it is more than a merely pragmatic theoretical virtue. It is a sign of truth. If plausibility is a function of scope and simplicity, then it would seem that naturalism is at least as plausible as theism, because the scope of naturalism is at least as small as the scope of theism and naturalism is in one important respect a simpler hypothesis than theism.

Concerning scope, notice that naturalism claims only that natural entities all *lack* supernatural causes. Theism, on the other hand, claims not only that all natural entities *possess* (proximate or remote) supernatural causes, but also that they share a single ultimate supernatural cause (at least a necessary cause if not a sufficient one), and further that this supernatural cause is omnipotent, omniscient, and morally perfect. Because of the great specificity of these claims, it is safe to conclude that naturalism does not have greater scope than theism. Of course, some (though not all) theists maintain that God *necessarily* exists, but that won't decrease the scope of theism and thus won't raise the intrinsic probability of theism because we don't know by rational intuition that God's existence is necessary.

Concerning simplicity, naturalism attributes one sort of uniformity to the world, namely, that the causes of all natural entities are themselves natural. Theism, on the other hand, postulates a supernatural realm in addition to the natural realm, just as Aristotle postulated a celestial world composed of quintessence in addition to a terrestrial one made of earth, water, air, and fire. This made Aristotle's physics less simple and so less likely to be true than any physics that could explain the facts equally well without dividing reality into two fundamentally different realms. Similarly, naturalism, by virtue of its simpler picture of reality, starts out with a higher probability than theism prior to considering the evidence for and against each. Of course, this conclusion is more than my Bayesian argument needs. What is needed, and what turns out to be a fairly modest claim if scope and simplicity are the correct criteria for assessing plausibility, is that theism not be more plausible than naturalism.

The Antecedent Probability of Evil

Now let us turn to the second premise of my Bayesian argument from evil, which states that F is antecedently much more probable on the assumption that naturalism is true than on the assumption that theism is true. The word "antecedently" is crucial here. What this means is that the probabilities being compared are not "all things considered" probabilities. Instead, an abstraction is being made. Premise (2) claims that, *independent of the observations and testimony upon which our knowledge specifically of F is based*, F is much more probable given naturalism than it is given theism. When assessing the probabilities in premise (2), however, one should take into account most of what one knows, including that we live in a complex universe containing living things, some of which are conscious and others of which are self-aware. Some philosophers believe that such facts are evidence favoring theism over naturalism. Even if that is so, it is not relevant to the evaluation of premise (2) of the argument, but instead is taken into account by the clause "other evidence held equal" in the conclusion of the argument.

Given a correct understanding of what the second premise asserts, it may seem intuitively obvious that it is true. I suspect, however, that a few philosophers would maintain that plausible theistic explanations (theodicies) can be given of the facts reported by F, explanations that boost the probability of F given theism sufficiently to undermine this premise. A greater number of philosophers would reject the second premise on the grounds that we are in no position to compare the probability of F given theism to the probability of F given naturalism. This sort of position is widely referred to as "skeptical theism." Given the popularity of skeptical theism, appeals to premise (2) being "intuitively obvious" will simply not suffice. Supporting arguments are needed, and I will sketch one such argument. (A second argument based on evolutionary biology, as well as replies to several objections, can be found in Draper 2007.)

One might plausibly claim that suffering, when it contributes in a biologically appropriate way to the flourishing of a human being or animal, is not all that surprising on theism. From a theistic perspective, it makes sense to say that we are *supposed* to suffer in this way. That's just the sort of organisms we are. But from a theistic perspective, it also makes perfectly good sense to say that sentient organisms are *supposed* to flourish. (Or at least this would make perfectly good sense if we did not already know that countless sentient beings do not flourish.) The argument for this has three premises. First, almost all sentient organisms are *capable* of flourishing in biologically realistic circumstances. This is proven by the fact that many do flourish and by the fact that the differences between those that do flourish and those that do not are in almost all cases relatively small. Second, sentient organisms have a good – they certainly can be benefited or harmed – and the failure to flourish is incompatible with achieving that good. Third, a God, being perfect in moral goodness, could not care more deeply about sentient beings achieving their good, and being perfect in power and knowledge, could not be better positioned to ensure that sentient beings achieve their good. Therefore, the fact, reported by F, that countless living organisms, including sentient beings, never flourish at all and countless others flourish only briefly is extremely surprising given theism. It is not what one would expect to find in a living world created by a being who qualifies for the title "God."

This argument makes two key assumptions. First, it assumes that, *other moral considerations held equal*, a wise and morally perfect creator would strongly prefer that every sentient being flourish for a significant portion of its life. Second, it assumes that the truth of the first assumption lowers the antecedent probability of F given theism. So-called "skeptical theists" may be inclined to challenge these assumptions on the grounds that it is *possible* that a God would have good moral reasons unknown to us to permit sentient organisms to languish. But this possibility only proves that claims about what a God would prefer must be prefaced with "other moral considerations held equal." It is also possible, *and no less likely*, that a God would have good moral reasons unknown to us to *prevent* sentient organisms from languishing – reasons in addition to the reasons that are known to us. Thus, contrary to what many "skeptical theists" seem to believe, the probability of F given theism will depend largely on the moral reasons concerning F that we know about, not on the ones we don't know about, and the reasons we know about lower the probability of F given theism and lower it significantly. Since no parallel reasons lower the probability of F given naturalism, it follows that F is much more probable given naturalism than it is given theism.

Conclusion

Although we have briefly examined the premises of my Bayesian argument from evil, we haven't yet looked at the two inferences in the argument. Bayes' theorem supports the inference from steps (1) and (2) to step (3) so long as the claim that F reports strong evidence favoring naturalism over theism is understood to mean that our knowledge of F increases the ratio of the probability of naturalism to the probability of theism many-fold. Of course, if theism were more probable than naturalism independent of all evidence, then the conclusion – step (5) – of my argument would not follow from its sub-conclusion, step (3). But step (4) of the argument states that this is not the case, that in fact naturalism is at least as plausible as theism. Therefore, step (5) follows from steps (3) and (4): in the absence of additional evidence besides F that *favors* theism over naturalism, theism is *very* probably false. Notice that it also follows that in the absence of additional evidence besides F that *strongly* favors theism over naturalism, theism is *probably* false.

In closing I should note that I do not mean to claim, even implicitly, that no offsetting or even outweighing evidence in support of theism exists. Indeed, I happen to believe that there is strong offsetting inferential evidence favoring theism over naturalism. Nor do I mean to claim that this other evidence must be *inferential*. A direct experience apparently of God, if one were fortunate enough to have one, could conceivably provide counterbalancing evidence. Of course, assessing one's *total* relevant evidence is an enormous and difficult task, but those who defend evidential arguments from evil instead of logical ones cannot avoid it – not if they hope to draw a categorical conclusion about the existence of God.

Questions for Reflection

Consider the following MT arguments for God's existence:

If God does not exist, then morality is not objective.
Morality is objective.
So, God exists.

If God does not exist, then the world contains no complex order.
The world does contain complex order.
So God exists.

1 What other MT arguments for God's existence can you think of?
2 Should MT arguments for God's existence be understood as logical arguments or as evidential arguments?
3 Do MT arguments for God's existence have weaknesses similar to the (alleged) weaknesses of MT arguments from evil?
4 Construct the most convincing Bayesian argument against naturalism that you can. Is it as convincing as Draper's Bayesian argument from evil against theism?
5 Skeptical theists doubt that that we are in a position to make the probability judgments upon which Bayesian arguments from evil depend. Suppose they are right. Does that also undermine the viability of probabilistic arguments supporting God's existence?

References

Alston, W. (1991) "The Inductive Argument from Evil and the Human Cognitive Condition." *Philosophical Perspectives* 5, 29–67.

Draper, P. (1989) "Pain and Pleasure: An Evidential Problem for Theists." *Nous* 23, 331–50.

—— (2007) "Natural Selection and the Problem of Evil." In P. Draper (ed.), *God or Blind Nature? Philosophers Debate the Evidence*. Forthcoming on the Secular Web at the following URL: www.infidels.org.

Mackie, J. L. (1955) "Evil and Omnipotence." *Mind* 64, 200–212.

Otte, R. (2003) "Rowe's Probabilistic Argument from Evil." *Faith and Philosophy* 19, 147–71.

Phillips, D. Z. (2004) *The Problem of Evil and the Problem of God*. London: SCM Press.

Pike, N. (1963) "Hume on Evil." *Philosophical Review* 72, 180–97.

Plantinga, A. (1974) *The Nature of Necessity*. Oxford: Clarendon Press.

Rowe, W. L. (1979) "The Problem of Evil and Some Varieties of Atheism." *American Philosophical Quarterly* 16, 335–41.

—— (1986) "The Empirical Argument from Evil." In R. Audi and W. J. Wainwright (eds.), *Rationality, Religious Belief, and Moral Commitment*. Ithaca, NY: Cornell University Press.

—— (1996) "The Evidential Argument from Evil: A Second Look." In D. Howard-Snyder (ed.), *The Evidential Argument From Evil*. Bloomington, IN: Indiana University Press.

Schellenberg, J. L. (2000) "Stalemate and Strategy: Rethinking the Evidential Argument from Evil." *American Philosophical Quarterly* 37, 405–19.

Swinburne, R. (2001) *Epistemic Justification*. Oxford: Clarendon Press.

Further Reading

Howard-Snyder, D. (ed.) (1996) *The Evidential Argument From Evil*. Bloomington, IN: Indiana University Press. (A significant collection of papers on the evidential argument from evil, skeptical theism, and theodicy.)

Hume, D. (1779) *Dialogues Concerning Natural Religion*. Various publishers. (A classic work by a philosophical giant, full of important insights on the design argument, the argument from evil, and the relationship between the two.)

Pike, N. (ed.) (1964) *God and Evil: Readings on the Theological Problem of Evil*. Englewood Cliffs, NJ: Prentice-Hall. (An excellent collection of papers primarily on the logical argument from evil.)

Rowe, W. L. (ed.) (2001) *God and the Problem of Evil*. Oxford: Blackwell. (Small and yet remarkably comprehensive, covering both logical and evidential arguments as well as skeptical theism, theodicies, and defenses.)

Swinburne, R. (1998) *Providence and the Problem of Evil*. Oxford: Clarendon Press. (A very ambitious defense of the free will theodicy.)

Chapter 11

A Naturalistic Account of the Universe

Quentin Smith

The Logical Impossibility of a Simple, Partless Being, Such as God, Causing Itself

The suggestion that the universe creates itself *ex nihilo* cannot be found in our current philosophical literature, and it has been a suggestion no atheist, agnostic, or theist has ventured to make. The reason this suggestion or claim has not been made is that it has seemed implausible and even obviously false. But the reason why this suggestion has not been made, and why it has seemed obviously false, is due to a surprisingly elementary mistake. Philosophers are used to thinking about complicated and complex theories, and they are used to finding mistakes in philosophical theories that are very subtle, sophisticated, and hard to detect. The elementary issues are often overlooked, and it is possible for a mistake to be "too elementary to be noticed."

What is this mistake? When wondering whether a self-caused being was possible or not, philosophers only thought about a simple being, a being without parts, and did not think about or develop a theory about the way in which a whole of parts can be self-caused. The contrast between the illogicality of a self-caused partless being and the logical coherence of holistic self-causation that requires a whole-part relation can be made manifest.

The statement or proposition that there is a self-caused simple, partless being is logically false (it is "viciously circular" in the logician's sense). If a being with no parts caused itself, a being we can call B, this means B caused B. This is a circular explanation, and this circularity is logically "vicious" (meaning it is illogical).

Theists have often stated that God is a simple, partless being, but they deny that God causes himself to exist. Theists and atheists have denied that anything can be an (efficient) cause of itself. Thomas Aquinas writes: "There is no case known (neither is it, indeed, possible) in which a thing is found to be the efficient cause of itself; for so it would be prior to itself, which is impossible" (Aquinas

1974: 1a.2.3, 489). Aquinas and others typically do not elaborate upon this problem, but presumably they do not mean *merely* that something cannot *temporally* precede itself, since they often conceive of God as timeless and they deny that God can cause himself (see Rowe 1998: 29–30) What, exactly, is the reason why God cannot cause himself?

There is one philosopher who is an exception to this tradition that God is not self-caused. Descartes claimed that God, although a simple, partless being, causes himself to exist. He did not mean that God, as a cause, exists in time and exists earlier than God, as an effect (which would imply the contradiction that God exists earlier than the first time at which he exists). Descartes meant that God timelessly or simultaneously causally sustains his own existence. In Descartes's terminology, God is the "efficient cause" (which approximately means *cause* in contemporary terminology) of his own existence:

> I have not said that it is impossible for anything to be its own efficient cause; for, although that statement is manifestly true when the meaning of efficient cause is restricted to those causes that are prior in time to their effects . . . it does not seem necessary to confine the term to this meaning in the present investigation. . . . If I did not believe that anything could be related to itself exactly as an efficient cause is related to its effect, so far should I be from concluding that any first cause existed. . . . [The first cause is] the cause of its own existence; such a cause I understand God to be. . . . Because He is the very Being who actually preserves Himself in existence, it seems possible to call Him without undue impropriety the *cause of His own existence*. (Descartes [1642] 1968: 13–14)

Descartes's claim that God causally sustains himself, that he is the cause of his own existence, is logically false, and this problem is more fundamental than any consideration or hypothesis that causes must temporally precede their effects. Causes are logically prior to their effects. What could this mean? The claim that God or any other being can be self-caused is often regarded as self-evidently or obviously logically fallacious, without the precise nature of the logical problem being explained. Even William Rowe, who has treated the issues of causation, God, and the universe at least as precisely as any other contemporary thinker, has noted that the problem about "priority" cannot merely be a problem about temporal priority, since Aquinas admits simultaneous causation, but that the problem is that "the cause" is "causally or perhaps metaphysically prior to it [the effect]" (Rowe 1998: 30). But what, exactly, does this mean? Since we shall explain the respect in which the universe is self-caused, it would be helpful to understand exactly why it is logically impossible for a simple, partless being, such as God, to be self-caused.

In fact, there are several logical problems with the concept of a self-caused Deity, but two of these problems involve arguments that will be relevant to the later discussion of a self-caused universe.

One reason why God cannot be self-caused is that God's *decision* to perform a causal act logically necessitates that God exists, such that God's existence is not causally necessitated by his *causal act* but is logically necessitated either by his *making a decision* to perform a causal act or by God *deciding* not to perform a causal act. Neither God nor anything else can make a decision to perform or not to perform some act unless it exists. This can be seen more clearly if we contrast two decisions. "God decides to cause something" implies "God exists" and "God decides not to cause something" also implies "God exists." This shows that God's existence is logically necessitated by God *deciding to* perform, or *deciding not to* perform, some causal act, which precludes his existence from being a possibility whose actualization is dependent upon and is a result of some *causal act he performs*.

I suggest the "causal or metaphysical priority" is not the priority of the *causal act* to the effect, since *it is logically impossible for there to be a causal act* whereby something simple causes its own existence. It is not logically possible for there to be God's act of causing God's existence and it is not logically possible to be something, the causal act, that is causally or metaphysically either prior or posterior to the act's effect, the existence of God. Rather, there is a *formal logical priority* of a *decision to perform or not perform some causal act* to God's existence in this sense: "God decides to perform some causal act" logically implies "God exists," and "God decides not to perform some causal act" also logically implies "God exists"; and yet "God exists" does not imply "God decides to perform some causal act" and "God exists" also does not imply "God decides not to perform some causal act." "God exists" is consistent with either decision, making God's decision about whether to perform or not to perform some causal act, not a consequence of God's causal activity, but a presupposition of God deciding to either perform or not perform some causal act. This is the contradiction in the idea of God causing himself to exist: "God causes himself to exist" implies the contradiction "God's existence is logically presupposed by God's causal acts and God's existence is not logically presupposed by God's acts but is a consequence of one of these causal effects." This shows that the idea of God or any other simple, partless being causing itself to exist is an explicit logical self-contradiction.

A second problem with the theory that God causes himself to exist is that a self-caused Deity would stand in an (allegedly) *causal* relation to himself, but this relation would be inconsistent with the logically necessary form of a causal relation. Suppose that a stone is thrown into a pond and that this causes a splash. The throwing of the stone is the cause C and the splash the effect E. A logically necessary form of this and any causal relation is illustrated by the example:

> If a stone is thrown into a pond (the cause C), then there must be a splash in the pond (the effect E).

Here the "must be" is not a logical necessity, but a causal necessity. It is also true that:

If there is a splash in the pond (effect E), there need not be a stone thrown into the pond. The splash could be caused by a branch falling into the pond (another cause C*).

In other words, the cause C causally necessitates the occurrence of the effect E. But E can occur without the cause C occurring and E could be the effect of some other cause C*. For any simple, partless being, be it God or some other being, this formal structure of a causal relation is violated. If we try to treat God as cause and effect, we have an explicit logical contradiction in the second sentence:

1   If God (the cause) causes God (the effect), then God (the effect) must exist.
2   But if the effect (God) exists, the cause (God) need not exist.

If we talk instead about God's *causal act* or God's *willing* or a divine volition, as the cause, and God's *existence* as the effect, then we have:

3   If God wills that God exist, then God must exist.
4   If God exists, there need not exist God's willing that God exists.

This last sentence ("If God exists, . . .") may not appear to express a logically self-contradictory proposition, but taken in the context of the total theory (e.g., Descartes's total theory), it does express a contradiction. If God is self-caused, then being self-caused would not be an accidental or contingent feature of God, but would be a logically necessary feature. Being self-caused would belong to the essence of God, such as being omnipotent. If we adopt a certain theory of names, we will say that the name "God" expresses the concept or sense expressed by the description, "the omnipotent, omniscience, perfectly free, self-caused, perfectly good being." Accordingly, the sentence "God exists but *is not causing* or willing himself to exist" expresses a logically self-contradictory proposition, since "God" expresses the concept of a being that *causes* itself to exist.

A self-caused Deity is a self-contradiction, since the relation called "causes itself to exist" has a structure that is logically incompatible with the formal logical structure of a causal relation. In the (alleged) divine self-causation relation, the existence of the effect not merely necessitates the existence of the particular cause, but this necessitation is a logical necessitation – a much stronger modality than the necessity that belongs to the causal relation. This cause also *logically* necessitates this effect; so the relation between them is one of logical equivalence. They are not causally related but logically related, much as there is a relation of logical equivalence between having three angles and being a closed three-sided figure.

There are many sorts of logic systems, so it should be specified that in modern logic this would be in the terminology of some philosophers of religion a "narrow logical necessity," i.e., a formal logical necessity of the sort in the "predicate logic" formulated by Frege, Russell, and Whitehead. But prior to the twentieth century or late nineteenth century, this would be a formal logical necessity in Aristotelian logic, and would be what Kant called analytic necessity and Hume called a statement about "relations among ideas." A statement that is formally logically necessary is true by virtue of its form (e.g., the statement: a whole of parts is not a partless being) and its negation is an explicit logical contradiction (a whole of parts is a partless being). This needs to be emphasized since, beginning about 1970, many philosophers began calling non-formal necessities or synthetic necessities "broadly logical necessities." I have elsewhere argued that a clearer terminology would reserve the term "logical" for formal logical necessities or possibilities and use "metaphysical necessities or possibilities" for non-formal necessities, which are often controversial, such as the (alleged) metaphysical necessity: *Jane is composed of cells whose DNA has the chemical structure X, Y, Z.*

This argument that God (or any other simple being) cannot cause himself to exist has more than passing interest. We will see in the next sections that an argument of the same form also shows that God cannot cause the universe to exist. But first, let us contrast this illogical self-causation relation that would obtain if a simple, partless being "caused itself," with the logical self-causation relation which would obtain if a complex being, a whole of parts, caused itself to exist.

The Logical Possibility of a Whole of Parts, Such as the Universe, Causing Itself

In contrast to God or any other simple, partless being, complex beings, wholes of parts, can cause themselves to exist. Since there are distinct beings or particulars in a whole, these distinct particulars may form a causal sequence, which each particular being caused by an earlier particular. I shall argue that there is at least one of these wholes, the whole universe W, that causes itself to exist. The statement that a whole, which we will call "W," creates itself is not a viciously circular causal explanation of the form "B creates B," which is the form applicable to a simple, partless being. Rather it is of the form "Each part of the whole, W, is caused by an earlier part of W, and the existence of the whole, W, that is composed of these parts is logically necessitated by the existence of its parts." Here "W" is the name of the single whole that is composed of the many parts; that is, W is composed of all these parts, but W is not itself a part of itself.

If one conceived wholes as sets, W would be an "improper subset of itself," but we shall consider the universe as a concrete aggregate (if only for the reason that if the universe is a set, it is an abstract object and cannot be caused by God or anything else, making the issue of whether this set is caused by God or uncaused to be based on a false premise: that a set is something that can be caused by anything).

The parts of the whole, W, are particulars or individual things and the sort of logical necessity that obtains between them and the whole is *de re* logical necessity (from *res* meaning "thing"). *De re* logical necessity is objective necessity of concrete things or structures of things that is intrinsic to the universe itself and does not belong merely to our ways of thinking about things or merely to abstract objects, such as propositions. *De re* necessity is the necessity of things possessing certain properties or standing in certain relations. The existence of the concrete whole W stands in a relation to the existence of the concrete parts of W, being logically necessitated by the existence of the parts.

By contrast, *de dicto* necessity is the necessity of a sentence (from *dicto* meaning "to be written down") or proposition being true. The proposition, "The parts of the whole, W, exist," logically implies the proposition, "The whole, W, exists." Accordingly, this proposition is necessarily true, "If the parts of the whole, W, exist, then the whole, W, exists."

The logical problems that arose in the attempt to conceive of God as self-caused are due to the fact that God is traditionally conceived as a simple being, as having no parts. If God were a whole, W, composed of parts, then God could be a self-caused being if each part of God is caused by another part of God. The existence of all these parts of God would logically necessitate the existence of the whole, W, that is composed of all these parts, where W is God. However, theists reject the idea that God is a whole composed of parts; they traditionally think that God is a simple, partless being and that the existence of God is uncaused. But the universe is a whole of parts; the universe consists of successive states of the universe and each of these states is caused by earlier states. The universe, in fact, will turn out to be the clearest example of a self-caused whole of parts.

There are two ways to argue that the universe is self-caused, dependent on whether one is a realist about individual wholes (i.e., one who believes that there is an individual or particular, the individual whole W, that is distinct from all of the successive states of the universe that are the parts of W). If one is a reductionist about wholes, then one will hold that there is no distinct individual, the whole, but that that "the whole W" is merely an abbreviation for "all the states."

Let us begin with a realist theory of wholes. In this case, "the universe W is self-caused" can be used in a way that is not illogical to express a true proposition, namely, that each part of W is sufficiently caused by earlier parts of W and the infinite existence or beginning to exist of W is logically necessitated by the existence of all of W's parts. The obtaining of this formal logical necessitation relation is the sufficient reason why the universe W exists. The traditional line of thinking about the cosmological argument for God's existence, going back at least to Leibniz and Clarke, begins with assumptions common to both theists and atheists. The theists and atheists agree that each state of the universe's existence is caused by earlier states of the universe's existence. Leibniz, Clarke and contemporary theists and atheists, such as Taylor, Swinburne, and Vallicella, observe that the whole universe, the whole W composed of these states, either is uncaused or is caused by God. Leibniz, for example, distinguishes between the extramundane reasons for the universe, the universe or aggregate, and the series of states that constitute this aggregate or whole: "The reasons of *the universe*, therefore, lie hidden in something extra mundane different from the chain of states or series of things, *the aggregate* of which constitutes *the universe*" (Leibniz [1697] 1951: 346, my emphasis). The universe is the aggregate or whole W that is composed of "the chain of states or series of things." We know why each state of the universe W exists; it is caused by earlier states. But why does the particular that is the whole of these, the particular W, exist?

Richard Taylor forms the issue clearly. He says "the world" is the whole of all existing things (except God), states, and states about the world W: "But it is at least very odd and arbitrary to deny of this existing world the need for any sufficient reason, whether independent of itself or not, while presupposing that there is a reason for every other thing that exists" (Taylor 1963: 87). Taylor, Leibniz, and others are realists about the whole W. There really is a particular being, W, that is distinct from all the particular states that compose it.

A reductionist theory of wholes denies this. Accordingly, there is a second kind of argument for the thesis that the universe is self-caused. This argument is called the *Reductionist Argument* since the whole is reduced to and identified with all the states and "W" is used merely as an *abbreviation* of "all the states that exist" or other plural phrases that refer to all the states. There is no individual W that is distinct from all the states, and whose existence is either uncaused, or caused by God, or logically necessitated by the existence of parts. In the Reductionist Argument, the universe is "self-caused" in the sense that the universe is not distinct from all the states and each state is causally explained by earlier states.

Below, I first state the Realist Argument for a self-caused universe and then the Reductionist Argument.

The Realist Argument for a Self-Caused Universe

Let us begin by adopting a realist theory of wholes. This argument supposes that there is a whole, an individual existent W, that is different from all the parts of the whole. In this case, the explanation of why the universe W exists is that its existence is logically necessitated by the existence of its parts, each of which is causally explained in terms of earlier parts.

W, the whole of all the parts, is not *causally* explained by all the parts, since its parts do not *cause* it to exist. Rather, the existence of all the parts of the whole W logically necessitate the existence of the whole W and in this sense the existence of the whole W is logically explained by the existence of the parts. It is a logical truth that if particulars actually stand in a relation to a whole W, a relation of actually being parts of W, then if these particulars actually exist, then W actually exists. Once the existence of each of these parts is causally explained, the existence of the whole is provided an explanation: the existence of the whole is logically necessitated by the existence of its parts, and each of its parts is explained by being causally necessitated by earlier parts. Why does the whole exist? It exists because its existence is logically necessitated by the existence of its parts, each of which is causally explained by earlier parts.

If each part (state of the universe) is caused by earlier parts, then the explanation of the existence of *each part* is that it is caused by earlier parts. But what explains the existence of *the whole universe W*? The answer is not, as theists think, that it is caused by an external cause, God. Nor are atheists correct in saying there is no explanation for its existence. Swinburne says this whole W is a set, but since sets are abstract objects and cannot be caused, we can charitably interpret him as meaning some sort of concrete whole or aggregate. Swinburne says that the "set" or whole of past states of the universe does need an external cause: "if the only causes of its past states are prior past states, *the set* of past states as a whole will have no cause and so no explanation" (Swinburne 1991: 124, my italics). Swinburne argues that there will be an explanation, however, if God causes the whole W of past states (p. 124).

I disagree. Rather, there is an explanation of W's existence in terms of the logic of wholes and their parts (this logic is called "mereology"). The whole universe W exists because each of its parts is caused to exist by an earlier part, and all of W's parts cannot be *parts of the whole W* unless the whole W exists. "All of the parts of the whole W exist" logically implies "the whole W exists."

The whole W cannot have an external cause, such as a Deity, since if its parts exist, that logically implies the whole exists, and no external cause can have any effect on the existence of something, the whole W, whose existence is logically prior to the causal activity of any external cause, such as God's causal activity. In fact, there cannot be an external cause of the whole W, since such a cause would imply a logical contradiction of the same sort as we discussed in explaining why God cannot be self-caused. First, note that the statement "there exists all the parts of W" logically implies "the whole W exists." Now note that, "there exists all the parts of W and God exists and causes something" entails "the whole W exists," *and, furthermore*, "there exists all the parts of W and God exists and does not cause something" *also entails* "the whole W exists." This shows that the part of both statements that entails "the whole W exists" is "all the parts of W exist" and the added clauses about God causing something or not causing something is logically irrelevant to the truth of "the whole W exists." W's existence cannot be an effect of God's act of causation since in every logically possible situation in which God exists and all the parts of W exist, "all the parts of W exist and God does not cause anything" entails "W exists." Thus, there is no logically possible situation in which God's causal activity is necessary for W's existence and there is no logically possible situation in which God's causal activity is sufficient for W's existence.

Since God is defined as "the cause of the universe," and God does not cause the universe, it follows that God does not exist. The positive result of the inquiry is that the logical certainty that *the universe as a whole has a cause* that philosophers had before Hume's criticism of arguments for an external cause is regained. We can now have a logically certain answer to the question: What caused the universe to exist?

The "logically demonstrable" answer – or "logically demonstratable," as philosophers from Aquinas to Leibniz and Berkeley phrased it – is that the universe (instead of being caused by an external cause) caused itself to exist, but not in the illogical sense applied to simple, partless beings, but in the logical sense applied to a complex being, the universe as a whole of successive states.

The Reductionist Argument for a Self-Caused Universe

If we adopt the theory that there is no individual W, no universe that is a whole that is a distinct existent from all of its parts, then the reason for the universe's existence cannot be that W's existence is entailed by the existence of W's parts. There are no parts and there is no whole in the sense of "parts" and "whole" that I used in the argument based on a realist theory of wholes. Consequently, either there is a different sort of sufficient reason for the universe's existence or else there is no reason at all.

Hume and others were mistaken when they said that once each part of any whole is explained, the whole is explained. But whether or not Hume was mistaken is irrelevant to the Reductionist Argument for a self-caused universe, since this argument implies that the universe is not the whole W and that there are not parts of the whole W. There is no individual, the universe W, which is a distinct existent from all of the parts of this individual. Rather, "W" or "the universe," does not refer to an individual, a whole that is distinct from all of its parts, but is used as an abbreviation of "all the states" or "S1 and S2 and S3, and all the other states" or "S1, S2, S3, etc.," where "S1" is a name of some state.

Each state includes the maximal three-dimensional space that exists at a time t, and includes all the other contingent concrete beings that exist at the time t, such as galaxies and organisms *as they are at the time t*. The sentence "S is a part of the universe" is stipulated (in the Reductionist Argument) to have the sense expressed by "S is one of all the states."

The states have various ordering relations among themselves. For example, each instantaneously existing three-dimensional (3D) space, each different maximal 3D space at each different time t, has a wider radius than all earlier 3D spaces, which is one way of suggesting a cosmological theory that space (or space-time) has been expanding since the Big Bang 15 billion years ago. Accordingly, we can have a consistent theory if we adopt the convention or stipulation that "the universe" does not refer to a distinct, individual existent, but is instead an abbreviation of "all the cosmic states." If the existence of each state has a sufficient reason by virtue of being caused by earlier states, then each state has a sufficient, causal explanation for its existence and there is no state that is either uncaused or that has an external or divine cause of its existence.

I have adopted the convention that "the universe" is an abbreviation of such plural expressions as "S1 and S2 and S3 and so on." There is no logical or empirical contradiction or problem that results from adopting this convention and one could argue by Ockham's razor – "do not postulate any more entities than is necessary" – that since there is no need to postulate an individual whole W, we should not posit an individual W and instead stipulate that "W" is an abbreviation of "all the states."

But there is no decisive reason to choose between the reductionist and realist theories of wholes. The Realist Argument could be justified by saying that second- and higher-order predicate logic is valid and these imply the existence of sets, which are distinct from their members. This is not a decisive argument, since one could not agree that this logic is valid or applicable to the universe; alternatively, one could provide the syntactics of higher-order predicate logic with a semantics that do not imply that there exist sets or wholes of any kind. One could postulate sets on the grounds that physics postulates them (this is W. V. O. Quine's argument). A set is an abstract object and since abstract objects cannot enter into causal relations, a set cannot be caused by God or some other external cause. One could solve this problem by substituting a concrete whole for a set, perhaps even a "sum" in the sense of mereological essentialism, which largely follows the same logic as sets except the "sums" are concrete wholes. Or one could argue on other grounds that the universe is a concrete aggregate, a whole, that is distinct from all its parts (Smith 1986).

The Big Bang Conceived as the Process of the Universe Causing Itself to Begin to Exist

Some philosophers may object that our universe cannot be self-caused, since current science shows that our universe *began to exist*. This scientific theory, called "Big Bang cosmology," holds that our universe (space and time, as well as all matter and energy) began to exist about 15 billion years ago in an "explosion" called "the Big Bang." Some philosophers allege that this theory does not permit a conception of the Big Bang as an event or process of the universe originally creating itself *ex nihilo* or causing itself to begin existing. It seems to me, however, that this allegation by some philosophers is made on the very general grounds that no universe can cause itself to begin to exist. They do not address the specific nature of the universe's beginning that is described by Big Bang cosmology. This is the key issue, since the very concept of the beginning of the universe in Big Bang cosmology, the concept of the universe's beginning in terms of *a Big Bang singularity*, implies (without additional metaphysical premises) that the universe's beginning to exist is self-caused.

It is the assumption of both atheists and theists that if Big Bang cosmology is true, either (1) the universe began to exist 15 billion years ago *without a cause* of its beginning, or else (2) there is a cause *external* to the universe that caused the universe to begin to exist. This external cause is usually identified with God. However, as I have suggested, there is a third alternative, (3) *the universe caused itself to begin to exist* and this third alternative is the one that Big Bang cosmology implies; the universe posited by Big Bang cosmology is the sort of whole that involves holistic, *self-initiating, self-causation.*

The crucial idea in Big Bang cosmology is that the Big Bang is a "singularity": To say that its beginning is a "singularity" implies that the universe begins to exist, but there is no first instant $t = 0$ at which it begins. The *cosmic singularity* is a hypothetical time $t = 0$ at which all the laws of nature, space, and time break down. The first instant $t = 0$ is hypothetical or merely imaginary because if it did exist, it would be a physically and logically impossible state, due to the breakdown of all laws, even the laws required for time to exist. If a state did exist at $t = 0$, it would have logically impossible features such as millions of tons of three-dimensional matter fitting inside a zero-dimensional point. This breakdown at the hypothetical $t = 0$ implies that there is no first instant $t = 0$ of the finitely old time-series, and it implies that each instant is preceded by earlier instants. An instant is a time that is instantaneous or has zero-duration. An interval is a time that is temporally extended and has a duration of a certain length, such as one hour or one minute. Since there is a Big Bang singularity, there is no instant $t = 0$ that is the first instant of the earliest interval in each sequence of temporal intervals of some length, such as a sequence of (non-overlapping) hours, a sequence of minutes, a sequence of seconds, etc. Before any instant in an earliest hour, minute, or second in one of these sequences, there is an infinite (continuum-many) number of other instants. Formulated in terms of instantaneous states of the universe, this means that before each instantaneous state of the universe, there are other instantaneous states, and each instantaneous state of the universe is caused by earlier instantaneous states. Accordingly, the universe causes itself to begin to exist in the sense that it began a finite number of years ago, say 15 billion years, but each instantaneous state in any earliest interval is caused to exist by earlier instantaneous states.

In terms of the Reductionist Argument for a self-caused universe, this means the universe causes itself to begin to exist in the sense that (1) each instantaneous state S is sufficiently caused by earlier states and (2) there are no instantaneous states that exist earlier than some *finite* number of equal-length, non-overlapping intervals. For example, each state is caused by earlier instantaneous states but no state exists earlier than 15 billion years ago.

In terms of the Realist Argument for a self-caused universe, this means that the states are parts of a whole, the individual W, and W causes itself to begin to exist in the sense that (1) each instantaneous part S of the whole W is sufficiently caused by earlier parts of W; (2) there are no instantaneous parts of the whole that exist earlier than some finite number of equal-length, non-overlapping intervals; and the existence of all these parts of the whole, W, entails the existence of the whole W.

Some contemporary theists, such as Burke (1984) and, most notably, Vallicella (2000), have argued that if the first instant $t = 0$ of the first second or minute after the Big Bang can be "deleted" (i.e., regarded as a non-existent), then the first instant of any second or minute can be deleted. This would allow one to say that any second or second-long process has no external cause, since (they allege) each of its instantaneous states would be caused by earlier instantaneous states that are internal to the second-long process. They say a cannonball's flying through the air could then be "causally explained" without referring to the relevant external event, the explosion of the gunpowder in the cannon, by saying that each instantaneous state of the ball's movement is caused by earlier instantaneous states of its movement, implying that the external event, the gunpowder explosion, is not the cause of the ball's movement.

Their mistake is failing to realize that the first second or first minute, in a maximal sequence of non-overlapping seconds or minutes, lacks a first instant $t = 0$ because of a unique circumstance, that there is a cosmic *singularity*. There is no cosmic singularity at the present second or present year or at any time in the past 14 billion years or so. There is no cosmic singularity either within the present second, or at a boundary of the present second, or external to the present second but "nearby" a boundary of the present second. There are also no cosmic singularities at any of the instants or intervals these philosophers mention. Big Bang cosmology implies the minute- or second-long processes of the sort they mention, such as the flight of a cannonball, *must* (according to the laws of nature) have a first instant. The first instantaneous state of the cannonball's movement is externally caused by the explosion of the gunpowder. There is a causal process, such as the ignition of the gunpowder, that occupies an interval that is temporally prior to the interval that includes the process that is the effect of the causal process, the "effect process" being the motion of the cannonball. The effect is a process that begins at the first instant of the later interval. This first instant is the beginning point of the interval of the cannonball's motion; in other words, it is the beginning point of the process that is the effect of the causal process of the gunpowder being ignited and exploding. This instantaneous boundary point is not only the first instant of the effect process caused by the ignition of the gunpowder; it also limits the earlier causal process in the sense that every instant of this causal process occurs before this first instant of the effect process. This is a fundamental causal law of Big Bang cosmology and the causal law breaks down only at singularities. Accordingly, if we assume Big Bang cosmology is true and that the universe began to exist 15 billion years ago, then we can understand how the universe originally caused or created itself and thereafter continuously created itself.

Questions for Reflection

1   In Descartes's argument that a simple being, without any parts, is "self-caused," what the does the word "self" refer to? According to Descartes, what

is related by the relation of *causation*; that is, what is the *cause* and what is the *effect*? Is there a logical error in Descartes's argument and, if so, what is the error (or errors)?

2   On the realist theory of wholes, what does "self" refer to in the expression "the universe is self-caused"? On the realist theory of wholes, is the distinct individual W, which is the universe *as an individual whole*, a cause, an effect, or neither? What are the items that are related by the relation of "causation;" that is, what are the causes and effects?

3   On the reductionist theory of wholes, what does "self" refer to in the expression "the universe is self-caused"?

4   If the universe begins to exist in a "Big Bang," in what sense does the universe "cause itself to begin to exist"?

References

Aquinas, T. (1974) "Summa Theologica." In A. Hyman and J. Walsh (eds.), *Philosophy in the Middle Ages.* Indianapolis, IN: Hackett Publishing Company.

Burke, M. (1984) "Hume and Edwards on Explaining All Contingent Beings." *Australasian Journal of Philosophy* 62, 355–62.

Clarke, S. (1738) *A Discourse Concerning the Being and Attributes of God.* 9th edn. London: Knapton.

Descartes, R. ([1642] 1968) "Reply to Objections I." In *The Philosophical Works of Descartes*, trans. E. S. Haldane and G. R. T. Ross. Cambridge: Cambridge University Press.

Leibniz, G. ([1697] 1951) "On the Ultimate Origination of Things." In P. Wiener (ed.), *Leibniz Selections.* New York: Charles Scribner.

Martin, M. (ed.) (2003) *The Impossibility of God.* Amherst, NY. Prometheus Books.

Rowe, W. (1998) *The Cosmological Argument.* Fordham: Fordham University Press.

Smith, Q. (1986) *The Felt Meanings of the World: A Metaphysics of Feeling.* West Lafayette, IN: Purdue University Press.

—— (1997) *Ethical and Religious Thought in Analytic Philosophy of Language.* New Haven, CT: Yale University Press.

—— (2006) "The *Kalam* Cosmological Argument for Atheism." In M. Martin (ed.), *The Cambridge Companion to Atheism.* Cambridge: Cambridge University Press.

Smith, Q., and W. L. Craig (1993) *Theism, Atheism and Big Bang Cosmology.* Oxford: Clarendon Press.

Swinburne, R. (1991) *The Existence of God.* Rev. edn. Oxford: Clarendon Press.

Taylor, R. (1963) *Metaphysics.* Englewood Cliffs, NJ: Prentice Hall.

Vallicella, W. (2000) "Could the Universe Cause Itself To Exist?" *Philosophy* 75, 604–12.

Further Reading

Lewis, D. (1987) *On the Plurality of Worlds.* Princeton: Princeton University Press. (David Lewis argued that every universe that is logically possible *exists*; this is based on his theory that if something is possible, it exists.)

Post, J. (1986) *The Faces of Existence: A Non-Reductive Physicalism*. Ithaca, NY: Cornell University Press. (John Post denies that the universe causes itself, but he says the universe is "The First Cause" in the sense that the universe contains the basic explanatory factors in every chain of explanations.)

Spinoza, B. (1985) "The Ethics." In *The Collected Works of Spinoza*, ed. and trans. Edwin Curley. Princeton: Princeton University Press. (Spinoza believes that nature as a whole necessarily exists and that the causal successions of physical and mental particulars in nature are infinite.)

Witherall, A. (2002) *The Problem of Existence*. London: Ashgate Press. (Witherall's book explores various ways to explain the universe's existence.)

Part III

The Nature and Attributes
of God

Chapter 12

The Coherence of Theism

Charles Taliaferro

The concept of God in Judaism, Christianity, and Islam is the object of sustained philosophical inquiry. Substantial philosophical work (constructive and critical) has focused on each of the divine attributes: omniscience, omnipotence, essential goodness, perfection, omnipresence, eternity, necessary existence, incorporeality, simplicity (not containing parts), freedom, praiseworthiness, beauty, and impassibility (not being subject to passions). There are abundant arguments for the coherence or incoherence of each of these attributes taken separately and of different combinations of attributes (e.g. Can an omnipotent being be essentially good?). By "coherence" I mean both *intelligibility* (Does the attribute make sense? Is it understandable?) and *possible truth* (Is it possible that there is a being with the divine attributes?). Some of the best philosophers working today argue that theism is coherent (Swinburne 1977) while others who are of equal caliber argue that theism is incoherent (Martin and Monnier 2003). Philosophers of all persuasions have been drawn to the debate because the theistic concept of God includes many of the key elements in almost any philosophy (omniscience draws on the concepts of knowledge and truth, omnipotence draws on our concept of agency, and so on) and because of the rich history of the debate itself.

The stakes in this debate are significant. If some version of the ontological argument is plausible (as I believe it is), then if there is reason to believe theism is coherent, there is some reason to believe that it is true. If, on the other hand, there is good reason to believe that theism is incoherent, then any plausible arguments for God's existence are moot. I further suggest that debate over the coherence of theism cannot be lightly brushed aside on religious grounds in the name of mystery. If one can form no coherent concept of God whatsoever, how can one pray to or worship or seek to live in concord with God? Religious practices and ethics do not seem to require *perfect* comprehension and clarity, but it is difficult to see how theistic practices and ethics could be sustained if one thinks God is completely incomprehensible or one adopts the position that, given our concepts, the idea of God is incoherent.

There are three major sections that follow. The first takes up the question of methodology. Just how are we to debate matters of coherence and incoherence? The second section highlights the difficulties facing those who argue for the incoherence of theism, while the third section addresses arguments for the incoherence of a central theistic attribute, the incorporeality of God.

A Coherent Framework

One way to determine whether some state of affairs is coherent is to determine whether it can be consistently described, pictured, imagined, or thought. In some cases, visual imagination may be helpful, but there are others where our powers of conception are greater; for example, we may readily conceive of a closed geometric object with 1,000 sides, but there is reason to believe that we cannot see or picture one as a whole.

The case of a round square is immediately seen to be impossible because its description involves a contradiction. This involves a positive apprehension of the impossibility rather than inferring its impossibility because of the difficulty in picturing one. Other states of affairs are less easy to judge. *There being a barber who shaves all and only those who do not shave themselves* takes a few minutes to determine that it is impossible, but other states of affairs are more vexing, such as, *there being something spatially extended but not colored; time travel; wisdom not being a virtue; an event that is not caused.* Assessing the coherence of these requires enormous, comprehensive attention to one's background theories of the elements involved, e.g., one's philosophy of time, space, virtue, and causation (Taliaferro 2001).

When it comes to debating the coherence of theism there is what may be called the framework of debate. Consider the divine attribute of existing necessarily. Most classical theists hold that God exists necessarily; God is not a contingent being, nor is God's existence derived from contingent laws and forces. If one assumes that the only possible candidates for necessarily existing objects are numbers (the number seven exists necessarily) and one assumes God is not a number, then one has reason to believe God cannot possibly necessarily exist. Having a framework in which to debate whether some state of affairs is coherent is not a problem in the sense that it impedes debate. Indeed, one could not even begin a debate about the coherence of theism without a framework. Given the important role of a framework, much debate will have to be focused on the status of the frameworks itself. So, for example, a theistic debate over God's necessary existence may have to take up the challenge that there are all sorts of necessarily existing objects (in addition to numbers, there are properties, propositions, and logical laws) and the counatercharge that to rule out God as necessarily existing from the outset is *ad hoc.*

In surveying the work on the coherence of theism, I suggest that the chief end has not been what may be called *mere* coherence. A case of mere coherence would be one in which all debaters conclude that there is some remote reason to think theism might be coherent (or might be incoherent). Bertrand Russell once wrote:

> I do not pretend to be able to prove that there is no God. I equally cannot prove that Satan is a fiction. The Christian God may exist; so may the Gods of Olympus, or of ancient Egypt, or of Babylon. But no one of these hypotheses is more probable than any other: they lie outside the region of even probable knowledge, and therefore there is no reason to consider any of them. (Russell 1957: 44)

This illustrates the problem with fighting over mere coherence. I believe that most philosophical theists want to establish more than the thesis that theism is no less coherent than ancient Egyptian gods, whereas most philosophical atheists who argue for the incoherence of theism want to show that theism is (as Russell claims) not a real possibility; they want to cast theism as an intellectually indefensible means of describing or explaining reality, even if it is a bare metaphysical possibility.

The Flexibility of Theism

A key reason why it is difficult to establish the incoherence of theism is owing to what may be called the flexibility of theism. Theistic tradition has fostered a host of alternative conceptions of each of the divine attributes so that if one analysis falters, there are others. For example, to establish that the attribute of being omniscient is incoherent one would need to consider at least five different concepts of what is involved in omniscience (Kvanvig 1986). The evident, historical flexibility of theism may stem from the open-ended nature of divine attributes. Thus, to claim that God knows the world does not by itself commit one to a specific theory of knowledge, belief, justification, knowledge acquisition, and so on. In this section I consider the flexibility that is displayed in the debates over the attributes of omnipotence, omniscience, and eternity.

Omnipotence

Customary analyses of this attribute include the following: A being is omnipotent if it can do anything whatsoever. Alternatively: A being is omnipotent if it can do anything consistently describable. Or: A being is omnipotent if it can do anything possible. These analyses create the following problems for the God of Judaism, Christianity, and Islam. Arguably some of the following appear to be possible for humans to undertake but not possible for God: ride a bicycle, build a statue too heavy for one to lift, commit suicide, and unjustly steal from someone. Monotheistic tradition conceives of God as incorporeal and essentially good (God can do no injustice). There are some strategies philosophers have employed to propose that God *can* do these acts: Perhaps God can become physically incarnate (as Christians believe) or restrict God's own power (perhaps God can create a massive statue and then elect to limit God's power so that God could not then lift it) or perhaps God *can* do unjust acts but chooses not to. But even if successful, still other puzzle cases can arise. For example: Can God do something that was not done by God? This "puzzle" makes it impossible for God to perform, for if God does some act, God does that act (for such cases, see Martin 1990).

In reply, many theists today follow the older tradition of Anselm and Aquinas, which does not construe "omnipotence" as sheer power, but as a kind of divine or perfect power. Power alone is not, on this view, praiseworthy or an excellence. So, the divine attribute of omnipotence is better conceived of in terms of possessing maximal (or unsurpassable) excellent power. It is not an excellence worthy of an unsurpassably perfect being to be able to ride a bike, create something too heavy for God to lift, commit suicide, or unjustly steal from someone. This relocation of the attribute of omnipotence in a philosophy of perfection has been especially welcomed by T. V. Morris and others who are working in the Anslemian tradition: Anselm famously held that God is a being greater than which cannot be conceived (Taliaferro 1998).

Omniscience

Philosophers have developed several arguments claiming that it is an incoherent thesis that God is all-knowing. In this chapter we will consider two. Here is an argument against divine omniscience on the grounds of divine perfection. This is an objection to the coherence of theism that explicitly targets those who promote an Anselmian understanding of God.

1   A perfect being is not subject to change.
2   A perfect being knows everything.
3   A being that knows everything always knows what time it is.
4   A being that always knows what time it is is subject to change.
5   A perfect being is therefore subject to change.
6   A perfect being is therefore not a perfect being.
7   Ergo, there is no perfect being (Kenny 2003: 212).

Where might the flexibility of theism come in? Arguably, one may challenge the first premise. Perhaps, in the abstract, one might think that a perfect being should be like an unchanging abstract object, but when one takes seriously religious tradition, there seems little objection to the thesis that God as a loving, merciful creator, changes. For Christians, there was a time before the incarnation and a time afterwards. The occurrence of change was (so it may be argued) a manifestation of perfect love, rather than an undergoing of imperfect movement (e.g., Leftow 1991).

Consider a second puzzle: If God knows what you will freely do tomorrow (let's refer to it as x), it is the case now that you will indeed do x. But if it is true now that you will freely do x, how can you also be free not to do x? Arguably, freely doing some act seems to involve you having a *bona fide* ability either to do the act or not. Some philosophers conclude that omniscience is incompatible with future free action.

This puzzle has generated a colossal number of replies. One may (1) deny that freely doing x involves an ability to do otherwise (Frankfurt 1969); (2) simply deny that there is any puzzle at all because God's foreknowledge of what you will freely do is the result of what you will freely do (Linville 1993); (3) deny that God foreknows the future – that is, because God is eternal or atemporal, God's knowledge is from the standpoint of eternity, and the future is as it were present to God (Stump and Kretzmann 1981).

I do not suggest that each or any of these replies is decisive; I am only seeking to convey different routes that the critic of theism will need to show are incoherent before being able to dismiss omniscience. An increasingly popular alternative is to (4) deny that omniscience pertains to future free action. Several philosophers argue that God is temporal and that future free actions are underdetermined. It is not true *now* that you will do x in 2100 because you neither have nor have not done x in 2100. As such, future free action is not something that can be known by any being whatsoever. Omniscience is then analyzed along the lines of unsurpassable knowledge or greatest knowledge possible; a being is omniscient if and only if it has unsurpassable knowledge (Swinburne 1977).

Eternity

As already implied in discussing the first two attributes, when it comes to God's relationship to time, philosophers have generated several positions including (1) the thesis that God is eternal insofar as God is not temporally extended. On this view, there is no before, during, or after for God. God's being is like an eternal present (Leftow 1991). Alternatively, (2) philosophers have proposed that God is temporally extended but without origin or end (Wolterstorff 1982). On this view, God is said to be everlasting. Finally, (3) it has been argued that God was eternal (without temporal extension) and then underwent temporal extension at creation (Copan and Craig 2005).

Without going into details, this list of possible positions will seem like only a menu from which to begin looking into the enormous literature on each attribute. Fair enough: my point in this section is limited only to making the assertion that there are indeed many alternatives to consider, and so the task of establishing that, say, divine eternity is incoherent will need to take seriously more than one viewpoint. In the next section, I focus more on the details of the arguments and counterarguments.

Essential Physicalism and Theism

While the previous section offered an overview of the different strategies involved in the coherence of theism debate, this section focuses on a more sustained challenge where theism appears to be less flexible. Several philosophers have argued that the very idea of a non-physical divine reality is incoherent. Consider four challenges: an argument from bodily organs, an argument from causation, the emptiness of theistic explanations, and the problem of individuation.

An Argument from Bodily Organs: In theistic religion, God is said to hear and see. These activities require bodily organs. As a non-physical being, God lacks organs; it is therefore incoherent to suppose God can see or hear. Bede Rundle puts the argument as follows:

> Someone who insists that God, though lacking eyes and ears, watches him incessantly and listens to his prayers, is clearly not using "watch" or "listen" in a sense we can recognize, so while the words may be individually meaningful and their combination grammatical, that is as far as meaningfulness goes: what we have is an unintelligible use of an intelligible form of words. God is not of this world, but that is not going to stop us speaking of him as if he were. It is not that we have a proposition which is meaningless because unverifiable, but we simply misuse the language, making an affirmation which, in the light of our understanding of the words, is totally unwarranted, an affirmation that makes no intelligible contact with reality. (Rundle 2004: 11)

An Argument from Causation: On this view, for God to causally affect the cosmos, God must be spatially proximate in the cosmos. If God is non-physical, God is not spatial; hence God cannot causally affect the cosmos. Rundle develops this argument in the context of a discussion of miracles. Imagine that the theist claims to be able to give coherent content to the idea that God acts in the world by describing God's miraculously healing someone's limb. The case is dramatic (a limb is completely regenerated after being placed in water) but even in this case, Rundle maintains that it would not be coherent to suppose that God's action brought about the miracle.

> The difficulty with a supernatural agent is that it requires one foot in both domains, so to speak. To qualify as supernatural it must be distanced from any spatio-temporal character which would place it in our world, but to make sense to us as explanatory of changes therein it must be sufficiently concrete to interact with material bodies. . . . Grant that it has a physical dimension, and there is the risk that what appeared to be a miraculous cause will become a familiar and more or less comprehensible denizen of the natural world. Rule that out as a possibility and we appear to have nothing which would qualify as a potential perpetrator of terrestrial change. The regeneration of a limb immersed in water cries out for explanation, so if all the usual possibilities are exhausted, it seems only rational to look in less well-charted directions. However, an unshakeable belief that there must be an explanation does

not ensure that the proposed supernatural hypothesis genuinely counts as one, that in calling something a miracle we are doing anything more than attaching a label inscribed "Awaiting Explanation." (Rundle 2004: 27–8)

The Emptiness of Theistic Explanations: It has been argued that theistic explanations are senseless, without any comprehensible content. Rundle writes: "To claim that God said, 'Let there be light', leaves us not one jot the wiser as to how light came about" (Rundle 2004: 28). Jan Narveson develops the objection as follows:

> It ought to be regarded as a major embarrassment to natural theology that the very idea of something like a universe being "created" by some minded being is sufficiently mind-boggling that any attempt to provide a detailed account of how it might be done is bound to look silly, or mythical, or a vaguely anthropomorphized version of some familiar physical process. . . . It is plainly no surprise that details about just how [creation] was supposed to have happened are totally lacking. . . . For the fundamental idea is that some infinitely powerful mind simply willed it to be thus, and, as they say, Lo!, it was so! If we aren't ready to accept that as an explanatory description – as we should not be, since it plainly doesnt explain anything as distinct from barely asserting that it was done – then where do we go from here? On all accounts, we at this point meet up with mystery. (Narveson 2003: 94)

If Narveson and Rundle are right, theistic claims about God's action do not have sufficient content to count as coherent, possible explanations for the existence of the cosmos or any cosmic changes.

Consciousness and Individuation: D. Z. Phillips contends that it is incoherent to suppose that God, as pure consciousness, can have thoughts or an identity. His reasoning is basically that to have thoughts requires a social context of language-users and to have an identity, similarly, requires a world in which a person individuate herself in relations to others.

> "Consciousness" cannot yield to identity of its possessor. Consciousness cannot tell me who I am. If it is supposed to pick me out, I'd need to experience a number of consciousnesses, which is absurd. If, on the other hand, consciousness is taken to mean my awareness of the world, or "there being a world for me," others are in that world just as much as I am. It is a world in which I may see others in pain, or cry out in pain myself, for example. . . . But God has no neighbors. It may be thought that he could identify himself for himself with a self-authenticating definition: "I am this." But this reverts to the initial difficulty. It falls foul of [the] critique of a magical conception of signs, the view that the meaning of a word or sound is a power inherent in them, rather than something that is found in their application. (Phillips 2005: 457)

Do these objections secure the incoherence of theism?

A theist might invoke an appeal to flexibility by claiming that God is physical. After all, Thomas Hobbes took such a position; Grace Jantzen has defended the thesis that the world is God's body, and some philosophers have revived Newton's proposal that space itself (as opposed to spatial objects) is a divine attribute. But assuming one retains the core classical thesis that God is non-physical, a different strategy is called for. One can begin by challenging the framework of the debate.

While some of these philosophers who argue for the incoherence of theism due to the unintelligibility of incorporeality are not physicalists, they all seem to hold that it is impossible for there to be any agent or intelligent force that is non-physical. In this sense, they adopt what may be called essential physicalism. According to this theory, it is impossible for there to be anything non-physical, or at least, it is impossible for there to be a non-physical agent. While different forms of physicalism have a large following in the contemporary philosophical community, there are signs of tension. We have yet to resolve the perennial problem of how it could be that a state of consciousness could turn out to be the very same thing as brain and physiological process. Michael Lockwood puts the problem in stark terms:

> Let me begin by nailing my colours to the mast. I count myself a materialist, in the sense that I take consciousness to be a species of brain activity. Having said that, however, it seems to me evident that no description of brain activity of the relevant kind, couched in the currently available languages of physics, physiology, or functional or computational roles, is remotely capable of capturing what is distinctive about consciousness. So glaring, indeed, are the short comings of all the reductive programmes currently on offer, that I cannot believe that anyone with a philosophical training, looking dispassionately at these programmes, would take any of them seriously for a moment, were it not for a deep-seated conviction that current physical science has essentially got reality taped, and accordingly, *something* along the lines of what the reductionists are offering *must* be correct. To that extent, the very existence of consciousness seems to me to be a standing demonstration of the explanatory limitations of contemporary physical science. (Lockwood 2005: 447)

Arguably, no current conception of the brain or our anatomy in physical-chemical terms captures conscious, subjective experience. Colin McGinn writes:

> The property of consciousness itself (or specific conscious states) is not an observable or perceptible property of the brain. You can stare into a living conscious brain, your own or someone else's, and see there a wide variety of instantiated properties – its shape, color, texture, etc. – but you will not thereby see what the subject is experiencing, the conscious state itself. (McGinn 1990: 10–11)

As Alastair Hannay writes, physicalism faces a serious problem when it comes to its effort either to eliminate or sequester consciousness. "The attitude of much physicalism [to consciousness] has been that of new owners to a sitting tenant.

They would prefer eviction but, failing that, are content to dispose of as much of the paraphernalia as possible while keeping busy in other parts of the house" (Hannay 1987: 397). The problem is that the very existence and importance of consciousness is as evident as it is hard to square with current forms of physicalism. It is impossible to resolve the credibility of physicalism here. I simply take note that the thesis that subjective experience is exclusively physiological is open to question. Alternative, non-physicalist accounts are making a comeback (Taliaferro 1994; Hasker 1999; Unger 2006). Now, theism asks us to consider something that extends far beyond human consciousness, but the prospects for the coherence of theism improve insofar as one can see that even human consciousness extends beyond what would be captured in an ideal physics. And if physicalism is at least open to question, the thesis that physicalism is necessarily true (essential physicalism) is even more open to question. Let's consider each of the objections.

Reply to the argument from bodily organs

Rundle appears to be making a grammatical point, as though religious believers who think an incorporeal God can hear prayers are misusing the word "hear." Religious believers have historically been quite explicit that God knows all states of the world (including prayers) without requiring some physical instrument or medium. While I doubt that "hearing" as a term grammatically requires "ears" (one might have auditions if the brain is appropriately stimulated even after losing one's ears), we can simply refer to *God's awareness or knowledge that prayers are being said* rather than assert that *God hears prayers*. St Anselm is representative of philosophical theists who explicitly contend that God knows all things but without bodily organs.

> Therefore, O Lord, although thou art not a body, yet thou art truly sensible in the highest degree in respect of this, that thou dost cognise all things in the highest degree; and not as an animal cognises, through a corporeal sense. (Anselm 1998: 57)

Anselm may be wrong, but it is not at all clear that he is making a grammatical error.

Whether or not Anselm is using bad grammar, imagine that it is necessary for human beings to have sense organs in order to hear or see. Even if we do need bodily organs, must all cognition, including God's, be so mediated? To insist on this would make the God of theistic tradition much closer to the Mesopotamian gods Bertrand Russell complained about, as noted above. Anselm's notion that God cognizes all things to the highest degree suggests that God's knowledge is direct and unmediated. Can we make sense of direct or immediate cognition? I think we can. Many of our cognitive states do not seem to require a bodily organ (apart from a functioning brain); so, reflection on mathematics, memory of the past, the exercise of imagination, our awareness of our own intentions, our visual experience during dreams, and so on, do not require mediating organs like a mathematic eye, a memory nose, imaginative tongue, or some inner organ that we move around to get a better look at our intentions and dreams.

Consider how Rundle might possibly reply: Look, you concede that in all of these human cases the brain functions as the organ. It may be that the brain is not like the eye or ear, but it is essential in mediating the knowledge. So, you lack a coherent case in which we cognize things in a direct, unmediated fashion.

Response: The brain is *causally required* in order for us to undertake the relevant tasks, but note that *the brain does not function as a cognitive mediator.* In other words, I do not know that I am intending to type these words just now by knowing what state my brain is in. I know directly in an unmediated fashion what I am intending. I suggest that in our own case we can discover the coherence of immediate cognition without sensory organs functioning as cognitive media. I suggest that in the absence of an argument that there could not be a being that had such immediate cognition to a maximal, unsurpassed degree (as Anselm thought), Rundle's case for theistic incoherence is unsuccessful.

Reply to the argument from causation

Rundle thinks that if we are going to explain something even in this spatio-temporal world, the cause must be spatio-temporal. Let's focus on the spatial component, for theists could draw on the "flexibility" outlined in section two and maintain that God is temporal. Assuming God is temporal, is there a conceptual problem with supposing God could bring about some change in a spatial world?

Consider the framework behind the objection. If we have reason to believe that our subjective states – such as intentional willing – are not explicitly observable or analyzable in terms of physical-chemical processes and behavior, we have in our own case an example of where causation is not exclusively and straightforwardly a spatial transaction. I believe that we do have a coherent, intelligible understanding of non-spatial causation when it comes to reasoning, the drawing of inferences based upon entailments. When you reason on the basis of some premises and reach a specific conclusion, you (presumably) embrace the conclusion *in virtue of* grasping the premises and their entailments (or in virtue of some implicit or explicit appeal to evidence and rules of inference). I suggest that this is a case of causation. The reason why you think the number "6" when someone asks you for the smallest perfect number (a number equal to the sum of its divisors including 1 but not including itself) is because of your reasoning that 6 = 1 + 2 + 3. Let's agree that you would not reach the conclusion without your (spatial) brain but, as with the case of immediate awareness above, the brain plays no role in the cognitive process of your realizing the answer to the question. We have, then, in our own case, an intelligible understanding how causation need not involve spatial processes.

I believe that the current state of physics has made it tougher to reject divine agency in the name of a straightforward concept of physical causation. Contemporary physics now allows for "action at a distance," waiving Newton's insistence that if object A effects B, there has to be a spatial contact (direct or by way of some other object C). With spatial contiguity waved as at least not necessary, it does not follow that there is or can be a non-spatial agent. But quantum physics has shaken up a "common sense" objection that we posses a complete understanding of causation so as to secure materialism. Witness the following entry for "Materialism" in the *Oxford Companion to Philosophy*:

> Photons and neutrons have little or no mass, and neither do fields, while particles pop out of the void, destroy each other, and pop back in again. All this, however, has had remarkably little overt effect on the various philosophical views that can be dubbed "materialism," though one might think it shows at least that materialism is not the simple no-nonsense, tough-minded alternative it might once have seemed to be. (Honderich 2005)

Reply to the emptiness of theistic explanations

An aggressive reply would be that we are far clearer about explanations in terms of intentionality (he turned on the light because he wanted to see his beloved) than in non-intentional explanations. This was Thomas Reid's view. At a time when contemporary physics does not (yet) have a full model of causal interaction, Reid's position is still worth considering. But a more modest stance would be that however advanced our explanatory models for human and general physical behavior, there must be retained *some* irreducible unique role played by intentions. Let's imagine your calling out "Let there be light!" is accounted for exhaustively by forces that include no beliefs, desires, intentions, or any mental states. Under these circumstances, our whole understanding of ourselves as agents would be undermined. It would mean that your calling out was not done in virtue of the beliefs and desires that you had. So, in reply, I suggest the theist may countercharge that explanations for human agency must still preserve the notion that persons have certain causal powers that are not eclipsed by physicalistic explanations. In the literature, these powers are sometimes put in terms of our ability to undertake *basic actions* (actions that do not require us to undertake a separate act in order to bring something about).

Reply to the consciousness and individuation objection

This objection seems to place God in the bizarre circumstance of not being able to have thoughts or self-understanding unless God is in a language-using community in which there is a publicly recognized context of acting in virtue of certain rules. It may be too hasty simply to deem this objection as overly anthropomorphic, but it is worth noting that in theistic religion God is understood to be unsurpassed in cognition and wisdom; such knowledge and wisdom is understood to be basic to God's nature and not derived or conferred upon God through instruction and training. There would be no place in the very concept of God to imagine God needing a counterpart to follow rules. Moreover, the essential uniqueness of God sets to one side the apparent need for God to be able to distinguish Godself from other gods. (The Christian theist here can suggest this further reply to Phillips: If one were to insist that self-awareness required interaction with other self-aware beings, the concept of God as triune – one substance, three persons – might fit the bill.)

Two other points can be made in seeking to overturn Phillips' charge of incoherence. First, the very terms Phillips introduces seem to set up a false, or at least peculiar, relationship between a person and his consciousness. My "consciousness" cannot tell me or not tell me who I am. It is not so much that I have consciousness, but I am conscious. And in being conscious of myself, I do not have to make an inference that I am not someone else. This can be a direct, immediate apprehension. If one were drawing an analogy with divine cognition, presumably it would be just such direct, immediate apprehension.

Second, Phillips is employing a very famous argument stemming from Wittgenstein. The so-called "private language argument" was designed to undermine the appeal to direct, evident awareness of the world that is not mediated by others, their use of language, and so on. I do not think the argument succeeds, for it cannot eliminate the need for an individual to have antecedent conscious self-awareness and the awareness of others. As A. J. Ayer writes:

> But unless there is something that one is allowed to recognize, no test can ever be completed: there will be no justification for the use of any sign at all. I check my memory of the time at which the train is due to leave by visualizing a page of the time-table; and I am required to check this in turn by looking up the page. But unless I can trust my eyesight at this point, unless I can recognize the figures that I see written down, I am still no better off. It is true that if I distrust my eyesight I have the resource of consulting other people; but then I have to understand their testimony, I have correctly to identify the signs that they make. (Ayer 1973: 41)

I think Ayer is correct that the whole business of checks and corrections with other people cannot take the place of the antecedent, proper trust a person must have in her own experiences. This illustrates the coherence of supposing that a subject may have cognitive access to the reality prior to any sort of linguistic usage and of submitting to the corroboration of other subjects. In short, you need in your own case to have a cognitive power to know of the world antecedent to checking in with your neighbors. Given that primacy in the human case, there is no reason to believe God requires neighbors to have cognitive power.

I suggest Phillips' criterion for self-awareness is itself flawed and it is therefore unable to form the foundation for the case against the coherence of theism.

Whether or not the theistic reply is successful, my hope is that the above exchange exhibits the ways in which arguments for the incoherence or coherence of theism can be structured in light of different philosophical frameworks.

Future Tasks

I suggest that debate over the coherence of theism sustains philosophical interest because, even if there is no God, it engages central convictions about the nature of persons, consciousness, the world, values, meaning, and metaphysics. It is a terrain that involves either fruitfully using the imagination, exposing the causes of when we have become bewitched by our own language, or bringing to light the ways in which language may be used to describe or refer to a divine transcendent reality.

Questions for Reflection

1   If God is eternal or in some way outside of time, can God act in time? Does divine eternity undermine the practice of petitionary prayer? For example, does it make sense to ask God to change the future if God is outside of time?

2   If God is omnipotent, God should be able to bring about any consistently describable state of affairs. But if God is essentially good, God cannot bring about states of affairs that are radically evil (that is, events that are unredeemable and only serve to magnify/intensify world evils). But if God cannot bring about radically evil states of affairs (which can be consistently described), then God is not omnipotent. Discuss.

3   In what respects can theistic arguments, such as the ontological, cosmological, or design arguments or an argument from religious experience, support the case for the coherence of theism?

4   What standards may be formulated as to when thought experiments are reasonable or unreasonable? Imagine someone claims not to be able to conceive of divine omnipresence or omniscience. When does failure of being able to form some understanding of these attributes become evidence that the concepts are incoherent or, alternatively, become some reason for thinking that the person simply has limited abilities of imagination and conception?

5   If you conclude that some divine attribute such as omniscience is incompatible with omnipotence or God's essential goodness, when does this become evidence that theism is incoherent as opposed to evidence that theism needs to be philosophically revised? For example, one might conclude that the concept of God gives central place to divine goodness, and then re-analyze what it

means to be omniscient or omnipotent. Compare a debate over the coherence of theism with debate over the coherence of other concepts (e.g. concepts in theoretical physics or in theories of justice – Plato, for example, makes the central task of the *Republic* a vast thought experiment in which one is asked to imagine the ideal, just state).

References

Anselm (1998) *St Anselm's Basic Writings*, ed. S. N. Deane. Chicago: Open Court.
Ayer, A. J. (1973) *The Concept of a Person*. New York: St Martin's Press.
Copan, P., and W. L. Craig (2005) *Creation Out of Nothing: A Biblical, Philosophical, and Scientific Exploration*. Grand Rapids, MI: Baker Academic.
Frankfurt, H. (1969) "Alternate Possibilities and Moral Responsibility." *Journal of Philosophy* 66, 829–39.
Hannay, A. (1987) "The Claims of Consciousness: A Critical Survey." *Inquiry* 30, 395–434.
Hasker, W. (1999) *The Emergent Self*. Ithaca, NY: Cornell University Press.
Hoffman, J., and G. S. Rosenkrantz (2002) *The Divine Attributes*. Oxford: Blackwell.
Honderich, T. (ed.) (2005) *Oxford Companion to Philosophy*. Oxford: Oxford University Press.
Kenny, A. (2003) "Omniscience, Eternity, and Time." In M. Martin and R. Monnier (eds.), *The Impossibility of God*. Amherst, NY: Prometheus.
Kvanvig, J. (1986) *The Possibility of an All-Knowing God*. New York: St Martin's Press.
Leftow, B. (1991) *Time and Eternity*. Ithaca, NY: Cornell University Press.
Linville, M. (1993) "Divine Foreknowledge and the Libertarian Conception of Human Freedom." *International Journal of the Philosophy of Religion* 33, 165–86.
Lockwood, M. (2005) "Consciousness and the Quantum World." In Q. Smith and A. Jokic (eds.), *Consciousness: New Philosophical Perspectives*. Oxford: Clarendon Press.
Martin, M. (1990) *Atheism*. Philadelphia: Temple University Press.
Martin, M., and R. Monnier (2003) *The Impossibility of God*. Amherst, NY: Prometheus.
McGinn, C. (1990) *The Problem of Consciousness*. Oxford: Blackwell.
Narveson, J. (2003) "God by Design?" In N. A. Manson (ed.), *God and Design*. London: Routledge.
Phillips, D. Z. (2005) "Wittgensteinianism, Logic and Reality." In W. J. Wainwright (ed.), *The Oxford Handbook of Philosophy of Religion*. Oxford: Oxford University Press.
Rundle, B. (2004) *Why There Is Something Rather than Nothing?* Oxford: Clarendon Press.
Russell, B. (1957) *Why I am not a Christian*. London: Allen and Unwin.
Stump, E., and N. Kretzmann (1981) "Eternity." *Journal of Philosophy* 78, 429–58.
Swinburne, R. (1977) *The Coherence of Theism*. Oxford: Clarendon Press.
Taliaferro, C. (1994) *Consciousness and the Mind of God*. Cambridge: Cambridge University Press.
—— (1998) *Contemporary Philosophy of Religion*. Oxford: Blackwell.
—— (2001) "Sensibility and Possibilia." *Philosophia Christi* n.s. 3, 403–20.
Unger, P. (2006) *All the Power in the World*. Oxford: Oxford University Press.

Wolterstorff, N. (1982) "God Everlasting." In S. Cahn and D. Shatz (eds.), *Contemporary Philosophy of Religion*. Oxford: Oxford University Press.

Further Reading

Gale, R. M. (1991) *On the Nature and Existence of God*. Cambridge: Cambridge University Press. (An important contribution.)

Helm, P. (1988) *Eternal God*. Oxford: Oxford University Press. (A defense of the eternity of God.)

Hoffman, J., and G. S. Rosenkrantz (2002) *Divine Attributes*. Oxford: Blackwell. (One of the best analytic treatments available.)

Hughes, C. (1989) *A Complex Theory of a Simple God*. Ithaca, NY: Cornell University Press. (One of the best books on the thesis that God is simple.)

Hughes, G. J. (1995) *The Nature of God*. London: Routledge. (An excellent overview of key divine attributes.)

Martin, M. (1990) *Atheism*. Philadelphia: Temple University Press. (An important case against the coherence of theism.)

Martin, M. and R. Monnier (2003) *The Impossibility of God*. Amherst, NY: Prometheus. (Over 30 essays by analytic philosophers arguing against the coherence of theism.)

Morris, T. V. (1987) *Anselmian Explanations*. Notre Dame: University of Notre Dame Press. (A significant collection of essays supporting the coherence of thinking of God as unsurpassably excellent.)

—— (ed.) (1987) *The Concept of God*. New York: Oxford University Press. (A highly useful collection of seminal essays.)

Quinn, P., and C. Taliaferro (1998) *A Companion to Philosophy of Religion*. Oxford: Blackwell. (Contains entries on each of the divine attributes and arguments for and against the coherence of theism.)

Swinburne, R. (1977) *The Coherence of Theism*. Oxford: Clarendon Press. (This is the single most important defense of the coherence of theism by an analytic philosopher.)

Taliaferro, C. (1994) *Consciousness and the Mind of God*. Cambridge: Cambridge University Press. (A defense of the coherence of theism, especially in light of divine incorporeality and omnipresence.)

Wierenga, E. (1989) *The Nature of God*. Ithaca, NY: Cornell University Press. (Systematic and of high quality.)

Chapter 13

The Impossibility of God?

Robin Le Poidevin

Reasons for Disbelief

What kinds of reasons might you have for denying the existence of God? One possibility is that you simply do not find the various arguments that have been put forward in favor of God's existence sufficiently compelling, and that there should be, as it is sometimes put, a "presumption of atheism" (Flew 1972). That is, the existence of God would be such an extraordinary fact that only the most convincing reasons would justify your accepting it. In the absence of such reasons, disbelief seems appropriate. However, this is less a firm rejection of God than a refusal, or at least a disinclination, to believe in his existence. It is not in itself a firm belief in God's non-existence.

Another possibility is that you think that the existence of God, as he is traditionally conceived, conflicts with certain very evident features of the world such as human and animal suffering, whether through deliberate cruelty or natural disasters. How, you might wonder, could there be an all-powerful and loving God who would permit such suffering? This problem, in one form or another, is known as the problem of evil (see chapter 10, The Argument from Evil). It is much more of a direct challenge to theism, the view that God exists, than the mere absence of compelling reasons in favor of theism. However, theists have a number of responses to this, including, for example, the suggestion that suffering is necessary for the development of a mature moral personality.

A third possibility is that you regard theological doctrine (the set of beliefs characteristic of a God-centred religion) as a whole as incoherent. That is, it does not tell a consistent story about God's nature and his relation to us. For example, Christian tradition tells us that God is the all-powerful creator, transcending the limitations of the created universe, and yet this same being became incarnate, that is, embodied, and appeared on earth in the person of Jesus Christ. How is this possible? How can an eternal, all-powerful, all-knowing, and transcendent being be, for a certain period in history, a human, limited in space, time, power, and knowledge? Again, Christian theists have a number of strategies for dealing with the apparent paradox here (Morris 1986). The incarnation involved, not God without qualification, but the second person of the Trinity. Properties of one member of the Trinity might not be shared by others. Becoming incarnate might have involved giving up some of the characteristic properties of divinity. Or perhaps Christ led, as it were, a dual existence. And so on.

A fourth possibility is that you regard the very concept of God himself, even in isolation from the other doctrines that define a particular religion such as Christianity, as incoherent. That is, you might think that the properties that are traditionally held to define God's nature cannot consistently be had by a single individual: they are incompatible (e.g., Blumenfeld 1978). Or perhaps one or other of the traditional properties is incoherent, even considered by itself. Of all the objections to the existence of God we have just summarized, this, arguably, is the most serious. For it suggests that the very idea of God contains an internal contradiction or paradox. It is not that the existence of God would conflict with other things we might want to say about the world, human existence, or religious belief, but that it makes no sense. If this line of reasoning is correct, what follows is not merely that God does not in fact exist, or that we have good reason to suppose that he does not exist, but that *he could not possibly exist*. God would be an impossible object. It is this line of reasoning that we will look at in this chapter.

God as the Most Perfect Being

According to the first of the Thirty Nine Articles of Religion in the 1662 *Book of Common Prayer*:

> There is but one living and true God, everlasting, without body, parts, or passions; of infinite power, wisdom, and goodness; the Maker, and Preserver of all things both visible and invisible. ([1662] 1981)

The Articles were intended, by the bishops who first formulated them in 1562, to capture the essential and defining principles of the then relatively new Church of England. The part of the First Article quoted here, however, contains the conception of God common to the great monotheistic religions of Judaism, Christianity, and Islam. Other elements, such as the doctrine of the Trinity (the part of the Article not quoted), are peculiar to Christianity, and reflect philosophical and theological disputes that followed the establishment of the Christian religion.

The Thirty Nine Articles as a whole might appear to be something of an eclectic mixture, a result of historical accident and theological compromise, but the properties listed above can, as St Anselm argued in his *Proslogion*, plausibly be represented as following from the central conception of God as the most perfect being possible (Charlesworth 1965: chs. 5–7). The argument in each case has a common form. Since knowledge is better than ignorance, the most perfect being will be *omniscient*, that is, know all things. Since capacity is better than incapacity, the most perfect being will be *omnipotent*, that is, be able to do anything. (This is refined later in the chapter.) Since good is better than evil, the most perfect being will be *omnibenevolent*, that is, perfectly good. Since it is better to be depended upon than to be dependent, it will not only be the case that the most perfect being will be independent of everything else, but also that everything else will be dependent on him for its initial and continued existence. Since to be unlimited is better than to be limited, a perfect being will be everlasting: there will be no times at which he does not exist. One might, indeed, regard this as a necessary condition of omnipotence (for a defense of this strategy, see Schlesinger 1985; for analysis of these properties, see Swinburne 1977; and Hoffman and Rosenkrantz 2002; regarding the historical development of these concepts, see Hughes 1995).

When it comes to the clause "without body, parts, or passions," the derivations are perhaps a little less straightforward. Why should it be part of our conception of a most perfect being that he be disembodied? Here we have to remember that according to Christian tradition, human beings have both a soul, capable of thought, and a body, a purely physical and unthinking substance (Swinburne 1986). Of these, it is the soul that is most intimately related to us as individuals. I am, said Descartes, essentially a thinking thing, and only contingently an embodied being (Descartes [1641] 1984: *Meditation* 2). Still, the body has an important role to play. The body is the intermediary between the soul and the world: we know what is going on in the world only through the world's acting on the body's sense organs, and information from those organs being communicated to the soul. Thus our knowledge of the world is *indirect*. But indirect knowledge is clearly inferior to direct knowledge, since it depends on some other (and in the case of the senses) fallible mechanism. A perfect being, then, will have only direct, and infallible, knowledge of the world. It has no need of a body to inform it of the state of things. Like us, it is essentially a thinking thing. But unlike us, it is not even contingently an embodied being. A body would be simply *de trop*.

So on the traditional view, although we are composite beings, our parts being a soul and a body, God simply has, or indeed just is, a soul. Lacking a body also brings with it the consequence that a perfect being would not have physical parts in the way that we have – arms, legs, and so on.

Perhaps the most surprising (and, for some, the least attractive) component of the First Article is the idea of God being "without passions." What this means is that God cannot suffer. For suffering, arguably, is an imperfection. To suffer is to be in a state that we would rather not be in: we desire not to suffer. But a perfect being could not be in a state he would desire not to be in, for, being perfect, he would only desire what is good, and for him to desire to be in a different state would imply that another state was better. A perfect being, however, can only be in the best state possible. Therefore, he cannot have such a desire, therefore he is *impassable* – incapable of suffering.

A property traditionally ascribed to God in Christian thought, but not made explicit in the Articles of Religion, is that of *necessary existence*: it is not even possible for God not to have existed (Adams 1983; Hughes 1995, ch. 1). Again, this is something we could derive from the idea of a perfect being. For a perfect being could not, like us, exist merely accidentally: that would suggest his existence depended on something else, on how things happen to turn out. But a perfect being is not dependent on anything else. Therefore, a perfect being, if he exists, exists of necessity. Indeed, we might argue that only a necessarily existing being would be truly worthy of worship (Findlay 1948).

This is certainly plausible, if controversial. What is decidedly controversial is the suggestion that we do not even need to qualify "God exists of necessity" with the words "*if* he exists." For Descartes, existence is built into the very notion of a perfect being, for existence is a perfection, and since God has all perfections, it follows that he exists. So we can infer God's existence simply from the definition of God as a perfect being. This is a version of the ontological argument (see chapter 8, The Ontological Argument; also Plantinga 1974: ch. 10; Mackie 1982: ch. 3). The crucial premise, however, may backfire, since it also forms the basis of an inverted ontological argument: if God exists, he exists of necessity; but it is clearly possible for him not to exist; therefore, his existence is impossible (Findlay 1948).

The portrayal of God in the First Article of Religion is not, then, simply an arbitrary list of properties, but a remarkably unified conception, the central idea being that of a perfect being. Is it, however, coherent? It is tempting to say that, since the properties all follow from the central idea of perfection, they must all be compatible with each other. But this would be too hasty. It may well be that there is some hidden incoherence in the very notion of a perfect being, and we can bring out this incoherence by showing that it entails a list of properties which could not be all held by a single being. Moreover, it may turn out that one or other of the properties itself contains a contradiction, or paradox. In the remainder of this chapter we will look at two kinds of difficulty for the notion of God as a perfect being: the first is an apparent conflict between, on the one hand, his being "everlasting" and "without body," and, on the other, his being the "Maker and Preserver" of all things; the second, some difficulties concerning "infinite power."

Space, Time, and Creation

In what relationship will God stand to time and space? God's role as creator suggests that he will be both timeless and non-spatial. For space and time, being part of the physical world, are arguably part of creation. And if the spatio-temporal framework is brought into being by the creative act, then the creator's existence cannot require the existence of that framework. God will transcend the boundaries of his creation. We should, therefore – this line of argument goes – think of his existence as non-spatio-temporal (Leftow 1991: ch. 12). For Anselm, God's timelessness is part of his perfection (Charlesworth 1965: ch. 13; for discussion see Pike 1970).

This, incidentally, gives us another reason for thinking of God as "without parts." To be extended in space is to have spatial parts, and vice versa. So a non-spatial being will lack such parts. And according to some contemporary philosophers, to be extended in time is to have *temporal* parts, and vice versa. The idea here is that what exists at one time cannot strictly speaking be identical with anything that exists at another time: when we think of a temporally extended object, what we have in fact is a continuous series of qualitatively similar and intimately causally related objects, each of which occupies only one time (Sider 2001). Whether we accept this idea or not, it is clear that a timeless being will lack temporal parts.

When we think of an "everlasting" thing, we naturally think of it as existing at *all* times: it just goes on and on. But thinking of God as being outside, or transcending, time, would be another way of approaching his everlastingness: the idea of temporal limits simply makes no sense as applied to God. This line of thought, however, seems to run contrary to the traditional conception of God as *omnipresent*: present at all times and in all places, an idea that finds expression in the Old Testament:

> Whither shall I go from thy spirit? Or whither shall I flee from thy presence? (Ps. 139:7)

> Can any hide himself in secret places that I shall not see him? Saith the LORD. Do I not fill heaven and earth? (Jer. 23:24)

Why, though, should we think of God as omnipresent? Unlike, for instance, omniscience, it does not seem to be something that follows immediately from the idea of the perfect being. However, it may be argued that two of his divine properties, namely omniscience and omnipotence, require omnipresence. If God knows something, he knows it immediately, without the intermediation of anything else. His influence on physical objects is similarly without intermediary. The directness of his knowledge and action might seem to require his actually being at the times and places he knows of, or affects. So omnipresence would then follow indirectly from his perfection.

Conflict with non-spatiality and non-temporality could be avoided here by saying that omnipresence is not something that explains, or enables, God's omniscience and omniscience; rather, talk of omnipresence is just a figurative way of drawing attention to the directness of his knowledge and power. He is "in" all places and "at" times just in the sense that he knows about, and can affect, things in those locations in a direct way (Swinburne 1977: ch. 7). In spite of Jeremiah's words, we do not have to think of God as literally filling time and space.

The trouble with this maneuver is that it makes the mechanism by which God affects the world quite mysterious. Is God's relation to the world a causal one? If so, then since causation is something that takes place in time and space (a direct cause is, in our experience, right next door to its effect), God has to operate within, not outside, the spatio-temporal framework. If the relation is not causal, then we do not know how to interpret the words "Maker and Preserver."

So here is our first serious conflict, making the notion of a creator of all things highly paradoxical. On the one hand, God's being responsible for the existence of space and time requires him to be independent of them, and so timeless and non-spatial. On the other, his being the creator of the world (in a causal sense), requires him to be in time and space. How might the theist respond to this challenge? We will look at two strategies.

Timelessness and Creation

Let us focus on the issue of timelessness, since non-spatiality is unlikely to raise problems not covered by what follows. The first strategy is to point out that only on a very narrow conception of causation does a cause have to be something located in time and space. Admittedly, when we think of standard cases of causation, we are apt to think in terms of events taking place at particular moments in time: a brick being thrown through a window causing it to break, a bolt of lightning causing a fire, an assassination causing a war, and so on. But we also sometimes think in terms of *agent* causation, where the cause cited is an individual or group of individuals: naughty Tim breaking the window, an assassin bringing about the death of a politician, a government raising taxes (Swinburne 1977: ch. 8; Swinburne 1994: ch. 3). Now, admittedly, these agents have the effects they do by acting in time, but is it a necessary truth that an agent has to be in time to bring about an effect?

In familiar cases, where the agent is in time, they are also part of the causal order of things. That is, as well as being the instigator of change, the agent is also impinged on by change, and often their actions are in response to recently received information. This timely reactiveness requires the agent to be suitably located in time. But suppose we consider a being who is *only* an initiator of change, who is not causally impinged on, and whose actions are not a result of reactivity to the world. Then, we might suppose, there is no need to regard such a being as acting in time. The effects, of course, are in time, but the cause is not (Stump and Kretzmann 1981).

Perhaps this is a coherent conception of an agent, but it does not sit particularly well with the traditional notion of a God who continues to have a relationship with the world. The idea of a pure cause who is not impinged on by the world is like that of a blind watchmaker who, having made the watch, is unaware thereafter of the time the watch is indicating. The point here is not just about omniscience. God could have perfect knowledge of every state of the world by virtue of having causally determined every aspect of it. In his unique case, knowledge of the world need not be acquired through the world's causally impinging on him. But this idea of God's determining every aspect of the world is, for many, a rather repugnant one. What becomes of free human action? Admittedly, there are philosophers – "compatibilists" – who believe that freedom is compatible with total causal determinism. But theists tend not to be compatibilists, for this would undermine the "free will" defense against the problem of evil: that evil is directly attributable to the free actions of human agents, and not to God (Swinburne 1986).

In addition, it is hard to square God's timelessness with his being a *person* (or, as the doctrine of the Trinity has it, three persons). If a timeless being had a mental life, it would be utterly different from any mental life we could conceive of.

There is yet another reason to resist the idea of a timeless God, and that has to do with the nature of time itself. An influential view of time in metaphysics, and one that corresponds to our intuitive conception of it, is that, whereas past and present have reality, the future does not. The future, as we might informally put it, is not "there" waiting to become present. There simply are no future facts, no way things are going to be, until they actually happen (Lucas 1989). And this goes naturally with a certain view of causation, that a cause, acting in the present, brings into existence its effect, which until then had no reality. On this view, one time, and one time only, is objectively and absolutely "now." It is hard to reconcile this with a timeless and all-knowing God (Padgett 1992). From the viewpoint (if that is the correct term) of a timeless God, all times are present – or at least no time more present than any other. But then, if the "unreal future" conception of time is correct, there is a division in reality of which God is unaware. Surely however, reality is as God sees it, and so, if time really is like this, it must be God's view of it as well. But God can only be aware of the division between past, present, and future by being in time (for historical background and discussion of these issues see Helm 1988; Leftow 1991; Taliaferro 1998: ch. 6).

It seems, then, that the conception of a timeless God will need to go together with a radically different view of time.

Divine Space and Time

A second strategy is to allow that God exists as a temporal, and indeed a spatial, being, and so able to enter fully into the causal order without completely determining that order, but to think of space and time as divine attributes. The conflict in the notion of creation arose as a result of thinking of space and time as themselves created, requiring God both to be independent of, and so outside, space and time, and yet nevertheless to be capable of causal interaction. But what if we consider space and time to be uncreated? God himself is not created, and so his essential attributes require no further explanation (given that God's existence is self-explanatory). Now if space and time are themselves attributes of God, then they would not be independent of God, and yet their existence would call for no explanation. Moreover, we would have a simple account of the traditional doctrine of divine omnipresence: God is everywhere because space and time themselves are just aspects of the divine existence.

Since space and time are intimately involved with physical theory, and we have become used to such expressions as "space-time curvature," "singularities in space-time," and so on, it may seem very odd to suggest that these expressions are actually describing God, or some aspect of him. But the notion of divine space and time has a long history, and was particularly prevalent in the seventeenth century. So, for instance, we find Isaac Newton, in the *Principia Mathematica*, offering the following characterization of God:

> He is not eternity and infinity, but eternal and infinite; he is not duration or space, but he endures and is present; and, by existing always and everywhere, he constitutes duration and space. (Alexander 1956: 167)

The sense in which he can constitute time and space, without being identical to them, is that he stands to them as an object does to its intrinsic properties. A similar view is echoed by an earlier writer, Henry More, one of the "Cambridge Platonists" (Jammer 1969).

This may seem uncomfortably close to pantheism: the view that God is identical to everything that exists. There is, however, a difference. Note that, on More's and Newton's view, God is not being identified with time and space: they are merely aspects of him – a position more akin to "panentheism" (see chapter 2, Religion and Science). And this still allows us to say that objects within time and space, although dependent for their very being on God, are nevertheless distinct from him.

Two Conceptions of Omnipotence

We turn now to another threat to the possibility of God, as traditionally conceived. This concerns the divine property of omnipotence, that of being infinitely powerful. Earlier, we characterized this as being able to do anything, but this needs refining. For one thing, God's own nature will restrict the kinds of action he can perform. Lacking a body, he will not be able to sit down. If he is timeless, he will not be able to change, and so on. It is better, therefore, to capture the notion of unlimited power in terms of what God is able to bring about (Swinburne 1977: ch. 9). As a first attempt, then, we could offer the following: a being is omnipotent if and only if, for any given state of affairs, that being can bring about that state of affairs. This will need refining further, however, as the following paradox shows:

An omnipotent being is one who can bring *anything* about. Therefore, an omnipotent being could, for example, bring it about *both* that the earth was flat *and* that the earth was round. But the earth *could not* be both flat and round. In more general terms, a genuinely omnipotent being would be able to bring about the impossible. But, by definition, it is not possible to bring about the impossible. Therefore, there could be no omnipotent being.

This paradox can be dealt with fairly swiftly, we might suppose. To be omnipotent is not to be able to bring about anything whatsoever, even absurdities, but rather to bring about anything that is a *logical possibility* (i.e., does not involve a contradiction). This is how Aquinas understands the matter:

> Whatever can have the nature of being falls within the range of things that are absolutely possible, and it is with respect to these that God is called all-powerful. (Aquinas 1967: 1a.25.3.4, p. 163)

We may therefore call it the *Thomist conception*. Since the earth's being both flat and round involves a contradiction, it is not a limitation on God's omnipotence that he cannot bring about such a state of affairs. For we cannot even form a coherent description of what it is he cannot do (Hughes 1995: ch. 4).

This is such an obvious and sensible approach that we might well feel that there is nothing more to discuss. However, it does raise quite deep issues about the nature of logical necessity. What is logically possible is determined by the laws of logic and mathematics. But if these are objective, absolute laws, and not just a human invention, then the question is whether they hold true independently of God. According to the Thomist conception, it seems that they do, for those laws determine the range of God's powers. But does this not undermine God's perfection? For we suggested that a perfect being would not only be independent of everything else, but also be such that everything depended on him. Surely it involves no absurdity to extend the scope of "everything" here to include, not just anything occupying space and time, but also all abstract things and truths: this, after all, is one reading of "Maker, and Preserver of all things both visible and invisible."

The view that God could be responsible for creating, not just the concrete world, but also abstract truths, is expressed by Descartes:

> . . . the power of God cannot have any limits . . . [but] our mind is finite and so created as to be able to conceive as possible the things which God has wished to be in fact possible, but not be able to conceive as possible things which God could have made possible, but which he has nevertheless wished to make impossible. The first consideration shows us that God cannot have been determined to make it true that contradictories cannot be true together, and therefore that he could have done the opposite. The second consideration assures us that even if this be true, we should not try to comprehend it, since our nature is incapable of doing so. (Descartes 1991: 231, letter to Mesland, 2 May 1644)

This conception of omnipotence, according to which God decides what shall be logically possible and what shall be impossible, we may call the *Cartesian conception* (for comparisons between Aquinas and Descartes, see Hughes 1995). The problem now is that when we try to explain how God's power extends beyond that of the logically or mathematically possible, we inevitably contradict ourselves. We have, then, a dilemma: either we accept the Thomist conception, in which case we have to posit something that is independent of God, thus undermining his perfection, or we adopt the Cartesian conception, in which case we cannot even coherently state the range of God's power. Descartes himself seems to concede this second horn of the dilemma when he says that "we should not try to comprehend it."

Two ways out of the dilemma suggest themselves. One is to deny that possibility and necessity are in any sense a feature of the world, and insist that they merely reflect constraints on meaningful discourse. Thus, the fact that we regard "All round objects have a shape" as a necessary truth is just to do with the meaning of the terms: if we can apply the term "round" to an object, then we can also apply the term "has a shape." We are not picking out some mysterious feature of the objects themselves. Indeed, the assertion would be true in the absence of any round objects. But if the necessity, or contradictoriness, of certain assertions is not a feature of the world itself, then we need not worry whether they are features that exist independently of God.

However, when we earlier wanted to draw the distinction between our existence and that of a perfect being, we suggested that, whereas our existence was merely accidental, or contingent, the existence of a perfect being was necessary: if he exists at all, he does so as a matter of necessity. That is what makes him both independent of the world, and also worthy of worship. If there is any merit in this line of reasoning, then it seems we do have to make room for a conception of necessity as part of reality itself, and not merely our descriptions of that reality. This is how Aquinas understands possibility and necessity (Hughes 1995: ch. 4). In addition, and independent of specifically theological concerns, we may want to recognize a class of truths which, while not being logically necessary in that their negation involves no contradiction, are nevertheless necessary in some sense. So, for instance, although it involves no explicit contradiction to suppose that the past can be affected, we do not regard this as a genuine possibility, since it is ruled out by the metaphysical relationship between causation and time. We might therefore say that it is metaphysically necessary that the past cannot be affected (Swinburne 1994: ch. 5). The question then arises as to whether metaphysical necessities are, or are not, independent of God.

The second way out of the dilemma, though possibly a rather obscure one, is to make the same kind of maneuver that we made when discussing God's relation to time. Perhaps the necessity of certain logical and mathematical truths is, like space and time, an attribute of God himself – in some way God constitutes those necessary truths (without, of course, being identical to them).

The Stone Paradox, and the Possibility of
Relinquishing Omnipotence

Another much-discussed paradox of omnipotence is known as the paradox of the stone, and runs as follows. An omnipotent being is one who can bring anything about. Therefore, an omnipotent being could create a stone that was too heavy for him to lift up. But if he could not lift it up, he would not be omnipotent. And if he could not make such a stone, he would not be omnipotent.

Thus stated, the paradox can be disposed of simply by adopting a *time-relativized* notion of omnipotence: a being is omnipotent at time *t* if and only if he can bring about any metaphysically possible state of affairs at or after *t*. (This is very close to one of Swinburne's analyses in 1977: ch. 9.) There is nothing incoherent in supposing that an omnipotent being could give up his omnipotence: after all, if he could not do so, would this not be a limit to his power?

Two difficulties now arise. To relinquish omnipotence is to change in some respect, and a purely timeless being cannot change. There appears, then, to be a conflict between timelessness and omnipotence. However, although we could not talk of a timeless being relinquishing any part of his powers, we could talk of his power being time-restricted, so that his power with respect to times after *t* is more restricted than his power with respect to times before *t*.

Whether we talk of relinquishing omnipotence, or omnipotence being time-restricted, however, this approach to the paradox depends on the being in question being merely *contingently* omnipotent. We can recast the paradox in terms of a necessarily or essentially omnipotent being – one who could not be otherwise than omnipotent. Such a being could not give up his omnipotence; so there is *already* a limitation on his power, which means that he cannot after all be omnipotent. Therefore, there can be no necessarily omnipotent being. (Again, this paradox requires us to take seriously the idea that some necessary truths – for instance, that God is omnipotent – are necessary because of some feature of reality, and not because of the conventions of language.)

This certainly looks quite distinct from the previous paradox we considered – namely, God's bringing about the impossible. There is nothing intrinsically incoherent in bringing about a state of affairs which restricts the possibilities of subsequent action – we do this all the time! The problem only arises when one imagines a necessarily omnipotent being doing so; thus the problem seems to be internal to the notion of omnipotence. A necessarily omnipotent being both can, and cannot, do anything that would limit his omnipotence. Of course, the specific case of the stone is a trivial one. But there are other, theologically significant, cases. It is crucial to traditional Christology that we can conceive of God's (more specifically, God the Son's) becoming incarnate, and according to the *kenotic theory*, we can only do this if God gives up some of his divine properties, such as omnipotence (see discussion in Morris 1986). But how can a necessarily omnipotent being do so? It would be very unfortunate for Christianity, however, if its own conception of God was in conflict with incarnational Christology.

It was pointed out earlier that God's own nature (for instance, lacking a body) would necessarily place restrictions on the range of possible actions. We could certainly formulate omnipotence so as to take account of this, as follows: a being is omnipotent if and only if he can bring about any state of affairs that does not conflict with his essential nature. But, at least in the case of God, such a definition (as Aquinas saw) risks circularity, since "omnipotence" is part of God's essential nature; so the definition becomes "God is omnipotent in the sense that he can bring about any state of affairs that does not conflict with his omnipotence, and other essential aspects of his nature."

The problem of formulation can be dealt with. Taking the various considerations raised in this and the previous section into account, we can offer something like this: "God is omnipotent in the sense that for any time t, God can bring about any metaphysically possible state of affairs at or after t that does not have the implication that, for any time t^*, later than t, there is some state of affairs that he cannot bring about at or after t^*."

There is, however, a deeper issue. However we choose to define the technical term "omnipotence," the question remains: *does* God's own nature restrict his own power in such a way that we are no longer prepared to describe him as all-powerful in the intuitive sense? Perhaps the most serious conflict concerns God's moral nature. If he is perfectly good, then necessarily he wills only what is good. If he is all-powerful, however, he can will what is not good. So he cannot be perfectly good and all-powerful (Geach 1973). Nevertheless, the nature of the constraint is quite different from the kinds of constraint that restrict our powers. There are things that we cannot physically do, such as live in a vacuum, or perform 100 arithmetical calculations simultaneously. God is not subject to these kinds of constraints. It would be physically possible for him to do what is not good, but, necessarily, he would not choose to do so (Swinburne 1977: ch. 9). Is this a limitation? Perhaps only if we think of the good as itself independent of God. But, employing a now-familiar maneuver, we could regard aspects of God's nature as constituting the good (just as other aspects might constitute space and time, or metaphysical necessity). If God is constrained to do what is good, he would not then be constrained by something which was independent of him. Of course, whether this conception of the relationship between God and the good makes sense is yet a further issue (see chapter 9, The Moral Argument).

Questions for Reflection

1 What properties would you expect a "perfect being" to have? Are there some properties that do not admit of a scale of perfection?
2 What problems does the idea of a God who exists in time and space pose?
3 Can a timeless being be causally responsible for anything?

4   What is it for a being to be omnipotent? Does the idea lead to paradox?
5   Are there logical, mathematical, or moral limits to God's power?

References

Adams, R. M. (1983) "Divine Necessity." *Journal of Philosophy* 80, 741–46. Reprinted in Morris (1987).
Alexander, H. G. (1956) *The Leibniz-Clarke Correspondence*. Manchester: Manchester University Press.
Aquinas, T. (1967) *Summa Theologiae*, trans. T. Gilby. London: Eyre and Spottiswoode.
Blumenfeld, D. (1978) "On the Compossibility of the Divine Attributes." *Philosophical Studies* 34, 91–103. Reprinted in Morris (1987).
Book of Common Prayer ([1662] 1981). Cambridge: Cambridge University Press.
Charlesworth, M. J. (1965) *St Anselm's Proslogion*. Oxford: Clarendon Press.
Descartes, R. ([1641] 1984) *Meditations on First Philosophy*. In J. Cottingham, R. Stoothoff, and D. Murdoch (eds.), *The Philosophical Writings of Descartes, Volume II*. Cambridge: Cambridge University Press.
—— (1991) *The Philosophical Writings of Descartes, Volume III: The Correspondence*, ed. J. Cottingham, R. Stoothoff, D. Murdoch, and A. Kenny. Cambridge: Cambridge University Press.
Findlay, J. N. (1948) "Can God's Existence be Disproved?" *Mind* 48, 176–83.
Flew, A. (1972) "The Presumption of Atheism." *Canadian Journal of Philosophy* 2, 29–46.
Geach, P. T. (1973) "Omnipotence." *Philosophy* 48, 7–20.
Helm, P. (1988) *Eternal God: A Study of God without Time*. Oxford: Clarendon Press.
Hoffman, J., and G. S. Rosenkrantz (2002) *The Divine Attributes*. Oxford: Blackwell.
Hughes, G. J. (1995) *The Nature of God*. London: Routledge.
Jammer, M. (1969) *Concepts of Space: The History of Theories of Space in Physics*. 2nd edn. Cambridge, MA: Harvard University Press.
Leftow, B. (1991) *Time and Eternity*. Ithaca, NY: Cornell University Press.
Lucas, J. R. (1989) *The Future*. Oxford: Blackwell.
Mackie, J. L. (1982) *The Miracle of Theism*. Oxford: Clarendon Press.
Morris, T. V. (1986) *The Logic of God Incarnate*. Ithaca, NY: Cornell University Press.
—— (ed.) (1987) *The Concept of God*. Oxford: Oxford University Press.
Padgett, A. (1992) *God, Eternity and the Nature of Time*. Basingstoke: Macmillan.
Pike, N. (1970) *God and Timelessness*. London: Routledge and Kegan Paul.
Plantinga, A. (1974) *The Nature of Necessity*. Oxford: Clarendon Press.
Schlesinger, G. N. (1985) "Divine Perfection." *Religious Studies* 21, 144–58.
Sider, T. (2001) *Four-Dimensionalism: An Ontology of Persistence and Time*. Oxford: Clarendon Press.
Stump, E., and N. Kretzmann (1981) "Eternity." *Journal of Philosophy* 78, 429–58. Reprinted in Morris (1987).
Swinburne, R. (1977) *The Coherence of Theism*. Oxford: Clarendon Press. Rev. edn. 1993.
—— (1986) *The Evolution of the Soul*. Oxford: Clarendon Press. Rev. edn. 1997.
—— (1994) *The Christian God*. Oxford: Clarendon Press.
Taliaferro, C. (1998) *Contemporary Philosophy of Religion*. Oxford: Blackwell.

Further Reading

Hughes, G. J. (1995) *The Nature of God*. London: Routledge. (An accessible and informed introduction to historical discussions of the properties of God by, among others, Aquinas, Ockham, and Descartes.)

Morris, T. V. (ed.) (1987) *The Concept of God*. Oxford: Oxford University Press. (A collection of important papers attacking or defending the coherence of the divine attributes.)

Swinburne, R. (1977) *The Coherence of Theism*. Oxford: Clarendon Press. Rev. edn. 1993. (A classic contemporary statement and defense of the traditional conception of God, with detailed analyses of omnipotence, omniscience, omnipresence, etc.)

—— (1994) *The Christian God*. Oxford: Clarendon Press. (Puts the position defended in his 1977 work in the context of an explicit account of metaphysical concepts, including substance, causation, time, and necessity. Also includes a discussion of the incarnation and the Trinity.)

Chapter 14

God, Time, and Freedom

Katherin A. Rogers

Introduction

Though the issue of the nature of time seems esoteric, I will argue that adopting a certain theory of time, "four-dimensionalism," allows for what may be the most satisfactory reconciliation between divine foreknowledge and human freedom – a consequence that is of great practical significance to theists. My project here is Anselmian in methodology and conclusions. Anselm of Canterbury (1033–1109 CE) addresses the dilemma of freedom and divine foreknowledge inherited from Augustine (354–430 CE) and Boethius (ca. 480–524 CE). The problem is this: If God is omniscient, he knows today that you will choose x tomorrow. When tomorrow comes, you cannot possibly choose other than x. If you choose y instead, then either God's "knowledge" was mistaken or the past is changed such that God knew that you would choose y. But both entailments are impossible. But if you cannot choose other than x, you are not free and morally responsible. Thus it seems we must give up either divine foreknowledge or human freedom.

Anselm offers an "eternalist" solution. By positing that God knows your choice from his perspective in eternity, we can preserve both divine foreknowledge and human freedom. This solution has been widely rejected. It is argued that, since we cannot change God's knowledge in eternity, if God eternally knows that you choose x tomorrow, you cannot choose otherwise and you are not free (Zagzebski 1991). I argue that, while this criticism does connect with Boethius' eternalist solution, Anselm proposes a different understanding of divine eternity and its relationship to time; God is outside of time and "sees" all of time not *as if it were* actually present to him, but *because it really is* actually present to him. Your choice of x tomorrow is the source of God's eternal knowledge. You bring it about, by choosing x tomorrow, that you cannot do other than choose x tomorrow. True, since God knows eternally that you choose x tomorrow, from our perspective God knows "today" that you will choose x tomorrow, and so there is a sense in which your choosing *x* tomorrow is necessary. But this is a necessity of which *you*, the choosing agent, are the author. So it cannot conflict with the most robust sort of freedom.

Anselm's solution does require that one adopt a four-dimensionalist under-standing of the nature of time (sometimes called the "tenseless view" or "eternal-ism") which holds that all times, what any given temporal perceiver at any given time (P at *t*) perceives as present, past, or future, are all equally real. What P at *t* perceives as the present does not have any privileged ontological status. Perceivers in 1007 and 2007 and 3007 each perceive their own time as present, but all of these "presents" exist equally. This follows from Anselm's understanding of divine eternity. If 1007 and 2007 and 3007 are equally present to God, then, since it is God's eternal act of thinking and willing that constitutes reality, they must be equally real.

Many contemporary philosophers of religion find four-dimensionalism too bizarre, insisting rather on "presentism." Presentism is the view that the present instant is all that exists. The past and future are absolutely non-existent. Some of these philosophers argue that presentism is the obvious theory imposed upon us by our immediate experience; so if the Anselmian understanding of eternity entails the falsity of presentism, God cannot be eternal in Anselm's sense, and the solution to the freedom/foreknowledge dilemma must lie elsewhere. In this chapter I defend Anselm, beginning with a few words about his commitment to a traditional concept of God and to a libertarian analysis of human freedom. Then I show why two key contenders in the contemporary debate, Open Theism and Molinism, entail the rejection of one or both of these commitments. Next I look at two non-Anselmian versions of the eternalist solution to the dilemma and argue that they, too, reject either traditional classical theism or libertarian freedom or both. Then I spell out Anselm's solution. I conclude the chapter with a discussion of the criticism that Anselmian four-dimensionalism conflicts with our experience of the world.

First, a word about Anselmian methodology: Anselm takes as his guiding prin-ciple and non-negotiable premise the absolute perfection of God. The theory which best coheres with this claim is preferable to any theory which conflicts with it, even if conflicting theories seem to accord better with "common sense" or our everyday experience. Of course if the cohering theory entails a logical contradic-tion, or undermines a fundamental pillar of Christian belief, it may have to be rejected, but the claim that God is perfect trumps evidence drawn from how things may appear to human beings when it comes to settling disputed questions like the nature of time.

God and Freedom

Anselm subscribes to what might be called "traditional" classical theism. Anselm's God is the immediate cause of all that is not himself. Everything that has ontological status is sustained in being by the will of God. In Anselm's universe, with one key exception to be discussed below, there are not even any propositions whose truth is independent of God. Math and logic are reflections of God as absolute being. Value is a reflection of God as absolute good. Propositions which are contingently true, such as those about the laws of nature or the existence of some creature, depend upon God's creative activity. A "divinity" confronted with truths independent of its nature or creative activity could not be God, the absolute author of all.

The key exception has to do with human freedom. Everything that has onto-logical status is immediately caused by God. However, if the proposition "Rogers sinned at *t*" is true, its truth is not up to God, but rather up to me, as is the truth of the proposition, "Rogers was capable of sinning at *t*, but refrained." Anselm (*On the Freedom of the Will*) holds that it is logically impossible that God should cause sin, since to sin is to will what God wills that you should not will. Thus the *choice* to sin, and hence the choice to refrain, must originate with the created agent. God sustains the agent in being, with every aspect of the choice which has any real existence – the faculty of the will and all of its motives. But moral choice involves the creature's attempt to succeed in pursuing two, competing, God-given motives, both of which cannot simultaneously be realized. The actual choice is simply the agent's success in pursuing one desire rather than the other. This "winning out" of one desire over another is indeed up to the created agent, but it is not some new existent *thing* with ontological status (*On the Fall of the Devil*).

Thus, without abandoning traditional, classical theism, Anselm offers an analysis of freedom which includes the two elements central to libertarianism: self-causation and open options. By "self-causation" I mean that the ultimate responsibility for the choice lies with the agent. The choice *originates* with the agent. It is not determined, where "determined" means caused by something not to be identified with the agent. So, for example, if God or the indeterminate motion of a particle in your brain over which you have no control, causes your choice, then your choice was determined. You cannot be ultimately morally responsible for it.

For Anselm it is this self-causation aspect which takes precedence. God inevi-tably does the best, Anselm holds, and yet he is free because his choices are entirely from himself (*a se*), since he exists in complete independence. What of "open options"? Creatures exist in complete dependence on God. Therefore, for the created agent to choose *from itself* it must have conflicting motives and it must be up to the creature which option it will choose. There cannot be anything outside its own choice which in any way causes or necessitates that it cannot choose otherwise. On Anselm's view, although God is the source of all that has ontologi-cal status, he has carved out a small space for created agency. The creature can only cling to the justice God has given it or throw it away by willing something else instead. This is not an ability which produces any new *thing* in the universe, but it is enough to ground moral responsibility.

Anselm's libertarian conclusions commit him to the view that there are events in the world which are neither caused, nor even wanted, by God. Moral choice originates with the created agent, who could really choose between alternative possibilities. Can this claim be reconciled with divine foreknowledge?

Open Theism and Molinism

Among philosophers of religion the contemporary debate over freedom and fore-knowledge is dominated by Open Theists and Molinists. Both hold that human beings have libertarian freedom. The Open Theists hold that it is just not possible to reconcile such freedom with divine foreknowledge and choose to deny that God knows the future (Hasker 1989; 1994). They are clear-sighted about the consequences of this position. David Basinger, explaining the practical implications of the view, writes that the future is so open that we cannot even count on God to offer us sound career advice since he cannot know what the economic situation will be five years hence (Basinger 1994).

Clearly the Open Theists have abandoned divine perfection as Anselm under-stood it. A God who does not know the future knows much less and can achieve much less than a God who does. It is sometimes argued that foreknowledge would not enhance God's power, since if it is the actual future he foreknows, he cannot make what actually does happen not to happen and so he cannot change anything (Basinger 1986; Hasker 1989; 1994). While Anselm would agree that knowing the future could not give God the ability to do the logically impossible and make what happens at t *not* happen at t, nonetheless it does give him enor-mous power to *bring about* what happens (Rogers 2007). So foreknowledge does enormously enhance God's power. Open Theism is not an option for anyone committed to a truly robust understanding of divine omniscience and omnipotence.

What of the other main contender: Molinism? Named for its apparent ori-ginator, Spanish philosopher Luis de Molina (1535–1600), Molinism claims that libertarian freedom can indeed be reconciled with divine foreknowledge. God has three sorts of knowledge. He has "natural" knowledge of all necessary truths and of all that is possible for him to create. He has "free" knowledge of what world he will actually create and of all that will actually happen. And he also has "middle" knowledge. "Middle" knowledge is God's knowledge of all that *would* happen given any possible creative choice he might make. Included within divine middle knowledge are the so-called "counterfactuals of freedom." These are propositions about what any possible free – *libertarianly free* – agent would choose in any possible situation. Since God has always known his own intentions regarding which possible agents he will actually create and which possible situations he will actually place them in, he has always known what free created agents will choose (Flint 1998; Freddoso 1988).

Critics of Molinism have found much to criticize in this theory. For example, there is the puzzle of the "grounding" problem. The proposition about the free choice is true before the free choice is actually the case and even in the absence of the free choice ever actually being the case, and so it is difficult to see what makes it true (Hasker 1989). Further, Molinism rejects the God of traditional, classical theism, and does not seem to manage to preserve true libertarian freedom. Traditional, classical theism held that all that exists in the universe is either God or dependent upon his will. The counterfactuals of freedom are neither. They exist co-eternally with God as an unchosen framework limiting his options. Thus the hypothesis of middle knowledge is inconsistent with the traditional, classical theist understanding of God as the creator of all.

Can this same charge be leveled against the Anselmian view? In Anselm's analysis the truth of "Rogers sinned at t" is up to me, not to God. Doesn't this claim entail the problem raised against Molinism? No. The difference is this: On Anselm's account the truth of the proposition about what the free agent chooses originates with the actual choice of the free agent. But the free agent exists only because God chose to create it. God chooses this "limitation" for himself due to his surpassing goodness in making creatures with a spark of the divine aseity. It is not, as with Molinism, a limitation imposed from outside upon God willy-nilly.

Moreover, Molinism cannot be reconciled with libertarianism whereby there cannot be anything outside an agent's own choice which in any way causes or necessitates that it could not have chosen otherwise. The Molinist can deny that there is anything in the history of the world which causally compels the agent to choose one option over another. But nonetheless there is something outside of its own choice that necessitates that it could not have chosen otherwise. The truth of the counterfactual of freedom exists from all eternity, and it is *not* based on the actual choice of the actual agent (Flint 1998). The agent cannot choose otherwise than as God foreknows he will choose. So the agent's choice is rendered necessary by something outside of the agent over which he has no control. Molinism does not succeed in reconciling libertarian freedom with divine foreknowledge (Hasker 1989).

Two eternalist attempts

What of the claim that the dilemma can be solved by positing an eternal God? I will argue that two, non-four-dimensionalist versions of the eternalist solution fail. Boethius, in his *Consolation of Philosophy*, is apparently the first philosopher to argue that if God's knowledge is eternal, then divine foreknowledge does not conflict with human free choice. In fact, the term "Boethian" is often applied to this approach. Boethius is not, however, attempting to reconcile divine foreknowledge with a *libertarian* understanding of human freedom. He never says that free will must involve self-causation or open options. The problem, as Boethius sees it, is this: while foreknowledge does not in itself compel the foreknown event to take place, it is evidence that the foreknown event must be the result of natural, necessitating causes which conflict with freedom. So if God foreknows an event, doesn't that mean that the event must happen by natural necessity and hence not be free?

Our mistake, says Boethius, is in thinking that God's knowledge is like ours and so must be based on a present understanding of the preceding causes which necessitate the future event.

God is eternal where eternity is "the whole, simultaneous and perfect possession of boundless life" (Boethius 1973: 5.6, 423). His knowledge,

> surpassing all movement of time, is permanent in the simplicity of his present, and embracing all the infinite spaces of the future and the past, considers them in his simple act of knowledge as though they were now going on . . . set far from the lowest of things it looks forward on all things as though from the highest peak of the world. (Boethius 1973: 5.6, 427)

But this is not the four-dimensionalist solution. What we call past, present, and future is not equally real and present to God. For Boethius, God sees future events "as though" they were present, not *because* they are present. And it most emphatically is not the case that God knows our future free choices because he "sees" us making them. "But now how upside-down (*praeposterum*) it is that it should be said that the cause of eternal foreknowledge is the occurrence of temporal things! But what else is it, to think that God foresees future things because they are going to happen, than to think that those things, once they have happened, are the cause of his highest providence?" (Boethius 1973: 5.3, 397). The creature cannot have any causal impact on God. Rather, ". . . God possesses this present instant of comprehension and sight of all things not from the issuing of future events but from his own simplicity. . . . For the nature of his knowledge as we have described it, embracing all things in a present act of knowing, establishes a measure for everything, but owes nothing to later events" (Boethius 1973: 5.6, 433).

God's knowledge is the cause of all. The Boethian thesis seems to assume both presentism and divine immutability. God knows all time and acts upon all of time *as if* it were all present to him. Boethius does not address the pressing questions: If God sees all time as if it were present to him, when in fact it is not, doesn't he see things wrongly? And, if presentism is true, but God sees all of time as if it were equally real and present, then he cannot know what time it is *now*. Worse, since God knows future choices as their cause, he must himself be the cause of sin. Boethius certainly does not succeed in reconciling divine foreknowledge with libertarian freedom.

Let us look, then, at a different eternalist solution. Brian Leftow does not propose a four-dimensionalist view, but rather appeals to the theory of relativity in suggesting that the perception of time may be relative to different perceivers (Leftow 1991; Stump and Kretzmann 1981). The "framework-relativity of simultaneity" may allow us to say that two events which are simultaneous in one frame of reference are not simultaneous in another. "If we take eternity as one more frame of reference, then ... [e]vents are present and actual all at once in eternity, but present and actual in sequence in other reference frames" (Leftow 1991: 234–5). Thus today and tomorrow, which are not simultaneous to us, might be simultaneous to God in eternity. He can know our tomorrow "at the same time" as he knows our today, and hence can be said to know our future.

But Leftow's approach is hard to square both with traditional, classical theism and with the claim that God can foreknow our *libertarian* free acts. The suggestion that God views things from "one more frame of reference" reduces the divinity to just one more inhabitant of the universe. Traditional, classical theism insists that it is God's vision which establishes reality. It is not that we see things one way and God sees them another, and there is no privileged perspective. If God sees all of what we call past, present, and future as equally present to him in his frame of reference, and hence equally real, then it *is* equally real and we have Anselmian four-dimensionalism.

Moreover, the libertarian claim is that your free choice originates with you. This means that the truth of the proposition which has your choosing as its subject must be grounded in your choosing. If, in your frame of reference, tomorrow has not come, then you have not chosen. There simply is no truth of the matter regarding the free choice. However, on Leftow's approach to the freedom/foreknowledge dilemma, there must be a truth of the matter today since we must be able to say today that God knows what you will choose tomorrow. If four-dimensionalism is not the case, then our future is absolutely non-existent today and, on the libertarian account, there just is no truth concerning your choice tomorrow. Reconciling libertarian freedom with divine foreknowledge requires not only that we hold that God is eternal, but also that we adopt a four-dimensionalist theory of time.

Anselm's Solution

Anselm is, to my knowledge, the first to adopt a four-dimensionalist understanding of time and the only major philosopher to incorporate this position in the attempt to solve the freedom/foreknowledge dilemma. The clearest statement of Anselm's four-dimensionalism comes in his last completed philosophical work, *On the Harmony of the Foreknowledge and the Predestination and the Grace of God with Free Will* (hereafter, *On the Harmony*). But the subject also comes up in his earlier works, the *Monologion* and the *Proslogion,* where Anselm explains that divine perfection entails eternity. Just as God is immediately present to all places, keeping them in being, he is immediately present to all times. God "is not in place or time, but all times and places are in Him." Regarding the past, present, and future "... everything is in you [God]. Nothing contains you, but you contain everything" (*Proslogion* 19).

In *On the Harmony* 1.5 Anselm discusses time and eternity as related to the dilemma of freedom and foreknowledge. He writes, "Just as the present time contains all place and whatever is in any place, in the same way the eternal present encloses all time and whatever exists in any time. . . . For eternity has its own unique simultaneity in which exist all the things which exist at the same place or time, and whatever exists in the different places and time." Things and events which exist in time are always there and present to God. It is not that propositions about them are known by God, or that God knows them through knowing what he himself intends to do. The things and events *themselves* exist in divine eternity. There is our temporal perspective, relative to each fleeting moment, from which our past is gone and our future has not yet come to be. And then there is the divine perspective which sees all as equally real. And it is the divine perspective which sees reality as it is – which, in fact, pervades and sustains reality as the cause of its being. Anselm's description above of divine eternity as a sort of fifth dimension, encompassing the fourth dimension of time, which itself contains the three spatial dimensions, makes this very evident. He is thus the first clear and consistent four-dimensionalist.

And so to Anselm's version of the eternalist answer to the freedom/foreknowledge dilemma: God does know today that you will choose x tomorrow. And so it is necessary that you choose x tomorrow. But God knows that you choose x because tomorrow is present to him. He "sees" you choosing x as you choose it. It is your actual choice which is the ultimately originating source of God's knowledge. The necessity which follows from God's knowledge is then a logical and "consequent" necessity which follows from the fact of the event. It is certainly not causally determining. And more than that. It is a necessity stemming from your own choice, what we might call a "self-imposed" necessity. It is you choosing x tomorrow which makes it the case that you cannot do other than choose x tomorrow. Surely the logical, consequent necessity of "if you choose x, then, necessarily, you choose x," does not conflict with libertarian freedom.

Above, in explaining libertarianism, I said that it must be up to the creature which option it will choose and there cannot be anything *outside its own choice* which in any way causes or necessitates that it cannot choose otherwise. On the four-dimensionalist understanding, God's foreknowledge does entail necessity, but it is a logical necessity coming from the fact of the agent's actual choice. God's knowledge in eternity is "fixed" in that he knows what happens at every moment in all of space-time. And his knowledge cannot be changed, just as what in fact happens cannot be changed; that is, it cannot be made not to happen. If x happens at t, x happens at t. But, in a four-dimensional universe, the fact that God's knowledge cannot be changed leaves room for a libertarian, free choice to be the cause of God's fixed and eternal knowledge. If this is correct, then Anselm has succeeded in reconciling divine foreknowledge with libertarian freedom within the universe of traditional, classical theism. And all it took was accepting the four-dimensionalist theory of time. Is that too high a price?

The Phenomenology of Four-Dimensionalism

Recent work on the question of divine eternity and the relationship of God to time, while not embracing four-dimensionalism, allows that if we adopt the four-dimensionalist view many of the difficulties raised by the claim that an eternal God interacts with our temporal universe disappear (Craig 1998). My impression is that most philosophers of religion reject four-dimensionalism, not because they discern some logical contradiction within it, but because they believe that it conflicts in some obvious and powerful way with our experience of the world. Though different versions of this point have been expressed in print, they have not been developed into full-blown criticisms. In this last section I sketch some of these claims and offer preliminary suggestions for how they might be answered.

One common way of expressing the criticism of four-dimensionalism is simply that our senses tell us otherwise. Alan G. Padgett writes, ". . . we are wise to accept the reality of past, present, and future as our senses present temporal passage to us . . . there is no sound reason to reject the evidence of our senses with respect to temporal passage" (Padgett 2000: 16–17). But time *per se* is not something sensible. What sensory evidence do we have for presentism over four-dimensionalism? The first point that occurs to the Anselmian is that, as Augustine pointed out in his meditation on the nature of time in *Confessions* 11, as soon as I try to grasp the nature of time I realize that it is a very strange phenomenon. Is four-dimensionalism any stranger than presentism? On the latter view all that exists is the present instant, which, it turns out, must be the extensionless point at which the non-existent future becomes the non-existent past. That is not how the world "feels" to me.

Surely the claim is not that past and future do not exist equally with the present because, in the present, I cannot perceive them. Of course I at t do not perceive what I at $t + 1$ perceive, but that does not entail that $t + 1$ is non-existent, but only that I cannot perceive it at t. I do not say, when in Philadelphia, that Chicago does not exist because I cannot perceive it.

Perhaps the charge is that we observe *change* and the four-dimensionalist view denies change (Hasker 2002). But the four-dimensionalist view does not deny change. In a sense the entire universe of space-time, and each thing in it, is immutable. Certainly whatever exists or happens at any t, exists or happens at t and it cannot possibly *not* exist or happen at t. But that's just the principle of non-contradiction. True, people often talk about "changing the course of the future," but that's sloppy language on any theory of time. On the presentist view there is no course to be changed, and whatever turns out to happen, turns out to happen. On the four-dimensionalist view there *is* a course which just is what it is. Either way nothing gets *changed*. Change, as we experience it, is just that some thing or state of affairs is different at t than at $t + 1$, but the four-dimensionalist has no difficulty at all with that.

Perhaps the criticism is that on the four-dimensionalist view there is no real coming into or passing out of being. Even the most ephemeral creature is "eternal" in some sense. But the four-dimensionalist does not deny that there is coming into and passing out of being in the sense that something that does not exist at t, but exists at $t + 1$, has come into being, and something that exists at t, but not at $t + 1$, has passed out of being. True, there is no *ultimate* coming into or passing out of being. All that, from our perspective, is, was, and will be, is immediately kept in being by God and present to his eternity. This way of looking at things has some odd implications, but I do not know what sort of sense evidence could be adduced against it.

Among the odd implications is the conclusion that temporal things have a more robust ontological status than presentism would grant them. Each existent is an ever-present reality sustained in being by the direct knowledge of God. The Anselmian, steeped in the standard medieval view that all that has being is good, will find this an entirely appealing entailment. It is good news that the trilobite and the T. rex, although they are not present in 2007, are not nothing. Certainly temporal things are not eternal as God is eternal. God's eternity consists in *not* being stretched out across time, but rather in being wholly present to all time "at once." The distinction between the temporal and the eternal is not destroyed, but nonetheless it turns out that we have a more robust ontological status than we might have thought – and good for us!

But here is a consequence which some Christians apparently find troubling. If each instant of our lives is ever-present to God's eternity, then what of our past sins? Suppose we have repented and been reborn in Christ? From the divine perspective, those acts of sin are never wholly expunged from the space-time universe. Perhaps we are saved at $t + 1$, but we sinned at t, and t is as real as $t + 1$. My response is that, yes, that is exactly the case. God sees your life as a whole and if you are now a saved sinner, the sin is as real as the salvation. That whole story is you and, from the divine perspective, no part of the story gets erased. I find this a wholesome entailment when it comes to how we should see ourselves. However firm one's hope of salvation, it seems appropriately humbling to recognize that, if one is saved, one is nevertheless, always and forever, a saved *sinner*. Moreover, in practice, when one thinks of oneself as four-dimensional, such that each instant of one's life is ever-present to God, there is an incentive to improve one's behavior *right now* in order to shorten the offensive segments of the time-worm that is oneself.

A final difficulty for the four-dimensionalist is raised by the "arrow of time." If each instant is equally real, what drives the ordering of events sequentially such that the past must be before the present, and the present must be before the future? How can we account for the objectivity of "before" and "after?" Why should it be that we inevitably experience $t + 1$ after t, rather than the other way around?

First, is the presentist really in a much better situation *vis-à-vis* the arrow of time? Some presentists point to the absolute difference between past and future, noting that the future is absolutely open while the past is absolutely fixed. But, to pose a question somewhat similar to Augustine's in *Confessions* 11, doesn't it seem a little odd to ascribe such properties to non-existence? One might say that, in the present, propositions about the past have a truth value, and propositions about the future do not. But regarding the past, isn't there a grounding problem? There is nothing at all in existence to ground the truth of the proposition about the past, so whence the radical asymmetry between past and future? If we say that the truth value of the proposition about the non-existent past is grounded in what was, seeing that what was and what will be are equally non-existent, there seems no reason to deny that the truth value of the proposition about the non-existent future is grounded in what will be. But then the asymmetry between the fixed past and the open future is lost. The presentist may have problems of his own with the arrow of time.

Of course that doesn't save the four-dimensionalist. He could just decide that our experience of the "arrow of time" is illusory, not reflecting any reality about the universe. But that would grant the charge that four-dimensionalism conflicts with ordinary experience, and it is too early in the debate to surrender the point. At least two moves spring to mind. The four-dimensionalist might hold that the objectivity of before and after is a brute fact. Four-dimensionalism does not *entail* that there is *not* an objective before and after. It only makes it difficult to see what additional hypothesis about the space-time universe explains the phenomenon. The theistic four-dimensionalist can add that perhaps God simply "sees" events as sequentially ordered into before and after – the explanation for the arrow of time is just that that is how God has established things.

A different approach might be to ground the objectivity of before and after in the objectivity of causal connections. The "before" is objectively different from the "after" because the after is a consequence of the causes at work in the before. In order to make this move one must allow that there is more to a "cause" than that it be constantly conjoined *and precedent* to an "effect." It is circular to explain the objective difference between "before" and "after" by appealing to the relationship of cause to effect, and then to explain the objective difference between "cause" and "effect" by saying that the "cause" is the one that comes *before*.

The Anselmian has no love for Hume's anemic brand of causation, since he is already committed to causes that exercise some power to produce their effects. God brings things into being. The created agent produces his choice and the actions which follow. How could I be to blame if the crime I have chosen to commit, though subsequent to, is not *produced by*, my choice? And there are good reasons to posit what traditional, classical theism called "secondary causes" – natural causes which do exercise power to produce their effects, although they and everything in the entire system is immediately sustained in both being and activity by God, the "primary cause." If causes are objectively different from their effects in that they produce them, and if at least one broad category of cause standardly comes before its effect, then there is a reality to before and after which could ground the arrow of time.

These are only tentative suggestions for defending four-dimensionalism against the charge that it is refuted by experience. I hope that the opponents of four-dimensionalism will work to develop the criticism, so that its defenders can construct more fully rendered responses. But suppose at the end of the day that four-dimensionalism is shown to be an ill fit with human experience? The Anselmian argues that four-dimensionalism is entailed by divine perfection and allows for the most adequate reconciliation between freedom and foreknowledge. If the way the physical universe *seems* to us cannot be reconciled with four-dimensionalism, perhaps it is better to allow that appearances can be deceiving than to give up God's perfection and abandon either his foreknowledge or our freedom.

Questions for Reflection

1 Why would a religious person believe that it is important that God know the future?
2 Why would a religious person believe that it is important that human beings have genuine freedom? And what do we mean by "genuine freedom"?
3 Why does divine foreknowledge seem to conflict with human freedom?
4 How might adopting a four-dimensionalist view of time, and positing that God is eternal such that all of time is "present" to him, allow a reconciliation between divine foreknowledge and human freedom?
5 On the level of human experience, the four-dimensionalist theory of time seems pretty strange. What might be some consequences of adopting four-dimensionalism? Can the strangeness be mitigated?

References

Anselm (1077–8) *On the Harmony of the Foreknowledge, The Predestination, and the Grace of God with Free Will*. Translations are my own from Anselm (1968) *Sancti Anselmi Opera Omnia*, ed. F. S. Schmitt, Stuttgart-Bad Cannstatt: F. Frommann Verlag.

Basinger, D. (1986) "Middle Knowledge and Classical Christian Thought." *Religious Studies* 22, 407–22.

—— (1994) "Practical Implications." In C. Pinnock, R. Rice, J. Sanders, W. Hasker, and D. Basinger (eds.), *The Openness of God*. Downers Grove, IL: InterVarsity Press.

Boethius (1973) *The Consolation of Philosophy*, trans. S. J. Tester. Loeb Classical Library edn. Cambridge, MA: Harvard University Press.

Craig, W. L. (1998) "The Tensed vs. Tenseless Theory of Time." In R. LePoidevin (ed.), *Questions of Time and Tense*. Oxford: Clarendon Press.

Flint, T. (1998) *Divine Providence: The Molinist Account*. Ithaca, NY: Cornell University Press.

Freddoso, A. (1988) *On Divine Foreknowledge*. Ithaca, NY: Cornell University Press.

Hasker, W. (1989) *God, Time, and Knowledge*. Ithaca, NY: Cornell University Press.

—— (1994) "A Philosophical Perspective." In C. Pinnock, R. Rice, J. Sanders, W. Hasker, and D. Basinger (eds.), *The Openness of God*. Downers Grove, IL: InterVarsity Press.

—— (2002) "The Absence of a Timeless God." In G. Ganssle and D. Woodruff (eds.), *God and Time*. Oxford: Oxford University Press.

Leftow, B. (1991) *Time and Eternity*. Ithaca, NY: Cornell University Press.

Padgett, A. (2000) "God the Lord of Time." *Philosophia Christi* 2nd ser. 2, 11–20.

Rogers, K. (2007) "Anselmian Eternalism: The Presence of a Timeless God." *Faith and Philosophy* 24, 3–27.

Stump, E., and N. Kretzmann (1981) "Eternity." *The Journal of Philosophy* 78, 429–58.

Zagzebski, L. (1991) *The Dilemma of Freedom and Foreknowledge*. Oxford: Oxford University Press (chapter 2).

Further Reading

Anselm (1077–8) *On the Harmony of the Foreknowledge, the Predestination, and the Grace of God with Free Will*. (Anselm's attempt to reconcile freedom and foreknowledge.)

Augustine (388–95) *On Free Will*, book 2. (Augustine's attempt to reconcile freedom and foreknowledge.)

—— (397–401) *Confessions*, book 11. (Augustine's meditation on the nature of time and the relationship of time to divine eternity.)

Boethius (ca. 519) *The Consolation of Philosophy*, book 5. (Boethius' attempt to reconcile freedom and foreknowledge.)

Hasker, W. (1989) *God, Time, and Knowledge*. Ithaca, NY: Cornell University Press. (Hasker's attempt to show that freedom and foreknowledge are irreconcilable.)

Zagzebski, L. (1991) *The Dilemma of Freedom and Foreknowledge*. Oxford: Oxford University Press. (Zagzebski's attempt to reconcile a type of freedom without open options and foreknowledge.)

Chapter 15

Divine Hiddenness, Death, and Meaning

Paul K. Moser

In the *Phaedo*, Plato claims that "those who really apply themselves in the right way to philosophy are directly and of their own accord preparing themselves for dying and death" (64a). This claim sounds very strange to us today. If Plato is right, contemporary philosophers have failed to "apply themselves in the right way to philosophy." So, maybe contemporary philosophers aren't true footnotes to Plato after all. Maybe they have missed his main point about the point of philosophy. Even so, the important questions regarding death are not about Plato.

What has death to do with philosophy? Or, more immediately, what has death to do with *us*, with us *as persons*, regardless of whether we are philosophers? Does death have an important lesson for us, even if we are inclined to ignore its lesson? Let's begin with the obvious: death happens.

The Reality of Death

Death is the cessation of *bodily* life. Some mind-body dualists, under Plato's influence, deny that death is the cessation of *mental* life. It is, however, the end of embodied life, at least as we know it. So, when we die, others will bury or cremate our bodies, even if they don't do the same to *us*, to our souls. Mind-body dualists and materialists agree on this much: bodily death happens. They disagree, however, on whether our bodily death allows for our mental survival.

We might deny that death happens. Still, we will die. We can run but we cannot hide from death. The reality of death marks the human predicament, wherever we go in space and/or time. Death is universal for humans. The reality of death is the reality of a pervasive destructive *power*. It destroys us at least physically, if not mentally and socially too. It sometimes is delayable, given the powers of modern medicine. Still, death seems unavoidable if we are left to our own resources. Its power seems immune to our best medicine and science. Death inevitably triumphs over humans and our powers.

What, if anything, is the significance of death? The answer depends on what exactly death is. One question is whether it is an *irreversible* destructive power. Is death forever? Given materialism about reality, it is: there is no coming back. If reality is uniformly material, entropy meets no lasting counterbalance, and death doesn't either. Our best physics tells us that in the long term the physical universe is destined to break down. The energy of the physical universe will naturally disperse if it is not counterbalanced. Consider, for instance, how a cube of ice will naturally melt in a heated room. The same ice cube does not ever return from its dispersion. The material world thus does not offer us, as the persons we are, a lasting alternative to death. It leaves us with dying and death, with the dispersing of bodily life. If we depend for our existence on bodily life, we too will be dispersed forever, given materialism (see chapter 11, A Naturalistic Account of the Universe).

Loss in Death

Given materialism, we will no longer be persons after our death. So, there is no lasting hope for *us*, regarding our future as persons. We have no lasting future; so, we have no lastingly good future. Our destiny is just the abyss of dispersed physical energy. We will then have, in the abyss, no value in ourselves because we will have ceased to exist. People who were once valuable will then no longer be valuable. We will no longer be important, or worthwhile. Our existence and value will have ceased, never to be recovered. Some people may remember us, but mere memories are not the persons we are. We ourselves will not survive in memories. We will be gone forever, dispersed and done for, given materialism.

The loss of us will be a real loss. Why? Because we now are valuable – that is, worthwhile and good – in many ways. We exemplify goodness in many respects, even though we exemplify evil too. So, our funerals will be a sad occasion for many people – not for *us*, of course, but for many others. Their sadness will correspond to the loss of us with regard to what *was* valuable about us, including our being alive. People who pretend that death is no loss at all are misguided, perhaps even self-deceived. They need a reality check from the spontaneous responses of people at funerals. One might spin the reality of death to fit a far-fetched theory, but the responses of the uninitiated at funerals are telling indeed.

Materialists might take an extreme position here. If our value as persons ceases at death, as it will given materialism, then our death is not important after all, because we aren't truly valuable. We are just insignificant energy centers waiting entropically (so to speak) to be dispersed. Such extremism is confused. The fact that we have no *lasting*, or ultimate, value, given materialism, doesn't entail that we have no value at all. We can still have *temporary* value, and we do, even though materialism makes our ultimate future bleak. Correspondingly, we can reasonably have *short-term* hope for our temporary well-being. Hope for our lasting, or ultimate, well-being would be misplaced. Materialism offers no basis for such hope. Entropy will leave us all without hope. The final hopelessness of materialism is palpable. Lasting meaning, or purpose, is likewise excluded. Camus (1955), for example, paints a powerful portrait of life without lasting meaning.

Our ultimately hopeless destiny, given materialism, is a reality beyond our power to change. We can't save ourselves or anyone else from the abyss of final dispersion and destruction. Our intelligence, however sophisticated, can't save us. Our philosophy, however profound, can't save us. Our willful drive, however resolute, can't save us. Nor can our families, friends, colleagues, or community save us, however well-intentioned they are. Death will leave us in its cold wake, regardless of our cleverness, drive, or acquaintances. Materialism, then, is less than cheery about death. Materialists should be too, at least as long as they embrace materialism. The grave is their destiny.

Outside Help

In the face of death, we can reasonably be hopeful only if we have outside help from a power that can overcome death. This would be *outside* help, because its power would be beyond us. We lack the power of our own to overcome death. The needed help would be actual help, not merely possible help. It would offer us the actual opportunity to overcome death, to survive the destruction brought by death.

Could an *impersonal* power save us from death? This would be a power without plans, intentions, or goals. It would enable us to survive destruction by death, but it would not do so intentionally, or purposively. It would happen blindly, in the way the wind, for instance, could blindly form a three-dimensional portrait of Mother Teresa's face on the sandy shoreline of Lake Michigan. The wind *could* do this, but we cannot count on it to do so. If it happens, it is unpredictable for all practical purposes and thus beyond what we can reasonably hope for. If it were to happen for Mother Teresa (against all odds), we could not reasonably assume that it will happen for another person too. We thus wouldn't wait on the shoreline for someone's portrait to emerge from the sand. If we did, our sanity would be questioned.

Our *grounded* hope in surviving death, *if* we have such hope, requires a ground for supposing that death will be overcome by us. This ground cannot be the unpredictable vicissitudes of local wind movements. It requires a ground predictable and trustworthy by us, that is, predictable and trustworthy in practice. The announced intentions of a reliable, trustworthy personal agent would offer such a ground. We know this from everyday experience, as we often form a grounded hope on the basis of the announced intentions of other persons. For example, I reasonably hope that my return home from the campus will be timely, given that a trustworthy friend has promised to give me a ride home. This hope has a basis different in kind from the basis for my wish that the wind inscribe a human portrait on the shoreline of Lake Michigan. My hope is grounded in a good reason; my wish is not.

Let's consider the kind of outside help that would come from a trustworthy personal agent who has the power to overcome death. I have said "would come," rather than "does come," to avoid begging a likely question: namely, "*Is* there actually such help?" Another likely question is: "If there's outside help from a personal agent, why would that agent allow death to occur in the first place?" Some people hold that such an agent, if genuinely helpful, would block death from the start. Here we have the beginnings of an analogue to the so-called problem of evil for theism (see chapter 10, The Argument from Evil).

Would a superhuman personal agent allow us to undergo death even though that agent seeks to help us to overcome death? If so, why? A noteworthy answer comes from Paul's epistle to the Romans: "The creation was subjected to futility, not by its own will, but by the will of the One who subjected it, in [the One's] hope that the creation will be freed from its slavery to decay and brought into the glorious freedom of the children of God" (Rom. 8:20–21). Let's unpack this.

Paul's reference to futility echoes the writer of Ecclesiastes: "Futility of futilities! All is futility" (Eccles. 1:2; 12:8). They have in mind what is ultimately pointless, in vain, when left to its own ways. Paul thus suggests that God introduced death to show that the ways of creation on its own are ultimately futile, pointless, meaningless. In particular, as a part of creation, we humans ultimately come to naught on our own. Death leaves us with a hopeless destiny if we are left to our own resources. All of our own projects and achievements, even our philosophical labors, will meet the same fate: futility. They are all destined for the abyss, never to be revived. This seems to be nothing but bad news, but is it really?

Paul suggests that a certain hope lies behind the futility of death: God's hope of freeing people from futility to enter the family of God. Death is portrayed as a means to bring about this hope. How can death, our death, lead to life, our life? How can such loss yield such good?

Dying to Live

Death can enable a needed learning curriculum for us if it serves the teaching purposes of an agent who can overcome death for us. What might such an agent have to teach us with death, our death? We all need instruction about our desperate situation when left to our own resources. We need to learn that all of our best intentions, efforts, and achievements will ultimately be futile, meaningless, if we are on our own. Death is the intended wake-up call to this humbling lesson. It shows that we cannot think, will, or work ourselves into lasting satisfaction by our own resources. It shows that we are fragile and even ultimately hopeless on our own. Death announces that we need outside help for lasting satisfaction and meaning. It solemnly warns us who remain: if we stay to ourselves, without outside power, we are done for, forever.

The reality of death fits perfectly with the view that we are creatures intended to depend on One greater than ourselves, on One who can overcome death for us. Such depending is just trust. It is faith, *not* as guesswork or a leap beyond evidence, but as willing reliance on One whom we need to overcome death, to live lastingly. What exactly is this reliance, and how does death bear on it?

For shorthand, let's introduce talk of "God" for the One in question. The slippery word "God" is a title, not a proper name. It signifies One who not only can overcome death but also is worthy of worship, i.e., unconditional commitment and adoration as our morally impeccable Maker and Sustainer. We can use a title intelligibly, even the title "God," without begging the question whether God exists. A title can have semantic significance owing to its connotation, even if it lacks denotation. So, our use of the term "God" as a title does not automatically ignore the qualms of atheists and agnostics.

Our trusting, depending, or relying on God appropriately is just willingly counting on God as our Savior and Lord, that is, as our Redeemer and Master. In counting on God thus, I commit to God as *my* God. I thereby commit to putting God's will over my will, just as Jesus did in the Garden of Gethsemane as he prayed to God: "Not what I will, but what You will" (Mark 14:36). In trusting God, I commit to dying to my own selfish ways to live to God's ways. In short, I resolve to die to my selfishness to live to God. This entails a commitment to reject selfishness, in particular, any selfishness that involves exalting my will above God's. In selfishness, I fail to honor God as God. I put myself and my ways first. The call to faith in God is, in contrast, a call to die to selfishness in order to live to One who can overcome death for us. Whatever else it is, it is *not* a call to leap beyond evidence, as if faith in God were necessarily defective from a cognitive viewpoint. Trust in God can, in principle, be at least as cognitively good as your trusting in your best friend.

Why assume, however, that I must die to my ways to live to God? Isn't this a perversely harsh understanding of what faith in God involves? Not if my own case is at all representative of the human condition. My problem is the human problem: deep-seated selfishness, the antithesis to the unselfish love integral to God's morally impeccable character. I'm also very good at hiding my selfish ways from myself and others. I tell myself stories of how they are reasonable and even good. Our inveterate selfishness qualifies us as morally deficient and thus disqualifies us immediately as God. The title "God," requiring a morally impeccable character of its holder, does not apply to ourselves. Even so, we have the persistent tendency to play God in at least some area of our lives. We pose as Lord over at least part of our lives, particularly in areas we deem vital to our well-being. One such area concerns how we treat our enemies, that is, our acquaintances who are a clear threat to our well-being. At best, we ignore them; at worst, we seek to destroy them. Rarely do we show them unselfish forgiving love, the kind of merciful love found in the true God (see Matt. 5:43–8). The risk is, we suppose, too great, too threatening to our comfort and well-being. We thereby choose against the ways of an all-loving God. We presume to know better. We thus play God. Trust in God is the refusal to play God.

Another area where we play God concerns what is to count as suitable evidence of God's reality. We presume to be in a position, on our own, to say what kind of evidence God *must* supply regarding God's reality. We reason, in agreement with Bertrand Russell and many other philosophers: If God is real, God would be revealed in way W. For instance, God would show up with considerable fireworks or at least pomp and circumstance. God, however, is not revealed in way W. Hence, God is not real. Russell (1970) thus anticipated his preferred response if after death he met God: "God, you gave us insufficient evidence." We thereby exalt ourselves as cognitive judge, jury, and executioner over God. God, we suppose, must be revealed on *our* cognitive terms. In such cognitive idolatry (see Moser 2002), we set up our cognitive standards in ways that preclude so-called "reasonable" acknowledgment of God's reality. Our cognitive pride thus becomes suicidal. We play God to our own demise. The reality of our impending death exhibits that without the true God, we are ultimately hopeless. We are then impostors in playing God.

We must die to our playing God, if we are to live lastingly. Death is our final notice. It calls us to the stark realization that our playing God will not last but will instead lead to the grave, once and for all. In shattering us, death ultimately ruins all of our projects too. The needed power for lasting life, then, is not from us or our projects. Only pride gone blind would lead one to deny this. Even in the face of death, our selfish pride endures. In the absence of the humbling effects of death, our pride would run wild indeed. Death reveals that what is lastingly important is not from us. It exposes our core insecurity (and impotence) about life itself, that is, our insecurity about the future of our lives. We know *that* our lives will end, but we have no idea of *when* they will end. Our end could come in 20 years or it could come in 20 minutes. This indefiniteness makes for insecurity and anxiety, at least when we honestly attend to the matter. As a result, we typically divert attention in ways that lead to indifference about death and related realities.

How Not to Approach Death

Avoidance and indifference toward death threaten all of us at times, in our fear, insecurity, and weakness. Blaise Pascal writes:

> the fact that there are men indifferent to the loss of their being . . . is not natural. They are quite different with regard to everything else: they fear even the most insignificant things, they foresee them, feel them, and the same man who spends so many days and nights in rage over the loss of some office or over some imaginary

affront to his honour is the very one who, without anxiety or emotion, knows he is
going to lose everything through death. It is a monstrous thing to see in the same
heart and at the same time both this sensitivity to the slightest things and this strange
insensitivity to the greatest. ([1660] 1995: sec. 681)

We ignore and become indifferent to death, because we know that our own
resources cannot overcome it. We know that death will triumph over us. So, we
conclude, let's just resign ourselves to it. We then fail to seek the needed solution
(the One who is the solution) in the right way.

Russell acknowledges the inadequacy of our own resources in the face of death,
but still recommends intentional and courageous "contemplation" of our fate in
death. He claims: "it remains only to cherish . . . the lofty thoughts that ennoble
[our] little day; . . . to worship at the shrine that [our] own hands have built." He
means the shrine that our *minds* have built. Russell also recommends that we
approach the dying "to give them the pure joy of a never-tiring affection, to
strengthen failing courage, to instill faith in hours of despair" ([1903] 1957: 18).
Faith? In what? Russell is silent, because he has no hope-conferring object of faith
to offer.

Russell's rhetoric may sound good, but he cannot deliver on it. The eternal
truths he loves passionately offer no hope to the dying. How could they? They
cannot overcome death for the dying. So, they are no basis for us to "instill faith
in hours of despair." Russell deserves credit for facing death as an immediate
problem even for philosophers. He has, however, no basis for his courage, his joy,
or his faith. His faith does not yield living through dying, because his faith has
no *object* of faith that can overcome death. The mere *attitude* of faith, being a
psychological human state, does nothing to overcome death. Russell, then, is not
helpful in solving the human plight. He offers no genuine help. He has no good
news for us, the dying.

Do we want outside help? Some of us don't. Thomas Nagel claims that the
existence of God poses a serious "cosmic authority problem" for us, so much so
that he hopes that God does not exist. Nagel writes: "I want atheism to be
true. . . . I hope there is no God! I don't want there to be a God; I don't want
the universe to be like that" (Nagel 1997: 130). Contrast this bold attitude with
the tempered attitude of the Yale surgeon, Dr Richard Selzer, who likewise is not
a theist: "Probably the biggest, saddest thing about my own life is that I never
had faith in God. I envy people who do. Life without faith is rather a hard proposition" (Selzer 2000). An undeniable hardship of life without God is that ultimately it all comes to naught, and we have indications of this futility of life. Selzer
rightly feels the pain of life without God. Somehow, Nagel doesn't. He evidently
misses the tragedy of a bypassed opportunity of a lastingly good life. Something
has gone wrong.

It would be a strange, defective God who didn't pose a serious cosmic authority
problem for humans. Part of the status of being *God*, after all, is that God has
unique authority, or lordship, over humans. Since we humans aren't God, the true

God would have authority over us and would seek to correct our profoundly selfish ways. Nagel confesses to having a fear of any religion involving God. Such fear seems widespread among humans, and all humans may share it at least at times. It stems from human fear of losing our supposed lordship over our decisions and lives. We want to be able to say, as the blindly arrogant song goes: "I did it my way." Willful children are very good at exhibiting this attitude, and adults can be too. Our attitude is: "It's my way, or no way." Human willfulness runs deeper than the reach of reason. One's willfulness, tragically, can be *consistently* suicidal. Reason is no panacea, after all. If it were, we wouldn't need God.

Our supposedly self-protective fear, confessed by Nagel, may *seem* to be for our own good. It blocks, however, our receiving a lastingly good life. Consider the existence of an all-loving God who sustains, and who alone can sustain, lastingly good life for humans. The existence of such a God is a good thing, all things considered, for us humans. Nagel hopes that there is no such God. In doing so, he hopes that something good, all things considered, for all of us does not exist. Such a hope against the reality of something good for us arises from Nagel's desire to have moral independence and authority. At least, I can't find a better diagnosis.

Nagel's desire is willful in a way that flouts good judgment. It rests on this attitude: "If I can't have my moral independence of God, even though God is all-loving and good for me, then I hope that God doesn't exist. I don't want to exist in a universe where God is the moral authority over me and others. I just won't stand for that kind of moral non-independence. If I can't be morally independent of God, then I just won't be at all." Nagel is willing to sacrifice something good for himself and others (namely, lastingly good life) for the sake of a willful desire to be morally independent of God. If, however, God is all-loving (as God is by title), this willful attitude is dangerously misguided. Its willfulness invites the needless destruction of suicide in a world blessed by the presence of an all-loving God. We thus have a case where willfulness blocks good judgment. This is a trademark of the human condition of *supposedly* self-protective fear.

Our attitudes toward God's existence are not purely cognitive in their origin and sustenance. Our *willfulness* looms large. Let's turn, then, to the role of *evidence* regarding God as the One who can overcome death for us.

Hidden Help

If God exists, God is hidden. Pascal was dead right: ". . . any religion which does not say that God is hidden is not true" ([1660] 1995: sec. 275). Jesus himself thanks God for hiding. After giving his disciples instructions regarding their preaching of the kingdom of God, Jesus prays as follows:

> I thank you, Father, Lord of heaven and earth, because you have hidden these things from the wise and the learned, and you have revealed them to infants. Yes,

Father, this seemed good in your sight. (Luke 10:21; cf. Matt. 11:25–6; Isa. 45:15)

If an all-loving God aims to help us to overcome death, shouldn't we all receive an explicit revelation of God's reality that is beyond reasonable doubt? Wouldn't an all-loving God appear clearly to dispel doubts about God's reality and the significance of human death?

We think we know what we *should* expect of an all-loving God. As a result, we confidently set the parameters for God's reality as if they were decisive regarding God's reality. We seldom ask, however, what *God* would expect of *us*. We'll do so here. An all-loving God would promote unselfish love, and thus would not settle for our simply knowing that God exists. I could know that God exists but hate God. Indeed, my hate toward God could increase as my evidence of God's reality increases. As I get more evidence of God as a genuine moral authority over me, I could easily deepen my hate toward God. This could come from willful insistence that I be my own moral authority at least in certain areas of my life.

Hate toward God is not good for anyone, including the one who hates God. It blocks a congenial relationship between a person and the only One who can overcome death and supply lastingly good life for that person. So, an all-loving God would not promote hate toward God. For the person resolutely opposed to God, more evidence of God's reality would typically be harmful. It would intensify and solidify opposition to God. Jesus thus advises his messengers not to cast his sacred message before resolute opponents, lest they trample it under foot (Matt. 7:6). Such a mean-spirited response by Jesus' opponents would be good for no one, not even the opponents. An all-loving God seeks to break willful opposition but not typically by means of a counterproductive direct assault on it. Instead, God typically invites us in various ways to come to our senses, and then waits. Since people aren't pawns, we should not expect universal success on God's part. Because people can freely reject God's invitation, some people might not ever come around to acknowledge God, despite God's best efforts.

What of "agnostics"? They withhold judgment regarding God's existence on the basis of allegedly counterbalanced evidence. They reportedly endorse agnosticism "for reasons of evidence." Typically, however, agnostics overlook the most important evidence of God's reality: namely, the reality of God's genuinely unselfish love in Jesus and thereby in the life of a person who yields to him as Lord and thus receives God's Spirit. This kind of love prompts the apostle Paul to make the following *cognitively* relevant point: "[Christian] hope does not disappoint, because the love of God has been poured out within our hearts through the Holy Spirit who was given to us" (Rom. 5:6). Paul thus identifies a kind of evidence that saves one from disappointment in hoping in God: the presence of God's Spirit accompanied by God's unselfish love. Followers of Jesus often fail to live up to the high calling toward God's holy love, but this does not challenge the distinctive evidence just noted.

Evidence from the presence of God's Spirit is akin to the evidence from conscience regarding, for instance, the goodness of a case of self-giving kindness and
the evil of a case of needless torture. Such evidence from conscience, although
genuine, does not yield a non-question-begging argument against skeptics, but
this is no defect in the evidence. In addition, such evidence can be suppressed by
us, and we will dismiss it if we *will* to do something in conflict with it. Still, the
evidence from conscience is genuine and salient. Likewise for the evidence of
God's Spirit, which comes typically with the conviction in conscience that we have
fallen short of God's unselfish holy ways.

Volitional factors loom large in acquiring evidence of God's reality. An all-
loving God would seek to be known *as God*, for the good of humans. So, God
would seek to be known as *our* God. God sent Jesus as living proof that God is
for us, not against us. The self-giving sacrifice of Jesus aims to alert us to God's
intervention on our behalf. In his journey from Gethsemane to Calvary, Jesus
resists ("dies to") selfishness in order to live to God. He subjects his will to the
unselfish will of his Father. This subjection of the will is cognitively as well as
morally significant. It highlights autobiographical factors in receiving evidence of
God's reality as God. As I yield to God's call to obey, as Jesus did, God emerges
as *my* God, and I thereby become God's servant and child. Only in such volitional
yielding on my part does God become *my* God. My firm knowledge of God as
my God thus depends on volitional factors concerning me, concerning my exercise
of my will in relation to God. I must yield my will in response to the convicting
and redirecting intervention of God's Spirit in my conscience. I can have no firm
knowledge of God as my God in a will-free manner. We tell ourselves that *if* God
appeared to us in an astonishing manner, *then* we would yield to God as God.
This, however, is doubtful, because we then have already set ourselves up as cognitive judge over God.

The evidence from the presence of God's Spirit does not yield a non-question-
begging argument for God's reality. This is no problem, because the reality of
evidence does not depend on a non-question-begging argument. For example, I
do not have a non-question-begging argument for my belief that I am awake now
(at least relative to an extreme skeptic's questions), but I still have good evidence
that I am awake now. Whether an argument is non-question-begging varies with
the questions actually raised in an exchange. Evidence itself is not exchange-relative
in this way. Our *having* evidence does not entail *giving* an answer of any kind. So,
we should not be troubled by our lacking a non-question-begging argument
relative to an agnostic's questions. We should rather identify the evidence suited
to an all-loving God who seeks volitional transformation rather than mere reasonable belief.

Commitment to the true God can yield unsurpassed explanatory value, at least
in certain areas of inquiry. Such a commitment, we might argue, makes the best
sense of who we are and of why we have come into existence. The reasonableness
of theistic belief is thus sometimes recommended as underwritten by an inference
to a best explanation. Still, the foundational evidence of God's reality is irreducibly

a matter of experiencing the presence of God's personal Spirit. This presence is not an argument of any kind. It is rather God's authoritative call on a person's life. If a call promotes hate, it is not from an all-loving God. False gods compete with the true God, and they are known by the standard of unselfish love.

Some agnostics will demand that we begin with mere "existence-arguments" concerning God. This is misguided. In the case of the true God, essence, character, and value must not be bracketed for the sake of mere existence-arguments. The present approach holds these together, thereby maintaining the explanatory, psychological, and existential distinctiveness of the evidence supplied by the Jewish-Christian God. Genuine existence-evidence regarding the true God comes not as a needed preliminary to, but instead *through*, the good news of what God has done for us in Jesus, in concert with the convicting and drawing power of God's Spirit. Proper conviction of God's reality comes through the transforming working of God's personal Spirit in conjunction with the good news of what God has done for us. So, we should begin not with mere existence-evidence but rather with evidence of what God has done and is doing in terms of His gracious personal calling through the good news of Jesus. We will thus avoid the risk of being diverted to deism, mere theism, or something else less robust than the reality of the true God and Father of Jesus. We will then highlight God's gracious offer of reconciliation to all people, even unsophisticated people, via the good news of Jesus. A person doesn't have to be able to follow intricate arguments to receive evidence of God's reality. This is good news indeed.

Arguments aside, the good news of Jesus need not be lost on people raised within non-theistic traditions. The convicting and drawing power of God's Spirit can begin to transform receptive people from any tradition, even receptive people who do not yet acknowledge this Spirit as the Spirit of the risen Jesus. When the good news of Jesus actually comes to the latter people, it will, in due course, bring them to acknowledge the work of God's Spirit within them as the work of the Spirit of the risen Jesus. The good news of Jesus has its base in a power that cuts much deeper than arguments and religious traditions: the transforming power of the Spirit of the living God.

Conclusion

For the person eager to follow God's ways, the available evidence is subtle but adequate. It is subtle in order to keep people humble, free of prideful triumphalism of the kind that destroys community. In our pride, we would readily turn a conveniently available God into a self-serving commodity. This tendency prompted Jesus to say that "it's an evil generation that seeks for a sign" (Matt. 16:4). The evidence available to us fits with the curriculum of death: the aim is to teach us to trust the One who alone can save us from death and corruption.

The lesson is that we must turn from our ways to get in line with the true God. This is difficult news, because we have a hard time trusting a God we cannot see.

We fear that our well-being and rationality will be at risk if we trust this invisible God. The truth of the matter is that our well-being and rationality are at risk and even doomed if we fail to trust God. Death serves as a vivid reminder. Without God as our trusted Savior, only death awaits us. As we die to our ways in order to live to God, we receive God as our Savior from death and corruption. Nothing can then extinguish us, not even death. Death leaves us, then, either with lives that are ultimately an empty tragedy or with a God subjecting this world to futility in order to save it. In sincerely hoping for the latter, we become open to a kind of evidence that will change us forever, even from death to life. If we have the courage to hope in God, we'll see that Plato was right: Philosophy done right prepares us for dying and death. It also leads to the One we need.

Questions for Reflection

1 What purpose, if any, could an all-loving God have in allowing human death? Could death be intended to be a wake-up call of some sort? If so, to what end?
2 If there is no personal God, what is the best story we could tell about the meaning, or purpose, of human life? Will this story recommend for or against ultimate despair, or hopelessness? Will it recommend against suicide?
3 Is it logically coherent to suppose that the existence of an all-loving God would be elusive, or hidden, to some extent? If so, what could God's purpose be in divine elusiveness? Might we be the problem here? If so, how?
4 How should we expect to be able to know the reality of an all-loving God? Are we already in a good position, given our selfish tendencies, to come to know God's reality? Or, might we need to undergo significant change as we come to know divine reality?
5 Barring coercion, could an all-loving God come to know us, given our selfish and dishonest ways? If not, should we expect to be able on our own to come to know God's reality? Do we have due cognitive modesty in this connection?

References

Camus, A. (1955) *The Myth of Sisyphus*, trans. J. O'Brien. New York: Knopf.
Moser, P. K. (2002) "Cognitive Idolatry and Divine Hiding." In D. Howard-Snyder and P. K. Moser (eds.), *Divine Hiddenness*. New York: Cambridge University Press.
Nagel, T. (1997) *The Last Word*. New York: Oxford University Press.
Pascal, B. ([1660] 1995) *Pensées*, trans. H. Levi. New York: Oxford University Press.
Plato (1969) *Phaedo*. In *The Last Days of Socrates*, trans. H. Tredennick. London: Penguin.

Russell, B. ([1903] 1957) "A Free Man's Worship." In *Mysticism and Logic*. Garden City, NY: Doubleday.

——— (1970) "The Talk of the Town." *New Yorker* (February 21), 29. Cited in A. Seckel (ed.) (1986) *Bertrand Russell on God and Religion*. Buffalo, NY: Prometheus.

Selzer, R. (2000) "Interview." *Teen Ink* (December).

Further Reading

Moser, P. K. (2002) "Cognitive Idolatry and Divine Hiding." In D. Howard-Snyder and P. K. Moser (eds.), *Divine Hiddenness*. New York: Cambridge University Press. (Identifies purposes of divine hiding.)

Pascal, B. ([1660] 1995) *Pensées*, trans. H. Levi. New York: Oxford University Press. (Acknowledges the relevance of human will to divine hiding.)

Russell, B. (1903 [1957]) "A Free Man's Worship." In *Mysticism and Logic*. Garden City, NY: Doubleday. (Statement of life in an accidental universe.)

Part IV
Emerging Themes

Chapter 16

Continental Philosophy of Religion

Bruce Ellis Benson

Introduction

That there is a body of thought properly termed "continental philosophy of religion" is a somewhat artificial and also relatively recent idea. On the one hand, it is largely analytic or Anglo-American philosophers who use the term "continental" to categorize philosophy done on – or inspired by philosophers from – the continent of Europe. That Europe encompasses markedly differing traditions frequently goes unnoticed. Further, since analytic and continental philosophies of religion diverge significantly in both methods and concerns, the latter cannot be seen as merely a "continental" version of analytic debates. Whereas analytic philosophy is largely concerned with the legitimization of religious belief – and so focuses on such issues as evidence and arguments for God's existence, the problem of evil, and the possibility of reconciling free will with divine foreknowledge – continental philosophers are far more concerned with basic questions of what religious belief is and how one properly speaks of and relates to God. In addition to these, one question very much in common to both traditions is the relation of faith and reason.

On the other hand, although such earlier continental figures as Immanuel Kant, G. W. F. Hegel, Johann Fichte, Ludwig Feuerbach, Søren Kierkegaard, Martin Heidegger, Gabriel Marcel, Maurice Blondel, and Paul Ricoeur wrote substantially on religion and theology, the 1991 publication of Dominique Janicaud's *The Theological Turn of French Phenomenology* (Janicaud 2000) and the so-called "return to religion" in European thought today can be read as signaling the flowering of a contemporary continental philosophy of religion in the past few decades.

Given both limitations of space and the remarkable nature of recent developments, our focus here will be primarily on these contemporary currents. However, we need to begin by setting these present discussions within an historical context. To that end, it is helpful to examine the relation of faith, reason, and the self as exemplified by Kant, Edmund Husserl, and Heidegger.

Faith, Reason, and the Centrality of the Self

Kant's deep ambiguity regarding faith and reason proves in many ways paradigmatic for future continental thought. His conflicted position – in which reason is alternatively subordinate or in control – ends up being a pattern that is either followed or criticized by those who come after him. In the *Critique of Pure Reason*, Kant famously claims that he "had to deny *knowledge* in order to make room for *faith*" (Kant [1787] 1998: Bxxx). As such, it seems that Kant gives faith the upper hand, implying that reason either is limited in ability or else must be kept in check (or both). Yet, in *Religion Within the Boundaries of Mere Reason*, faith must now submit to reason. Of course, Kant had earlier worried about the forces of "enthusiasm" and "dogmaticism" (Kant [1787] 1998: Bxxxiv); so this turnabout is not completely unexpected. Whatever one thinks of the orthodoxy of Kant's later position, reason clearly gains hegemony over faith, which means (practically) that it is reason's decision as to what can and cannot be accepted from the Christian tradition.

This privileging of reason is in effect a privileging of the self and can likewise be found in Kant's essay "What is Enlightenment?" in which Kant claims that "enlightenment" occurs when one is able to rely solely on one's own reason. As he puts it: "Have the courage to make use of your *own* understanding! is thus the motto of enlightenment" (Kant [1784] 1996b: 17). When Kant virtually repeats this formula in the *Critique of the Power of Judgment*, he makes it clear that autonomous reason is the exact opposite of "heteronomy of reason" in which one's judgment is "led by others" (Kant [1790] 2000: 174–5). With Kant, not only does reason occupy a position of mastery over faith but also my own reason takes precedence over that of others. Still, what complicates Kant's position is that God – not being a proper object of phenomenal knowledge – is never truly revealed and thus not available to human knowing.

Although Husserl wrote relatively little on religion, his phenomenology is illustrative of a basic philosophical ideal that has provoked much discussion among contemporary continental philosophers of religion. This ideal actually goes back at least as far as Plato, but it is well described by the phrase used by medieval philosophers, "*adaequatio intellectus et rei*" (literally, "adequation of the intellect and the thing"). Husserl's version of this ideal can be worked out in terms of intentionality and intuition. On Husserl's account, when we perceive an object, we "intend" that object in the sense that it is the object of our thought and thus "intuited." According to Husserl, thought is always "intentional" in the sense that "consciousness is always of something" (Husserl 1967: 13). Naturally, there are degrees to which we can intend something – degrees of what Husserl would call "intuitive givenness" – that extend all the way from a nearly "empty" intuition of an object to one in which the object is very much present to consciousness, so much so that it is "itself there," "immediately intuited" (Husserl 1973: 57). In such a case, the act of thinking (*noesis*) would be equivalent to its object (*noema*). Ultimately, the ideal for knowledge is what Husserl terms "the principle of all principles:" "*everything originarily offered* to us *in 'intuition' is to be accepted simply as what it is presented as being*, but also *only within the limits in which it is presented there*" (Husserl 1983: 44). The goal, then, is that our knowledge of an object be "pure," without any interpretative elements being added. Yet, as neutral as this ideal might sound, later philosophers like Emmanuel Levinas and Jean-Luc Marion point out that intuition is still guided by certain "limits," to which Husserl himself alludes. It is those limits that threaten to undo the very purity of intuitive given-ness that Husserl seeks, which would mean that the subject has a kind of "control" over the object known.

In effect, Heidegger provides a similar pattern to that of Kant, though precisely in reverse. In an early lecture titled "Phenomenology and Theology" (1927), he claims that Christian theology – since it is a distinct "science" – has faith as its *positum*. Theology arises *from* faith and has as its purpose the cultivation and clarification of faith. Accordingly, "*theology is a positive science, and as such, therefore is absolutely different from philosophy*" (Heidegger 1998c: 41). Theology concerns faith; philosophy concerns reason. "Faith does not need philosophy," says Heidegger, yet then he goes on to claim that "the *science* of faith as a *positive* science does" (p. 50). At least in terms of its basic concepts, theology needs the "correction" of philosophy, which "*functions only as a corrective to the ontic, and in particular pre-Christian, content of basic theological concepts*" (p. 52). So philo-sophy gains the upper hand over faith and theology.

Heidegger seems to move from this position in his "Letter on Humanism" (1946). In the same way that language cannot be controlled or owned by the speaker, so Heidegger sees thought as beyond our control. As he puts it, "think-ing, in contrast, lets itself be claimed by being so that it can say the truth of being" (Heidegger 1998b: 239). Theologically, his "solution" puts God within the limits of being, for he claims that "only from the truth of being can the essence of the holy be thought" and "only in the light of the essence of divinity can it be thought or said what the word 'God' is to signify" (p. 267). So philosophy has not truly relinquished control. However, in "The Onto-theo-logical Constitution of Meta-physics" (1957), Heidegger realizes the true gravity of philosophy taking control over theology. Heidegger argues that the ontological difference – the difference between "being" itself and various "beings" – forms the basis of Western meta-physics and that this difference has taken a distinctly theological form. "Metaphys-ics is theology, a statement about God, because the deity enters into philosophy. Thus the question about the onto-theological character of metaphysics is sharp-ened to the question: How does the deity enter into philosophy, not just modern philosophy, but philosophy as such?" (Heidegger 2002: 55) In effect, God is the ultimate foundation of metaphysics, as both the final entity in the chain of beings and the first cause. Far from being an honor, this means that "the deity can come into philosophy only insofar as philosophy, of its own accord and by its own nature, requires and determines that and how the deity enters into it" (p. 56). In other words, philosophy has been in control of God all along. "God" is only what can be thought by the human mind. Of course, this "god" is not the God of Abraham,

Isaac, and Jacob but the abstract "god of the philosophers," a human fabrication. Heidegger recognizes that "man can neither pray nor sacrifice" nor "fall to his knees in awe nor can he play music and dance before this god" (p. 72), for one would be simply worshiping oneself. Once again, philosophy has attempted a kind of mastery in which faith is turned into reason.

Levinas and the Other

Philosophy's move to master the other – whether human or divine – is of foremost concern to Levinas. Whereas philosophers have traditionally taken metaphysical or epistemological questions to be primary, Levinas insists that *ethics* – the relation to the other – is first philosophy. In place of Kant's emphasis on autonomy of the self, Levinas thinks that one acts aright by acting *heteronomously*, so that the other curbs my freedom. Clearly, Levinas is working with a very different notion of freedom when he says, in *Totality and Infinity*, "the presence of the Other, a privileged heteronomy, does not clash with my freedom but invests it" (Levinas 1979: 88). On Levinas's account, I am free when I serve the other. But who is this "other"? In an important sense, Levinas cannot really answer this question, for the other appears as a "face" that "is present in its refusal to be contained" (p. 194). Instead of fitting within the phenomenological categories of consciousness that we use to "make sense" of what we encounter, the face resists all such categorization. Even more enigmatically, the paradigmatic figure of the other for Levinas is the widow, the orphan, and the stranger, all of whom exercise a power over me by being "absolutely defenseless" (Levinas 1987: 21).

These ethical concerns are likewise significant for religion. According to Levinas, the other "is indispensable for my relation with God. . . . The Other is not the incarnation of God, but precisely by his face, in which he is disincarnate, is the manifestation of the height in which God is revealed" (Levinas 1979: 78–9). Thus, it is in this relation to the other that God is revealed to us, meaning that this relation constitutes "religion" for Levinas. Of course, the intertwining of the relation to the human other with the relation to God raises a difficult question: if both are "infinitely other," then where exactly does one draw the line that separates them? In his early writings, Levinas provides little to answer this question. However, in his essay "God and Philosophy," he addresses this explicitly: "God is not simply the 'first other', the other par excellence, or the 'absolutely other', but other than the other, other otherwise, other with an alterity prior to the alterity of the other, prior to the ethical bond with the other and different from every neighbor, transcendent to the point of absence" (Levinas 1996: 141). So God is the ultimate other whose being can in no way be circumscribed. Unlike the god of the philosophers, whose being is perfectly elucidated by metaphysics, "the God of the Bible signifies the beyond being, transcendence" (p. 130).

While highly sympathetic to Levinas's ethical and religious concerns, Jacques Derrida criticizes him both for his hyperbolic conception of otherness and for his attempt to go beyond traditional metaphysical categories. First, in "Violence and Metaphysics," Derrida contends that it is only *because* I can identify the other as another "ego" that I am able to perceive the other as a human "Other, and not a stone" (Derrida 1978: 125). Levinas is attempting to get beyond the conception of the other found in Husserl, in which the other is taken to be simply analogous to the self. While there is a danger in any conception of the other in which the other is merely a reflection of the self, there is likewise a danger in making the other so very other as to lose exactly those characteristics that make the human other worthy of treatment *as* human. Second, and much more important, Derrida wonders whether Levinas can really leave the rationality of Greek philosophy behind. Insisting that even when one tries not to philosophize "one still has to philosophize," Derrida contends that we who are indebted to the long tradition of Greek metaphysics cannot simply abandon those concepts (p. 152). In other words, what could it mean to think "otherwise," as Levinas suggests we do.

In response to the second charge, although Levinas acknowledges that philosophy "compels every other discourse to justify itself" and that even "rational theology accepts this vassalage," he refuses to submit (Levinas 1996: 129). One might think that Levinas would then take refuge in "faith," but he insists that even the "faith/reason" dichotomy has been set up on philosophy's terms, making faith inferior to reason. Levinas likewise resists any "domestication" of either God or revelation by way of philosophy. " *Not to philosophize would not be 'to philosophize still,'*" he retorts (p. 148). Yet Levinas also draws on philosophy for precursors to his idea of absolute otherness. From Plato, he appropriates the idea of the Good as "beyond being" (*epekeina tes ousias*) for thinking about God. Thus, God is that which cannot be categorized or thematized by any characteristics common to being. From Descartes, Levinas takes the idea of the infinite God that Descartes finds within his mind. Just as Descartes concludes that he could never have "imagined" such an infinite God, so Levinas argues that Descartes's recognition of such a God is an example of God "breaking into" human consciousness. But here a problem emerges. In the same way that it seems likely that Descartes has an idea of an infinite God precisely because of being raised as a Christian, so it would seem that Levinas's God is distinctly theological and, more to the point, Jewish. Indeed, Levinas speaks of "the revealed God of our Judeo-Christian spirituality" who "shows himself only by his trace, as is said in Exodus 33" (Levinas 1996: 359). Janicaud contends that in Levinas "phenomenology has been taken hostage by a theology that does not want to say its name" (Janicaud 2000: 43). If Janicaud is right, Levinas is essentially doing theology under the guise of philosophy. But, long before Janicaud, Derrida had already asked (rhetorically): "Independent of its 'theological context' (an expression that Levinas would most likely reject) does not this entire discourse collapse?" (Derrida 1978: 103) In the end, Levinas is fundamentally a theological thinker who appropriates philosophical language for a distinctly theological cause: to snatch faith back from philosophical dominance and thus "make room for faith."

Derrida and the Messianic

Questions of faith and reason become increasingly important in the thought of Derrida as he becomes more deeply influenced by Levinas. Given this Levinasian concern, Derrida claims that "deconstruction" has always been about doing justice and goes so far as to say "*deconstruction is justice*" (Derrida 2002a: 243). Of course, justice is always delayed and deferred for Derrida, which means it has a "messianic" structure pointing us to the future. Deconstruction likewise embodies this messianic logic. Although "deconstruction" is difficult to define, Derrida is adamant that it is not really a "method;" rather, it is the possibility of questioning, modifying, and reformulating of all formulas and beliefs precisely because formulas and beliefs are always inadequate. In "Force of Law," Derrida argues that deconstruction operates in the service of justice by continually asking whether laws serve justice. For Derrida, justice is a kind of regulative ideal that is so absolute that it cannot be deconstructed. While law is intended to embody justice, since doing justice means taking an infinite responsibility for the other, laws can never be more than imperfect attempts to instantiate justice. Given that imperfection, Derrida calls for a heightened vigilance and sense of responsibility.

Derrida's concern for justice is both ethical and religious in nature, and he ties those two aspects together in *The Gift of Death*. Responding to Jan Patocka's claim that Christian ethics represents the explicit taking of responsibility over the secrecy and mystery of the cultic, Derrida insists that there is likewise something mysterious at the heart of Christianity. Yet, since Derrida argues that ethical responsibility is ultimately to the singular other rather than some universal rule, it is difficult to specify exactly wherein this responsibility lies. "*Donner la mort*" (literally, "to give death") is the euphemistic French expression for suicide, but Derrida reinterprets it as sacrificing of oneself for the other. At the heart of Christianity, argues Derrida, is such a sacrifice. Yet, in order to be a true sacrifice, that sacrifice must be done in secret. Re-reading Kierkegaard's account of Abraham's near-sacrifice of Isaac, Derrida argues that Abraham is forced to act in secret, in the sense that he cannot "explain" his action by recourse to law. According to any standard of morality, killing one's own son is highly irresponsible, to say the least. But for Derrida this secrecy – and sacrifice – can be ascribed to all ethical actions. The moment one speaks is the moment one "loses the possibility of deciding or the right to decide. Thus every decision would, fundamentally, remain at the same time solitary, secret, and silent" (Derrida 1996: 60). Responsibility is essentially aporetic for Derrida, because it is somewhere between accounting for one's action (the ethical, the universal) and not accounting for one's action (the non-ethical, the singular). Moreover, neither morality nor faith can be characterized as an economic exchange. Although God rewards Abraham, he does not "pay him back." It is only *after* Abraham is ready to sacrifice his son – without any hope of reward – that he is rewarded. The logic here is the logic of the gift, something given without calculation or expectation and thus a true sacrifice. Of course, Derrida recognizes that such a gift is not just difficult but "*the* impossible," "the very figure of the impossible" (Derrida 1992b: 7). For Derrida, the entire structure of Christianity – both its morality and its faith – partakes of this logic. Or else it only *appears* to do so. Derrida closes *The Gift of Death* with an open question: does giving in secret, as Jesus instructs his disciples to do (Matt. 6), end up being a gift, or it is just a calculating way of getting back *even more?*

However one answers that question, it is clear that Derrida himself rejects the logic of any specific "messianism" (whether Christian, Jewish, or Islamic) as too violent and definitive. Instead, he seeks an open sort of faith that does not prescribe any specific messiah and so is generally messianic, which he defines as "the opening to the future or to the coming of the other" that comes as an "absolute surprise" (Derrida 2002a: 56). Specifically, Derrida speaks of a "nondogmatic doublet of dogma . . . a *thinking* that 'repeats' the possibility of religion without religion" (Derrida 1996: 49). Given that this is a "nondogmatic" version of religion, it is no wonder that Derrida speaks of "my religion about which nobody understands anything." Even though he says "I quite rightly pass for an atheist," he also claims "I pray, as I have never stopped doing" (Derrida 1993: 154–5, 56). Like Augustine, Derrida sees himself as grappling with the question "what do I love when I love my God?" Derrida brings together Kant's desire to make room for faith and his attempt to construct a religion within the bounds of reason in an interesting way. While Derrida champions faith, he is critical of any sort of "dogmatic faith" that "claims to know" and thus "ignores the difference between faith and knowledge" (Derrida 2002a: 49). Moreover, like Kant, Derrida is interested in a faith that is primarily moral in nature. It is not clear, though, how Derrida can have "faith" without any dogma. Even though being too dogmatic is a danger that can lead to fundamentalism, it would seem that faith must have some "object" of belief. Or, to put this in Derrida's own terms, the danger for Derrida is that undecidability threatens to turn into indecision. Further, for someone who is so concerned about protecting particularity, appropriating the logic from concrete messianisms implies a disregard for the singularity of messianic beliefs. Strangely enough, despite the fact that Derrida has often been perceived as some sort of "relativist," the question can be asked whether Derrida instead makes justice and faith so ideal and transcendent that they can never adequately take concrete form. In the end, then, it would seem that the requirements of reason squeeze out the possibility of faith for Derrida. As much as he appears to be the champion of faith, it is a faith that always is "to come" and so one that never seems to materialize.

Marion and Idolatry

Marion is just as attuned to the nuances between faith and knowledge as Derrida, though his own Roman Catholicism proves decisive for both his theological and philosophical positions. Much of the discussion we have seen in Levinas and Derrida is re-worked in Marion in terms of the idol and how it differs from the icon. Already in *The Idol and Distance*, Marion interprets Friedrich Nietzsche's proclamation of the "death of God" as the death of the god of the philosophers – i.e., nothing more than an idol that "does not have any right to claim, even when it is alive, to be 'God'" (Marion 2001: 1). Marion identifies a variety of such onto-theological gods: Plato's form of the Good, Aristotle's "thought thinking itself," Plotinus's One, Kant's "moral founder," and Hegel's *Geist*. Quoting Heidegger's rhetorical question "will Christian theology decide one day to resolve to take seriously the word of the apostle and thus also the conception of philosophy as foolishness?" (Marion 1998a: 288), Marion claims: "To take seriously that philosophy is a folly means, for us, first (although not exclusively) taking seriously that the 'God' of onto-theology is rigorously equivalent to an idol" (Marion 2001: 18).

This distinction between idols and icons is central to *God Without Being*. Like a mirror, the idol reflects us and so points us back to ourselves. The idol is precisely what satisfies the gaze, for the idol proves itself adequate to the consciousness that intends it. In contrast, "the icon summons sight in letting the visible . . . be saturated little by little with the invisible (Marion 1991: 17). In effect, the icon is like a window that allows us to look outside of ourselves. Since Paul terms Christ the "icon" of God (Col. 1:15), Marion concludes that he is the "norm" of all icons, which are for him examples of "saturated phenomena." Earlier, we noted that Husserl's "principle of all principles" is that the object before one's consciousness be allowed to appear just as it is but "within the limits" of consciousness. In opposition to this latter restriction, Marion claims that some phenomena "exceed" the limitations of consciousness. Here the problem is that intuition is simply incapable of taking in all that appears before it. The lack of *adaequatio* is not due to the object but the *subject*. Although there are various types of saturated phenomena, Marion is concerned specifically with "revelation." Yet, for clarification purposes, Marion calls on Kant's analysis of the "aesthetic idea," which "furnishes much to think," so much so that "no determinate thought, or concept, can be adequate" to it (Marion 2000: 196). In the same way that the person who escapes from Plato's cave is "bedazzled" by the sun, so intuition is overcome with sheer excess. "Something is experienced as unbearable to the gaze because it weighs too much upon that gaze. . . . What weighs here is not unhappiness, nor pain nor lack, but indeed glory, joy, excess" (p. 200). In effect, the ego is de-centered and loses control by this sheer revelatory force of the saturated phenomenon.

When Marion speaks of "double idolatry," the first form of idolatry is clearly onto-theology. In this respect, Heidegger is an ally. Yet Marion reads Heidegger as introducing his own version of idolatry: "Beyond the idolatry proper to metaphysics, there functions *another* idolatry, proper to the thought of Being as such" (Marion 1991: 41). God is still in submission to "Being" in the later Heidegger, as we noted in his "Letter on Humanism." In contrast, Marion wants "to think God without any conditions, not even that of Being" (p. 45). The move Marion makes is very similar to that of Levinas's attempt to think "otherwise." Instead of thinking of God in terms of being, Marion suggests thinking of God in terms of *agape*, in which God comes to us as *gift* and so cannot be controlled. Marion breaks with Husserl over the limits of consciousness and its control over what appears to consciousness. Even more significantly, Marion contends that "givenness" is central to phenomenology and that "the phenomenon therefore manifests itself insofar as it gives itself" (Marion 2002a: 248). He contends that phenomenological givenness is absolutely prior to – which means it cannot be controlled by – consciousness. In fact, the call of God effectively displaces the ego as the center of the world. As the one called – the *interloqué* – I am called upon to answer. Thus, there is a strange reversal in that my *logos* is "deposed from autarchy and taken by surprise," which "prohibits the *interloqué* from comprehending" in the sense of a full and proper adequation (Marion 1998: 201).

Rightly relating to God requires both an appropriate silence and also a speech in which "predication must yield to praise," meaning that "faith neither speaks nor states" (Marion 1991: 106, 183). Here Marion clearly moves in the direction of negative theology. Of course, Marion's turn to negative theology – or *apophasis*, the "*via negativa*" – must be set in the context of Derrida's discussion of negative theology. Already in the essay "Différance," Derrida admits that his thought is occasionally nearly "indistinguishable from negative theology." Yet he notes, while deconstruction and his notion of *différance* (which combines the notions "to differ" and "to defer") concern the very possibility of presence to consciousness and thus thought and language *in general*, negative theology is quite specifically concerned with theological language that asserts a "superessentiality beyond the finite categories of essence and existence" (Derrida 1982: 6). In "How to Avoid Speaking: Denials," Derrida considers the logic of negative theology, primarily its explicit denial that ends up being an assertion. Negative theology turns out to follow the logic of Plato's "beyond being." Thus, like Plato, Dionysius "asserts" that "God is the Good that transcends the Good and the Being that transcends Being" (Derrida 1992a: 113). In "Sauf le Nom," Derrida characterizes this logic of "apophatic boldness" as "going further than is reasonably permitted. That is one of the essential traits of all negative theology: passing to the limit, then crossing a frontier." And yet, at the same time, "negative theology empties itself by definition, by vocation, of all intuitive plenitude" becoming in effect "*kenôsis* of discourse." Negative theology, then, is the converse of Husserl's *adaequatio*: not a "full intuition" but "an empty or symbolic intending" – an "inadequation" (Derrida 1995: 36, 50).

Whereas Derrida thinks that – ultimately – there is only "assertion and negation," Marion wishes to argue for a "third way" that goes beyond them. On his account, "the language of praise plays its own game" (Marion 2001: 193). When Derrida claims that negative theology places God back in metaphysics by way of a "superior, inconceivable, and ineffable mode of being" (Derrida 1982: 6),

Marion responds that "negative theology, at bottom, does not aim to reestablish a 'superessentiality,' since it aims neither at predication nor at Being" (Marion 2001: 230). Whether Derrida or Marion is right depends upon how we construe "*hyperousios*," either as utterly outside Being (Marion's view) or the highest possible being, however far removed from all other beings (Derrida's view). Marion holds out for the possibility of a language of praise that goes beyond the true and false logic of predication. Yet Derrida counters: "Even if it is not a predicative affirmation of the current type, the encomium [praise] preserves the style and the structure of a predicative affirmation" (Derrida 1992a: 137). Although Derrida thinks that a "pure" prayer – addressed to no one – is possible, he thinks praise must ascribe some particular qualities to some particular God. It is hard, though, to see how even prayer could be so directionless, let alone praise. Thus, it is difficult to see how Marion can convincingly argue for a third way.

To whatever extent a negative theology has a particular religious orientation (Christian or otherwise), to that extent it can be located within a particular religious tradition – however "unorthodox" or unusual it may be in that context. This problem, though, leads us to another one that Marion faces. For Marion insists that the source of the "call" to the *interloqué* is likewise radically indeterminate. As he puts it, "the requirement to neither know nor name God in terms of presence traverses the entirety of Christian theology" (Marion 2002b: 150). In an important sense, Marion sees himself as being more rigorously phenomenological than Husserl in that he insists that the object – in this case, God – appears to consciousness outside of any limits imposed by us. Yet Derrida questions whether there can be a "pure form of the call" (Derrida 1992b: 52) and, in discussion with Marion, insists that phenomenology always requires "limits" or what Husserl terms the "horizon" (Derrida 1999: 66). Alternatively, Janicaud accuses Marion of importing his phenomenological horizon from theology, so that "despite all the denials, phenomenological neutrality has been abandoned" (Janicaud 2000: 68).

Even if God cannot be adequately known or named, that does not lead to the conclusion that no knowledge or identity *at all* is possible. It would seem that *some sort* of assertions regarding God must be possible and are necessarily implied by God-talk of any kind. Yet, if Marion is right that de-nomination "ends up as a *pragmatic theology of absence*" (Marion 2002b: 155), then what content can theology have? Further, if no predication or naming is possible, then what separates the idol from the icon? Indeed, can this very distinction be rigorously maintained? Rather than simply deny predication, it may be better to rethink it. If Aristotle is right that philosophy begins in awe or what Marion terms bedazzlement, then perhaps predication *never* gets to the point of "comprehension," in which all that is known is perfect adequation. Instead of awe simply being replaced by theory – as Aristotle would have it – awe would then always remain a part of the experience of understanding and predication regarding God. True, all that can be said regarding God comes radically short of full adequation. Yet praise results precisely when the limits of predication are acknowledged. Thus, a properly circumspect predication emerges that recognizes itself – like John the Baptist – as "bearing witness" to that which can never be comprehended.

Conclusion

With Marion, we find philosophy right back at the problem raised by Kant and Heidegger – just how "independent" faith is from reason. Moreover, Marion is likewise back at the question in effect raised by Husserl: whether the phenomenon is able to appear directly to consciousness without any limitations imposed by reason. So where does continental philosophy of religion go from there?

One direction is that exemplified by Marion, who attempts to free faith from the control both of reason and the horizon of consciousness. Other French philosophers – who have only recently been translated into English – have taken such route. So, for instance, in *The Word and the Cross* Stanislas Breton argues that the "logic" of the cross represents a "foolishness" that starkly contradicts the wisdom of the world. Similarly, in *I Am the Truth: Toward a Philosophy of Christianity* Michel Henry claims that "living is possible only outside the world, where another Truth reigns" (Henry 2003: 30). And Jean-Louis Chrétien emphasizes the centrality of God's call in *The Call and the Response*, arguing that the call inevitably calls human reason into question.

Going in a very different direction, Gianni Vattimo finds himself able to embrace faith only because he sees its structure as kenotic. Instead of limiting reason to make room for faith, in *Belief* Vattimo argues that Christian faith is itself "weak" and that this weakness is exemplified by the incarnation. In a similar move, the atheist Marxist Slavoj Zizek argues that the very logic of Christianity is such that "it has to sacrifice itself – like Christ, who had to die so that Christianity could emerge" (Zizek 2003: 171). Christianity's ultimate telos is that it overcomes itself. Although just as much an atheist as Zizek, Alain Badiou appropriates St Paul as a thinker of a "*universal singularity*" (Badiou 2003: 13). Reading Paul's move as a radical break with Jewish law and Greek reason, Badiou sees Paul's new universal order as standing in opposition to the emphasis on particularity in Levinas, Derrida, and Marion.

Contemporary continental philosophy of religion, then, can be seen as a continuing discussion of issues raised by Kant, Husserl, and Heidegger. Such is where it stands poised today.

Questions for Reflection

1 If philosophy has long had the tendency of limiting God (in terms of God's being or ability to appear), then how successful are recent continental philosophers in overcoming that tendency?

2 Can Levinas truly go beyond traditional metaphysical concepts/intentionality
   and create an alternative space for thinking "otherwise"? How much does his
   emphasis on the sheer "otherness" of God effectively mitigate the possibility
   of a valid experience of God?
3 Does Derrida's "religion without religion" turn out to be another way of
   "letting God in" only on philosophy's terms? To what extent is he like Kant
   in this respect?
4 What does Marion both gain and lose by replacing predication with praise?
   How helpful does the notion of the "saturated phenomenon" prove for
   rethinking theology?
5 In what ways do the emphases in Levinas, Derrida, and Marion on radical
   otherness, undecidability, and absence relate to current global religious and
   political phenomena, such as fundamentalisms of various sorts?

References

Badiou, A. (2003) *Saint Paul: The Foundation of Universalism*, trans. R. Brassier. Stanford: Stanford University Press.

Breton, S. (2002) *The Word and the Cross*, trans. J. Porter. New York: Fordham University Press.

Chrétien, J.-L. (2004) *The Call and the Response*, trans. A. A. Davenport. New York: Fordham University Press.

Derrida, J. (1978) "Violence and Metaphysics: An Essay on the Thought of Emmanuel Levinas." In *Writing and Difference*, trans. A. Bass. Chicago: University of Chicago Press. Originally published 1964.

—— (1982) "Différance." In *Margins of Philosophy*, trans. A. Bass. Chicago: University of Chicago Press. Originally published 1968.

—— (1992a) "How to Avoid Speaking: Denials," trans. K. Frieden. In H. Coward and T. Foshay (eds.), *Derrida and Negative Theology*. Albany, NY: State University of New York Press. Originally published 1987.

—— (1992b) *Given Time I: Counterfeit Money*, trans. P. Kamuf. Chicago: University of Chicago Press.

—— (1993) *Circumfession*. In G. Bennington and J. Derrida, *Jacques Derrida*. Chicago: University of Chicago Press.

—— (1995) "Sauf le Nom." In T. Dutoit (ed.), *On the Name*. Stanford: Stanford University Press. Originally published 1993.

—— (1996) *The Gift of Death*, trans. D. Wills. Chicago: University of Chicago Press. Originally published 1992.

—— (1999) "On the Gift: A Discussion between Jacques Derrida and Jean-Luc Marion." In J. D. Caputo and M. J. Scanlon (eds.), *God, the Gift, and Postmodernism*. Bloomington, IN: Indiana University Press.

—— (2002a) "Force of Law: The 'Mystical Foundation' of Authority." In G. Anidjar (ed.), *Acts of Religion*. New York: Routledge. Originally published 1989.

—— (2002b) "Faith and Knowledge: The Two Sources of 'Religion' at the Limits of Reason Alone." In G. Anidjar (ed.), *Acts of Religion*. New York: Routledge.

Heidegger, M. (1998a) "Introduction to 'What is Metaphysics?'" trans. W. Kaufmann. In W. McNeill (ed.), *Pathmarks*. Cambridge: Cambridge University Press.

—— (1998b) "Letter on Humanism," trans. F. A. Capuzzi. In W. McNeill (ed.), *Pathmarks*. Cambridge: Cambridge University Press.

—— (1998c) "Phenomenology and Theology," trans. J. G. Hart and J. C. Maraldo. In W. McNeill (ed.), *Pathmarks*. Cambridge: Cambridge University Press.

—— (2002) "The Onto-theo-logical Constitution of Metaphysics." In *Identity and Difference*, trans. J. Stambaugh. Chicago: University of Chicago Press.

Henry, M. (2003) *I Am the Truth: Toward a Philosophy of Christianity*, trans. S. Emanuel. Stanford: Stanford University Press.

Husserl, E. (1967) *The Paris Lectures*, trans. P. Koestenbaum. 2nd edn. The Hague: Martinus Nijhoff.

—— (1973) *Cartesian Meditations*, trans. D. Cairns. The Hague: Martinus Nijhoff.

—— (1983) *Ideas Pertaining to a Pure Phenomenology and a Phenomenological Philosophy*, book. 1, *General Introduction to a Pure Phenomenology*, trans. F. Kersten. The Hague: Martinus Nijhoff.

Janicaud, D. (2000) *The Theological Turn of French Phenomenology*, trans. B. G. Prusak. In *Phenomenology and the "Theological Turn:" The French Debate*. New York: Fordham University Press. Originally published 1991.

Kant, I. ([1793] 1996a) *Religion Within the Boundaries of Mere Reason*. In *Religion and Rational Theology*, trans. and ed. A. W. Wood and G. Di Giovanni. Cambridge: Cambridge University Press.

—— ([1784] 1996b) "What is Enlightenment?" In *Practical Philosophy*, trans. and ed. M. J. Gregor. Cambridge: Cambridge University Press.

—— ([1781/1787] 1998) *Critique of Pure Reason*, trans. and ed. P. Guyer and A. W. Wood. Cambridge: Cambridge University Press.

—— ([1790] 2000) *Critique of the Power of Judgment*, trans. P. Guyer and E. Matthews and ed. P. Guyer. Cambridge: Cambridge University Press.

Levinas, E. (1979) *Totality and Infinity: An Essay on Exteriority*, trans. A. Lingis. The Hague: Martinus Nijhoff. Originally published 1961.

—— (1987) *Collected Philosophical Papers*, trans. A. Lingis. Dordrecht: Kluwer.

—— (1996) "God and Philosophy." In A. T. Peperzak, S. Critchley, and R. Bernasconi (eds.), *Basic Philosophical Writings*. Bloomington, IN: Indiana University Press. Originally published 1975.

Marion, J.-L. (1991) *God Without Being*, trans. T. A. Carlson. Chicago: University of Chicago Press. Originally published 1982.

—— (1998) *Reduction and Givenness: Investigations of Husserl, Heidegger, and Phenomenology*, trans. T. A. Carlson. Chicago: University of Chicago Press.

—— (2000) "The Saturated Phenomenon," trans. T. A. Carlson. In *Phenomenology and the "Theological Turn:" The French Debate*. New York: Fordham University Press.

—— (2001) *The Idol and Distance: Five Studies*, trans. T. A. Carlson. New York: Fordham University Press. Originally published 1977.

—— (2002a) *Being Given: Toward a Phenomenology of Givenness*, trans. J. L. Kosky. Stanford: Stanford University Press.

—— (2002b) *In Excess: Studies of Saturated Phenomena*, trans. R. Horner and V. Berraud. New York: Fordham University Press.

Vattimo, G. (1999) *Belief*, trans. L. D'Isanto and D. Webb. Stanford: Stanford University Press.

Zizek, S. (2003) *The Puppet and the Dwarf: The Perverse Core of Christianity*. Cambridge, MA: MIT Press.

Further Reading

Benson, B. E. (2002) *Graven Ideologies: Nietzsche, Derrida and Marion on Modern Idolatry*. Downers Grove, IL: InterVarsity Press. (An account and critique of the theme of idolatry in Nietzsche, Derrida, and Marion, set in the context of the thought of Husserl, Heidegger, and Levinas.)

Caputo, J. D. (1997) *The Prayers and Tears of Jacques Derrida: Religion without Religion*. Bloomington, IN: Indiana University Press. (A reading of Derrida as a person of faith.)

Carlson, T. A. (1999) *Indiscretion: Finitude and the Naming of God*. Chicago: University of Chicago Press. (A discussion of God-talk from Hegel, Heidegger, and Dionysius to Derrida and Marion.)

De Vries, H. (1999) *Philosophy and the Turn to Religion*. Baltimore: Johns Hopkins University Press. (A thorough account of the recent return to religion in continental thought.)

Hart, K. (2000) *The Trespass of the Sign: Deconstruction, Theology, and Philosophy*. New York: Fordham University Press. (An exploration of deconstruction's usefulness for theology.)

Horner, R. (2005) *Jean-Luc Marion: A Theo-logical Introduction*. Aldershot: Ashgate. (An introduction to Marion as theologian.)

Westphal, M. (2001) *Overcoming Onto-theology: Toward a Postmodern Christian Faith*. New York: Fordham University Press. (A collection of essays that appropriate postmodern thought for Christian faith.)

Chapter 17

Eastern Philosophy of Religion

Gavin Flood

Eastern philosophy of religion covers philosophy in the continents of South and East Asia, including the countries of India, Tibet, China, and Japan. We cannot, of course, offer a comprehensive coverage of this great diversity which spans 3,000 years, but we can offer some account of central philosophical concerns that arose in the histories of South and East Asia. Indeed, some of the most fruitful developments occurred through the cross-fertilization of ideas, particularly with the spread of Buddhism from India to China. But we first need to say something of the category "philosophy" in an Eastern context (King 1999; Ram-Prasad 2005). The history of philosophy in the West has until recently not recognized the philosophy that developed in India and China. Although in many ways sympathetic to "Eastern" thinking, Heidegger is able to write that there is no non-European philosophy, philosophy being "in essence Greek" that gives rise to science and technology (Halbfass 1988: 168). Although Heidegger is speaking about the world domination of European technological and scientific modes of thinking, his perception of philosophy being the exclusive domain of the West has only been slowly eroded. It depends, of course, on what we mean by "philosophy." If we take philosophy to be characterized by rationality or systematic thinking about the world and the human situation, then clearly philosophy has been an important feature of Eastern civilizations. Both India and China have strong rationalist traditions; both developed science, mathematics, medicine, linguistics, logic; both raised questions about human meaning, whether God exists, the nature of self and world; and both developed systematic answers to those questions. While "Eastern philosophy" is a contested category, for our purposes we can take it to refer to the systematic, rational inquiry about questions of knowledge, existence, and human purposes that emerged in India and China from an early period.

Perhaps one of the reasons for the non-recognition of Eastern philosophy in Western university philosophy departments has been its exegetical nature. Indian philosophy, which carried through into China, was expressed primarily through commentaries and sub-commentaries on texts regarded as revelation. Much Hindu philosophy is commentary upon foundational sacred texts of the tradition and Buddhist philosophy is likewise primarily commentary on the works of foundational thinkers or texts purporting to be the word of the Buddha. Such a hermeneutical philosophy was also a feature of Western scholasticism and the histories of philosophy East and West have more points of similarity as regards method or process when seen in a historical perspective. We shall begin our survey by examining some of the ways in which the questions about the reality of self, world, and transcendence were addressed firstly in India and then in China.

Philosophy in India

Metaphysical speculation developed early in the history of South Asia. Hymns of praise to gods who were the focus of sacrifice became collected in a group of texts written in an early form of Sanskrit known as the Veda (literally, "knowledge"), the earliest of which was probably composed around 1200 BCE. Some of these hymns contain early philosophical speculation, especially one hymn which poses the question of origin, whether in the beginning there was being (*sat*) or non-being (*asat*) and speculating that he who is in highest heaven knows or "perhaps he does not know" (*Ṛg-veda* 10.129). Later layers of the Veda, particularly a group of texts called Upaniṣads (800–400 BCE) which offer more systematic inquiry, develop this theme of "being," speculating about the essence of the universe as a supreme power (*brahman*) with which the individual self (*ātman*) is identical (e.g., *Chāndogya-upaniṣad* 6.2.1–2). Such texts became extremely influential in the history of philosophy with later philosophers writing learned commentaries on them – reading the texts in the light of their own philosophical positions. Of particular importance is the *sūtra* literature, which stands at the beginning of the commentarial traditions. A *sūtra* is a terse, pithy verse which summarizes the teachings of a philosophical tradition upon which commentaries were written. A commentary (*bhāṣya*) is an explanation of the sūtras along with shorter glosses (*vṛtti*) and further explanations (*vārttika*). An author might also write an auto-commentary on his own verses. The scholastic nature of the Indian philosophical tradition is central to understanding it, and new ideas were presented in a way that showed that they were, in fact, old ideas contained within the earlier texts.

These traditions of exegesis developed in the first millennium CE and continued into the later medieval period. It is here that we find a semantic equivalent for the term "philosophy" in *darśana* from a verbal root *dṛś*, "to see." *Darśana* is a system of thought expressed through Sanskrit commentaries on revealed scriptures, on sūtras, and in independent treatises which shared a common language and common themes of debate. Another term, *ānvīkṣikī* could be rendered "critical inquiry" or "investigative science" and is applied particularly with reference to logic (*nyāya*) (Halbfass, 1988: 263–86; Ganeri 2001: 7–17).

By the later medieval period different systems of philosophy had been classified into six which accepted the Veda as revelation (*astika*) and those which rejected it (*nāstika*). These six orthodox systems of philosophy grouped into three pairs, namely Sāṃkhya-Yoga, Mīmāṃsā-Vedānta, and Nyāya-Vaiśeṣika, came to be known as the Hindu *darśana*s, although they do not exhaust the Hindu systems. It will be useful simply to list the six schools here.

- Sāṃkhya – the enumeration school. It posits a dualism between self (*puruṣa*) and matter (*prakṛti*) which are eternally distinct. The purpose of life is to free the self from the bonds of matter. This is a foundational tradition of Indian philosophy and later schools adopt its terminology, especially its categorization or enumeration of the elements of the universe, the *tattvas*.
- Yoga – this is the school codified by Patañjali in his *Yoga-sūtras*. It assumes the dualism of Sāṃkhya but adds the Lord (Īśvara) as a special kind of soul that was never bound and which becomes the focus of meditation.
- Mīmāṃsā – the tradition of exegesis on the Veda. This school is realist and pluralist, claiming that the purpose of the Veda is to tell the observant Brahmin what to do and what not to do. Ritual injunction (*vidhi*) is the main function of revelation which tells humanity how to perform the sacrifice, other narrative dimensions of the text being merely explanations (*arthavāda*) providing encouragement for performing the injunctions.
- Vedānta – the tradition which develops from the Upaniṣads (the "end of the Veda"). This tradition is also known as the later (Uttara) Mīmāṃsā and differs significantly in privileging sections of revelation about knowledge (*jñāna*) from injunction. A key text is the *Brahma-Sūtras* by Bādarāyaṇa on which key philosophers commented. There were three main schools of Vedānta. Advaita or non-dual Vedānta, whose main exponent was Śaṅkara (788–829 CE), maintains the reality of the one absolute with which the individual self is identical. Viśiṣṭādvaita, qualified non-dualism, whose main exponent was Rāmānuja (1017–1137), maintains the self is distinct from God and yet participates in and is sustained by God. Finally Dvaita or dualist Vedānta expounded by Madhva (1238–1317) maintains a strict dualism between self and Lord. There is then, quite a range of views presented within the Vedānta tradition although the predominant sectarian affiliation is devotion to Viṣṇu.
- Nyāya – the tradition of logic concerned primarily with questions of epistemology. For the Nyāyika the world is real and causes our perception of it. Our perception may grasp the same object through different senses, and the mind coordinates them, giving coherence or continuity to our perception of the world and ourselves. The Nyāya also developed logic and the syllogism.
- Vaiśeṣika – the atomist school. The world is a plurality of realities that comprise imperceptible atoms. The tradition is concerned with mapping these constituents or categories (*padārtha*) which can be known independently of

the self. Knowledge of the categories furthermore leads to human contentment
and freedom from limitation.

These six do not exhaust the traditions of Indian philosophy. An important
text of the fourteenth century, the *Compendium of All Philosophies* (*Sarvadarśanasaṃ-
graha*) by Mādhava (ca. 1340 CE) describes 16 different schools, including
Śaiva ones (whose focus is the deity Śiva) along with different schools of Buddhism
and Jainism. The Śaiva schools form a dualist tradition (the Śaiva Siddhānta) as
well as a monist tradition (the Pratyabhijñā) which reads the revelation of the
Siddhānta through the lens of its monistic metaphysics. Within each school there
could be considerable diversity. For example, on the one hand there was the
non-dualism of Śaṅkara who claimed that self and absolute are not distinct,
and on the other there was Madhva who argued for a strict dualism between self
and absolute.

The great diversity of Indian philosophical traditions needs to be emphasized.
Indeed, one of the characteristics of the philosophical schools is that they did
not wish so much for agreement with each other but wished to establish the
truth of their own positions through argument and exegesis. Discourse or *vāda*
becomes a characteristic of these traditions which sought their own conceptual
clarity and demarcation from other, rival schools (Clayton 1992). Such a demarcation was possible because of the shared language of Sanskrit, a shared
philosophical terminology, and a shared number of philosophical concerns
(Ram-Prasad 2001). Of particular importance is speculation about the means of
valid knowledge (*pramāṇa*) which most of the philosophical schools deal with.
These methods are six, namely perception (*pratyakṣa*), inference (*anumāna*),
verbal authority (*Śabda*), analogy (*upamāna*), presumption (*arthāpatti*), and
non-apprehension (*abhāva*). Different schools accepted or rejected different
kinds of valid knowing and they provided the ground for debate about
questions of existence and non-existence, unity and plurality, and the nature
of language. These means of knowing were used in the rational pursuit of
goals, and all schools shared a confidence in rational inquiry. A person who
pursues rational methods to reach a goal is rational (Ganeri 2001: 10). Perception
gives knowledge of the world, but perception alone can mislead or deceive and
so we need to reason as well. Thus from the perception of smoke on a mountain,
we can infer that there is fire there too. But even these forms of knowing are
not sufficient, and we have to trust the verbal authority of an authoritative
person (*āpta*) and more specifically the word of the revealed scriptures. While these
three are the primary means of knowing accepted by most schools, others accept
analogy (smoke on the mountain implies fire as in a kitchen), presumption (a kind
of inference, for example, if Devadatta is fat and we never see him eat, then
he must eat at night), and non-apprehension (not seeing a pot in the kitchen is
the non-apprehension of the pot). Not all schools of philosophy accept all six; the
materialists, as one would expect, only accept perception as arriving at true
knowledge.

The *darśanas* linked rational inquiry with the goal or ends of life. In traditional Hinduism there are four aims of a person (*puruṣārtha*), namely the pursuit of social and moral obligation, especially as regards one's social class and stage of life (*varṇāśrama-dharma*), the pursuit of wealth (*artha*), the pursuit of pleasure, especially sexual pleasure (*kāma*), and the pursuit of salvation or liberation (*mokṣa*) (Flood 1997). This last goal is often regarded as the highest good, especially by the philosophical traditions, and we find a repeated trope that the purpose of the particular philosophical tradition is the freeing of the self from suffering or, more specifically, the freeing of the self from the cycle of birth and death (*saṃsāra*) impelled by the force of one's action (*karma*). While, no doubt, many Indian philosophers were simply concerned with philosophical questions for their own sake, generally philosophical inquiry in the Indian traditions is not content with merely understanding the world but claims that knowledge or correct cognition is a liberating force that can free a person from the bondage of limiting constraint; the constraints of their particular socio-historical situation or their particular, habitual mental apparatus and desire which denies the self its freedom. Reason becomes instrumental in gaining liberation from the world. Central to the denial of freedom insofar as we are limited by it, but also central to the erasure of that denial, is language.

Language and Consciousness

Language is a central concern and theme of Indian philosophical speculation. Language in the sense of uncontrolled, conceptual thought is part of the force that keeps a being bound in the cycle of transmigration because, according to many traditions, the uncontrolled mind leads to the pursuit of self-centered desires and so helps to form attachments which keep us bound. Yet language can also be liberating in the sense that correct reasoning (through language) can dissolve dilemmas and therefore dissolve suffering. Furthermore, contact with the sacred language of revealed scripture is transformative. The "perfected" language which is Sanskrit articulates the revelation from a transcendent source. This revelation to humanity is a linguistic revelation which gives injunctions and prohibitions to the human community. Indeed, the absolute (*brahman*) is associated with sound and the famous syllable *oṃ* or *aum* connects the ineffable absolute with the particularity of language in the human world (*Māndukya-upaniṣad* 10.2). This sound pervades the world and pervades or holds together all of language as a leaf is held together by a stalk (*Chāndogya-upaniṣad* 2.23.3).

Speculation not only upon the content of the Veda but upon the very nature of language itself developed very early in the Indian tradition. There is a sophisticated science of language in place by the fifth century BCE, and by the fifth century CE we have a developed philosophical school of grammar expressed in the work of Bhartṛhari for whom grammar is used in the service of philosophy. The study of grammar in a philosophical context becomes a method of liberation, and the old idea that language links the human world of transaction to the divine is developed by him. The truth of the self and world is the absolute as sound, the idea that an ultimate reality is primarily expressed as sound and in language. This sound absolute (*śabdabrahman*) is clouded by our ignorance, but once that cloud is dispelled through the study of language and grammar, we can perceive the timeless source of language (which Bhartṛhari calls "the seeing one," *paśyantī*) which then manifests in a subtle form as mental speech governed by the power of time (the intermediate, *madhyama*), and finally in gross speech, the most differentiated aspect of speech and time ("the elaborated one," *vaikharī*) (Houben 1995: 278). This structure of language is cosmological in the sense that language is integral to the very nature of the universe as a hierarchical entity in which lower forms are manifestations and solidifications of higher, more subtle forms.

Bhartṛhari links these speculations to a theory of meaning as disclosure (*sphoṭa*). At the level of uttered speech, a meaning is apprehended in a sudden flash of comprehension or intuition and the sentence appears as a complete unit. Indeed there was some dispute over whether meaning occurs at a sentence level or is revealed at word-level from which sentence meaning is built up (Raja 1963: 95–148). The Grammarian school maintained that the larger units of language have more semantic density up to the sound absolute which is a totality of meaning. Human language is a fragmentation of this sound absolute. A significant idea in these speculations is that language is inseparably bound to that to which it points. Thus in complete contrast to the twentieth-century linguistics of Saussure, where a word is a sign which bears an arbitrary relationship to its referent, for *sphoṭa* theory there is an intrinsic connection (which is implied by the high status of Sanskrit as a sacred language).

Speculation about language is a kind of philosophy of religion for the Grammarians as the inquiry into language is an inquiry into the nature of existence, the nature of time, and the nature of that which is beyond time. These ideas flow into all schools of Indian philosophy, especially non-dual Śaivism where speculation about language is also speculation about consciousness.

Consciousness (*cit, caitanya, saṃvit*) is the focus of a number of Indian philosophies. Some schools, notably Advaita Vedānta and the Pratyabhijñā, identify consciousness with the foundational reality of self and world. In the Pratyabhijñā, for example, supreme truth or meaning of the world is that all subjects and objects are appearances of pure consciousness. This pure consciousness according to thinkers such as Abhinavagupta (975–1025) and his student Kṣemarāja appears in the two forms of limited subjectivity (the subject of first person predicates, as in "I am performing the sacrifice" or "I see the pot on the mat") and objectivity (the pot on the mat). We know this through revelation, through reasoning, and through the recognition (*pratyabhijñā*) that one is, indeed, identical with pure consciousness. But unlike the Buddhist idealists, the stream of cognitions must rest in a cognizer for the Śaiva exegete, which is pure subjectivity (*ahantā*).

God

Among the *darśanas*, not all are concerned with a God in the sense of a power that stands outside of the universe and is its cause. Even the non-dualist systems are not theistic insofar as they deny the ultimacy of any *theos* which is subordinated to the impersonal power of the absolute (*brahman*) in the case of Advaita Vedānta or to a universal consciousness or pure subjectivity in the case of the Pratyabhijñā. Advaita Vedānta glosses *brahman* as being (*sat*), consciousness (*cit*), and bliss (*ānanda*), while the Pratyabhijñā glosses Śiva as pure consciousness. Apart from the non-dualist systems which relegate God as a distinct being and creator to a lower order, there are explicitly atheistic systems such as the Materialists, the Buddhists, the Jains, Sāṃkhya, and Mīmāṃsā, the latter two still being contained within the fold of vedic orthodoxy. But there were traditions that explicitly defended the idea of God and presented strong philosophical proofs, not dissimilar to those developed in the West (see part II, The Existence of God). Of particular importance is the Nyāya tradition.

In his *Nyāyakusumañjali* the philosopher Udāyana (ca. 1050–1100 CE), who combined both Nyāya and Vaiśeṣika systems, offers a number of arguments to establish the existence of an all-powerful, omniscient God who creates, maintains, and destroys the universe over and over again. We can outline three here. Firstly, a causal argument: the world is a combination of atoms and eternal, infinite substances which are unconscious. Furthermore, the world comprises things which are themselves compounds. Each unconscious compound is an effect of a cause, but this cause itself must be conscious and intelligent because it directs the combination of atoms. The cause must also be omniscient in order to know what the combinations of these infinite atoms could be. That cause is God who is like a conscious carpenter controlling the unconscious axe. Secondly, Udāyana offers an argument from sentient beings. The world has to be created in order that souls can work out the fruits of their action (*karma*) which exists as an unseen potential (*apūrva*). It therefore needs direction by an intelligent agent, which is God. Thirdly, an argument from scripture is that the Vedas are authoritative revelation whose author must be God because he alone could know the truths that the Vedas impart.

As with all theistic arguments, Udāyana's must be seen in the context of their occurrence and are arguably supports of faith rather than attempts to convert the atheist philosophers. Thus if a thinker did not accept the validity of revelation, then he would not accept Udāyana's arguments for the existence of God from the Veda. Udāyana also offers arguments about the nature of God. God is a substance because he is endowed with the property of intelligence as other substances are endowed with properties. However, the properties of God are quite distinct from the properties of ordinary souls and so God is a different kind of self. In response to the question "why does God create the universe?" Udāyana responds that activity, the creative impulse, is part of the nature or essence (*svabhāva*) of God just as the earth upholds things because it is its very nature to do so (Chemparthy 1972; Potter 2004: 581–88; Tachikawa 1982).

Such theistic arguments are, of course, rejected by the *nāstika* traditions, namely, Buddhism, Jainism, and Materialism, all of which remain strongly atheistic in their orientations. But it is not so much atheism as rejection of the Veda that characterizes these traditions and takes them outside the fold of the Hindu schools. To these traditions we briefly turn now.

Philosophies Outside the Vedic Fold

The Materialists, Jains, and Buddhists are placed together as a group only by the Hindu traditions which reject them. But they do form part of a wider movement in the first millennium BCE in which wandering holy men and philosophers known as *śramaṇa* (or Pali *samana*) expounded their views in contrast to the Brahmins. The *śramaṇa* traditions did not align themselves with each other even at the time of the Buddha (died ca. 400 BCE) and maintained quite distinct positions, arguing as much with each other as with the Brahmanical traditions. Unfortunately, no texts of the Materialists have so far come to light and we know their position and arguments only from their opponents. Generally they seem to have maintained that only perception leads to valid cognition and they rejected all immaterial realities that could not be perceived, specifically an immaterial self (*ātman*) and transcendent God. Thus it followed that the purpose of life was primarily worldly success (*artha*) and pleasure (*kāma*).

The Buddhist and Jains were different, being religious paths as well as philosophical views. Along with their Hindu counterparts they share the view of life as suffering and advocate that there can be an end to suffering. Like the Hindu traditions they accept rebirth, but unlike the Hindu traditions Buddhism rejects an eternally reincarnating soul and, along with the other *nāstika* schools, rejects the authority of the Veda. In some ways the doctrines of the Jain tradition are closer to the Hindu philosophies, differing in their understanding of *karma* as a substance that adheres to the soul which must be washed clean through detachment, non-violence, and asceticism. But let us focus here on two schools of Buddhist philosophy which the Hindu philosophers critically engaged with, namely the Madhyamaka and Yogācāra traditions of Mahāyāna Buddhism.

Like the Hindu *darśanas*, the Buddhist philosophies followed a pattern of *sūtra* and philosophical teachings about the sūtras in commentaries (*śāstra*). While Buddhism rejects the Veda as revelation, the Mahāyāna nevertheless had its own texts that were highly revered and which the Mahāyāna believed to be the word of the Buddha. A group of texts that were especially important and influential, not only in India but in China too, were the perfection of wisdom sūtras (Prajñāparamitā) composed in the early centuries CE. The Madhyamaka is the *śāstra* for these texts, of whom the most important philosopher and founder is Nāgārjuna (ca. 150 CE).

Nāgārjuna in his root verses on the Middle Way (*Mūlamadhyamaka-kārikās*) composed a text that is foundational to the later Buddhist traditions. In this text he responds to the earlier tradition of the Abhidharma which had maintained that the flow of temporal reality is made up of discreet entities or *dharmas* which come into existence at each moment and immediately go out of existence. It is this flow of *dharmas* that comprises our experience of ourselves and world. Nāgārjuna criticized the Abhidharma primarily on two accounts. Firstly, it is contradictory to maintain both a doctrine of causation and a doctrine that each thought moment is discreet and has an essence or "own-being" (*svabhāva*). Something with essence could not cause something else with essence as there could never be a connection between them. Something that is caused is less real for Nāgārjuna than something not caused, and since everything is caused in the sense of being interdependent, reality has no foundation upon which other things depend (Potter 1991: 237–8). For Nāgārjuna causality is interdependence which itself lacks substance or is empty of substance. The true nature of existence is emptiness (*śūnyatā*); existence is empty of essence and empty of self; thus the wisdom (*prajñā*) of enlightenment is waking up to emptiness and the realization that the limit of the ultimate state or *nirvāṇa* is the limit of the phenomenal state or *saṃsāra*. If emptiness is reality, there cannot, in the end, be a distinction between emptiness and human experience of the world. Enlightenment is freedom from conceptualization that attributes essence to self and world, a freedom achieved through the application of the rational method (*prasaṅga*) which demonstrates the unwanted consequence of foundationalist views (Bhattacharya 1998; Burton 1999; Potter 1991; Siderits 2003).

Nāgārjuna was an extremely influential thinker at the beginning of the Mahāyāna Buddhist traditions in India, Tibet, and China. The doctrine of emptiness expounded by Nāgārjuna has been called, not without justification, the central philosophy of Buddhism (Murti 1955). While the Madhyamaka tradition drew on scriptural resources known as the perfection of wisdom (*prajñāparamitā*) sūtras, a second important tradition drew on a different group of sources. This was the Yogācāra or Vijñānavāda school which maintained a doctrine of consciousness-only, whose scriptures were texts such as the *Saṃdhinirmocana-sūtra*. This text teaches that the Buddha's final message is not simply that of emptiness. At first the Buddha taught the Four Noble Truths and basic Buddhist teaching and the turning of the first wheel of the teachings or *dharma*. Then he taught a more advanced teaching about emptiness in the Prajñāparamitā literature (the second turning of the wheel). Finally, the third turning of the wheel of *dharma* is the teaching of the *Saṃdhinirmocana* which claims that at least one thing has essence (*svabhāva*) which is pure consciousness. The Yogācāra school emphasizes consciousness, especially as understood in the context of meditation (*yoga*), and arrives at the basic doctrine of consciousness-only (*citta-mātra*) (Williams and Tribe 2000: 152–4). In order to avoid the problem of nihilism in the philosophy of emptiness, we need to understand the mind as having three aspects (*trisvabhāva*), the constructed aspect of the unenlightened who perceive distinct subjects and objects of consciousness, the dependent aspect (*paratantrasvabhāva*) or the flow of consciousness as a series of mental events upon which a subject-object dichotomy is projected, and thirdly the perfected aspect (*parinispannasvabhāva*), reality experienced in meditation as pure consciousness. This state is identified with emptiness, but emptiness is here understood as the emptiness of distinct subject and object of experience (Williams and Tribe 2000: 156–8). Another way of describing this consciousness-only teaching is in the doctrine that the different kinds of human consciousness through the senses (eye-consciousness, ear-consciousness, and so on) rest on an underlying or storehouse-consciousness (*ālayavijñāna*).

Yet this idealist version of Buddhism still operates within the parameters of fundamental Buddhist ideas, particularly the view of a person as having no essence. Vasubandhu (ca. 400 CE) articulated an idealist philosophy against the earlier Sautrantika view (i.e., that external atoms cause our perception), arguing that the mental series of cognitions do not need either an external world to cause them or a substantive self, the flow of cognitions being aware of themselves. A rigorous logical school developed from Yogācāra considerations fused with Madhyamaka arguments in the philosophies of Diṅnaga (ca. 480–540 CE) and Dharmakīrti (ca. 600–660 CE). Diṅnaga wishes to maintain a commonsense understanding of the world but to divest it of ontological commitments (Ganeri 2001: 98). He argued that reality comprises a flux of momentary particulars (*dharmas*) which we directly perceive in the first moment of perception but which subsequently our minds project through a conceptual, linguistic apparatus. The first moment of perception is without construction (*nirvikalpa*) but all subsequent moments, after the object of perception has ceased to exist, are constructed (*savikalpa*). Thus he accepts the doctrine of momentariness (and thereby emptiness) along with the idea that the mind constructs reality (and thereby consciousness-only) (Williams and Tribe 2000: 120; Hattori 1968).

Madhyamaka and Yogācāra Buddhism continued to develop in Tibet and China. Madhyamaka in particular became important in the philosophical expression of Chan Buddhism (later Zen in Japan), where Buddhism blended well with indigenous Chinese traditions of Taoism and Confucianism. Finally we must turn briefly to these East Asian developments.

Philosophy in China

The fundamental concerns of Indian philosophy were about ontology and epistemology. The Indian philosophers focused on the fundamental being of world and self, the processes of perception, the relationship between perception and world, the possibility and nature of a transcendent reality, and the ways in which cognition can lead to freedom from bondage. In contrast, Chinese philosophers were much more concerned with ethics and the establishing of harmonious relationships within society. In contrast to the formal logic developed in India, while some such as the Mohists did develop logic, China laid more stress on literary, moral, and political discourse which was less abstract and more focused on the human world (Liu 2006). Indeed, Wing-Tsit Chan characterizes Chinese philosophy as "humanism" that "professes the unity of man and Heaven" (Chan 1963: 3). The traditions of Taoism and Confucianism developed between the sixth and third centuries BCE along with a wide variety of philosophies in what was called "the Hundred Schools," a period during which, according to Mencius, "unemployed scholars indulge in unreasonable discourse" (Yu-lan 1952: 132). The traditions became more firmly established from the Han dynasty (206 BCE – 220 CE) through to the eleventh century, with Buddhism first being transmitted to China in the first century CE. Neo-Confucianism absorbed these religions from the eleventh century to modernity. While philosophy in China is predominantly concerned with social harmony and values, there also developed a strong and unparalleled scientific tradition (Needham 1956). For current purposes we can survey Chinese philosophy within the broad parameters of Confucian, Taoist, and Buddhist traditions.

The *Analects* (*Lun-yü*) of Confucius (K'ung fu-zu 551–479 BCE) contain some of the fundamental concerns of Chinese philosophy, namely moral values as the foundation of social and political order. Social and political harmony is maintained by each person knowing and fulfilling the role allotted to them as son, father, priest, subject, wife, daughter, or king. The highest virtue is *jen*, "love" or "humanity," which embraces a number of qualities such as filial and fraternal love, cultivation, loyalty, and duty. If people cultivate these qualities, then social harmony is achieved and hierarchy of society corresponds to the natural moral order. Unlike India, while corresponding to a moral order, the social hierarchy is not linked to a hierarchical cosmology. Following in the tradition of the master, Mencius (Meng-tzu, 371–289 BCE), in the book that bears his name, advocated the Confucian moral order and the idea that human beings are innately disposed towards the good revealed, for example, in our natural reaction to save a child about to fall into a well. If we look within us, we can perceive our innate goodness which can be developed in the correct environment, that is, the correct moral order ensured by the just state with the just ruler. Mencius's political philosophy of the just king ensures the moral order and encourages the cultivation of goodness within persons (Yu-lan 1952: 119–27).

Similarly concerned with conduct but with an emphasis on the forces of nature, the classic source of Taoism is Lao-tzu's *Tao te ching* ("the Way and its Power"). Lao-tzu simply means "old master" and the text, composed around the fourth century BCE, is the work of a number of authors over a period of time. The central doctrine expressed in pithy aphorisms is that there is a pervasive first principle whereby all things are produced, and the goal of life is to live in harmony with this principle called *tao*. The text tells us:

There is a thing, formless yet complete. Before heaven and earth it existed. Without sound, without substance, it stands alone without changing. It is all pervading and

unfailing. One may think of it as the mother of all beneath heaven. We do not know
its name, but we term it *Tao*. Forced to give an appellation to it, I should say it was
"Great." (Yu-lan 1952: 177)

The term *tao* means "way" and came to refer to the way of human morality or
conduct. The wise person must conduct life so as to be in harmony with the *tao*
which in practical terms means a stilling of the self and the development of an
inner perception of the *tao*. The stilling of the self is also linked to action by non-
action: "*tao* never does, yet through it all things are done" (Yu-lan 1952: 178),
a kind of quietism which had political implications for the ruler in a time of social
upheaval and war, and which was the political context for the production of the
text. The next great treatise of Taoism is the fourth century BCE *Book of Chuang-
tzu*. Chuang-tzu accepts the notion of the *tao* as found in Lao-tzu but emphasizes
the forever changing nature of the universe. These patterns of change occur in
accordance with two principles or powers, the active, masculine energy or *yang*
and the passive, feminine energy or *yin*. The purpose of life is to find happiness
through harmony with the nature of things and to extend this happiness after
death to immortality in another form. Wisdom is being at one with the universe
and its constant change.

We can see that these doctrines accord well with Buddhism and, indeed, there
was mutual influence and points in common, particularly techniques of mystical
consciousness such as breathing techniques and non-activity (*wu-wei*). Buddhism
slowly spread from India to China, and texts were translated into Chinese. There
are two major trajectories of popular Buddhism in China: the pure land tradition
(Chng-t'u) which claimed that human liberation comes through faith in the
Buddha Amitabha (Amit'o in Chinese) and Ch'an, a meditation school based in
the monasteries. Within this context various Buddhist philosophies developed,
traditionally 10 schools, of which four become major developments. These
four are the consciousness-only school (Wei-shih), the Hua-yen, the Tien-tai, and
the Chan.

The consciousness-only school is the Vijñānavāda doctrine that the duality
between subject or self (*wo* which translated *ātman*) and object (*fa* which translated *dharma*) of consciousness is erroneous. Enlightenment is realizing that consciousness evolves and that this evolution is empty. Yet the truth is even more
subtle than this, and one must avoid, according to K'uei-chi (632–82 CE), the
doctrine of "emptiness," on the one hand, and "being," on the other (Yu-lan
1952: 301–2). The Hua-yen school is based on the teachings of the *Hua-yen ching*
("Flower Ornament Scripture") which is a translation in 420 CE of the Sanskrit
Avataṃsaka-sūtra. In China Hua-yen became extremely important and formed
into a system by Fa-tsing (643–712 CE). The realm of *dharmas* connotes the
entire universe which is characterized by interpenetration. All things are co-existent
and interrelated, each *dharma* or existent thing comprising six features of univer-
sality, specificity, similarity, difference, integration, and disintegration. Thus the

arising of one *dharma* entails the arising of all others and the arising of all entails the arising of one (Chan 1963: 407; Chang 1971). Not unlike the Hua-yen, the Tien-tai (Japanese Tendai) attempted a synthesis of Buddhist philosophies and maintained that absolute truth, identified with the Buddha, is a unity of phenomenal existence and the ultimate state or goal. The absolute and the phenomenal interpenetrate each other and both are real. Finally, Chan (Japanese Zen) was traditionally introduced into China in 520 CE by Bodhidharma although the most important Chinese teacher, the last in a line of patriarchs, was Hui-neng (637–713 CE). Although Chan is predominantly, although not only (Faure 1994), concerned with meditation, the philosophy of Nāgārjuna was important and his *Madhyamakakārikās*, along with a commentary, was translated into Chinese (409 CE) by Kumarajīva as the *Chung-lun* (Bocking 1995). There was some reaction against Buddhism by Neo-Confucianism which sought political and social reform and saw Buddhism as a threat to social harmony in its doctrines of celibacy, asceticism, and the denial of the person. Returning to earlier Confucian ideas, thinkers such as Chou Tun-yi (1017–73 CE) and Shao Yung (1011–77) advocated the way as the universal principle active within nature and within human beings. These ideas were systematized by Chang Tsai (1020–77 CE) who stressed the unity of man and heaven (Yu-lan 1952: 434–97).

Eastern Philosophy and Modernity

With the massive impact of Western modernity on the East through colonialism, the spread of technology, and the development of public education in the university system, Eastern philosophy has absorbed Western philosophy. For example, philosophy departments in India are concerned with philosophical problems originating in the history of Anglo-American and European philosophy whereas traditional Indian philosophy has had less impact on the West. In China, philosophy was influenced by visits from Bertrand Russell and John Dewey, along with Chinese students studying philosophy in the West, and the revolution ushered in interest in Marxist philosophy. Of course there has been some impact the other way, particularly of Indian philosophy on Romantic German philosophers such as Hegel, Schlegel, and later Nietzsche (Halbfass 1988; Macfie 2003), and in more recent years Indian philosophy has had some presence in analytic philosophy, especially logic (e.g., Matilal 1986; Ganeri 1999; Chakrabarti 1997). The philosophy of religion in particular is beginning to take seriously the contribution of Eastern philosophy to debates (e.g., Griffiths 2001).

Questions for Reflection

1   Is the category "Eastern Philosophy" meaningful or even useful?

2   Specify the different philosophical problems that have occupied philosophers
    in India and China.
3   How do Indian and Chinese philosophers deal with the problem of evil? Is
    there such a problem in those traditions?
4   What are the differences and similarities in the way philosophy is done East
    and West?

References

Bhattacharya, K. (ed.) (1998) *The Dialectical Method of Nagarjuna: Vigrahavyavartani*.
    Delhi: MLBD.
Bocking, B. (1995) *Nagarjuna in China: A Translation of the Middle Thesis*. New York:
    Mellen Press.
Burton, D. (1999) *Emptiness Appraised: A Critical Study of Nagarjuna's Philosophy*.
    Richmond: Curzon.
—— (2004) *Buddhism, Knowledge and Liberation*. Burlington, VT: Ashgate.
Chakrabarti, A. (1997) "Rationality in Indian Philosophy." In E. Deutsch and R. Bontekoe
    (eds.), *A Companion to World Philosophies*. Oxford: Blackwell.
Chan, W. (1963) *A Sourcebook in Chinese Philosophy*. Princeton: Princeton University
    Press.
Chang, G. C. C. (1971) *The Buddhist Teaching of Totality: the Philosophy of Hwa Yen
    Buddhism*. University Park, PA: Pennsylvania State University Press.
Chemparthy, G. (1972) *An Indian Rational Theology: Introduction to Udayana's
    Nyayakusumanjali*. Leiden: E. J. Brill.
Clayton, J. (1992) "Thomas Jefferson and the Study of Religion." Inaugural Lecture.
    Lancaster: Lancaster University.
Faure, B. (1994) *The Rhetoric of Immediacy*. Princeton: Princeton University Press.
Flood, G. (1997) "The Meaning and Context of the Purusarthas." In J. Lipner (ed.), *Fruits
    of our Desiring: An Enquiry into the Ethics of Bhagavad Gita for our Time*. Calgary:
    Bayeux Press.
Ganeri, J. (1999) *Semantic Powers: Meaning and the Means of Knowledge*. Oxford:
    Clarendon Press.
—— (2001) *Classical Indian Philosophy*. London: Routledge.
Griffiths, P. (2001) *Problems of Religious Diversity*. Oxford: Blackwell.
Halbfass, W. (1988) *India and Europe*. Albany, NY: State University of New
    York Press.
Hattori, M. (1968) *On Perception: Being the Pratyaksaparicccheda of Dignaga's
    Pramanasamuccaya from the Sanskrit Fragments and the Tibetan Versions*. Cambridge,
    MA: Harvard University Press.
Houben, J. E. M. (1995) *The Sambandha-samuddesa (a Chapter on Relation) and
    Bhartrhari's Philosophy of Language: A Study of Bhartrhari Sambadha-samuddesa in the
    Context of the Prakirna-prakasa*. Gonigen: E. Forsten.
King, R. (1999) *Indian Philosophy: An Introduction to Hindu and Buddhist Thought*.
    Edinburgh: Edinburgh University Press.
Liu, J. L. (2006) *An Introduction to Chinese Philosophy*. Oxford: Blackwell.

Macfie, A. L (ed.) (2003) *Eastern Influences on Western Philosophy: A Reader*. Edinburgh: Edinburgh University Press.

Matilal, B. K. (1986) *Perception: An Essay on Classical Indian Theories of Knowledge*. Oxford: Clarendon Press.

Murti, T. R. V. (1955) *The Central Philosophy of Buddhism*. London: Allen and Unwin.

Needham, J. (1956) *Science and Civilization in China*. Cambridge: Cambridge University Press.

Potter, K. H. (2004) *Presuppositions of India's Philosophies*. 2nd edn. Delhi: MLBD.

—— (ed.) (1991) *Encyclopedia of Indian Philosophies*. Vol. 4, *Indian Philosophical Analysis Nyayavaiseika from Ganesa to Raghunath Siromani*. Delhi: MLBD.

Raja, K. (1963) *Indian Theories of Meaning*. Madras: Adyar.

Ram-Prasad, C. (2001) *Knowledge and Liberation in Classical Indian Thought*. Basingstoke: Macmillan.

—— (2005) *Eastern Philosophy*. London: Cassell.

Siderits, M. (2003) *Personal Identity and Buddhist Philosophy: Empty Persons and Buddhist Philosophy*. Burlington, VT: Ashgate.

Tachikawa, M. (1982) *The Structure of the World in Udayana's Realism: A Study of the Laksanavali and the Kiranavali*. Dordrecht: Kluwer.

Williams, P., and A. Tribe (2000) *Buddhist Thought*. London: Routledge.

Yu-lan, F. (1952) *A History of Chinese Philosophy*, 2 vols. Princeton: Princeton University Press.

Further Reading

Chan, W. (1963) *A Sourcebook in Chinese Philosophy*. Princeton: Princeton University Press. (This book provides a historical anthology of Chinese philosophy in translation. A very useful and readable resource.)

Chemparthy, G. (1972) *An Indian Rational Theology: Introduction to Udayana's Nyayakusumanjali*. Leiden: E. J. Brill. (An excellent account of Indian philosophical theism.)

Ganeri, J. (2001) *Classical Indian Philosophy*. London: Routledge. (A very good account of Indian philosophy that presents philosophical problems in a way familiar to readers of Western philosophy.)

King, R. (1999) *Indian Philosophy: An Introduction to Hindu and Buddhist Thought*. Edinburgh: Edinburgh University Press. (A good introduction to the main schools that also attempts to place the study of Indian philosophy in the context of modernity and postcolonial discourse.)

Liu, J. L. (2006) *An Introduction to Chinese Philosophy*. Oxford: Blackwell. (A clear, well-written introduction.)

Potter, K. H. (2004) *Presuppositions of India's Philosophies*. 2nd edn. Delhi: MLBD. (First published in 1974, this is still an engaging account of Indian philosophy.)

Prasad, C. (2005) *Eastern Philosophy*. London: Cassell. (An excellent introduction that gives an account of the philosophical moves and traditions in Eastern philosophy, making those concerns relevant to a contemporary, Western readership.)

Smart, N. (1964) *Doctrine and Argument in Indian Philosophy*. London: Allen and Unwin. (A good, clear account of the major schools. The book avoids Sanskrit terms in the text using only English with an appendix giving Sanskrit terms.)

Williams, P., and A. Tribe (2000) *Buddhist Thought*. London: Routledge. (A very good, systematic survey.)

Yu-lan, F. (1952) *A History of Chinese Philosophy*, 2 vols. Princeton: Princeton University Press. (This is the classic account of Chinese philosophy. An informative and comprehensive history.)

Chapter 18

Feminist Philosophy of Religion

Pamela Sue Anderson

Context: Feminism in Philosophy

It is highly significant for feminist philosophers that philosophy of religion touches and crosses other branches of philosophy, including moral philosophy, epistemology, metaphysics, philosophy of science, philosophy of language, and the history of philosophy. Feminism in all of the latter has been characterized by critical thought and action for change. This means the transformation of the concepts and practices which have excluded, or have had pernicious effects on, women. Feminism in philosophy of religion follows suit, confronting similar obstacles to change, especially epistemological and ethical barriers. Feminism has challenged in a deep and fundamental manner those philosophical ideals which have both objectified women and led to self-fulfilling beliefs about the divine.

A first contention of feminist philosophers of religion is that men have been propped up by their ideal of the divine made in their own image and so have failed to attend adequately to reality, to real objects and subjects (Anderson 2003). A second feminist contention is that philosophy of religion should keep gender in mind while rethinking the nature of cognition, the role of contextual values in shaping epistemic practices, and the metaphysical assumptions which have generated epistemic injustices (Harris 2005).

The first contention derives from the discovery of "the man of reason" who, as Janet Martin Soskice observes, "in various guises trudges through the works of early modern philosophy, [as] a disengaged self in the disenchanted universe" (Soskice 1992: 60). She continues: "this . . . agent of science gains control, even in his *moral life*, through 'disengagement' and objectification [of the surrounding world but also of his own emotions, fears, and compulsions];" and "indeed this miracle of self-mastery is a familiar figure in the texts of spiritual theology" (pp. 60–1). Genevieve Lloyd demonstrates that this man of reason personifies the subject's self-image in the history of Western philosophy (Lloyd 1993). Iris Murdoch recognizes this figure well before Soskice and Lloyd (Murdoch 1970:

80). To her credit Murdoch also sees the link between moral philosophy and religious ideals. And Lloyd's account of the imagery of reason is informed by Michèle Le Doeuff's reading of the essential, but un-thought elements in the history of philosophy (Le Doeuff 1989: 27–32; cf. Lloyd 2000).

The double discovery of the man of reason imagery and of the symbolic exclusion of women from philosophy motivated twentieth-century feminist critiques. However, progressive change in philosophy has never been straightforward, and feminism in philosophy was strongly resisted in the twentieth century by Anglo-American analytic philosophers who defined themselves in terms of a norm of neutrality. These philosophers assume that clear and rigorous philosophical reasoning is without any political or gender bias; feminists call this "male-neutral" and mean unwittingly male (Anderson 1998: 13). In addition, feminism covers a whole range of different feminist voices and views. So feminism in philosophy is not clearly any single thing. And yet in the context of reading any particular text or branch in philosophy, feminism seeks a singular, critical focus in order to elucidate examples of the philosopher's gender-bias. The object of feminist critique is not only what has been excluded. I will return to this point when I consider the second contention in terms of three sets of reciprocally related issues for feminism in philosophy of religion. These latter issues will raise questions concerning the use of such essentially contested concepts as reality and the divine.

Philosophers, though, can no longer simply ignore the distinctive role of gender, or "sexual difference," in their thought and action (Anderson 1998: 5–9, 98–105; 2001: 195–202). Twentieth-century feminist philosophers of religion confronted a gender-biased or sexist picture of the human and the divine. A sex/gender distinction shaped the ways in which the traditional problems, beliefs, and arguments in philosophy were and often still are constructed (cf. Anderson 1998: 5–13). Philosophy of religion not only emerges in a history of patriarchal traditions which exclude and devalue women, but like the rest of philosophy it forms rational conceptions by opposing male to female, and masculine to feminine. Both the privileged, male history of reason and the masculine symbols of religion determined the dominant form of twentieth-century philosophy of religion. When asked about contemporary philosophy of religion in the English-speaking world at least, philosophers would still be correct to list the standard topics found in the most popular anthologies and textbooks such as the following: arguments for and against the existence of the theistic God who is a person without a body (i.e., a spirit), who is eternal, is perfectly free, omnipotent, omniscient, perfectly good, and the creator of all things; the nature and attributes of this God; the justification of religious belief as knowledge; the nature of religious or mystical experience; the problem of evil and the question of theodicy; the problem of religious language; the hope for immortality; and the relation of faith to reason. But, arguably, these topics have shaped, and continue to shape, a male picture of religion and reality. One feminist assumption is that every philosopher who defends the existence of this God and his traditional attributes has at least subliminally envisioned the divine as male. This gendering raised issues about our conception of human relationships, emotion, and desire.

In the end, the gendering of philosophy of religion has forced a range of new philosophical questions about how men and women live; how human beings as embodied – as sexed – fulfill their yearnings for love, goodness, and perfection. Both sex and gender have been put under interrogation. Some of these questions may have been raised against a backdrop of reductive accounts of Christian theism. But at the very least this interrogation began a process of critical review of theism, its gender-biases and contradictory aspects. As a result, new, more inclusive accounts of theism have also accompanied more radical dealings with a personal God. Yet feminists do not agree in their critiques of philosophy of religion; women philosophers differ at least as much as any other group of philosophers in the history of the field.

Gender: An Accidental Property?

Despite the presence of feminism as a movement for change, neither gender nor sex in philosophy of religion has yet become part of the general concern of philosophers or of feminists. This is true for each of the latter constituencies for equally fundamental, yet opposite reasons. As already suggested, these reasons are bound up with those gendered ideals of philosophy which have become the norms for critical thought and action. Ideals of neutrality and of gender keep male analytic philosophers and female (feminist) believers or critics apart; often they are at odds.

On the one hand, it is not uncommon for contemporary feminists, who could be women or men, to assume that the patriarchal nature of Western religions, especially traditional Christianity, should become part of past history. The secular view is that men and women can achieve progress in giving equal recognition to each other, whatever one's class or ethnicity or one's sexual or religious orientation. On the other hand, analytic philosophers of religion who are committed to a distinctive norm of neutrality in their philosophical thinking have strongly resisted political commitments. Their rational (neutral) arguments for theism are taken to demonstrate that the traditional conception of God is neither male nor contradictory.

However, a question remains whether the God who is without a body, impassable, omnipotent, omniscient, eternal, omnibenevolent is unwittingly male. Certain feminists contend that this God is the gender ideal for man; and "the only diabolical thing about women is their lack of a God and the fact that, deprived of God, they are forced to comply with models that do not match them" (Irigaray 1993: 64; also 61–4). This gender distinction depends on two essentially different sexual natures: one female and another male, each requiring a god in her or his own image, respectively.

In contrast to the unwitting maleness of the unchanging omni-conception of God, some Christian theologians argue that God is vulnerable or passible. How can the former, impassible conception of a personal God be reconciled with a passible conception of divine love? Can either conception of God be non-contradictory and non-male? Or, does either demonstrate something true about the gender of the theist's personal God? If the impassible conception is shown to be unwittingly male, would we want to say that the passible conception of divine love gives female attributes to a personal God? Once we start to raise questions about whether God's personal nature is vulnerable to suffering, or even to love, then gender issues are bound to be raised about our conceptions of God. And with gender comes the question of whether "he" is sexed or not.

Nevertheless, while Christian analytic philosophers of religion have claimed that their arguments are neutral and rational, secular feminist philosophers have claimed to be fully rational and ethical (but perhaps not neutral) in their rejection of theism. For example, the secular feminist supports certain norms of critical thinking and concrete action. These norms derive from the desire to ameliorate women's lives and resist religious commitments precisely because the latter support traditional forms of patriarchal oppression, notably those of gender inequality. Education for the secular feminist philosopher means allowing women to think for themselves and to make their own commitments.

To address the two diverging points of view on gender neutrality and on gender inequality, it is useful to assess T. J. Mawson's recent endeavor to remain a "sensible theist" and "clear-headed" in his choice of the gender pronoun "he" to refer to God. Mawson claims in apparent innocence – and supposed fairness – that as long as one is "conceptually clear-headed," no patriarchal bias will be implied by calling God "he" (Mawson 2005: 19–20). He conceives gender as an accidental property even though God's personhood is essential. In Mawson's words, "no sensible theist has ever thought that God really did have a gender" (p. 19). This is something worth debating. Does this mean that gender is a contingent aspect of persons and as such not necessary? If so, this implies that gender like the body is inessential for both human and divine persons. But the problem remains that we inevitably give God "his" gender as soon as we speak about "him" as a personal deity. It remains unclear, then, how we know what is essential for personhood. Embodiment, gender, and sex must each have some role in any other account of *personal* relationships. What conditions are necessary to know a person? Which attributes are essential for personhood?

In *The Philosophical Imaginary*, Le Doeuff explores the issue of "the non-essential" in philosophy. With incisive wit, her chapter on "Long Hair, Short Ideas" demonstrates the role played by imagery in the exclusion of women from philosophy, its practices, its institutions, and its authority (Le Doeuff 1989: 27–32). She uncovers a decisive feminist problem in the history of philosophy: a woman has not been imagined to be a subject who could have her own ideas or could think in her own place. So when it comes to philosophy, woman is by definition the non-essential. The essential subject is defined as male, or male-neutral, while woman, or her gender, is the non-essential. The recognition of this problem of gendering philosophy has been deeply significant for both the internal and the external critiques of Western philosophy by feminist philosophers.

In turn, philosophy of religion is gendered insofar as the un-thought elements – notably asides in texts about women and, say, sin, or false knowledge – have been assumed to lie outside of the rationality which makes up the core arguments of Western philosophy. Yet the fact of the matter is that these un-thought elements remain *essential to* the philosopher and not merely accidental; that is, they are essential in defining what is rational and coherent at the risk of both rationality and non-contradiction (Le Doeuff 1989; Anderson 1998: 9–11, 50–53). The decisive point is that the essential in philosophy, whether knowledge or rationality, is undermined when the concrete lives of men and women are wrongly ignored as philosophically insignificant. Instead of gaining knowledge and increasing rational coherence, maintaining ignorance – or uncritical assumptions – concerning gender undermines the philosophical claim to complete and clear knowledge.

Feminist philosophers of religion have uncovered knowledge of gender in the cultural upshot of debates in both philosophy and philosophical theology. The significance of the gendered imagery in philosophical and theological texts goes back at least to the Genesis story with the narrative about Eve's eating the fruit of the tree of knowledge and so taking the easy and wrong route to knowledge. This story illustrates with a single paradigmatic act the gendering and sexing of knowledge; women are excluded by having taken the wrong way to knowledge. But then, who exactly has true knowledge of right and wrong, or goodness and sinfulness? What is the correct route to knowledge? When it comes to cognitive claims concerning gender – including God's relation to gender – men alone certainly do not have an answer. Instead they have excluded questions of gender insofar as they have excluded woman and all that is associated with her attempts to gain knowledge. Granted, this is a bit elliptical; nevertheless, are Mawson and those who agree with him any more clear-headed about gender and God than those theologians who have feared and excluded women, like Eve, from the source of knowledge? Perhaps over the centuries women have learned more about gender by going their own hard way to knowledge.

If Le Doeuff is right about women's exclusion from philosophical knowledge, claims to clarity could too easily disguise the matter which would give us clarity about gender and the knowledge of gender. Have we begged the question of the gender of knowledge? Ironically the price for tolerable clarity could be a total lack of clarity – that is, opaqueness – concerning the significant questions about the (gendered) limits of rationality and knowledge. Clarity can, in this way, hide serious muddles and worse – that is, pernicious falsehoods about the actual subjects and practices capable of acquiring knowledge and justifying beliefs. We can easily deceive ourselves about gender and other sexual and social biases. Moreover, the past texts in philosophy of religion not only tell us something about the past of philosophy, but offer essential material for transforming the future subjects of philosophy. A textual and historical exploration of imagery forces reflection upon our beliefs about the subjects of philosophy and the actual shape of our gendered self-images. For feminist change to succeed, both men and women in philosophy must recognize themselves as materially and socially located.

Leaving Le Doeuff here, let us push forward the concern with the feminist critiques of the contemporary situation in philosophy of religion. This touches the internal process of the identity formation of men and women in relation to the divine. If philosophy is going to remain true to its original reflexive nature, then it will have to recognize the relevant and reciprocally related aspects of its material and social locatedness. This means teasing out the ways in which gender has shaped the concepts and the epistemological practices in philosophy of religion.

Neglected Issues in Philosophy of Religion

Stepping back to see the larger picture of Western philosophy helps to locate where we can begin to unravel a whole web of fundamental issues concerning women in philosophy of religion. These issues relate to philosophical method, to the historical locatedness of philosophy, and to the inevitability of the philosopher's political commitment (cf. Anderson 2003). These three resonate with epistemological and metaphysical questions faced by contemporary positivist and post-positivist, foundationalist and anti-foundationalist, philosophers.

First of all, religion has been a significant source of gender inequality, and each religion has employed methodological tools for legitimating gender inequality more widely. Feminists within and outside of religious communities have generated critiques of the androcentrism inherent in religious practices. Yet ignorance of the feminist critiques of this androcentrism and the methodological practices, such as the empiricist-inductive methods of justification which reinforce the sexism in philosophy, demonstrates a failure of philosophers of religion to be reflexive about fundamental dimensions of their own self-image. In this case, they lack awareness of how their religious beliefs have been shaped by both their epistemic practices and their assumptions concerning gender.

It is important to assess the curious failure to be reflexive about the religious dimensions of the philosopher's own self-image. For example, women, insofar as they are less than ideal agents, are left out of practices of moral reflection, if the imagery of the "God's eye point of view" is employed to their detriment (Anderson 2005; Taliaferro 2005). Roughly, the unchecked male biases of the all-knowing, impartial point of view lead to epistemic injustice for women, as long as the latter can never be even considered as adequate to the ideal.

Second, feminist critiques and reconstructions of philosophy of religion face issues related to the locatedness of the epistemic practices including the contextual values of religious epistemology. These include changing philosophical assumptions concerning the status of evidence and the role of often unacknowledged values which have undermined the reports of female investigators. Crucially, early in the twentieth century, philosophy of religion was to a large extent modeled on positivist methods and values. The internal critiques of positivism in the 1960s and 1970s forced scientists and at least some philosophers of science, and notably certain feminist philosophers, to develop post-positivist research. This latter changed the philosophical focus from any naïve forms of empiricism to fine-grained, discipline-specific and practice-specific studies of belief, acquisition of religious knowledge, and assessment of knowledge-making practices and methodologies.

Third, feminism in philosophy of religion confronts a resistance from those philosophers who do not recognize their own political commitments. A good example of this resistance to feminism in philosophy is the positivist who ignores the post-positivist informed epistemologists. Typically the positivist philosopher contends that a "feminist philosopher" is a contradiction in terms: the feminist who is political is incompatible with being a positivist philosopher who claims to be non-political. This incompatibility determines a recent disagreement between the feminist continental philosopher of religion, Grace M. Jantzen, and the analytic non-feminist philosopher, Paul Helm. The published disagreement between Helm and Jantzen focuses on a methodological preoccupation of analytic philosophy of religion with belief and its justification or warrant; this is a focus which Jantzen rejects and a concern which Helm insists she cannot reject. The apparent mutual incomprehension in this "debate" reflects one possible, political barrier between the analytic and the feminist philosopher (cf. Anderson 2003).

A less radical way to recognize the gendered nature of philosophy of religion is taken by women who engage with the master's own tools within analytic philosophy. For example, Sarah Coakley exploits some of the blind spots in the dominant school of Anglo-American philosophers of religion for feminist ends (Coakley 2002; cf. Anderson 2002). For her part in this process of gendering, Coakley examines the arguments of William Alston, Richard Swinburne, Alvin Plantinga, and Nicholas Wolterstorff with an eye to any significant gendered ways of knowing. She unravels the gendered standpoints concealed in Alston's notion of doxastic practice of Christian devotion, exploits the places in Swinburne's argument for the existence of God where he exposes a "soft" epistemic center, say, of reliance on others or on trust, and brings out the elements of vulnerability expressed in Wolterstorff's and Plantinga's proper basicality. Her contention is that despite themselves (male) philosophers bring in what they elsewhere devalue as "feminine" forms of subjectivity, including trust, vulnerability and suffering. Traces of traditionally feminine qualities indicate places at which feelings, including erotic passion, reveal a bodily relationship between human and divine. Clearly, this gendering of our ways of knowing is revealing and significant for feminist philosophy of religion.

Nevertheless, if this practice is extended beyond the focus upon this core group of Anglo-American analytic philosophers of religion, the content of gender(s) becomes problematic; that is, the gender properties cannot be fixed to men or women. Think of this distinction between the hard, masculine ways of knowing and what has been thought to be the soft epistemic center of male philosophers.

Next, take the theologian Paul Fiddes who argues strongly for divine passibility. Fiddes pictures a vulnerable, suffering God who could not be the ideal for the assumed masculine, hard knowing or for the immutable deity. Arguably, Fiddes's conception of divine vulnerability reflects the stereotypical female way of knowing, yet it might also be a patriarchal account which stresses the soft, feminine dimension of God's (maternal) love, divine suffering, and forgiveness (Fiddes 2000). Whatever the interpretation of this alternative of God as mutable, this counter-example supports the fact that the gender ideals have been imposed in stereotypical fashion which could be both unfair and inaccurate.

So, can a gendering of the hard and the soft ways of knowing as, respectively, male and female really make sense? Fiddes's conception of the God who suffers with us and in whom we participate, empathizing together as human and divine in loss and love, can be highly attractive to women and to men. But in being unlike the timelessly unchanging God of traditional theism, does this make it feminine or feminist? It could well be feminist-friendly, and yet not achieve the feminist goal of changing the pernicious effects of patriarchal practices on women.

With this illustration of gender's variability, the question of whether gender is an essential or accidental property of God re-emerges. Nevertheless, the philosophical significance of gender does persist at a deeper level. Take the topic of forgiveness. The philosophical problem with forgiveness rests in the logical and conceptual difficulty of, on the one hand, finding forgiveness pointless if the wrongdoer has atoned for his or her offense and, on the other hand, unjustified if no atonement is made for the offense. Now, think of an abused wife for whom forgiveness is problematic because of a seriously destructive lack of self-respect which the abuse has generated over a long period of time. Should the wife in fact continue endlessly to "love" her husband despite the perpetual abuse and remain in the marriage only to suffer ongoing abuse? A patriarchal account of Christian marriage would have to answer in the affirmative about forgiving and staying married; although this is likely to include trying to change the husband, years of abuse will not make change easy or certain. However, forgiveness of the husband by the wife might be justified once the wife has left the husband and once she is free of (self)-destructive abuse. This woman's forgiveness could be given in order to repair her own emotions and self-esteem; leaving the marriage for safer circumstances could enable the woman to forgive either if the former husband atones for his sinful abuse in some way, or if no atonement is made but she is able to understand without having to sustain his continual abuse. The crucial point here is that the gendered nature of the abuse had to be recognized first of all; the patriarchal nature of the marriage had not only allowed the abuse to continue but perpetuated a self-destructive situation. In the end, knowledge of the gender relations informs how and why the abused wife should act (1) out of proper self-love and (2) for reasons of rejecting an oppressive form of patriarchal marriage.

This example says something about both gender and forgiveness. Forgiveness is an act done out of love for another and/or oneself as another, but only out of "justice" in the specific sense of seeking mutual recognition by understanding and changed emotions; this means neither strictly distributive nor exclusively retributive justice. The knowledge gained about gender would be consistent with an empathetic God and practices of forgiveness which reveal human-divine vulnerability. Mutual empathy allows those who have been wronged and those who seek to change to come together in the creative power of divine love. The gender comes into this illustration most strongly at the point where the inequality between the man and the woman is recognized; and this recognition challenges both the patriarchal conception of marriage, which allows abuse to go on unchecked, and the formation of the woman's self-identity and, potentially, the man's reformed identity. The change sought by feminists would be to ameliorate conditions for women and ultimately to create a new identity for men and a transformation of their relations to women.

A Politics of Spiritual Practice

Returning to Coakley, we can observe that her contribution is not just to the feminine, soft spots in religious epistemology, but to a politics of prayer. The political power of prayer as a spiritual practice is anticipated by secular moral philosophers and is appropriated by contemporary feminist theorists who advocate a politics of bodily practices. Murdoch finds prayer to be a powerful ethical practice directed to the good (cf. Murdoch 1970: 55–6). Murdoch describes the activity of prayer to illustrate a point about the philosophical practice of attending to an independent reality and, ultimately, to goodness: "whatever one thinks of its theological context, it does seem that prayer can actually induce a better quality of consciousness and provide an energy for good action which would not otherwise be available" (Murdoch 1970: 83). Whether Christian or not, this conception of the power of prayer identifies a transformative potential for women and men, especially in their relations to God or goodness. In recent years, the shift in feminist philosophy of religion to ritual practices, as in a "politics of piety," is compatible with activities built upon a fundamental intuition about attention to a transcendent reality; in turn, these activities shape attention to real objects and subjects (cf. Mahmood 2005).

Yet other criticisms of Coakley arise. In her gendering of the practices of Christian mystics, the feminist continental philosopher-theologian Jantzen poses a serious challenge to Coakley's spiritual practice. Such spirituality

> allows mysticism to flourish as a secret inner life, while those who nurture such an inner life can generally be counted on to prop up rather than to challenge the status quo of their workplaces, their gender roles, and the political systems by which they are governed, since their anxieties and angers will be allayed in the privacy of their own heart's search for peace and tranquility. (Jantzen 1995: 346)

Nevertheless, Coakley still maintains the powerful nature of an inner life's vigil, insisting that the intense nature of submission to the divine can be subversive (Coakley 2002).

The contemporary feminist theorist Saba Mahmood goes further with her politics of piety. She captures a critical challenge for those feminist philosophers of religion who seek not to impose their own politics on others: "I understand the political demand that feminism imposes to exercise vigilance against culturalist arguments that seem to authorize practices that underwrite women's oppression. I would submit, however, that our analytical explorations should not be reduced to the requirements of political judgment" (Mahmood 2005: 195). Mahmood contends, "By allowing theoretical inquiry some immunity from the requirements of strategic political action, we leave open the possibility that the task of thinking may proceed in directions not dictated by the logic and pace of immediate political events" (p. 196). She concludes: "what I mean to gesture at is a mode of encountering the Other. . . . [T]his . . . requires the virtue of humility: a sense that one does not always know what one opposes and that a political vision at times has to admit its own finitude in order to even comprehend what it has sought to oppose" (p. 199).

The question is whether a vigilance of prayer, or any politics of piety, can change the status quo in philosophy of religion. Practices of devotion, even submission to divine goodness, are contentious, yet significant for the most recent debates in the field of feminist philosophy of religion. Philosophical study of bodily practices has been decisively transformed by Foucauldian accounts of subject formation (cf. Asad 1993).

A common polemic heard amongst feminist philosophers of religion today is that we should move away from an exclusive preoccupation with religious belief to a concern with religious practices. It is also not uncommon for academics to argue that the distinctive shape of modern philosophy, which gave philosophy of religion its preoccupation with defending belief, is secular as opposed to the more religious writings of pre-Enlightenment philosophical theology. The problem is that if we accept either Western philosophy's gender and ethnic exclusivity or modern philosophy's secularity, then it becomes doubtful whether philosophy of religion can shape the ethical and political concerns of contemporary feminists. The issue is not only with beliefs about God, but with questions about reality, ethical formation, and practical rationality.

To sum up, despite theoretical disagreements at a certain level of philosophical debate, the political and practical understanding of feminist philosophers of religion has begun to transform the field. This means collaborative exchanges have been able to confront the necessary, yet contested, nature of core concepts and spiritual practices. Examples of this contestation appear in the different critical responses to the early feminist critiques of certain gender-neutral assumptions in traditional theism. In particular, the question concerning the nature of reality and divine existence, especially knowledge of the embodied reality of human and divine relations, continues to generate change, as well as lively debate (cf. Hollywood 2004; Coakley 2005).

Conclusion

Significant new philosophical methods of analysis are addressing the role of desire and emotion in the ethical formation of gendered subjects by way of their bodily and spiritual practices. The diverse range of feminist interventions into philosophy of religion offers the potential for global understandings of gender, belief, and ritual practices. But feminism in philosophy of religion also rereads past dead philosophers as formidable as Kant and Hegel on reality, reason, and the divine. Thus feminism in philosophy of religion is opening doors to greater understanding of major philosophical conceptions from the past in novel and more inclusive ways for the future.

For instance, this broadening of philosophical and gender concerns has provided the opportunity to fill the lacunae in *A Feminist Philosophy of Religion* (Anderson 1998) concerning the nature of the reality and meaning of divine existence in the wake of post-positivist, but also of post-structuralist, forms of feminism. Working together, analytic and continental feminist philosophers of religion can contribute to the significant ways in which spiritual practices shape not just subjectivity, but intersubjectivity. Instead of excluding intimacy with the divine from the significant social dimensions of our embodied experiences, feminist philosophers have moved beyond the narrow confines of positivist forms of philosophy of religion (Anderson 2005; Coakley 2005: 516–25). To give philosophical labels, post-Hegelian feminist philosophers redirect feminist philosophers of religion to think with and beyond Kantian philosophy about realism as well as bodily and spiritual practices (Butler 1997; Hollywood 2004).

The decisive question is, what (gender) concepts should be employed to re-conceive the reality of the divine? In reply, we can be actively hopeful. Feminist philosophy of religion would seem to be at the cutting edge of debates in the Anglo-American world, in Europe, and across the globe when it comes to women, their ethical formation and spiritual practice. Ideally novel answers and new bodily practices will emerge as long as the dialogue is critically open and attentive to the other.

Questions for Reflection

1   How have feminist critiques of philosophy of religion changed our understanding of the nature and role of reason?
2   If gender is an accidental property of God, what does it mean to say that personhood is an essential property?

3 Can we sustain the belief that God is both impartial and omni-percipient without falling into incoherence?
4 How might critical consideration of epistemic injustice in the practices in philosophy of religion change the field?
5 What is meant by the claim that "the only diabolical thing about women is their lack of a God"?

References

Anderson, P. S. (1998) *A Feminist Philosophy of Religion: The Rationality and Myths of Religious Belief*. Oxford: Blackwell.

—— (2001) "Gender and the Infinite: On the Aspiration to Be All There Is." *International Journal for Philosophy of Religion* 50, 191–212.

—— (2002) "Feminist Theology as Philosophy of Religion." In S. F. Parsons (ed.), *The Cambridge Companion to Feminist Theology*. Cambridge: Cambridge University Press.

—— (2003) "Feminism in Philosophy of Religion." In D. P. Baker and P. Maxwell (eds.), *Explorations in Contemporary Continental Philosophy of Religion*. Amsterdam: Rodopi.

—— (2005) "What's Wrong with the God's Eye Point of View: A Constructive Feminist Critique of the Ideal Observer Theory." In H. A. Harris and C. J. Insole (eds.), *Faith and Philosophical Analysis: The Impact of Analytical Philosophy on the Philosophy of Religion*. Aldershot, Hants: Ashgate.

Asad, T. (1993) *Genealogies of Religion: Discipline and Reasons of Power in Christianity and Islam*. Baltimore, MD: Johns Hopkins University Press.

Butler, J. (1997) "Stubborn Attachment, Bodily Subjection: Rereading Hegel on the Unhappy Consciousness." In *The Psychic Life of Power*. Stanford, CA: Stanford University Press.

Coakley, S. (2002) *Powers and Submissions: Spirituality, Philosophy and Gender*. Oxford: Blackwell.

—— (2005) "Feminism and Analytic Philosophy of Religion." In W. J. Wainwright (ed.), *The Oxford Handbook of Philosophy of Religion*. Oxford: Oxford University Press.

Fiddes, P. (2000) *Participating in God: A Pastoral Doctrine of the Trinity*. London: Darton, Longman and Todd.

Harris, H. A. (2005) "Does Analytical Philosophy Clip Our Wings? Reformed Epistemology as a Test Case." In H. A. Harris and C. J. Insole (eds.), *Faith and Philosophical Analysis: The Impact of Analytical Philosophy on the Philosophy of Religion*. Aldershot, Hants: Ashgate.

Hollywood, A. (2004) "Practice, Belief and Feminist Philosophy of Religion." In P. S. Anderson and B. Clack (eds.), *Feminist Philosophy of Religion: Critical Readings*. London: Routledge.

Irigaray, L. (1993) "Divine Women." In *Sexes and Genealogies*, trans. G. C. Gill. New York: Columbia University Press, 55–72.

Jantzen, G. M. (1995) *Power, Gender and Christian Mysticism*. Cambridge: Cambridge University Press.

Le Doeuff, M. (1989) *The Philosophical Imaginary*, trans. C. Gordon. London: Athlone.

Lloyd, G. (1993) *The Man of Reason: "Male" and "Female" in Western Philosophy*. London: Routledge.

—— (2000) "Le Doeuff and History of Philosophy." In M. Deutscher (ed.), *Michèle Le Doeuff: Operative Philosophy and Imaginary Practice*. New York: Humanity Books. Reprinted in G. Lloyd (ed.) (2002) *Feminism and History of Philosophy*. Oxford: Oxford University Press.

Mahmood, S. (2005) *Politics of Piety: Islamic Revival and the Feminist Subject*. Princeton: Princeton University Press.

Mawson, T. J. (2005) *Belief in God: An Introduction to Philosophy of Religion*. Oxford: Oxford University Press.

Murdoch, I. (1970) *The Sovereignty of Good*. London: Routledge and Kegan Paul.

Soskice, J. M. (1992) "Love and Attention." In M. McGhee (ed.), *Philosophy, Religion and the Spiritual Life*. Cambridge: Cambridge University Press. Reprinted in P. S. Anderson and B. Clack (eds.) (2004) *Feminist Philosophy of Religion: Critical Readings*. London: Routledge.

Taliaferro, C. (2005) "The God's Eye Point of View: A Divine Ethic." In H. A. Harris and C. J. Insole (eds.), *Faith and Philosophical Analysis: The Impact of Analytical Philosophy on the Philosophy of Religion*. Aldershot, Hants: Ashgate.

Further Reading

Anderson, P. S. (1998) *A Feminist Philosophy of Religion: The Rationality and Myths of Religious Belief*. Oxford: Blackwell. (The first published monograph on feminist philosophy of religion.)

Anderson, P. S., and B. Clack (eds.) (2004) *Feminist Philosophy of Religion: Critical Readings*. London: Routledge. (A collection of essays by contemporary women authors giving voice – in a "dinner party" motif – to their different, often conflicting points of view for this new field of feminist debate in philosophy.)

Coakley, S. (2002) *Powers and Submissions: Spirituality, Philosophy and Gender*. Oxford: Blackwell. (A collection of lectures and essays, engaging Christian theism from a feminist perspective but with the tools of analytic philosophy; unearths the epistemological and spiritual power in vulnerability and other gender soft spots.)

Jantzen, G. M. (1995) *Power, Gender and Christian Mysticism*. Cambridge: Cambridge University Press. (A highly significant and popular study of the social construction of Christian mysticisms, employing the continental philosopher's methods of genealogy and deconstruction to demonstrate the links between gender and power.)

Mahmood, S. (2005) *Politics of Piety: Islamic Revival and the Feminist Subject*. Princeton: Princeton University Press. (One of the most recent interventions into feminist theoretical debates about the spiritual and political practices of Islamic women, employing methods derived from Foucault and Asad rather than liberal feminism.)

Appendix

Leading Philosophers of Religion

The lists of contemporary philosophers of religion in the following charts are by no means exhaustive. They are intended to be used as a tool to begin studying in the respective fields.

Table 1 Science, diversity, and religious knowledge

Religion and science	Religious diversity	Reformed epistemology	Religious experience
Ian Barbour	David Basinger	William Alston	William Alston
Philip Clayton	Gavin D'Costa	Kelly James Clark	Jerome Gellman
Ernan McMullin	Paul J. Griffiths	George Mavrodes	Gwen Griffith-Dickson
Arthur Peacocke	John Hick	Alvin Plantinga	William E. Mann
John Polkinghorne	Harold Netland	Nicholas Wolterstorff	William Wainwright
Mikael Stenmark	Joseph Runzo	René van Woudenberg	Keith E. Yandell

These charts were inspired by the excellent work of Charles Taliaferro in his *Evidence and Faith: Philosophy and Religion since the Seventeenth Century* (Cambridge: Cambridge University Press, 2005).

Table 2 Arguments for and against God

Cosmological	Design	Ontological	Moral	Naturalistic accounts of the universe	Problem of evil: supportive of theism	Problem of evil: critical of theism
William Lane Craig	Robin Collins	Charles Hartshorne	Robert M. Adams	Daniel C. Dennett	Marilyn McCord Adams	Paul Draper
William L. Rowe	Elliot Sober	Norman Malcolm	Paul Copan	J. L. Mackie	John Hick	Michael Martin
Quentin Smith	Stephen T. Davis	Graham Oppy	C. Stephen Evans	Kai Nielsen	Daniel Howard-Snyder	Derek Parfit
Richard Swinburne	John Leslie	Alvin Plantinga	George Mavrodes	David Papineau	Alvin Plantinga	William L. Rowe
Richard Taylor	Richard Swinburne	William L. Rowe	John M. Rist	John Searle	Richard Swinburne	Quentin Smith
			Linda Zagzebski	Quentin Smith	Peter van Inwagen	Michael Tooley

Table 3 The nature and attributes of God

Divine simplicity	Divine eternity	Omniscience	Omnipotence	Divine goodness
David Burrell	William Lane Craig	Marilyn McCord Adams	Harry Frankfurt	Robert M. Adams
Brian Davies	William Hasker	John Martin Fisher	Alfred J. Freddoso	C. Stephen Evans
Norman Kretzmann	Paul Helm	Thomas Flint	Joshua Hoffman	Laura L. Garcia
Brian Leftow	Brian Leftow	Alfred J. Freddoso	George Mavrodes	Paul K. Moser
William E. Mann	Alan Padgett	William Hasker	Nelson Pike	Philip L. Quinn
Jay W. Richards	Katherin A. Rogers	Nelson Pike	Gary Rosenkrantz	Charles Taliaferro
Eleonore Stump	Linda Zagzebski	Edward R. Wierenga	Edward R. Wierenga	Linda Zagzebski

Table 4 Emerging themes in philosophy of religion

Eastern	Continental	Feminist
Roger Ames	Ellen T. Armour	Pamela Sue Anderson
Chung-ying Chen	Bruce Ellis Benson	Sarah Coakley
Gavin Flood	John D. Caputo	Harriet A. Harris
Paul Griffiths	Dominique Janicaud	Grace M. Jantzen
Sallie King	Jean-Yves Lacoste	Kathleen O'Grady
Arvind Sharma	Jean-Luc Marion	Rosemary Radford Reuther
Paul Williams	Merold Westphal	Janet Martin Soskice

Index